1989 REPORT

REPORT BY JOSEPH C. WHEELER
Chairman of the Development Assistance Committee

DEVELOPMENT CO-OPERATION in the 1990s

EFFORTS AND POLICIES OF THE MEMBERS
OF THE DEVELOPMENT ASSISTANCE COMMITTEE

DECEMBER 1989

ORGANISATION FOR ECONOMIC CO-OPERATION AND DEVELOPMENT

Pursuant to article 1 of the Convention signed in Paris on 14th December, 1960, and which came into force on 30th September, 1961, the Organisation for Economic Co-operation and Development (OECD) shall promote policies designed:

- to achieve the highest sustainable economic growth and employment and a rising standard of living in Member countries, while maintaining financial stability, and thus to contribute to the development of the world economy;
- to contribute to sound economic expansion in Member as well as non-member countries in the process of economic development; and
- to contribute to the expansion of world trade on a multilateral, non-discriminatory basis in accordance with international obligations.

The original Member countries of the OECD are Austria, Belgium, Canada, Denmark, France, the Federal Republic of Germany, Greece, Iceland, Ireland, Italy, Luxembourg, the Netherlands, Norway, Portugal, Spain, Sweden, Switzerland, Turkey, the United Kingdom and the United States. The following countries became Members subsequently through accession at the dates indicated hereafter: Japan (28th April, 1964), Finland (28th January, 1969), Australia (7th June, 1971) and New Zealand (29th May, 1973).

The Socialist Federal Republic of Yugoslavia takes part in some of the work of the OECD (agreement of 28th October, 1961).

In order to achieve its aims the OECD has set up a number of specialised committees. One of these is the Development Assistance Committee, whose Members have agreed to secure an expansion of aggregate volume of resources made available to developing countries and to improve their effectiveness. To this end, Members periodically review together both the amount and the nature of their contributions to aid programmes, bilateral and multilateral, and consult each other on all other relevant aspects of their development assistance policies.

The Members of the Development Assistance Committee are Australia, Austria, Belgium, Canada, Denmark, Finland, France, the Federal Republic of Germany, Ireland, Italy, Japan, the Netherlands, New Zealand, Norway, Sweden, Switzerland, the United Kingdom, the United States and the Commission of the European Communities.

Publié en français sous le titre :

COOPÉRATION
POUR LE DÉVELOPPEMENT
RAPPORT 1989

DEVELOPMENT CO-OPERATION IN THE 1990s:
POLICY STATEMENT BY DAC AID MINISTERS
AND HEADS OF AID AGENCIES

1.   The Members of the Development Assistance Committee (DAC), joined by the World Bank, the International Monetary Fund and the United Nations Development Programme, met on 4th-5th December 1989 at the level of Development Co-operation Ministers and Heads of Aid Agencies. They agreed on the following policy statement on the orientation of their development co-operation in the 1990s.

2.   It is the essential conclusion of DAC's work on Development Co-operation in the 1990s that the vicious circle of underdevelopment that links high population growth, poverty, malnutrition, illiteracy and environmental degradation can be broken only through economic and developmental strategies and policies which *integrate* the objectives and requirements of

- Promoting sustainable economic growth;
- Enabling broader participation of all the people in the productive processes and a more equitable sharing of their benefits;
- Ensuring environmental sustainability and slowing population growth in those many countries where it is too high to permit sustainable development.

3.   The developing countries themselves are ultimately responsible for their own development. In particular, the effectiveness of their policies and institutions is central to their development successes and failures and the eventual attainment of self-reliance. External assistance can only be subsidiary to their own development efforts. However, depending on their increasingly diversified individual circumstances, adequate aid is essential, together with international policies which underpin an expansion of trade, investment and capital flows.

4.   The future orientation of development co-operation should be shaped by a constructive dialogue among developed and developing countries. We put forward this policy statement as a contribution to such a dialogue. A more comprehensive analysis is given in the 1989 DAC Chairman's Report on Development Co-operation in the 1990s.

*
* *

THE DEVELOPMENT IMPERATIVE – A CENTRAL GLOBAL PRIORITY

5. The developed and other economically advanced countries cannot live in isolated enclaves of prosperity in a world where other countries face growing mass poverty, economic and financial instability and environmental degradation. Not only is this unacceptable on humanitarian grounds; the future well-being of developed countries is linked to economic progress, preservation of the environment and peace and stability in the developing world.

6. In the coming decade and beyond developing countries will face unprecedented demographic and environmental pressures. Some 850 million people will be added to the Third World population in the 1990s, an *increase* which will exceed the total existing population in the OECD area, with a continuing rapid trend towards urbanisation and cities of a size which present new challenges. Poverty remains a pervasive phenomenon in most developing countries, affecting altogether about one billion people. At the same time, the world's ecosystem is in danger, requiring decisive action and possibly profound adaptations in economic activity in both developed and developing countries. And the serious human and economic effects of narcotics production and use present another major challenge for both developed and developing countries.

7. In this perspective, development co-operation must become in the 1990s a more central political concern, in both developed and developing countries.

8. With the improvement in world economic conditions, a better East-West political climate, progress in the solution of a number of regional conflicts (with a hope also of permitting a reduction in heavy military expenditure burdens), a development towards more open and democratic societies and more effective policies across a range of developing countries, there may be opportunities for more progress in the 1990s than there was in the 1980s.

9. Member governments recognise the importance of the fundamental political changes in Central and Eastern Europe and will support the important process of economic reform in these countries. This support will not diminish their determination to give high priority to their development co-operation with the Third World.

KEY ORIENTATIONS FOR DEVELOPMENT POLICIES AND DEVELOPMENT CO-OPERATION IN THE 1990s: GROWTH, PEOPLE AND ENVIRONMENTAL SUSTAINABILITY

10. Integrating the requirements of economic growth, participation of people and environmental sustainability implies a set of consistent and mutually reinforcing approaches in a range of key policy areas, as set out below.

Working with Developing Countries towards Broad-Based Economic Growth

11. Without broad-based economic growth the basic structural and social transformations which make up the process of development (including a widening preference for smaller families) will not occur.

12. The decade of the 1980s has witnessed world-wide a new climate of economic liberalisation. The need for properly functioning markets and appropriate prices and incentives, for sound fiscal and monetary policies and for structural adjustment on a continuing basis as prerequisites for effective resource use, growth and employment, is now better recognised in many countries. It is primarily these changes towards more effective policies which hold out promise for more progress in the 1990s than there was in the 1980s.

13. In designing and implementing policy reform programmes, full account needs to be taken of deep-seated structural problems and developing countries' social, demographic and political environment. The timeframe has to be realistic and ways must be found of mitigating adverse effects on the most vulnerable groups.

14. Economic growth requires carefully prioritised infrastructure investment and the build-up or rehabilitation of productive capacity in agriculture, industry and other sectors, with greater scope for private enterprise. In a number of areas closer regional co-operation would improve opportunities for fuller use of economic potentials. For those countries highly dependent on a few primary commodity exports, the key to development must be greater attention to diversification and to the role of markets. In poorer developing countries in particular, with insufficient domestic financing and limited external debt-servicing capacities, official development assistance has an important role to play in laying the basis for improved growth.

A New Emphasis on Stimulating Productive Energies through Investing in People and Participatory Development

15. Stimulating the productive energies of people, encouraging broader participation of all the people in the productive processes and a more equitable sharing of their benefits, must become more central elements in development strategies and development co-operation.

16. Investing in people is essential for economic growth and greater equity:
   - Higher priority is needed for making available, on the widest possible scale, sustainable and effective education and training, basic health care, and credit and advice for small farmers and entrepreneurs including women.
   - Improved food security and adequate nutrition through broad-based agricultural and rural development, creating increased production and incomes, remain an elementary development co-operation objective.
   - More active participation of women in the process of development at all levels is an essential element of sustainable, participatory development.
   - The drug problem must be tackled decisively to prevent human potential in developing countries from being destroyed or directed into illicit activities.

17. We will seek opportunities to work with developing countries towards promoting conditions for a dynamic productive sector, strengthening the role of individual initiative, private enterprise and the market system, and more generally, drawing the whole population into the active life of their countries. The transition from an economy which is stifled by over-regulation, and by powerful state and private monopolies, to an economy where the productive energies of people are motivated and can find legitimate expression is a complex challenge.
   - There is a vital connection, now more widely appreciated, between open, democratic and accountable political systems, individual rights and the effective and equitable operation of economic systems.

- Participatory development implies more democracy, a greater role for local organisations and self-government, respect of human rights including effective and accessible legal systems, competitive markets and dynamic private enterprise.
- More open competitive systems will improve effective resource use, growth and employment, and will create more favourable conditions for a more equitable income distribution.

18. New emphasis on participatory development does not imply bypassing governments. Indeed, effective development requires strong and competent governments and public services. At the same time, a more determined emphasis on individual initiative and private sector promotion will require less "governmentalised" channels of aid, building on national and local non-governmental institutions, as a part of government-to-government co-operation. Forms of development co-operation which contribute to more participatory decision-making processes include:

- Associating users through appropriate organisations with the design and implementation of aid financed projects;
- Promoting co-operatives and similar associations and NGOs;
- Co-operation in strengthening legal and judicial systems and democratic institutions of government.

Contributing to Environmentally Sound and Sustainable Development and Slowing Population Growth: Central Tasks for Development Co-operation

19. Contributing to environmentally sound and sustainable development is a central task for development co-operation in the 1990s. Without major action, irreparable damage could be done to the resource base and natural environment in developing countries. The problems could become increasingly intractable and expensive, compromising current and future development prospects. In developing countries, poverty is both a cause and result of environmental degradation. The imperative of protecting the environmental resource base for the benefit of today's and future generations is thus in itself a compelling reason for economic and social development. Without broad-based development, policies and practices securing sustainable use of natural resources will be difficult to attain.

20. It is essential that all countries actively participate in confronting global environmental issues. The industrial countries bear a special responsibility. But developing countries must also take action. They are directly concerned, both as sources and potential victims of global environmental degradation. Combating deforestation and desertification, protecting the ozone layer, more rational use of land and water resources, more efficient and rational energy production and use and appropriate treatment of toxic wastes and materials are among the central concerns.

21. Assisting developing countries in identifying and managing environmental problems at the level of policies and of specific programmes and projects must be a priority task for aid. The integration of environmental concerns into development projects and programmes, while increasing benefits, will often result in increased costs requiring the mobilisation of additional financial resources and technological transfers, including from donors.

22. There is an imperative need to slow population growth in those many countries where it is too high to permit sustainable development. Offering people in developing countries the opportunity to plan the size of their families, now taken for granted in the industrialised countries, is essential to avoid an aggravation of already difficult social, economic and

environmental problems. DAC Members are ready to help developing countries to establish, fund and implement effective population strategies and programmes as a matter of priority.

THE IMPORTANCE OF EFFECTIVE OECD ECONOMIC POLICIES FOR DEVELOPMENT

23. Following the serious international recession of the early 1980s, growth in world output and trade has improved markedly. The more positive medium-term economic prospects for OECD countries hold the promise of a better world environment for development in the 1990s. Nevertheless, at the beginning of the new decade, high real interest rates and persisting protectionist pressures are negative factors in the development outlook. The OECD countries accept that their international responsibilities require on their own part effective domestic and external adjustment and a strong political commitment to international economic co-operation, including the effort, through the Uruguay Round of trade negotiations, to strengthen the open, multilateral world trading system for the benefit of all countries.

24. We will work to secure a greater degree of coherence in policy-making, economic and increasingly now also environmental, with regard to the impact on developing countries.

25. Resolving debt problems and restoring capital flows remains a central, urgent task. Debt problems and slow growth continue to constrain development progress in a range of low and middle-income countries. These problems must be resolved as soon as possible, in the particular context of each debtor country, based on treatment of the fundamental structural and economic policy problems associated with them. Our governments are committed to continuing the co-operative effort to this end, as reflected by the recent strengthening of the debt strategy.

26. Strong adjustment and reform efforts undertaken by the debtor countries themselves remain the key to their recovery. Action by our countries to improve fiscal and external balances and action by debtor countries to restore economic confidence will together, in time, lead to a healthier level and pattern of capital flows to debtor countries, with lower real interest rates, increased direct investment and, of particular significance, the return of flight capital.

STRENGTHENING THE AID EFFORT

27. We intend to adapt our aid to help implement development assistance strategies along the lines set out above. In view of the growing diversity of developing countries we will strengthen our efforts to adapt and differentiate aid policies and modalities according to specific highly varied country needs and circumstances. We will ask our staffs to review policies and operational instructions in the light of this policy statement taking account also of the supporting material in the 1989 DAC Chairman's Report.

28. We reaffirm our determination to work with developing countries, the competent international institutions and other donors, to improve aid co-ordination in accordance with

the 1986 DAC aid co-ordination principles and to ensure a more coherent aid effort, properly integrated with the economic strategies, environmental requirements and public management of the recipient countries. In particular:

- We will seek further to improve aid quality. We reaffirm the 1988 DAC Principles for Project Appraisal; we will promote the evaluation of aid-financed projects and programmes and strengthened aid administrative capacity and take other measures as required.
- We will plan and manage our aid increasingly in the context of co-ordinated support for larger sectoral programmes, objectives and policies.
- We will encourage our operational staffs to participate effectively in efforts at improving local aid co-ordination and aid management.
- We reaffirm the principle that developing countries themselves must be at the centre of the aid co-ordination process and declare our readiness to help developing countries strengthen their capacity to co-ordinate and manage aid and to take increasing responsibility for aid implementation.

29. We acknowledge that the orientations set out above imply significant investments in physical and social infrastructure as well as support for policy reform. We acknowledge the significant degree of institutional reform implied in strengthening public management and dynamic enterprise sectors. We recognise that the nature and quality of technical assistance will often have to be significantly rethought and upgraded to contribute better to longer-run institution-building requirements.

30. The aid volume performance of individual DAC Members in recent years has varied considerably. While other capital flows have faltered, overall DAC aid has expanded in line with aggregate DAC GNP to reach about $50 billion. We express our appreciation for the efforts of NGOs in mobilising an additional $3-4 billion each year in voluntary contributions.

31. We recognise that in view of the huge development tasks ahead, which have been identified above, substantial additional aid efforts will be required both quantitatively and qualitatively. We welcome the increased efforts of DAC Members in this respect. We note the target already established by international organisations for the future level of official development assistance (0.7 per cent of GNP) and stress the importance of increased financial flows for development. Collectively, we shall seek to achieve further substantial increases in the aggregate level of aid.

32. We believe that the improvement in economic conditions in our countries, growing awareness among our publics of the interrelated problems of poverty, population growth and environmental degradation and the adoption of effective policies and programmes on the part of developing countries to address these issues enhance the climate for more positive aid volume responses. We will continue to review our aid efforts closely in the DAC.

During the past year, the Development Assistance Committee has devoted a major part of its work to a review of priorities for development co-operation in the 1990s. This 1989 Report, which is the 28th annual report on the efforts and policies of the Members of the Committee, reflects the Committee's findings.

The work of the Committee culminated in the adoption by the DAC High-Level Meeting, on 4th-5th December, of a statement on policy orientations for development co-operation in the 1990s. The text is set out at the front of this report.

In accordance with earlier practice, Part 1 of the report is written by the DAC Chairman himself. I have divided my commentary into two chapters. In Chapter I, I comment on three issues relevant to the longer-term future. In Chapter II, I comment on aid levels and other matters of more immediate interest.

Part 2 of the Report is the basic document made available to aid ministers and administrators for their consideration at the DAC High-Level Meeting. While written by the Secretariat it reflects the dialogue of the past year and the Members themselves should take much of the credit for this important work.

Part 3 of this Report provides customary information on trends and resource flows for development. It is followed by the standard DAC reporting tables.

The Report is issued on my authority and I take responsibility for its content. The OECD Secretariat's Development Co-operation Directorate, under the leadership of Mr. Helmut Führer, makes this Report possible and does most of the work, which I gratefully acknowledge.

Joseph C. Wheeler

Also available

FINANCING AND EXTERNAL DEBT OF DEVELOPING COUNTRIES — 1988
SURVEY (September 1989)
(43 89 03 1) ISBN 92-64-13261-9, 228 pages.   £14.50   US$25.00   FF120   DM50

EXTERNAL DEBT. Definition, Statistical Coverage and Methodology (1988)
(43 88 02 1) ISBN 92-64-13039-4, 178 pages   £7.00   US$12.00   FF60   DM26

VOLUNTARY AID FOR DEVELOPMENT: The Role of Non–Governmental
Organisations (1988)
(43 88 05 1) ISBN 92-64-13153-1, 154 pages   £11.00   US$20.00   FF90   DM39

Development Centre

ONE WORLD OR SEVERAL? Edited by Louis Emmerij (1989)
(41 89 04 1) ISBN 92-64-13249-X, 320 pages   £19.50   US$34.00   FF160   DM66

"Development Centre Studies" Series'

FINANCIAL POLICIES AND DEVELOPMENT by Jacques J. Polak (1989)
(41 89 01 1) ISBN 92-64-13187-6, 234 pages   £17.00   US$29.50   FF140   DM58

DEVELOPING COUNTRY DEBT: THE BUDGETARY AND TRANSFER
PROBLEM by Helmut Reisen and Axel van Trotsenburg (1988)
(41 88 01 1) ISBN 92-64-13053-5, 196 pages   £14.00   US$26.40   FF120   DM52

RECYCLING JAPAN'S SURPLUSES FOR DEVELOPING COUNTRIES by
T. Ozawa (1989)
(41 88 05 1) ISBN 92-64-13177-9, 114 pages   £11.00   US$19.00   FF90   DM37

"Development Centre Seminars" Series

THE IMPACT OF DEVELOPMENT PROJECTS ON POVERTY. Seminar organised
jointly by the OECD Development Center and the Inter American Bank (1989)
(41 88 07 1) ISBN 92-64-13162-0, 100 pages   £9.00   US$16.50   FF75   DM33

DEVELOPMENT POLICIES AND THE CRISIS OF THE 1980s edited by
Louis Emmerij (1987)
(41 87 03 1) ISBN 92-64-12992-8, 178 pages   £11.00   US$23.00   FF110   DM47

To be published

EXTERNAL DEBT STATISTICS: The Debt and other External Liabilities of
Developing, CMEA and Certain other Countries and Territories at End–December
1988 and End–December 1989

GEOGRAPHICAL DISTRIBUTION OF FINANCIAL FLOWS TO DEVELOPING
COUNTRIES. Disbursements. Commitments. Economic Indicators 1985–1988
Bilingual

TABLE OF CONTENTS

Part 1

CHAIRMAN'S OVERVIEW

I. LOOKING TOWARD THE NEXT CENTURY 11

   1. Moving Away from Lopsided Development: An Emerging Consensus on Population and Environment 11
   2. The Importance to Development of a New Relationship between Society and the Individual   15
   3. Poverty, Malnutrition and Agriculture 17

II. CURRENT ISSUES IN THE WORK OF THE DEVELOPMENT ASSISTANCE COMMITTEE 25

   1. Official Development Assistance in 1988 25
   2. Official Development Assistance in the Context of Total Resource Flows to Developing Countries 29
   3. Perspectives on Aid Management: A Fresh Look at Technical Co-operation 31
   4. The Maturing of Africa's Structural Adjustment Effort 33
   5. A Fresh Look at ODA for Least Developed Countries 36
   6. South Asia 37
   7. The Fourth United Nations Development Decade 39
   8. The Thailand Conference on Education for All 39

Part 2

DEVELOPMENT CO-OPERATION IN THE 1990s: WORKING WITH DEVELOPING COUNTRIES TOWARDS SUSTAINABLE AND EQUITABLE DEVELOPMENT

I. INTRODUCTION 43

PROGRESS, PROSPECTS AND PRIORITIES

II. THE DEVELOPMENT PROGRESS MADE AND THE CENTRAL DEVELOPMENT CO-OPERATION POLICY PRIORITIES FOR THE 1990s 45

   1. The Development Progress Made 45
   2. The Development Challenges Ahead 50
   3. The Central Development Co-operation Policy Priorities for the 1990s 53

III. WORLD ECONOMIC PROSPECTS AND ADJUSTMENT CHALLENGES 57

   1. Fundamental Long-Term World Economic Trends and the Major Adjustment Challenges for Developing Countries 57
   2. The Importance of Effective OECD Economic Policies and the Need for Improved Consistency with Development Co-operation Aims 59

IV. DEVELOPMENT CHALLENGES IN MAJOR REGIONS 61

1. The Basic Phenomenon of Country Diversity 61
2. East and South-East Asia 61
3. China and India 62
4. Other Asian Low-Income Countries 65
5. Latin America 65
6. Middle East and North Africa 66
7. The Special Case of Sub-Saharan Africa 68
8. Pacific Islands 69

POLICIES FOR BROAD-BASED GROWTH, PARTICIPATORY DEVELOPMENT
AND ENVIRONMENTAL SUSTAINABILITY

V.   WORKING WITH DEVELOPING COUNTRIES TO ACHIEVE
     BROAD-BASED ECONOMIC GROWTH 71

1. Effective Policies for Broad-Based Growth: Structural Adjustment in the Perspective of the
    1990s 71
2. Frameworks for International Co-operation for Encouraging Effective Development Policies   73
3. Encouraging Regional Economic Integration 75

VI. STIMULATING PRODUCTIVE ENERGIES THROUGH PARTICIPATORY
     DEVELOPMENT 77

1. The Notion of Participatory Development 77
2. A Larger Role for a Productive Private Sector: The Contribution of Market Forces and
    Private Enterprise to Development 78
3. Broadening the Base of Development Co-operation: Working with Non-Governmental
    Partners 82

VII. LAYING THE BASIS FOR BROAD-BASED GROWTH IN KEY SECTORS 85

1. Economic Infrastructure 85
2. The Energy Sector in a Development Perspective 85
3. The Central Role of Productive Agriculture 87
4. Science and Technology in the Service of Development 90
5. The Challenges and Opportunities of Urbanisation 91

VIII. STRATEGIES FOR EQUITABLE DEVELOPMENT 95

1. Achieving Equitable Development through Efficient and Broad-Based Growth, Participatory
    Development, Productive Employment and Investing in People 95
2. Creating Productive Jobs: The Basis of Equitable Development 95
3. Improved Food Security as an Elementary Objective of Development 97
4. Improving Access and Affordability of Essential Economic and Social Services 98
5. Implications for Aid 99

IX. A NEW EMPHASIS ON INVESTING IN PEOPLE 101

1. Human Resources: A Strategic Development Investment 101
2. Education 101
3. Meeting Basic Health Needs 104
4. The Need for Drug Abuse Control 105
5. Enhancing the Role of Women in Development 106
6. Institution-Building: A Key Priority for Development Co-operation 107
7. Helping Developing Countries to Abate Unsustainable Population Pressures 109

X.   BUILDING CONSENSUS ON ENVIRONMENTAL ISSUES 113

1. The New Awareness of Environment as a Critical Problem for Development 113
2. Strategies and Programmes for Sustainable Natural Resource Use: An Urgent Need 115

3. International Actions in Specific Areas 116
4. The Energy-Environment Dilemma 117
5. The Global Dimension of Environment: Longer-Term Challenges and Risks 118
6. OECD/DAC Action 121

IMPLICATIONS FOR RESOURCE MOBILISATION AND THE AID SYSTEM

XI. THE FINANCIAL CHALLENGES AHEAD 125

1. Current Realities: International Capital Flows, the Diversity of Country Situations and the World Economic Environment 125
2. Sustainable and Equitable Development in the 1990s: The Financial Dimension 128
3. Improving the Supply and Allocation of Capital at the Global Level in the 1990s 129
4. Dealing with Debt Overhangs 130
5. Foreign Direct Investment 131

XII. IMPLICATIONS FOR THE FUTURE ORIENTATION OF THE AID SYSTEM 133

1. The Capacity of the Aid System to Respond to the Emerging Challenges 133
2. The Contribution of Aid 134
3. Aid Volume Requirements and the Outlook for Aid 135
4. Improving Prospects for Self-Reliance 138
5. Co-ordination: Working Towards Concerted Donor and Recipient Efforts 138
6. Working with Developing Countries towards Effective Project Selection and Design 140
7. The Need for a Strong Multilateral System 141
8. Co-operation with More Advanced Developing Countries 143
9. Co-operation with Non-DAC Donors 144

Part 3

TRENDS IN RESOURCE FLOWS FOR DEVELOPMENT

I. FINANCIAL RESOURCES FOR DEVELOPING COUNTRIES:
1988 AND RECENT TRENDS .... 14.

1. Total Net Financial Resource Flows to Developing Countries 149
2. Aid Volume Trends and Prospects for DAC Members 153
3. Trends in Aid Patterns for Individual DAC Members 156

II. AID FROM NON-DAC SOURCES 173

1. Overview 173
2. Non-DAC OECD Countries 173
3. CMEA Countries 175
4. Arab Countries 178
5. Other Donors 181

III. MULTILATERAL AID: A TREND CONTINUES 185

1. Donors' Attitudes and Contributions 185
2. Trends in Disbursements 189
3. Current Replenishments of the Development Banks 189
4. Recent Policy Reviews 192

STATISTICAL ANNEX 197

7

TEXT TABLES AND CHARTS

Chart 1	Aid by the Major Donor Groups	26
Chart 2	Net ODA from DAC Countries in 1988	28
Table 2-1	Economic and Social Trends in Developing Countries, 1965-87	46
Table 2-2	Projected Population Growth in Developing Countries, 1965-2025	47
Chart 3	Comparative Per Capita Income Growth of Selected Groups of Developing Countries	48
Chart 4	Improvements in Life Expectancy between 1965 and 1987	48
Chart 5	Population in 1965 and 2000	49
Chart 6	Poverty	51
Table 2-3	Population in Urban Areas, 1950-2000	92
Table 2-4	Megacities in Developing Countries	92
Table 2-5	Growth of Labour Force in Developing Countries, 1990-2000	96
Table 2-6	Public Educational Expenditure	102
Table 2-7	Global Primary Energy Consumption and Carbon Dioxide Emission, 1986	119
Chart 7	Comparative Energy Consumption in 1986	120
Table 2-8	Balance of Payments on Current Account	126
Table 3-1	Total Net Resource Flows to Developing Countries	150
Chart 8	Total Net Resource Flows from all Sources by Type 1980-1988	151
Table 3-2	Key Totals for ODA Flows from DAC Countries	153
Table 3-3	Changes in Real Terms in DAC ODA and Capital Subscription Payments, 1986-88	154
Table 3-4	ODA Performance of DAC Countries in 1988 and Recent Years	157
Table 3-5	Aid from Non-DAC Donors	174
Table 3-6	CMEA Countries' Estimated Net Disbursements to Developing Countries and Multilateral Agencies	176
Table 3-7	ODA Net Disbursements by Arab Donors	178
Table 3-8	ODA Net Disbursements by National Arab Aid Agencies including Loans and Grants Administered on behalf of the Government	179
Table 3-9	Main Recipients of Known Net Disbursements of Bilateral and Multilateral Arab Aid	180
Table 3-10	Net Disbursements by Multilateral Arab/OPEC Funds and Banks	180
Table 3-11	Total ODA Contributions to Multilateral Development Agencies and Funds from DAC Member Countries 1979-88	186
Table 3-12	DAC Members' ODA Contributions to Multilateral Development Agencies and Funds as Percentage of Total ODA, GNP and of Total DAC Multilateral ODA, 1980-88	187
Table 3-13	DAC Members' Shares of Total DAC Funding of the UNDP and of DAC Extra-budgetary Financing of the Specialised Agencies, 1981-88	188
Table 3-14	The Composition of Net Disbursements of Concessional and Non-Concessional Flows from the Main Multilateral Agencies, 1981-82 and 1987-88	190
Table 3-15	Composition of Grant Expenditures on Operational Activities for Development of the United Nations System, 1980-81 to 1988	191

Part 1

CHAIRMAN'S OVERVIEW

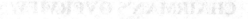

I

LOOKING TOWARD THE NEXT CENTURY

During the past year the DAC's nineteen Members have been discussing the major development issues likely to impinge on the aid process during the next decade. The dialogue has taken place under the title: "Development Co-operation in the 1990s". We are devoting most of the 1989 Report on the Efforts and Policies of the Members of the Development Assistance Committee to this subject.

Part 2 of the Report constitutes the basic document resulting from the DAC's year-long debate. The goal has been to bring together in a coherent conceptual framework a state-of-the-art assessment of the aid system in the perspective of the challenges of the 1990s. At their High-Level Meeting in December 1989, the DAC's aid ministers and administrators had this document before them as a basis for their own concise policy statement.

The DAC Chairman in this chapter provides his personal views on three issues related to priorities for the 1990s and beyond.

1. MOVING AWAY FROM LOPSIDED DEVELOPMENT: AN EMERGING CONSENSUS ON POPULATION AND ENVIRONMENT

In a recent article by Harlan Cleveland and Lincoln P. Bloomfield, they wrote:

"The elegant economist Barbara Ward spoke of our time as 'the hinge of history' and she wrote that the biosphere of our inheritance and the technosphere of our creation were out of balance:

'The door of the future is opening onto a crisis more sudden, more global, more inescapable, more bewildering than any ever encountered by the human species. And one which will take decisive shape within the life span of children who are already born.'

"She was writing in 1971. Everything that has happened since those words were written reinforces their prescient wisdom. For it was not as clear then as it is now, that (in Roger Revelle's memorable image) we humans are conducting a giant experiment of which we cannot even guess the outcome."[1]

The population and environment consensus which is now taking shape calls for a fresh look at development strategy and a new dimension of urgency. Newly understood imperatives challenge our complacency.

I recall a mission to Nepal in 1968. The magic of a helicopter ride north of Katmandu deposited a group of us near a hillside village about five days' walk from the nearest road. We visited the village clinic where, strewn over the floor, were empty penicillin phials. Our post-war technology had found its way to one of Earth's more remote villages.

The penicillin was one of a series of technological innovations which set in motion an exciting but asymmetrical process of development in which many children lived who would have died. Population increased. In Nepal's micro-economies, largely cut off from the outside world — even from the next valley — by the necessity to transport traded items on human backs, the old environmental balance was upset. Farming was extended uphill through the cutting of new terraces. With less forest land and more demand for wood, women walked farther to find firewood. More cattle also ate more fodder cut from young tree branches. The resulting deforestation in the Himalayan hills now affects water flows and exacerbates flood conditions hundreds of miles below in the Gangetic and Brahmaputra river systems. Nepal unwittingly exports soil to India and Bangladesh. Whole hill-sides slip down, taking away terraces and villages. Nepal's hill agriculture is increasingly unsustainable.

The news in the world of development is not that these asymmetrical processes are taking place. The quotation from Barbara Ward's writings nearly two decades ago reminds us that the problem has been known a long time. What is new is that these issues are now better understood by broad segments of our populations, and, at long last, are being translated into mainstream politics. A heightened sense of urgency is propelling a new consensus about environmental issues among the decision-makers in developing countries and industrial countries alike. Today's development process is now recognised as being lopsided (the word is Barbara Ward's); symmetry must be restored.

In industrial countries we have optimistically assumed that we were at least moving in the right direction in coping with environmental issues. We have nearly completed the demographic transition. Population growth in some industrial countries has almost stopped and in others is generally under 1 per cent. We have increased energy efficiency, though we know we can do much more. We have succeeded in cleaning up the air around many of our cities, although the record on this score is mixed. With effluent control, many rivers have been made cleaner. Concentration of agriculture on our high-potential lands has permitted us to re-forest large tracts of marginal land.

Our optimism has now been hit on the head with a new set of concerns. We have discovered acid rain. We now see much more clearly the indispensable protective function of the ozone layer. There is a general perception, being tested out by our scientists, that a process of air-warming — the greenhouse effect — will, over the long run, change the climate. Rich delta areas, or even whole countries, could be submerged by rising ocean levels. Furthermore, industrial-country officials recognise that the solutions to such problems are no longer uniquely in their hands — these are world-wide issues and solutions will increasingly involve developing countries.

Psychologically, there is a new perception as to who is "we". The concept of "we" has moved from the family to the tribe or community to the nation or grouping of nations, and finally now to Earth as a whole. Perhaps from a values point of view the most important message of the Brundtland Report, *Our Common Future*, is the ethical assumption that all 10 billion people expected to inhabit the Earth by the middle of the next century will have an equal right to the use of Earth's limited resources.

Only now are we tackling the problem of how 10 billion or even more people can live on our planet. In a world where many decisions which affect us all must be made by hundreds of millions of individuals rather than simply by a few central authorities, we face the challenge of reaching a consensus among those millions of decision-makers consistent with a sustainable development process. We seek this consensus in a dynamic world in which our technical understanding is severely limited. Our confidence that our value systems, our management processes, and our science and technology can be adapted, improved and brought to bear quickly enough, is being put to the test.

There is a basic paradox in the development strategy implied in *Our Common Future*. The paradox is that, although development is resource-utilising and therefore puts pressure on the sustainability of our forests, our soils, our water and our air, yet it is only through a process of development that we can achieve the balance which will save us. Suddenly we are in a hurry. We must hurry through the demographic transformation if we are to achieve some reasonable relationship between numbers of people using resources and the capacity of those resources to sustain us. We must hurry to make fuller use of our best agricultural areas if we are to stop the misuse of low-potential areas which should be utilised for forests or grazing or left alone altogether. We must hurry to apply known technology and to develop new technology if we are to provide 10 billion people a decent living, without destroying our fragile biosphere. Implicitly, this means we must hurry to achieve improved health, which itself involves moderation in the number of births. We must hurry to bring education to all of our populations because this is essential to our other objectives. We must hurry to create the conditions for job creation and income growth because, without efficient production and adequate income, the development process cannot be sustained.

What we have simplistically sought in terms of a demographic transition is now seen much more broadly as a transformation away from a traditional balance characterised by low population densities, by a light use of our environmental inheritance, and by a generally miserable set of circumstances in which most children born could be expected to die within a few years. The new balance, if we achieve it, will be one which involves much greater densities in human population, much more intensive, but still sustainable, use of our natural resource inheritance, and, in the end, a new demographic balance — a full life balance — in which each family has less children but where children born can expect to live 70 or 80 years in reasonably good health and with generally adequate nutritional intake. The new balance, of course, would be ever-changing, perhaps captured in a concept of dynamic symmetry. The world which is coming in the next century will be one requiring significant changes in values, driven by environmental imperatives, but consistent with the global ethic that we all deserve access to a "good life" process.

The consensus on environment and population as issues dealt with most effectively in the framework of a broad-based and quicker development process will surely add energy and clarity of purpose to developing-country strategies. Rapid and environmentally sustainable growth will require more finely tuned policies, more efficient technologies, and more financial resources. Strategies emphasizing the "enabling" of populations to give them the knowledge and capacity to make choices consistent with sustainability will favour programmes for universal education, public health and employment. In general, enabling strategies call for a broad-based incomes approach with agricultural development playing a major role rather than a narrower approach confining growth to only parts of the society. There will be more participation of developing-country populations, not simply as a result of changing governmental structures, but perhaps driven even more by increasing access to education and to information about how others live. The television revolution in the villages of the developing countries accelerates this process. Concern about environment will not be limited to the populations of donor countries, but will be internalised into the total development process.

Perhaps the greatest enemy of symmetry or balance in the development process is a complacent short-term view of our interests. We seem to have difficulty in looking at issues in intergenerational terms. Satisfaction of today's wants — the "now-now" syndrome — too often takes precedence over what makes sense for our grandchildren. If we drag out the process of access to a decent life, we also extend the time period when people, in their desperation, will cut down forests and cultivate inappropriate land areas. We put off the day when communities will be able to afford sanitary facilities or controls on effluents. We also postpone the goal of a demographic transition, of improved health and better education. Success in achieving a symmetrical development process is not fore-ordained. There is growing evidence that we are not now on course toward a sustainable civilisation for all 10 billion people expected in the next century. Only a recognition of the issues and an understanding of the needed changes in course will get us to the dynamic balance needed to pass on a sustainable process to future generations.

Highlighting the need for speed in obtaining symmetry brings a clearer focus to a number of issues for both developing countries and donors. Development strategies at the country level need to be designed to move quickly toward a broad-based approach, reaching the whole population. This means a democratisation of the education process rather than reserving education to the elites. Donors need to consider how they can support sector strategies for education which give a higher priority to primary and basic education and training. It means a democratisation of the health process rather than devotion of most government resources to urban-privileged groups. Donors should consider this in evaluating projects. It means fast but sustainable development of high-potential agricultural areas, including the provision of necessary infrastructure, rather than a slower process which keeps people on fragile eco-systems. It means making the best possible use of limited resources by defining land tenure and encouraging individual enterprise. It means moving quickly to conserve fast-disappearing water sources. It means speeding up the search for technology which will be energy efficient and resource saving. It means challenging developing-country communities to come up with programmes which will at the same time accelerate the development process and achieve greater restraint in the way limited natural resources are utilised. While we have no choice but to "use" natural resources, they must be used in such a way that they can continue to be available for future generations.

During the past year the United Nations has reported that earlier projections on population growth have had to be revised upwards. Thus, the hope that world population might level off at 10 billion is now less likely to be realised. The twenty-first century may see us reaching closer to 15 billion. This news should be as compelling as the news on the ozone layer and earth-warming, but it clearly is not. In industrial societies we are no longer concerned about rapid population growth in our countries. Some even worry that our growth is too slow. Developing-country growth is far away, "over there", impinging on us directly only in terms of illegal migration. In developing countries, too, the population issue has been politically unrewarding. One can hope for a whole new order of priority to measures which directly and indirectly will reverse the recent slow-down of progress in achieving the demographic transition. Existing complacency on this issue is completely inconsistent with a symmetry-seeking strategy. Perhaps attitudes will change as our perception of interrelationships increases.

One hopes these new perceptions will lead to support for new priorities and new strategies. As industrial countries themselves face up to questions of automobile- and industry-created pollution, phase out the production of chlorofluorocarbons and otherwise demonstrate the political courage to deal effectively with environmental issues, they will be in a stronger position to urge action by others. Donors need to provide funds to developing countries in support of broad-based growth. They need to provide not only good quality support but fully adequate support. Surely, if we are serious about supporting a development process which achieves the new dynamic symmetry which we now know is a matter of global urgency, then we must look again at our priorities.

2. THE IMPORTANCE TO DEVELOPMENT OF A NEW RELATIONSHIP BETWEEN SOCIETY AND THE INDIVIDUAL

Over recent decades, issues of human rights and democratic practices have become more important in international discourse. In aid relations, however, the issues have often been muted. Since many developing countries have remained in a pre-democracy stage of political development, aid agencies could only deal with them on their own terms. It has been hoped that the development process itself might cause an evolution toward more open and accountable systems. W. W. Rostow wrote nearly twenty years ago: "Just as the healing role of modernization as an ideology makes democracy more possible, modernization, in its most technical sense, is assisted by the spread of democratic process and responsibilities to the people — when done in the right way"[2]. Rostow wrote in a period of relative pessimism about the advent of democratic institutions. Today, his faith that in time the populations of developing countries — in their own way — would fashion democracy seems more justified.

It has been refreshing to hear more frequent voices from developing countries themselves speak in clear terms about matters we have too often befuddled in our own aid-related discourse.

15

One of the most articulate voices in the new debate has been Hernando de Soto, President of the Institute for Liberty and Democracy in Lima, Peru. The basic message conveyed by Mr. de Soto is that the donor community has forgotten its own history. We now take for granted many institutions, processes and traditions which are critical to the effective operation of society. Here are some of his examples.

— In industrial countries most property is titled by government. This is often not the case in developing countries. Without titles, people hesitate to invest and property cannot be used as collateral.
— In industrial countries it is very easy to establish limited liability corporations. In many developing countries, red tape virtually precludes the small entrepreneur from gaining the benefits of incorporation.
— In industrial countries most laws and regulations are adopted after a transparent process of advance publication and public hearings. In many developing countries they are issued by the executive branch without an opportunity for interested individuals or groups to comment and without advance publication in newspapers.

De Soto argues that Latin American law does not allow for public participation in government. Just as European mercantilism was replaced by modern democracy, so do existing systems in developing countries need to change to make democracy and markets work for everyone. This means opening up economic participation, creating institutions to decentralise and deregulate government power, and creating institutions to control and make accountable the monopolistic exercise of government power. It means public education to mobilise support for change[3].

For many societies, de Soto observes that communism has been the path followed to replace mercantilism, but even the principal communist states seem now to have recognised the need for greater security of tenure and contracts, due process of law, accountability, and open systems of criticism and correction.

Now that the word "democracy" has become an acceptable word to use in development circles, we are also hearing more often concerns about "corruption". There is also a more open discussion of the level of developing-country military expenditures and the military administrations which often occur when the armed forces become large compared with other societal groups[4]. We are even beginning to hear that one-party systems do not work. The connection between open democratic and accountable systems and the effective operation of economic systems is being made more forcefully. More developing-country voices seek political evolution toward more democratic forms. Take, for example, the following from the "African Alternative Framework to Structural Adjustment Programmes for Socio-Economic Recovery and Transformation" adopted in a Joint Statement by African Ministers of Economic Planning and Development and Ministers of Finance in a meeting in April 1989 in Addis Ababa.

"As stated in the *Khartoum Declaration*, basic rights, individual freedom and democratic participation by the majority of the population are often lacking in Africa. This pervasive lack of democracy also makes mobilisation and effective accountability difficult. This is one important sense in which Africa needs more democratic political structures in order to facilitate development. As the *Abuja Statement* noted, Africa has to draw strength from political cohesion and new political

16

perspectives that emphasise the democratisation of the African society and increased accountability of those entrusted with responsibility. All these have critical implications for the decision-making process and leadership structures in Africa. The existing patterns of social differentiation and political organization tend to encourage a rather narrow base for decision-making and the lack of the popular debate over basic national development policies and their implementation. Hence, the *Khartoum Declaration* observed that 'the political context for promoting healthy human development has been marred, for more than two decades, by instability, war, intolerance, restrictions on the freedom and human rights of individuals and groups as well as overconcentration of power with attendant restrictions on popular participation in decision-making'. All these impose severe constraints on motivation for high productivity."[5]

With the now more general recognition and acceptance of the importance of accountability in the making and implementing of rules and regulations and of the need for public participation, donors are offering more help in these areas. We hear of projects for land titling, for helping build judicial systems, for legal training, for help with electoral systems, for strengthening legal rights for women, and for strengthening parliamentary institutions. There is an increasing interest in decentralised decision-making characterised by the strengthening of local government, the encouragement of popular organisations and greater scope for the private sector. As education becomes more general in society and as entrepreneurship and market forces become more appreciated, the internal forces for reform are strengthened. A quiet revolution may be in process which can have profound implications for development. While economic and political monopolies of power will resist this revolution, and while history tells us that there will be both backward and forward movements, we seem to be in a period when democratic processes are advancing. This phenomenon is reflected in donor thinking about development co-operation in the 1990s.

3. POVERTY, MALNUTRITION AND AGRICULTURE

In the 1990s we need a strategy to reduce significantly the number of hungry people. Since most hungry people live in rural areas and are hungry because they lack the income to buy food, the strategy should focus on agricultural growth and employment creation.

The whole question of poverty and hunger is fraught with a confusion of facts and images. The confusion is getting in the way of purposeful action. Perhaps the term "poverty" is unfortunate since its definition varies from one society to another. Whatever its definition, it is frequently said the world harbours about one billion people living in a state of absolute poverty. It is also often said that the number is increasing. Unfortunately, definitional problems and the lack of reliable statistics make it hard to know whether or not the numbers are increasing. But there is general consensus that between 15 and 20 per cent of the world's population lives in intolerable conditions.

17

Perhaps the simplest measure of poverty is malnutrition. While existing statistics here are also less than completely reliable, they are good enough to permit some generalisations. They suggest that about 700 million people do not eat enough to lead a fully productive life. Even if this is wrong by some considerable margin, it is sufficiently right to tell us that a problem exists which in good conscience we cannot ignore.

To get at the question of hunger, we must overcome an image problem. Industrial-country populations think of hunger in terms of television pictures of emaciated and dying people in Ethiopia and Sudan. Those pictures propelled donor action to provide emergency food. We have all watched the drama in Sudan this past year, where the Secretary-General of the United Nations asked the head of UNICEF to co-ordinate the effort to get food positioned in Southern Sudan before the rains. It would be a callous world which did not respond to such needs.

But most of the 700 million are not hungry because of drought or civil war. Most are hungry in a much less dramatic way because they lack assets and employment. I think of my most recent visit to Bangladesh when I met a landless family living outside a village about four hours from Dhaka. Mother, father and six or seven children obviously did not get enough to eat. Yet there was plenty of food in the market. Their problem was that they had inadequate income to buy the food. Most of the 350 million hungry people in South Asia, 150 million in Sub-Saharan Africa, 75 million in China, and most of the rest spread among other Asian countries, North Africa and Latin America, are rural poor lacking land on which to grow food and lacking income with which to buy it. According to a recent World Bank study on "Poverty, Adjustment and Growth in Africa", two-thirds of the rural population in Africa remain below the absolute poverty level[6]. Most of these are malnourished. They are malnourished every year — not just in time of drought or war.

In most developing countries a large portion of national income is generated by agriculture-related employment. Any strategy to increase growth rates must be supported by accelerated growth in agriculture. Thus, at bottom, the most important single action donors could take to reduce hunger would be to support developing-country strategies to increase agricultural production and in this way and by other means to increase income in rural areas. Any such strategy must, of course, be linked to general growth strategies, which see urban and rural areas as inseparable parts of an integrated whole. High-technology agriculture needs urban development and urban development needs the impetus of agricultural growth[7].

Food strategies discussed over the years since the 1974 World Food Conference have tended to concentrate on food availability for the market or for emergency feeding rather than on nutrition and income questions. Gradually, though, attention has shifted in the direction of the developing-country farmer, the problems of employment and income, and the issue of hunger.

The World Food Council is now discussing malnutrition rather than simply market availability of food. In 1988 the Council met in Nicosia and adopted a Cyprus Initiative Against Hunger in the World. In 1989, meeting in Egypt, they adopted the Cairo Declaration. Among other things, the Council urged each country toward "the elimination of starvation and death caused by famine; a substantial reduction of malnutrition and mortality among young children; a tangible reduction in chronic hunger; and the elimination of major nutritional-deficiency diseases". The World Food Council President's report emphasized that "hunger will not be overcome unless the hungry have access to adequate employment or income producing opportunities."

No one argues that we will not need to continue to confer together about food for emergencies, food for market needs, problems of port capacity and timing of deliveries. The new clearer focus needed, though, is to consider how development strategies and aid packages, including food and non-food components, can be focused on rapid growth in incomes for those who are hungry. This means faster agricultural development. More money needs to be spent on rural infrastructure.

We should consider an overlay of complementary strategies which, taken together, add up to faster increases in agricultural production, the creation of on-farm and off-farm jobs, and improved nutrition — all critical to our broader anti-poverty goals. For example, a country needs policy and investment strategies for:

— production of major crops
— animal husbandry
— marketing
— fertilizers
— rural investments (irrigation, roads, power, communications, etc.)
— agricultural research
— seeds
— agricultural extension
— land tenure
— agricultural savings and credit
— use of donor-provided and own-purchased foods for assuring adequate supplies consistent with food price policies
— encouraging entrepreneurs.

Supplementary strategies which indirectly support agricultural production goals and also contribute to nutrition goals would be needed for:

— use of food and nutrition supplements for targeted low-income groups (for example, "under 5" groups, schoolgoers, pregnant and lactating mothers and people unable to work)
— reducing morbidity and mortality, including primary health care and use of the latest technologies such as inoculations, oral rehydration and iodine supplements to salt
— vitamin-enhancing programmes
— drinking water and sanitation
— education (including nutrition education)
— family planning
— women in development.

There are good reasons why such a "complementary strategies" campaign to reduce dramatically the number of hungry people should be as attractive to donors as to developing countries themselves.

By supporting an income-generating programme to combat malnutrition and hunger, we would work on something which industrial-country populations, which must provide

19

part of the funding, can understand better than vaguer concepts of poverty and development. The key is the connection between growing food and giving people a chance to work to feed their families.

Though one might initially guess that such a strategy would not gain the support of the agricultural communities in donor countries, this perception may be wrong. It is true that in recent years there have been concerns expressed that an agriculture-led strategy in developing countries would reduce markets for OECD-country food producers. But research completed by the International Food Policy Research Institute (IFPRI) and others tells us that actual experience has been the opposite. According to the United States Department of Agriculture, total developing-country production of cereals (excluding China) increased from an annual level of 275 million tons in the early 1960s to 485 million tons in the early 1980s. During the same period, developing-country cereal imports tripled from 34 million tons to 101 million tons. The group of countries with the highest food production growth rates, increasing from 64 million tons to 136 million tons, increased cereal imports from 14 million tons to 41 million tons. The reason for this seemingly paradoxical result is that additional incomes lead to both additional direct consumption of grain and more livestock consumption. A kilo of meat requires several kilos of grain to produce. Thus, strategies for broad-based agriculture-led job-creating growth, which enhance nutrition for developing-country populations, will lead to higher levels of trade in agricultural commodities — not to mention higher levels of trade in general. For example, an analysis of India's perspective planning suggests that a shift toward an employment-oriented strategy resulting in a moderate improvement in income distribution would increase demand for foodgrains by 6 million tons by the year 2000. Such an approach could make the difference between India's being a country marginally surplus in foodgrain and being a substantial importer. Thus, a determined effort to reduce hunger is also an excellent trade development programme[8].

One can imagine a country interested in such a hunger-reducing, employment-creating, agriculture-focused strategy taking up the question in the framework of their consultative group. Indicating a desire to embark on such a strategy, they could ask the donors to agree in principle to a long-term commitment along the following lines: the developing country would articulate a strategy which would cover all the sub-strategies needed. Donors would agree to help support the rural infrastructure and other sub-strategies in need of funding. They would also acknowledge the fact that there would be a period of increased economic activity for the whole economy which would not be matched right away by increased production, leading to induced imports which would need to be financed. Inevitably, food production would vary from year to year. While at least a portion of food imports required to meet increased demand could be provided as food aid, these would have to be adjusted to reflect fluctuations in production and to support the developing country's agricultural price policies. The financing of induced non-food imports would be appropriate for commodity or programme assistance. The donors would need to agree to a general magnitude of financing to match recipient performance, but would have to be flexible as between food and non-food assistance. The World Food Programme and the World Bank would work with the donors and the recipient to assure full co-ordination. While the individual components of such a strategy have each been part of past development efforts, the new features would be a greater clarity of objectives, better co-ordination of the elements, and a more ambitious scale of operation. The concept of a "development contract", put forward by Norway's Minister for Foreign Affairs, Thorvald Stoltenberg, might well be used for such a programme[9].

Such a strategy could be designed to achieve very positive environmental benefits. Rural infrastructure is often of direct environmental help. For example, water-saving measures such as land levelling, water spreading, and improved irrigation structures all are both environmentally positive and needed to increase agricultural production. Then there are drinking water and sanitation projects. The programme could also involve needed efforts on reforestation. Also, by concentrating on developing high potential lands, it may be possible to reduce pressure on marginal lands more appropriate for less intensive use.

For some donors food aid is attractive politically. Such a programme would use large amounts of food because consumption of food would usually increase sooner and faster than agricultural production. Also, food could be used for special feeding programmes for under-five populations and for school-goers as part of an accelerated education effort. Up until now, however, some donors have insisted on running food programmes separately from other aid, which has meant that the amounts of food (or proceeds from the sale of food) to pay labour for work done in building rural infrastructure has varied from year to year depending upon the weather or depending upon other factors which determined how much food a country needed to import. While food can be useful to support development, unless it is flexibly combined with other forms of aid or with local resources, a coherent and sustained development effort becomes difficult to implement. As H. W. Singer has written: food aid "will only have its maximum impact if it is better linked with other forms of assistance (financial, technical, health assistance, trade, etc.) and, above all, better integrated into recipient countries' development plans and policies"[10].

In the past we have tended to think of getting at the hunger problem by direct feeding. This essentially welfare approach is fully appropriate for emergency situations and for non-employable persons. But, that approach does not help most of the hungry people. The approach suggested here meets the criteria for sustainable development. It is a hunger strategy, an agricultural strategy, and, beyond these, it is an economic strategy. It puts people to work, including the landless. It creates capital and helps develop a financial infrastructure. It supports an efficient production process. It creates a healthy, dynamic synergy between rural and urban areas.

While an employment approach to improving nutrition may not have all of the emotional appeal of direct feeding of people caught in an emergency, the connections among hunger, unemployment, and low agricultural productivity ought to be understandable politically in both developing and donor countries. Definitions of degrees of malnutrition are now sufficiently precise and the incidence of malnutrition sufficiently measurable that developing-country governments should be able to monitor progress with low-cost sample surveys. A concerted effort involving the countries where most hunger occurs could significantly reduce the number of malnourished people in the next decade. Aside from the direct benefits in reducing hunger, such a programme would have very positive spin-offs in terms of developing-country overall growth, in terms of linked income enhancement in urban areas, and in terms of long-term commercial markets for donor-country products.   It would also provide significant environmental benefits.   Yet, there are many obstacles to be overcome, including political indifference and social rigidities, the need to bring together many policy strands to make the strategies work, the need for co-ordination with many donors, and the need for adequate funding provided flexibly and over time.   None of these is an insuperable problem.

NOTES AND REFERENCES

1.   This quotation is from *The Future of International Governance: Post-War Planning without the War First* by Harlan Cleveland and Lincoln P. Bloomfield, and printed in "Multilateralism and the United Nations", Journal of Development Planning, No.17, Department of International Economic and Social Affairs, United Nations, New York, 1987, page 8.

2.   *Politics and the Stages of Growth*, W. W. Rostow, Cambridge University Press, 1971, page 298.

3.   For a brief description of the work and findings of the Instituto Libertad y Democracia (ILD) see "Constraints on People: The Origins of Underground Economies and Limits to Their Growth" by Hernando de Soto in *Beyond the Informal Sector: Including the Excluded in Developing Countries*, Jerry Jenkins, Editor, ICS Press, San Francisco, California, 1988.

4.   See, for example, "National Policies for Development in Poor Countries" by Philip Ndegwa in *One World or Several*, edited by Louis Emmerij, President, OECD Development Centre, OECD, 1989, page 137.   Ndegwa discusses the interrelationships between democracy and development, emphasizing the need for public participation, for a development strategy aimed at people in all parts of a country, for suppressing corruption and tribalism, and for education of the people about development problems.

5.   "African Alternative Framework to Structural Adjustment Programmes for Socio-Economic Recovery and Transformation", United Nations Economic Commission for Africa (E/ECA/CM.15/6/Rev.3) 1989, paragraph 24.

6.   "Poverty, Adjustment and Growth in Africa" by Ismail Serageldin, The World Bank, 1989.

7.   For this discussion I have drawn especially from work of the International Food Policy Research Institute.   See their 1987 and 1988 Reports and "Food and Development: The Crucial Nexus" by John W. Mellor in *Economic Impact*, Number 61 and "Ending Hunger: An Implementable Program for Self-Reliant Growth" by John W. Mellor (forthcoming). See also "Food Security in Sub-Saharan Africa - Proposal for a Nutritional Security Strategy to be followed by Financial Co-operation, prepared by a KfW Study Group" by H. H. Prestele, *et al*, Kreditanstalt für Wiederaufbau, Frankfurt am Main, May 1989 and "Poverty, Adjustment and Growth in Africa" by Ismail Serageldin, World Bank, 1989.

8.   See International Food Policy Research Institute, 1987 Report pages 15-16, and the following short papers issued by IFPRI: "Trends of Cereal Production and Trade in Developing Countries" by Leonardo A. Paulino, IFPRI; "Livestock-Feedgrain Linkages in the Developing Countries" by J. S. Sarma, IFPRI; "Agricultural Growth and Import Demand in the LDCs" by Alain de Janvry and Elisabeth Sadoulet, University of California, Berkeley; "Effects of Income Growth and Distribution Changes on the Demand for Foodgrains in

India" by J. S. Sarma and Vasant Gandhi, IFPRI, "Third World Food Markets: Options for Agricultural Exporters? An Overview" by Nurul Islam, IFPRI; and "The Effects of Agricultural Growth in Developing Countries on Imports: Some Policy Implications" by Earl D. Kellogg, Consortium for International Development, and Richard H. Kodl, United States Department of Agriculture.

9. See "Toward a World Development Strategy" in *One World or Several*, *op. cit.*, page 241.

10. See "Food Aid: Development Tool or Development Obstacle?" by H. W. Singer, Institute of Development Studies, University of Sussex, published in *Irish Studies in International Affairs*, Vol.2, No.3, p.59.

II

CURRENT ISSUES IN THE WORK OF THE
DEVELOPMENT ASSISTANCE COMMITTEE

1. OFFICIAL DEVELOPMENT ASSISTANCE IN 1988

The Members of the Development Assistance Committee provided about $48 billion of official development assistance (ODA) in 1988 compared with $41.5 billion in 1987. This represents an increase of 16 per cent in nominal terms, or 7.6 per cent when measured at 1987 prices and exchange rates. This healthy increase was welcome news, coming as it did after a year in which, in constant prices and exchange rates, ODA had actually dipped by 1 per cent.

DAC ODA now represents just above 85 per cent of world aid, a significant increase over previous years. Reports on the basis of which CMEA assistance is estimated have been late this year. The OECD Secretariat assumes that the 1987 level held. In the case of Arab aid, there was another significant reduction from $3.3 billion in 1987 to $2.3 billion in 1988. Including smaller amounts from others, world aid came to about $56 billion. All of these figures are in terms of net ODA expenditures by donors rather than in terms of ODA receipts by developing countries, the difference consisting of two principal factors: funds made available to multilateral institutions in excess of the amounts multilateral institutions actually disbursed; and the cost to donors of their aid administration. ODA receipts by developing countries from all sources totalled over $51 billion. Total receipts, when measured at constant prices and exchange rates, have fallen slightly each year since 1985 in spite of the increase in ODA receipts from DAC Members during this period of over 5 per cent.

In 1988, there was a substantial temporary increase in official development assistance made available to multilateral institutions. A bunching of deposits in 1988 partly explains why in 1987 DAC Members recorded a modest decrease in ODA in volume terms. This bunching may also have a negative impact on ODA levels for 1989. Thus, it is important not to put too much stock in one year's figures; it is better to look at experience over a longer period.

Chart 1 shows aid in terms of 1987 prices and exchange rates. It shows the steady increase of DAC ODA in real terms over the past ten years. For the ten-year period 1979-88 the average annual increase in DAC ODA was just over 3 per cent, about the

25

Chart 1. **AID BY THE MAJOR DONOR GROUPS***

$ Billion

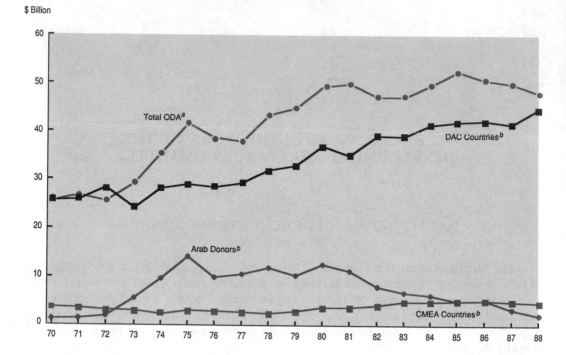

* ODA at 1987 prices and exchange rates.
a) Bilateral ODA and grants and concessional loans from multilateral agencies.
b) Bilateral ODA and ODA contributions to multilateral agencies.

same as real growth in GNP during this period. The increase was higher at the beginning of the decade than during the past five years. For the ten years as a whole, DAC increases almost exactly compensated for the reductions in Arab assistance, which in 1975 had been nearly $14 billion at 1987 prices and exchange rates, and which stayed over $10 billion into 1981, coming down to about $2 billion in 1988. CMEA aid has shown a gradual rise over this period, but of modest significance from the point of view of total disbursements.

As might be expected, the performance of the individual Members of the DAC varied. Table 3-4 in its last column provides useful information on effort over the past five years. In this period, Finland and Italy both increased aid volume (measured at 1987 prices and exchange rates) by roughly 16 per cent annually. Canada, Denmark, France, Japan, the Netherlands, Norway, Sweden, and Switzerland also chalked up increased aid levels during this period.

In terms of absolute volume, the improved record of Japan is the most important. Japan has a medium-term aim of reaching the DAC average ODA/GNP ratio by 1992.

By implication, this would mean an aid level of about $12 billion at the end of the period.

Most Members of the DAC adhere, at least in principle, to the 0.7 per cent target adopted in the United Nations. Denmark, the Netherlands, Norway, and Sweden all exceed this level, and Finland's aim is to reach it in 1989. France has reached it if aid to their overseas territories is included. Without the overseas territories, French aid is 0.5 per cent of GNP and France has announced its determination to reach 0.7 per cent as soon as possible.

The OECD Secretariat has found no reason to revise its earlier medium-term projection of a gradual average annual increase in DAC Members' ODA in the coming years of perhaps 2 per cent in real terms. This is heavily dependent on the continuing determination of Japan to increase its effort. Since we do not expect any further significant reductions in Arab assistance, if the DAC achieves this level of performance, the decade-long pause in the growth of world aid levels could be transformed into modest growth. New aid expected from Korea and Taiwan will also help. Firmer projections are not possible.

The DAC Chairman, of course, hopes that Members will not only continue to achieve their recent combined growth in ODA of over 2 per cent, but will substantially exceed this.

There are good reasons why DAC Members might decide to provide more assistance in the future. The recent tendency toward settlement of regional and country disputes might cause some Members to increase their total effort in order to initiate programmes in countries which have not been seen as high priorities for assistance in recent years. The list of candidates for new or increased aid is quite long and includes countries or regions of significant size. Afghanistan, Ethiopia, Indochina and Sudan are possibilities. In most cases, including these, further progress in settling internal or regional disputes will be needed before high levels of aid will make sense. But, there is so much movement in so many places that it is hard to believe it will be long before a number of countries which have received low donor priority in recent years will be able to make constructive use of increased levels of development aid. Of course, it is also our experience that countries earlier thought to be high priorities for development assistance have changed that status for one reason or another, and this experience too is likely to be repeated. But in general the direction seems positive.

Some donors have opened up for aid eligibility countries earlier taken off their lists because of growing oil revenues. Nigeria is an example. Then, one can expect a new impetus for aid as a result of the deepening concerns about world environmental issues. This will open up the need for new kinds of assistance, or for giving a higher priority to some traditional forms. For example, the donors have agreed in principle to provide assistance for the transfer of technology related to the ozone layer convention. It can be expected that similar indications of priority will be given in connection with the major determinants of earth-warming.

In the preceding chapter I urged a new look at the question of hunger, emphasizing the need for a determined effort to increase agriculture productivity through a programme of rural infrastructure investments. A serious effort here would justify both shifts in strategy in use of current levels and increased amounts as well.

Chart 2. NET ODA FROM DAC COUNTRIES IN 1988

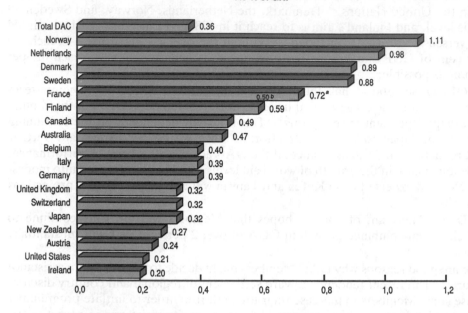

As % of GNP

Total DAC	0.36
Norway	1.11
Netherlands	0.98
Denmark	0.89
Sweden	0.88
France	0.50 b 0.72 a
Finland	0.59
Canada	0.49
Australia	0.47
Belgium	0.40
Italy	0.39
Germany	0.39
United Kingdom	0.32
Switzerland	0.32
Japan	0.32
New Zealand	0.27
Austria	0.24
United States	0.21
Ireland	0.20

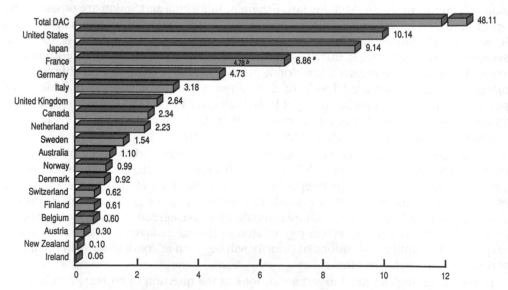

$ Billion

Total DAC	48.11
United States	10.14
Japan	9.14
France	4.78 b 6.86 a
Germany	4.73
Italy	3.18
United Kingdom	2.64
Canada	2.34
Netherland	2.23
Sweden	1.54
Australia	1.10
Norway	0.99
Denmark	0.92
Switzerland	0.62
Finland	0.61
Belgium	0.60
Austria	0.30
New Zealand	0.10
Ireland	0.06

a) Including DOM-TOM.
b) Excluding DOM-TOM.

Finally, there is a new awareness of an ironic development in aid priorities. Developing countries which did not succeed in managing their debt have become the recipients of extra assistance in response to their efforts at economic reform. Meanwhile, those which have all along exercised special prudence in the management of debt and have continued to meet repayment schedules are now often receiving smaller proportions of donor aid portfolios. Yet some of these countries could make very good use of more aid. Though their levels of imports have been going up, these levels could be allowed to increase faster if prudent management was supplemented by more concessional aid. This would permit accelerated programmes, for example, for rural infrastructure and for investments in education and health. Some large but low-income countries in Asia fall in this category of countries operating reasonably well but under their potential. Since some of these countries also harbour large proportions of the world's poor people, it is possible that a new consideration of priorities will give rise to a willingness to increase total aid levels.

I cite these factors not to predict that levels of ODA higher than the Secretariat expects are likely, but rather to emphasize that the need for higher assistance levels may well be increasing. One would not wish to rule out the possibility that donors might give these factors greater weight in their decision-making processes in the decade ahead.

A fuller description of ODA performance will be found in Part 3 of this report.

2. OFFICIAL DEVELOPMENT ASSISTANCE IN THE CONTEXT OF TOTAL RESOURCE FLOWS TO DEVELOPING COUNTRIES

A description of the role of ODA in the larger context of total resource flows is contained in Chapter XI of the basic paper on development co-operation in the 1990s (which is published as Part 2 of this report). See also Chapter I of Part 3. In addition, the reader is referred to *Financing and External Debt of Developing Countries, 1988* (OECD, 1989). Chapter II of that publication contains an analysis of broad trends and a discussion broken down by income groups and geographic regions.

A decade ago the Brandt Commission's report noted that more than two-thirds of resource flows to developing countries were on commercial terms, that is private bank loans, direct investments, and export credits. Less than one-third were on concessional terms. They recommended that ODA be dramatically increased. This would have reversed these proportions.

In the following decade the proportions changed in an unforeseen way without the hoped-for substantial increases in aid. Instead, the non-concessional flows dried up. ODA receipts from all sources held about steady, but became a much more important proportion of total flows — increasing from 30 per cent in 1979 to 50 per cent in 1988.

While ODA in no way compensated for the loss of non-concessional flows, the fact that ODA levels were maintained in this period avoided disaster for many countries, providing an essential safety net. ODA became even more valuable at the margin.

It should be an important goal of the next decade to establish the conditions for a full resumption of non-concessional flows. Table 3-1 tells us that over the past three years total net resource flows, measured in constant prices and exchange rates, have held about steady. Perhaps these levels represent the bottom of a trough and we can now hope for recovery. Of course, world-wide statistics such as these summarise widely varying individual country experience. Recovery will come at the country level as financial institutions respond to improved earnings capacity. That will happen one country at a time. The role of ODA in implementing the policies needed for confidence-building and in financing the infrastructure and institution-building needed by the private sector will be especially important in the years ahead. Adequate ODA, supporting developing countries' own efforts, will help lay the foundation for private sector and export credit agency confidence.

Here are some interesting highlights of recent experience.

— Total net resource flows have been more or less stable since 1986 when measured in constant prices and exchange rates. This reflects continued increases in nominal terms from the low point reached in 1986.

— Both multilateral and bilateral non-concessional disbursements increased.

— In 1988 there was a positive net flow of export credits for the first time since 1985, partly explained by a building-up of arrears in repayments.

— Net foreign direct investment in 1988 stabilized at its 1987 level after the recovery in that year.

— Net bank lending to Asia rose in 1988, but declined slightly to Latin America and Sub-Saharan Africa.

— An estimated $2 billion of interest arrears were capitalised by official creditors in 1988.

— IMF repayments exceeded new credits by $4 billion in 1988. A positive factor in the near term will be the substantial increase in disbursements under the Structural Adjustment Facilities, which are expected to increase from 1987 and 1988 levels of $0.5 billion to $3 billion in 1990.

— Debt stock is now increasing at a modest rate of about 3 per cent annually. Major contrasts by region reveal that Asian low-income countries (especially China, India and Indonesia) have been continuing to receive large inward capital flows, and hence have seen significant increases in debt stock over the past three years. Sub-Saharan debt stock has increased both because of sustained new lending and because of consolidation of arrears. Net indebtedness has fallen in East and South-East Asia and increased at a low rate in Latin America.

— There was a substantial increase in interest payments in 1988 due both to significant payments of interest arrears and to the rise in international interest rates.

— Debt forgiveness actions by DAC Members on ODA debt are progressively reducing ODA debt service to negligible levels for most debt-distressed poorer countries.

3. PERSPECTIVES ON AID MANAGEMENT: A FRESH LOOK AT TECHNICAL CO-OPERATION

In 1988 the DAC adopted its landmark Principles for Project Appraisal. These were published in the 1988 Report. Of course, each of the DAC's Members has for a long time had policies and procedures for the identification, planning and approval of projects. The special importance of this document, which is what makes it a landmark, lies in the fact that it is a common set of principles on which all DAC Members have agreed. As developing countries seek a more co-ordinated approach to development, they can use our new principles as a basis for their dialogue with the donor community.

One of the basic points stressed in the Principles for Project Appraisal is the primary role of the recipient country. The Principles are quite clear that "while project financing decisions are taken jointly by donors and recipients, responsibility for project identification, design and implementation rest with the recipient. Strengthening the capacity of recipient countries through training and institutional development for project appraisal, design and management, including budgeting and auditing, is an important objective for donor/recipient co-operation."

In discussing this issue on several public occasions during the past year, I have stressed the need for developing countries to take the matter of aid management more seriously. Recalling that 50 developing countries now receive more than 10 per cent of their GNP from aid, I have argued that management of the resulting portfolio is worth the appointment of one of a country's best people to head it, and worth giving the aid management staff support and rights of communication on a regular basis at the level of the prime minister and the cabinet. Models for such strong central aid management units are to be found in developing countries, particularly in Asia. The United Nations Development Programme has a special opportunity to encourage exchanges of experience in implementing its strengthened management support programme.

Many Members of the DAC have used the DAC's new Principles for Project Appraisal in a critical review of their own procedures. But, if dramatic progress is to be made in improved project appraisal, selection and design, such principles will need to be adopted in each developing country. While we can hope that the DAC's principles will be helpful in this process, of course they would need to be adapted and changed to meet each country's requirements. I hope the DAC's initiative in adopting these principles will trigger a new look at policies and procedures for managing aid in many developing countries.

The Principles for Project Appraisal were drafted and discussed within the DAC primarily with investment projects in mind. Subsequently, as we have turned our attention to issues involved in providing technical assistance, we have recognised that the Principles are often equally suitable for technical assistance programmes.

The DAC held a meeting on technical assistance in November 1988. At that meeting, we reached a number of tentative conclusions (see Section 6 of Chapter IX in Part 2). We then decided that a process of extensive consultation with others, especially with representatives of developing countries, would be helpful before reaching final conclusions. One important consultation was held in October 1989 under the auspices of the German Foundation for International Development. With this background and with the further dialogue within Member agencies, the DAC hopes to reach conclusions about improving technical co-operation policies and procedures in the course of 1990.

It is worth recalling that more than $10 billion is now being programmed for technical assistance activities, either in free-standing projects or as a part of projects supported by capital assistance.

Technical assistance has been severely criticised within donor countries. While there is general agreement that technical assistance plays a critical role in technology transfer, in institution-building, and in improving the skills of developing-country people, we know that technical assistance is a difficult process, involving very large numbers of people in donor and recipient agencies.

Donors are aware that developing countries are also worried that, together, donors and recipients are not getting full value for money from this form of assistance. Technical assistance has been subjected to careful review in a series of cluster meetings of African ministers of planning over the past two years. Criticisms were articulated in a consolidated report presented to a joint meeting of ministers of planning and UNDP resident representatives in the Africa region in Addis Ababa in April 1989. The ministers argued that the impact of technical co-operation has been insufficient in terms of building lasting capacity of national institutions. Because African governments had weak co-ordinating and management staffs, technical co-operation tended to be "donor driven". They also noted how much donors are spending on technical co-operation compared with their own expenditures. In some countries, donor costs for technical assistance are comparable to the wage bill of the whole civil service. Even developing-country support for technical assistance projects becomes a significant percentage of the budget. The situation has been subjected to new strains in the context of budget-reducing structural adjustment programmes. These by no means complete the list of concerns.

In June 1989, the DAC sponsored with the OECD Development Centre a joint seminar on development co-operation in the 1990s. At that seminar, an African minister made a forceful presentation on the need for a new look at technical assistance. The positive response of the Members to the Minister's initiative suggests that there is strong commitment among us for our review. There seems now to be considerable agreement between the developing countries and the Members of the DAC on the diagnosis. We all want technical assistance to be designed to strengthen institutional capacity of developing countries. This means that technical assistance should less frequently be used to fill gaps in personnel availability and more frequently used to help developing-country personnel to reach the stage where they can operate without outside help. It probably means fewer long-term advisers and more short-term advisers to developing-country operators. It means hiring more advisers from the recipient country and helping to provide incentives for the return of skilled expatriates. It probably means emphasizing building the capacity for training in developing countries with less emphasis on training in donor-country institutions.

But agreement on the diagnosis does not automatically bring agreement on the cure. While the use of better technical assistance programming criteria can be helpful, the answer will probably lie mostly with improved developing-country aid management, including better co-ordination among ministries and with donors. It may be the recipients' policies which, in the end, will change the situation and bring more value for money from this enormous resource.   If real change is to be made, there will be a need to focus on some of the policy issues involved in a general strengthening of national management.   The question of pay scales is fundamental and, of course, is directly related to the size of the civil service.   In the 1990s, many countries need to undergo structural adjustment of their management at least as dramatic as the economic structural adjustment measures they have been taking over the past several years.   But, since we are dealing with the livelihood of large numbers of people, there may be a need to strike deals with the donor community which will help provide the political room developing countries will need in order to undertake the necessary reforms.   Attributes of such a strategy could include a medium-term rationalisation of numbers of employees (but beginning immediately), selective important increases in wages, improved in-service and university training facilities, and special steps to ease the lot of those who will not be part of the system after the reforms have been implemented.   At the same time, governments should implement new policies on the kind of technical assistance they want.   Because such reforms are often critical to the success of structural adjustment programmes, the World Bank has already been discussing these broader policy issues in a number of developing countries.   The potential role of the UNDP in this field is increasingly acknowledged (see Section 4 of Chapter III in Part 3).   In addition to its increased focus on government management, it has been seeking greater rationality on the technical assistance process through its National Technical Co-operation Assessments and Programmes (NATCAPs).   One can hope that early in the 1990s the recipient and donor communities can both improve their policies and, country by country, apply them in such a way that technical assistance can play a more effective role in realising the important goals of self-sufficiency and sustainability.

4. THE MATURING OF AFRICA'S STRUCTURAL ADJUSTMENT EFFORT

One is still bemused by the enormity of the issues raised by the on-going debate about Africa.   In response to the problems left in the wake of terrible weather, commodity price collapse and over-extended debt, the United Nations adopted UNPAAERD — the United Nations Programme of Action for African Economic Recovery and Development 1986-1990.   The World Bank established SPA — the Special Programme of Assistance for Debt-Distressed Low-Income Countries in Sub-Saharan Africa.   The IMF decided, in effect, to refinance short-term debt with ESAF — the Enhanced Structural Adjustment Facility.   The bilateral donors agreed to support these institutions and to increase bilateral assistance in support of structural adjustment programmes.   They also have taken important measures providing debt relief.   These efforts have been financing the urgent actions needed when the patients have been in the emergency ward.   They provide transfusions in the form of immediate fast-disbursing assistance to finance critical import requirements.

In the debate on structural adjustment it is sometimes forgotten that adjustments are essential because the status quo is unsustainable. Also forgotten is the position of the developing country as the decision-maker. Very early in this new era of adjustment a debate arose under the terminology of "adjustment with a human face", in which it was suggested that the adjustment programmes which usually called for fiscal stringency were having a disastrous impact on health, education and nutrition programmes. In the light of this debate, the entire donor community has come to agree that more attention needs to be paid to these factors by developing countries and donors alike. Existing developing-country sectoral programmes, however, are often constructed in such a way that additional funds would not necessarily provide much relief to the broader population. If a sector programme is geared to helping the already better-off portion of the population, supplementary funding of such programmes would be largely wasted if evaluated in terms of how they help the population at large. Everyone agrees as to the importance of developing sector strategies which, in addition to focusing on the whole population, will rationalise personnel levels and salaries, provide for cost-recovery to take some of the pressure off central government budgets, and face a myriad of quality issues. The most discussed beginning of this process has been in the field of education in Ghana, but this approach is needed in many countries and in many sectors.

Meanwhile, the ambitions of the earlier period to turn things around very quickly have been modified by experience. It takes time to mount structural adjustment programmes and the results take time in coming. Structural adjustment needs to be a sustainable and continuing process.

One of the most important aspects of the structural adjustment effort has been the high level of co-operation among the bilateral donors under the leadership of the World Bank. Six-monthly meetings with the donors have reviewed progress of the SPA and have been used to consider improvements in the way that aid is provided so that funds could move very quickly and recipient-government bureaucracies could be relieved of some of the pressures occasioned by many unique donor policies and procedures. The system was used for the donors to nudge each other not only to speed things up but also to do more. While it is too early, of course, to reach seasoned judgments about these matters, the preliminary results seem very promising. Donors have untied increasing proportions of their assistance. They have often provided their funds as cofinancing. They have worked together to improve procurement and disbursement procedures.

In 1989, the World Bank issued a report entitled "Africa's Adjustment and Growth in the 1980s" citing recent growth rates and improvements in external balances in countries undergoing structural adjustment programmes in Africa. But progress on GNP growth and external account balances is not necessarily, or at least not speedily, translated into improvements in the conditions of life of the populations of the countries involved. The World Bank report drew fire from African ministers of finance and planning. Together, these ministers have come up with an "African Alternative Framework to Structural Adjustment Programmes for Socio-Economic Recovery and Transformation", issued by the Economic Commission for Africa. The basic message of the ECA Report is that structural adjustment programmes must be "holistic", addressing basic economic, social, and political weaknesses, if they are truly to transform the economic predicament of African countries. When the debate went public the President of the World Bank held a meeting with a number of UN agencies in May in order to define the issues and discover to what extent general consensus existed on them. The resulting press release suggested that the area of consensus was in fact quite broad. Supporting this conclusion is the World Bank's latest study entitled "Sustainable Growth with Equity: A Long-Term Perspective for Sub-Saharan Africa" which suggests important elements of a strategic agenda for the 1990s. It emphasizes the need to take account of the social impact of reforms, the need for investment to accelerate growth and the need for measures to ensure sustainability. Over time Africa's production structures need a fundamental transformation. The strategy should be people-centred with human resource development and meeting of basic needs as top priorities.

One comes away from the debate feeling that it is of the utmost importance that the momentum of structural adjustment be continued, that financing be fully adequate, that we move faster to a consideration of sectoral issues and the requirements for infrastructure, and that the effort be seen as one requiring sustained attention during the 1990s rather than one with a three- or four-year time span. We all need to stay with these efforts well beyond the emergency room phase.

Continuing the analogy, it is well recognised that the attitudes and participation of the patient are the most important factors in long-term treatment and cures. Economic health begins and ends with the policies and management of the developing countries themselves. The rest of us can only help. It is in this context that one can find reason to appreciate the on-going debate. The donor community will learn from the points of view put forward in the African document. The existence of the African Alternative Framework will invigorate the country-by-country debate, with the result that pro-grammes which are finally agreed upon will more probably reflect the convictions of the individual African countries and, therefore, have a better chance to be implemented effectively. This is the positive side. The more troubling side is the reflection in the document of lines of thinking which no longer carry conviction. For example, it is hardly consistent with a drive for sustainable and nationally determined development to ask that aid be used for an extensive period of time to maintain subsidies or to support poorly functioning state enterprises. While the case can be made that the capacity of the private sector in most African countries is insufficient in the short run to permit implementation of simplistic privatisation strategies, it can equally be wondered if Africa's private sector is not being sold too short in the document's willingness to put off grasping the nettles of economic reform until some undefined time in the future. In the end, of course, this debate will not be held on a continent-wide basis encompassing widely divergent country circumstances. The report itself acknowledges these differences. The lesson to be applied at the country level is that donors in countries where they are heavily involved need to have an increasingly sophisticated understanding of the real situation of each individual country. Blanket prescriptions need to be avoided, with strategies pursued fully consistent with local circumstances. Individual African countries need to work vigorously to broaden and deepen aid management capacity so that their voices will be fully taken into account in the dialogue which must characterise the important donor-recipient relationship[1].

5. A FRESH LOOK AT ODA FOR LEAST DEVELOPED COUNTRIES

With the UNCTAD-sponsored, French-hosted, second major international meeting on aid to least developed countries taking place in Paris in September 1990, Members are reviewing their experience over the past decade.   The United Nations now lists 42 countries as least developed.   Together they have a population of about 400 million.

At the 1981 meeting on least developed countries, most donors agreed that it would be desirable to strive to provide 0.15 per cent of their GNP to least developed countries. At that time, the list of countries was somewhat shorter.   In 1988, DAC donors achieved about 0.09 per cent, little more than half of the goal.

In spite of this apparent shortfall in performance, aid represents a very important portion of the least developed countries' income.   Half of the 42 countries in 1987 received ODA equivalent to more than 20 per cent of their GNP.   ODA was equivalent to between 10 and 20 per cent of GNP for another third of the countries.   The rest received between 5 and 10 per cent.   This compares with a global developing-country average of about 1.5 per cent of GNP.

In looking at the geographic location of the least developed countries in relation to their level of dependence on ODA, we find that half of the very dependent group of least developed countries (receiving aid equivalent to more than 20 per cent of their GNP) are located in the broad belt of countries just south of the Sahara, stretching from Cape Verde to Somalia.   Absent from this group were Ethiopia and Sudan which nevertheless received about 15 per cent of their GNP from aid.   Both countries have been beset by internal strife and much of the aid to those countries has recently been for emergency assistance.

The other half of the very dependent "over 20 per cent" category are countries consisting of groups of islands.   There are a number of small Pacific countries as well as the Comoros, Cape Verde, and Sao Tome & Principe, the last two already included in the group consisting of the belt of countries just south of the Sahara.   The nine countries consisting of island groups in the list of least developed countries have a total population of less than 8 million.

With these levels of aid dependency, it can be argued that the main issue in aid relationships with the least developed countries is not the level of effort by the donors measured in terms of the percentage of donor-country GNP going to the least developed group.   Rather, it would seem the world community might address other questions.

First, given the proper focus of development on achieving self-reliance and sustainability, what strategies might be pursued in order to use aid toward these ends more effectively?

Second, given the very high levels of aid dependence, it seems likely that additional aid is primarily to be achieved by improving the absorptive capacity for the constructive use of aid.   What steps can be taken to improve aid management in this group of countries?

Third, given the number of countries in this group in the broad belt just south of the Sahara, it would seem useful to review performance in these countries as a group and consider what changes in aid strategy would make sense.   In this connection, the continuing work of the Club du Sahel and the Permanent Interstate Committee for Drought Control in the Sahel (CILSS) should be very helpful.

Fourth, given the concentration of countries characterised by groups of islands in the over 20 per cent dependency group, it would seem useful to look at this group together. It is notable that the small Caribbean island states are not characterised as least developed. This is probably due to their location near North America and to their often close ties with European countries, but we might see whether there are lessons to be learned from this group which would have application to others. For some of these island states dependency is so great that real economic independence may eventually come in the form of endowments, where the stream of income from investments would be used to cover some of the recurring costs of education, health and transportation. The efficiency of these services is often very adversely affected by problems of distance and access to small population groups.

Fifth, while there may be little that the donor agencies can do to deal with internal problems which make it difficult to provide assistance for development, it is worth noting that five large least developed countries (Afghanistan, Burma, Ethiopia, Mozambique and Sudan), representing a third of the least developed group's population, could well become more important recipients of assistance once conditions have been established which would make it possible to translate aid into development progress.

Sixth, in terms of population the largest country among the least developed is Bangladesh, which contains about a quarter of the population of the group. Bangladesh gets about 10 per cent of its GNP from ODA. About half of its population is classified as living in a state of absolute poverty. Most donors are already giving Bangladesh a high priority in their allocations and there might be potential for increased allocations if funds could be absorbed. It might be useful to consider what set of actions would strengthen aid management and the policy framework to enable efficient use of more funds. Since the recent disastrous floods, renewed consideration is being given to possible strategies for better control of floodwaters, which could call for substantial resources.

The least developed countries as a whole tend to have the weakest structures of administration and the lowest standards of health, education and nutrition. Infrastructure is generally at a rudimentary level. Donors will have a chance to reflect on how their assistance might be better designed to be helpful as they prepare for the 1990 Conference.

6. SOUTH ASIA

In May 1989 the DAC held a meeting to discuss aid policy issues related to South Asia. The review was concerned with the area included in the South Asian Association for Regional Co-operation (SAARC) — Bangladesh, Bhutan, India, Nepal, Maldives, Pakistan and Sri Lanka. All are low-income countries.

South Asia as a whole has had reasonable success with development. Recent growth rates have averaged about 5 per cent. South Asian grain production has about kept up with market demand. There has been substantial industrial growth and exports

37

have increased. Steady progress has been made on literacy and life expectancy. Through prudent management South Asian countries have avoided the debt crisis.

With all of its forward movement, this region, which represents about 20 per cent of world population, is still very poor and is considered to be performing under its potential. Per capita income is about $300. Agricultural successes have been most notable in irrigated areas, but have largely left out significant parts of countries — particularly in the case of India. Growth in production of oilseeds and pulses has lagged. Investments in health and education are low in general and particularly so in Pakistan. (Sri Lanka has done much better in this respect.) Military expenditures compete with economic investment for scarce funds. Industrial growth has not been sufficiently linked with rural areas. The still high population growth rates, adding 22 million people each year, are of deepening concern. One-third of the population lives in extreme poverty — about half the world's poorest people live in South Asia. There are serious environmental problems.

There has been recent interest among the SAARC countries in giving increasing attention to programmes which would attack poverty. This would imply a shift in investment priorities toward rural areas, with more going for agriculture-related rural infrastructure, improvements in rural services, education and health. Aside from giving these programmes budget priorities, most observers conclude that more needs to be done on land reform and on dealing with hitherto intractable social cleavages. SAARC is considering the establishment of regional achievement goals for education, village electrification, road connections, safe drinking water supplies, and contraceptive use, following up the setting of similar goals for child health.

At the macroeconomic level, most South Asian countries are in the process of cautiously liberalising, implying a greater export orientation, a more open environment for both foreign and domestic investment, and an attempt to achieve more efficiency. There is room to speed up this process. The 1990s should see greater scope for closer economic ties with the faster growing economies to the East. As Japan has been important in the development of the newly industrialising economies, so may East Asia in general be an engine for growth in South Asia.

Donors continue to allocate to South Asia a fairly high proportion of their funds, but the share of total aid has gone down. Allocations in no way reflect South Asian population levels or the fact that such a large proportion of the world's hungry people live in this subcontinent. Aid is a much smaller proportion of recipient GNP in South Asia than is the case for most low-income countries. The proportion of bilateral assistance going to South Asia has gone down since the early 1970s from about 16 per cent to about 8 per cent. The mix of multilateral assistance has tended to become less concessional. Thus, if donors were willing to make an increased effort, South Asia offers an opportunity for translating aid into development progress. At the same time, the relatively good management by the South Asian countries could be improved. Money alone will not produce the results. But a combination of policy improvement and significant new resources could go a long way toward reducing poverty levels.

Elements of a programme to both raise rates of growth and tackle rural poverty would be:

— Political reform characterised by decentralising decision-making and broad popular participation;

— Economic measures to encourage industrial efficiency and provide an enabling environment for small entrepreneurs reaching all the way to the village level;
— Land reform and programmes to provide assets to the landless;
— More rural infrastructure, including further expansion of irrigation and programmes to improve yields in rainfed areas and for a broader range of crops;
— Broad-scale investments in people and basic needs — health, family planning, literacy, nutrition, water, sanitation and, in all of these, measures to empower women;
— Environment-related programmes preserving or improving forest, soil and water resources.

The World Bank is completing a study on the Gangetic Basin, which will address the question of geographic disparities in development progress in India and suggest an approach for future programmes. This, and similar studies for other areas could well provide the conceptual framework around which government and donor actions could be co-ordinated.

It would be wrong to expect early changes in donor policy toward development in South Asia. But the review proved useful in reminding donor decision-makers that the countries of South Asia remain very poor, containing half of the world's poorest people. Their relatively prudent economic management makes them good potential recipients where donor policy is to look for the most efficient places to use funds to reduce poverty[2].

7. THE FOURTH UNITED NATIONS DEVELOPMENT DECADE

In recent months most institutions involved in development have been considering policy for the decade of the 1990s. The most comprehensive review takes place in the United Nations, as it prepares the International Development Strategy for the fourth United Nations Development Decade. The first major debate will take place in the Special Session of the UN General Assembly devoted to International Economic Co-operation scheduled for the Spring of 1990. The Development Assistance Committee work on Development Co-operation in the 1990s represents our intellectual contribution to the United Nations process. I will not here go into a discussion of the issues, since the basic analytical paper, which constitutes Part 2 of this report, together with the High-Level Meeting statement scheduled to be adopted by DAC ministers and aid administrators on 5th December 1989, speak for themselves.

8. THE THAILAND CONFERENCE ON EDUCATION FOR ALL

In March 1990 a conference jointly sponsored by UNESCO, UNDP, UNICEF and the World Bank will be hosted by the Government of Thailand. I discussed the question of investing in people in the 1988 Report, arguing that developing countries and donors alike have probably been neglecting the importance of people-related programmes, including primary education. The neglect is not simply financial. For developing countries "interest politics" often favours higher education for urban populations over primary education in rural areas. For donors, the prejudicing factors may be the appropriate desire to reflect recipient priorities and the fact that rural education is local-currency intensive, and therefore less appealing for aid use than technical assistance expenditures for more specialised education and training. Many developing countries have never thought through their strategies, instead simply making annual adjustments in the budget in reaction to immediate political forces.

The hope for the Thailand Conference is that it might forge a consensus comparable to the one articulated for health at Alma Ata in favour of a serious drive for achieving minimum educational goals for the whole population. Such an approach implies comprehensive education reforms to raise quality, to allocate available resources more effectively and to address remaining problems of access. With few exceptions, assuming both international co-operation and a serious effort by countries to mobilise their own resources and make necessary reforms, it is possible for each country to provide at least primary education for most children and to reduce illiteracy substantially over the next decade. While the health strategy has by no means avoided misallocations of scarce health monies, it has played a very useful role in strengthening forces in developing countries, in the World Health Organisation and UNICEF, and in bilateral and multi-lateral aid agencies, which favoured a more ubiquitous approach to providing health services.

The DAC plans to hold a meeting on education strategies in 1991. This will be a useful opportunity to consider how donor aid policies should be changed as a result of the education-for-all initiative expected to emanate from the important meeting in Thailand.

NOTES AND REFERENCES

1. As participants in the structural adjustment process apply themselves to individual country situations, they appreciate more the political aspects of adjustment. For a new look at these issues see *Fragile Coalitions: The Politics of Economic Adjustment*, Joan M. Nelson and contributors, U.S.-Third World Policy Perspectives No.12, Overseas Development Council, Transactions Books, 1989.

2. A few paragraphs cannot do justice to a subject so vast as South Asia. Recent reviews looking at South Asia include: "Operational Approaches to Asia's Development Agenda", an address presented to OECD on 22nd June 1989 by Attila Karaosmanoglu, Vice President Asia Region, the World Bank; and "Development Strategy for South Asia for the 1990s and Beyond", a background paper prepared for the DAC by Mohammed Syeduzzaman, 23rd May 1989. Another significant opinion from the area, relevant to India, is "Eighth Plan: Some Strategic Perspectives", text of the J. N. Tata Memorial Lecture, delivered by Abib Hussain, Member, Government of India Planning Commission, at the Indian Institute of Science, Bangalore, 12th April 1989.

Part 2

DEVELOPMENT CO-OPERATION IN THE 1990s: WORKING WITH DEVELOPING COUNTRIES TOWARDS SUSTAINABLE AND EQUITABLE DEVELOPMENT

I

INTRODUCTION

During the past year DAC Members have reviewed the major development issues ahead with a view to reaching a consensus on the orientation of aid programmes for the coming decade.   Their objective was to bring together strategic thinking in governments so as to assist in the design of more effective aid, better tuned to evolving needs in developing countries, and to address the critical problem of the financial requirements of developing countries arising from the challenges of the 1990s.

The material published here, which has been prepared by the OECD Secretariat, reflects this work.   After a very brief summary of past development achievements, it identifies the fundamental development challenges for the 1990s and the ensuing central development co-operation policy priorities in key areas as they emerge from DAC discussions.

In keeping with the vocation of the DAC, the review centres on the role of official development assistance and the aid system.   Consequently, it focuses on the problems and needs of developing countries which are major recipients of aid.   The role of aid and the aid system, however, is put into the context of the larger concept of development co-operation and, indeed, the totality of economic and financial relations with developing countries.

This review brings together, in a coherent conceptual framework, the results of the work of the DAC in recent years on the range of central aid issues.   It therefore constitutes a "state of the art" assessment of the aid system in the perspective of the challenges of the 1990s.

The task of development and development co-operation is unfinished.   Unprecedented demographic and environmental pressures make the problem of improving the life of the masses of people in developing countries even more difficult.   Still, with the improvement in world economic conditions, a better East-West political climate, progress in the solution of a number of regional conflicts (with a hope also of permitting a reduction in heavy military expenditure burdens) and more effective policies across a range of developing countries, there may be opportunities for more progress in the 1990s than there was in the 1980s.   The last decade was a period of major change in the orientation of developing country policies and aid approaches.   These critical re-orientations remain to be carried through.   The process of repair and recovery and of policy reform will have to continue in the 1990s.

There are two major recurrent themes throughout the review: the diversity of the needs and problems over the wide range of developing countries and the linkages between issues and policies.

Development co-operation policy approaches need to take full account of the diversity of country situations ranging in a wide spectrum from the "newly industrialising economies" (NIEs) to the "least developed countries" (LLDCs). While respect for country specificities is essential, some policy generalisations remain useful. Indeed, there is a core programme of economic/financial and structural policies which is similar not only for the range of developing countries but also for industrial countries.

The theme of the review, working with developing countries towards sustainable and equitable development, brings together and underlines the strong linkages between the elements of what should be achieved in the period ahead:

— Improved economic growth as the indispensable basis for broader achievements;
— Stimulating productive energies through participatory development;
— Laying the basis for broad-based growth through adequate institutions and infrastructure;
— A more determined equity and anti-poverty orientation in economic and development policies;
— A new emphasis on investing in people;
— Stronger concern with environmentally sustainable development and natural resource use;
— Increasing the responsiveness of the aid system;
— Effective OECD economic and structural adjustment policies contributing to a favourable world economic environment for developing countries.

II

THE DEVELOPMENT PROGRESS MADE
AND THE CENTRAL DEVELOPMENT CO-OPERATION
POLICY PRIORITIES FOR THE 1990s

1.   THE DEVELOPMENT PROGRESS MADE

The 1980s are often referred to as a decade of crisis and depression for many developing countries.   Per capita income and employment losses in a range of developing countries, especially in Africa and Latin America, were indeed deeper and more sustained than those of Europe and the United States during the Great Depression of the 1930s. Many factors, ranging from deep-seated structural adjustment problems and policy deficiencies to debt burdens and world economic slowdown during the early part of the 1980s, are at the root of these difficulties.   But the picture is diverse, and some developing countries, especially in Asia, have weathered the difficult 1980s remarkably well.

Taking a more medium-term perspective, substantial progress has been made in improving standards of life and human welfare in a broad range of developing countries at all levels of income.   Taking the period of the past two decades together, most developing countries, with the major exceptions of the African low-income countries, Bangladesh and some other low-income countries in Asia and the Western Hemisphere, have made substantial progress in production, incomes and important social indicators. Serious poverty remains, however, even in some countries which have achieved good aggregate economic growth.   While institutional weaknesses, inadequate infrastructure and human resources development remain serious constraints to development in many countries, improvements have been made in these areas on which further progress can be built.

Taking developing countries together, their average annual GNP growth rate during the past two decades exceeded 5 per cent, substantially higher than that of OECD countries.   In spite of rapid population growth, average per capita incomes increased by about 3 per cent, again higher than OECD growth, and produced a doubling of per capita income during this period.   However, development levels and progress differ greatly among countries to the extent that global averages have little meaning.

— The greatest successes have been achieved in much of South-East Asia in economic growth, participation in the world economy, trade and perhaps social development.

45

Table 2-1. ECONOMIC AND SOCIAL TRENDS IN DEVELOPING COUNTRIES, 1965-87

	Real growth rates			GNP 1987	GNP per capita		Life expectancy		Total exports of goods and services 1987
	Per capita GNP 1965-87	GNP 1965-87	Population 1965-87		1965*	1987	1965	1987	
	Per cent			$ billion	Dollars		Years		$ billion
ASIA AND PACIFIC............	3.8	6.0	2.0	1 133.2	180	430	44	62	334.4
South-East Asia	5.5	7.7	2.1	339.9	710	2 430	57	67	240.5
NIEs*a*	6.5	8.4	1.8	264.9	890	3 790	59	70	203.9
Others*b*	3.7	6.2	2.4	75.0	460	1 070	55	65	36.6
Asian LICs	3.4	5.6	2.0	786.6	150	320	43	62	91.8
China	5.2	7.1	1.8	313.7	90	290	41	69	40.1
India	2.0	4.2	2.2	242.8	190	310	44	57	14.0
Bangladesh	0.4	2.9	2.5	17.4	150	160	44	50	1.4
Indonesia	3.7	6.0	2.1	76.5	200	450	43	57	18.8
Pakistan	2.4	5.4	2.9	36.1	210	350	44	52	5.0
Philippines................	1.1	3.8	2.7	34.6	460	590	56	63	9.2
Others....................	0.3	2.6	2.3	65.4	320	340	46	60	3.3
Pacific*c*	1.0	3.3	2.3	6.7	950	1 200	47	56	2.1
LATIN AMERICA	2.1	4.4	2.3	730.2	1 090	1 760	57	66	123.8
Central America and the Caribbean	2.1	4.7	2.5	214.5	970	1 560	56	66	49.9
Mexico	2.2	5.0	2.8	149.4	1 100	1 820	59	68	29.8
Others...................	1.3	3.5	2.2	65.1	870	1 170	51	64	20.2
South America	2.0	4.3	2.2	515.7	1 170	1 850	57	66	73.8
Brazil	3.6	6.0	2.3	285.9	900	2 030	56	65	28.7
Argentina.................	0.2	1.7	1.5	74.5	2 270	2 370	65	70	8.4
Others....................	0.9	3.3	2.4	155.4	1 190	1 470	55	65	36.7
AFRICA	0.9	3.6	2.7	329.4	480	590	44	53	55.6
Sub-Saharan Africa	0.3	3.1	2.7	184.3	380	410	43	50	33.9
Nigeria	1.1	3.8	2.6	66.2	480	620	41	51	8.0
Ethiopia	0.8	3.3	2.5	5.5	100	120	45	46	0.6
Zaire......................	−1.6	1.1	2.8	5.0	220	150	44	52	2.0
Sudan	−1.2	1.5	2.8	7.6	440	330	40	49	0.5
Tanzania	0.3	3.5	3.2	5.4	210	230	42	53	0.5
Kenya	1.7	5.5	3.8	7.3	220	330	49	57	1.8
Ghana.....................	−1.3	1.1	2.4	5.3	530	390	50	54	0.9
Sahel Group*d*	−0.2	2.1	2.4	10.7	290	270	40	46	2.4
Other LICs*e*.................	−0.3	2.3	2.7	33.7	330	310	44	50	8.1
MICs*f*	0.4	3.4	3.0	37.6	930	1 020	43	52	9.2
North Africa	1.9	4.5	2.6	145.1	870	1 330	49	61	21.7
Egypt	2.7	5.2	2.4	35.9	380	710	48	61	7.2
Others*g*	1.6	4.3	2.7	109.1	1 310	1 890	49	61	14.4
MIDDLE EAST	2.4	5.6	3.1	408.4	2 060	3 560	50	61	74.9
Memo items									
Developing countries, total......	2.9	5.1	2.2	2 601.2	360	700	46	61	588.7
LLDCs	0.4	2.8	2.5	91.4	210	230	42	51	11.0
OECD countries	2.4	3.2	0.8	11 068.6	7 620	13 140	69	75	2 534.5

*   GNP per capita for 1965 is derived from the 1987 figure (Atlas method) by applying real growth rates of GNP per capita for the period 1965-87. This is a very approximate method and precaution should specifically be applied for inter-country comparisons.
a) Hong Kong, Korea, Singapore, Taiwan.
b) Malaysia, Thailand.
c) Oceania, including Papua New Guinea.
d) Burkina Faso, Cape Verde, Chad, Gambia, Guinea Bissau, Mali, Mauritania, Niger, Senegal.
e) Benin, Botswana, Burundi, Central African Republic, Comoros, Djibouti, Eq. Guinea, Guinea, Lesotho, Liberia, Madagascar, Malawi, Mayotte, Mozambique, Rwanda, Sao Tome & Principe, Sierra Leone, Somalia, Togo, Uganda, St. Helena, Swaziland, Zambia, Zimbabwe.
f) Angola, Cameroon, Congo, Ivory Coast, Gabon, Mauritius, Namibia, Reunion, Seychelles.
g) Algeria, Libya, Morocco, Tunisia.
Source: World Bank, OECD and IMF.

Table 2-2. PROJECTED POPULATION GROWTH IN DEVELOPING COUNTRIES, 1965-2025

	Average growth rates			Absolute population			
	1965-88	1988-2000	2000-2025	1965	1988	2000	2025
	Per cent			Millions			
ASIA AND PACIFIC	2.2	1.7	1.1	1 627	2 678	3 298	4 318
South-East Asia......................	2.2	1.3	0.8	74	122	142	174
NIEs[a].............................	1.8	1.0	0.5	34	51	57	65
Others[b]...........................	2.5	1.5	1.0	40	71	85	109
Asian LICs.........................	2.2	1.7	1.1	1 549	2 550	3 149	4 132
China..............................	2.0	1.2	0.6	700	1 104	1 286	1 493
India	2.3	2.0	1.3	487	819	1 043	1 446
Bangladesh	2.4	2.7	1.8	63	110	151	235
Indonesia	2.3	1.5	0.9	105	175	208	263
Pakistan	3.2	2.9	2.0	56	115	162	267
Philippines	2.7	2.3	1.5	32	59	77	111
Others	2.0	2.3	1.4	106	168	222	317
Pacific[c]	2.4	1.9	2.0	3	6	7	12
LATIN AMERICA	2.5	1.9	1.4	223	394	495	702
Central America and the Caribbean[h] ...	2.8	2.1	1.5	71	134	171	249
Mexico	3.0	1.9	1.4	43	85	107	150
Others	2.4	2.2	1.7	28	49	64	99
South America.......................	2.4	1.9	1.4	151	260	324	453
Brazil..............................	2.5	1.8	1.3	82	144	179	246
Argentina	1.5	1.2	0.9	22	32	36	45
Others[i]...........................	2.6	2.1	1.6	47	84	109	162
AFRICA.............................	2.9	3.1	2.4	299	576	829	1 517
Sub-Saharan Africa	2.9	3.3	2.6	238	465	681	1 302
Nigeria	2.7	3.5	2.6	58	106	159	301
Ethiopia	3.0	2.7	2.4	23	45	61	112
Zaire	2.5	3.2	2.8	19	34	49	99
Sudan	2.5	2.9	2.3	14	24	34	60
Tanzania...........................	3.2	3.8	3.1	12	25	40	85
Kenya	3.6	4.2	2.9	10	23	38	78
Ghana	2.6	3.1	2.4	8	14	20	37
Sahel Group[d]	2.7	3.0	2.5	22	40	57	105
Other LICs[e]	3.2	3.1	2.6	56	116	168	319
MICs[f]	3.5	3.1	2.6	17	38	55	106
North Africa	2.7	2.4	1.5	61	111	148	215
Egypt.............................	2.4	2.2	1.4	30	51	67	94
Others[g]..........................	2.9	2.6	1.6	31	60	81	121
MIDDLE EAST	3.2	3.1	2.4	60	123	178	319
Memo items							
Developing countries, total	2.4	2.0	1.4	2 208	3 771	4 801	6 856
LLDCs	2.6	2.9	2.2	233	417	586	1 011
OECD countries	0.8	0.5	0.3	697	846	900	961

a) Hong Kong, Korea, Singapore.
b) to g) See footnotes to Table 2-1.
h) Excluding Cuba and DOM/TOM.
i) Bolivia, Chile, Colombia, Ecuador, Guyana, Paraguay, Venezuela.
Note: Demographic projections throughout this report are based on the medium variant of United Nations forecasts. In 1988, the medium projection for year 2000 was revised upwards from 6.1 to 6.25 billion. In 1989 the Executive Director of UNFPA reported to the UNDP Governing Council as follows: "Without enhanced intervention in the future, it is unlikely that United Nations population projections using the medium variant will be realised; rather it is more likely that the demographic scenario depicted in the high variant will come about. Should the latter happen, the annual increment to world population in the year 2000 would be 114 million, instead of the 97 million of the medium variant, soaring to 128 million by 2025 (instead of 81 million). In short, by 2025 the population of the world could be as high as 9.4 billion instead of 8.5 billion—a difference of almost a billion people [DP/1989/37, 14th April 1989]." Thus, questions are beginning to be raised about the realism of the medium variant projections as a planning instrument, not least in view of demographic developments in China, India, and particularly in Sub-Saharan Africa.
Source: United Nations, World Population Chart 1988 and Demographic Yearbook.

Chart 3. COMPARATIVE PER CAPITA INCOME GROWTH OF SELECTED GROUPS OF DEVELOPING COUNTRIES
1965 - 1987, per cent per annum

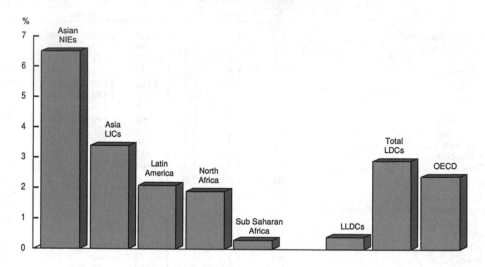

Note: For detailed data see Table 2.1.

Chart 4. IMPROVEMENTS IN LIFE EXPECTANCY[1] BETWEEN 1965 AND 1987

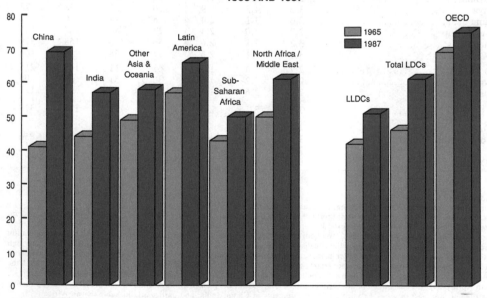

1. Years of life expected at birth. See Table 2.1.

Chart 5. **POPULATION IN 1965 AND 2000**

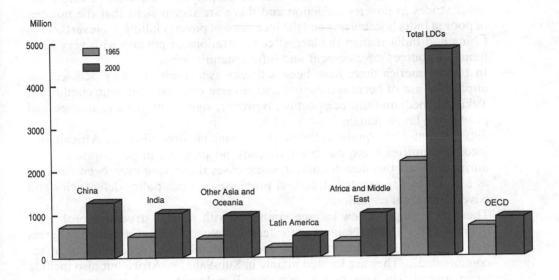

POPULATION IN YEAR 2000
(OECD + Developing Countries)
Total = 6.1 billion

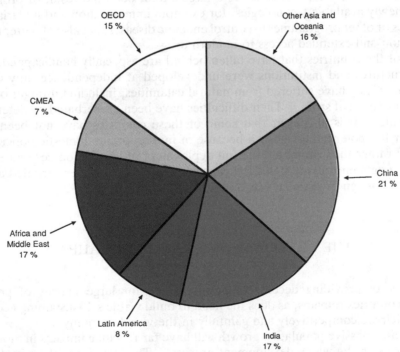

Note: For detailed data see Table 2.2.

— China and India, the most populous developing countries, have made significant advances in agricultural and industrial development. China has made enormous strides in poverty reduction and there are recent signs that the number of poor in India is stabilizing and the incidence of poverty falling. Nevertheless, China and India remain the largest concentrations of poverty with very large human resources development and infrastructure needs.

— In Latin America there have been setbacks as a result of policy deficiencies, imprudent use of borrowed capital and adverse external economic conditions. Taking a medium-term perspective, however, significant gains in income and production levels remain.

— Sub-Saharan Africa presents the most worrying picture. For the African low-income countries there has been virtually no progress in per capita income during the past two decades and in some cases there have even been declines as a result of deep-seated structural problems, serious policy deficiencies and adverse external conditions.

— There is a range of low-income countries with special structural problems, defined by the United Nations as the least developed countries, where progress has been very slow and for which special international action has been recommended. They are located mainly in Sub-Saharan Africa but also include some countries in Asia, such as populous Bangladesh, and Latin America.

There have been major health achievements over the past few decades in developing countries. Death rates have been declining; life expectancy increased from about 40 years in 1950 to 60 today. This has to a large extent been the result of programmes exploiting newly available technologies, for example immunisation and malaria control programmes or other programmes to control endemic diseases, but also of better nutrition and sanitation and extended access to modern drugs.

Many of the countries that have fallen behind are especially handicapped. Their political structures and institutions were undeveloped at independence only one generation ago. They have suffered from natural calamities, including drought or floods, and from war and civil strife. Their difficulties have been exacerbated by deteriorating terms of trade. It is also clear that some of these countries have not been able to exploit their full potential for growth because of inappropriate domestic policies which discouraged rather than promoted the full deployment of local resources and energies. Their limited agricultural and industrial capacities thus were further curtailed and both domestic and foreign investment was discouraged or distorted.

2. THE DEVELOPMENT CHALLENGES AHEAD

The task of providing decent conditions of life for large masses of people in developing countries remains, as does the need to build viable self-sustaining economies able to participate competitively and gainfully in the world economy.

Continuing massive population growth will have far-reaching impacts in most developing countries on the whole development process. The increase in the population of developing countries was 570 million in the 1960s and 720 million in the 1980s. Some 850 million people will be added in the 1990s. The population *increase* in developing countries in the 1990s will exceed the total existing population in the OECD area. In the 1990s, population growth in Sub-Saharan Africa will be some 200 million and in low-income Asia about 500 million. Several African countries at present double their population in twenty years or less. In rapidly rising populations, the proportion of young people and, as a result of improved living standards, of elderly people also is relatively large, creating high dependency ratios with far-reaching economic and social implications.

Poverty continues to be a pervasive phenomenon in most developing countries. Malnutrition, precarious housing, inadequate access to basic health and education facilities, insecure and badly paid jobs are the conditions of life of very large proportions of people in low-income countries; but this is also the condition of life of many people in middle-income countries.

Quantification of poverty is a precarious exercise. It is roughly estimated that the number of the world's poor today has grown to around 1 billion people. Over half live in the populous regions of South Asia (about 350 million) and East Asia (about 150 million). They are concentrated in rural regions with high population densities such as the Gangetic Plain of India, the delta region of Bangladesh, the island of Java

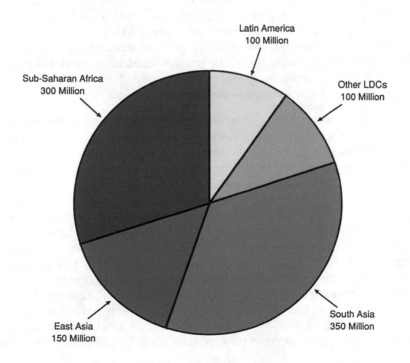

Chart 6. **POVERTY**
(1 Billion poor people)

51

in Indonesia and Central Mindanao of the Philippines. Poverty is extensive in the resource-poor areas in western India and north-western China. It is a largely rural phenomenon in Sub-Saharan Africa (about 300 million people), where poor, fragile soils and underdeveloped farming techniques predominate. In Latin America (about 100 million people) rural landlessness arises more from inequalities in landholding than population pressures, while in urban areas poverty exists in sizeable enclaves. Some 100 million people live in absolute poverty in North Africa, the Middle East and the resource-poor areas in western Pakistan, but for the most part they are dispersed in smaller, less visible areas of poverty in rural and urban areas.

Major trends and problems that are likely to characterise the development environment, and which will therefore figure centrally in donors' policies in the years ahead, will be more fully identified later in the report. They include the following.

— The massive population increases and pervasive poverty problems referred to above.
— Continued heavy debt burdens in many developing countries, especially in Sub-Saharan Africa and Latin America; these problems are to a large extent the manifestation of more deep-seated economic, social and political bottlenecks.
— Low levels of physical and human investment in many countries, which, unless raised, will undermine longer-term development prospects.
— World economic adjustment challenges arising from the globalisation of trade and technological advances, with particular problems for less resilient, commodity-dependent, low-income countries.
— A continuing rapid trend towards urbanisation and the associated problems.
— A very large increase in the demand for new jobs in developing countries, with consequential requirements for investments, and a likely strengthening of the need to export and of migration pressures.
— Continuing institutional weaknesses in many developing countries.
— Overload on the capacity of the environment in many developing countries, including the problem of deforestation and desertification, and the global dimensions of environmental degradation.

Growing tensions are likely to arise from the increasingly dualistic character of societies in many developing countries, with an expanding modernised and largely urban middle class on the one hand and the masses of slum-dwellers and rural poor on the other. Dualism is largely the inevitable side effect of modernisation and openness to the industrialised world through international trade, investment, globalisation of mass media as well as aid. But inequalities have been exacerbated by policies. Many developing countries, especially the low-income countries among them, face the fundamental challenge of developing forms of economic and social organisation and lifestyles which secure reasonable conditions of life for the masses of their people and their growing expectations in the face of the likely persistence for many years to come of relatively low levels of production and incomes and severe financial constraints. In the same vein, developing countries are concerned to reconcile the requirements of modernisation with the preservation of their cultural values and identities. In this perspective, considerably greater caution is indicated in using data on GNP growth and average per capita incomes, with their emphasis on aggregate material production and consumption, as measures of comparative development progress. Developing countries need to improve their analytical concepts and capacities and their data base in this area.

Catering for the growing masses and improving their lot and preserving the natural resource base pose enormous challenges. Major investments are required in production capacities, economic infrastructure, resource preservation and rehabilitation, and human resources development, including, as a central issue, upgrading the role of women as a strategic requirement for progress in more productive agriculture, health, fertility reduction and environmental protection. On the more hopeful side, country comparisons show the potential existing in most developing countries for improving, through effective policies and incentive systems, the mobilisation of domestic material and human resources and their more productive use.

3. THE CENTRAL DEVELOPMENT CO-OPERATION POLICY PRIORITIES FOR THE 1990s

Working with developing countries for broad-based sustainable and equitable development is identified as the guiding theme for setting the development co-operation priorities for the 1990s. The notion of "sustainability" has become central in the debate on development and aid strategies. It provides a useful emphasis on the need to be concerned with the *longer*-term impacts of policies and measures and the *structural* requirements of development. It encompasses the economic, social, financial and institutional viability of development strategies and economic policies. Recently awareness has been growing of the resource base and the environment as aspects of sustainability. The notion of sustainability is also closely related to the concept of self-reliance. Indeed, the ability of countries to sustain their economies without continuing dependence on external financial and technical assistance remains the ultimate objective of development co-operation. The related objectives of participatory development, of ensuring broad participation and sharing in the contribution to development and in its benefits and in providing decent conditions of life, income and employment for the masses of the people, including vulnerable and underprivileged groups, are the ultimate test of the success of development and development co-operation.

This report argues, as one of its main theses, that the attainment of broad-based growth and of sustainable and equitable development requires that they be made integral parts of development strategies and policies in all areas and at all stages.

This report will examine the central development challenges and the ensuing development co-operation priorities for the 1990s. Singling out a few priorities would be misleading in view of the complexity of the tasks ahead and the diversity of country situations. Patient and persistent work is required on the broad front of development issues. It is nevertheless useful at this stage to highlight some of the central requirements which call for new and more determined emphasis in the orientation of development assistance programmes.

— Helping developing countries in their own efforts to improve their economic and development policies and, even more fundamentally, their policy-making capacity, must remain a high priority for development co-operation.

53

— In the same vein, helping developing countries in strengthening the institutions required for effective development — in central and local government, in health and education and other essential services, in private business and the financial system — must remain one of the most important aims of development co-operation in the 1990s. This is essential for self-reliance, the ultimate objective of development co-operation.

— Co-operation for broad-based growth and participatory development means seeking opportunities in the dialogue with developing countries for using aid to promote conditions for a productive and dynamic enterprise sector and more generally to strengthen the role of individual initiative and the market mechanism.

— There are vast and growing requirements for urban and rural infrastructure.

— This review offers suggestions for policy orientations for equitable development as a basis for policy dialogue with developing countries and as an indication of opportunities for donor assistance which emphasize:

- Market and efficiency-oriented growth policies and their effective implementation by strong and competent governments;
- Enhancing opportunities for productive employment;
- Improving access and affordability of essential economic and social services to the masses of the people, including the poor, and their financial sustainability;
- Human resources development — investing in people — must be central in development co-operation strategies emphasizing broad-based growth and participatory development; improvements in health care, water and sanitation, family planning services, and especially education not only contribute to an improved quality of life; they are also indispensable for longer-term development;
- Improved food security and adequate nutrition levels, mainly through increases in productive income and agricultural and rural development, remain an elementary development co-operation objective;
- In the 1980s the role of women in development became a new priority in development co-operation; while progress has been made, the 1990s have yet to see this growing recognition of women's essential role in development translated into operational action;
- Development co-operation emphasizing sustainable and equitable growth has a role to play in helping developing countries to make universally available the opportunity to regulate fertility, thereby enhancing the welfare of mothers and children and reducing the excessive burden of population growth on development;
- A more equitable and participatory orientation of policies and resource allocation is not likely to occur without a minimum of democratic processes and economic and political pluralism through a broader sharing of economic and political responsibilities; there are forms of development co-operation which contribute to this process (e.g., using less "governmentalised" channels of aid, associating end-users through appropriate organisations with the

design and implementation of aid-financed projects, and promoting co-operatives and similar associations and NGOs).

— Contributing to environmentally sustainable development is a major new challenge for development co-operation in the 1990s. It is essential to build consensus on this issue with developing countries taking into account also the global dimensions of this problem. The first priority is to help developing countries integrate sustainable resource management into their development strategies and programmes.

— More attention needs to be paid to helping developing countries to cope with problems of drug abuse.

— Developing countries will need the support of an effective international aid system to meet the challenges of the 1990s. This review highlights the need for aid adaptation and differentiation in the following areas.

- Substantial additional aid efforts will be required not only quantitatively but also qualitatively.
- Working towards effective co-ordination and integration of donor and recipient efforts will become even more important in the 1990s as the dimensions and complexities of the development task increase.
- Donors and recipients will have to work together to improve the conditions for effective aid use, to reduce aid intrusiveness and to preserve prospects for self-reliance.
- With the growing complexity of the development and development co-operation task in the 1990s strong multilateral institutions as focal points for coherent efforts and policy dialogues are essential.

— Effective economic and structural adjustment policies of OECD countries are vital for an improved external economic environment of developing countries and their constructive integration into the global multilateral trade and investment system. They largely determine the prospects for export earnings and the availability and cost of external capital. They are central to a satisfactory solution of structural adjustment and debt problems. The machinery of government in OECD countries for ensuring consistent policies needs to be strengthened. In very broad terms, the key impacts of OECD economic management decisions and co-operation will be felt in the following areas:

- Success in achieving improved growth;
- Improving macroeconomic investment, expenditure and savings balances, with their impact on the availability and distribution of international capital and on real interest rates;
- Improving trade and structural policies; in particular, the outcome of the Uruguay Round will be of critical importance in resolving long-standing problems, including problems in the areas of agricultural and commodity trade and services.

III

WORLD ECONOMIC PROSPECTS
AND ADJUSTMENT CHALLENGES

1. FUNDAMENTAL LONG-TERM WORLD ECONOMIC TRENDS
AND THE MAJOR ADJUSTMENT CHALLENGES
FOR DEVELOPING COUNTRIES

The fundamental long-term economic trends which are likely to have an impact on developing countries through the 1990s are:

— Reasonable prospects for moderate economic growth in industrialised countries, partly because of productivity improvements flowing from the spreading of new technologies and continuing national efforts to increase the flexibility of OECD economies;

— The high real interest rates for international capital experienced in the 1980s may moderate early in the new decade, given appropriate policy shifts and the impact of demographic factors on household savings in OECD economies, but seem unlikely to fall to the relatively low levels of the 1950s and 1960s;

— The further globalisation of trade, finance and production structures, closely linked with the revolution in information and communication technologies and the rising importance of service industries and intellectual property;

— Rising competition in commodity production because of slowing growth in demand in industrialised countries, resulting from the falling commodity-intensity of manufacturing output with the advent of new materials and advances in design technologies, more efficient organisation and investment on the supply side, and potentially, in the agricultural field, the impact of biotechnology;

— The continued evolution of a multipolar world economy, with Japan and Europe assuming more weight and responsibility and the Asian region generally playing a dynamic role, while the role of Latin America will depend on the sustained application of effective economic policies as the debt problem is treated, the current economic and political reform efforts in Eastern Europe could add a further dimension to the evolution of the global economy;

— Trade, investment and technology issues will become increasingly interrelated and complex, both empirically and at the political level;

— Diverging demographic trends between developed countries and different groups of developing countries which are likely to have an increasing impact on economic patterns and decisions; differences in labour supply will influence the location of industries and choice of technology;
— Environmental problems and international action to deal with them might also have far-reaching economic consequences.

The capacities of developing countries to cope with the challenges of, or to take advantage from, the fundamental trends enumerated above vary greatly.   There is an important range of countries, including the Asian NIEs, the ASEAN countries, China, India, and a number of middle-income countries, who are either actually or potentially significant participants in an advanced international economy, dominated no longer by "vertical" trade but by intra-industry trade in manufactures, technology and services. Some other developing countries could begin to climb the bottom rungs of the ladder, in trade in textiles and other labour-intensive manufactured products, as they are vacated by other developing countries moving further up the ladder.   This process is already beginning to emerge in the Asian region, as the Asian NIEs, following to some extent in the trail of Japan, create space for other countries to move up behind; in fact a classic example of international economic diversification and integration.   The role of the Asian NIEs in this process has been central and their further adjustment and adaptation will be critical to its continuation.   The Asian NIEs have thus been instrumental in helping to spread growth around the Asian region and generally have contributed greatly to the dynamic recovery of world trade and growth in the 1980s.

It is clear that a critical factor in enabling developing countries to participate dynamically in world trade, and thus to adjust to the fundamental long-term forces now in play, is a flexible, robust business sector.   The individual business unit is the key institution for intermediating between national capacities and the world economy, thus enabling a nation's resources to be developed to take advantage of, rather than be submerged by, the evolution of international markets.   The Asian NIEs have succeeded by fostering a national context in which the business sector can flourish; strong business units in turn provide the capacity for these economies to adapt to and profit from technological change and patterns of demand.

In the smaller, weaker developing countries, a strong business sector is absent. These countries are therefore not in a position to cope effectively with the powerful new forces in the world economy.   Indeed, technological advances in manufacturing processes may diminish the advantages of low labour costs, making it more difficult for the less advanced developing countries to gain entry into the world markets for manu-factured goods.

The countries which fall into this category are highly commodity-dependent in general.   Their problem is not so much commodity dependence per se, but the fundamental institutional and human resource weaknesses that underly their situation. They are inceasingly vulnerable to other developing-country commodity producers with stronger institutional systems and business sectors, who are able to lower the costs of commodity production by employing advanced management and technological skills. Policy measures focused on commodity markets at the international level are not only difficult to implement, but are not directed at the real problems facing weaker developing countries.

A fundamental response to the situation of the weaker developing countries therefore must centre on the basic development tasks which will over time help these countries to participate more effectively in the world economy, the development of human resources, the building of institutions and infrastructure and the fostering of a market-based enterprise economy. It is for this reason that these themes have emerged as basic orientations for development co-operation in the 1990s.

2. THE IMPORTANCE OF EFFECTIVE OECD ECONOMIC POLICIES AND THE NEED FOR IMPROVED CONSISTENCY WITH DEVELOPMENT CO-OPERATION AIMS

Effective, coherent economic policies of OECD countries are vital for an improved external economic environment of developing countries. They largely determine the prospects for export earnings and the availability and cost of external capital. They are central to a satisfactory solution of the debt problem. In very broad terms, the key impacts of OECD economic management decisions and co-operation will be felt in the following areas:

— Success in achieving improved growth;
— Improving macroeconomic investment and savings balances (including the balance in the public sector) which have an impact on the availability and distribution of international capital and on real interest rates;
— Improving trade and structural policies; in particular, the outcome of the Uruguay Round will be of critical importance in resolving long-standing problems, including in the areas of agricultural and commodity trade and textiles.

It is important to establish coherent approaches to development co-operation in which broader OECD economic, trade, financial and structural policies (in particular in agriculture) and official development assistance reinforce each other in assisting developing countries to participate effectively in world trade and investment. The machinery of government in OECD countries for ensuring consistent and effective overall policies towards developing countries needs to be strengthened. Much depends on the success of co-operative efforts to wind back and correct policy-induced structural distortions in a number of key OECD economies which have helped to entrench major external imbalances and promote protectionist pressures. Without timely and coherent adjustments in fiscal and monetary policies for example, real interest rates may stay at high levels or even rise further, offsetting efforts to ease debt problems, and affecting exchange rates in a perverse direction which could add further to trade tensions. Failure to arrest the pressures for "managed trade" and unilateral trade measures would seriously undermine trade and investment prospects for developing countries and put in question the credibility of OECD Members' advocacy of trade policy reform in developing countries. Moreover, the costs imposed on developing countries by existing industrial country protection are already, according to some estimates, very considerable.

New issues of policy consistency are arising in ensuring compatibility of economic growth and development with the protection of the environment.

The notion of policy consistency has implications also for the relations between aid and export promotion. Attempts to use aid for commercial advantage will produce trade distortions but may also impair the developmental value of aid. Some progress has been made in introducing effective disciplines in this area and there has also been some movement in the direction of untying aid. But the danger of misallocation of aid persists, and requires sustained monitoring.

Recently, interest has been expressed in the OECD in developing dialogues with developing countries with a significant potential impact on the OECD area, such as the NIEs. Taking a longer-term view, a considerably broader range of developing countries will emerge as significant trade and investment partners and, in a wider interpretation of the interdependence notion (including such concerns as the global environment and political stability), the developments in poorer developing countries will also have an impact on the OECD area.

One of the important tasks for the years ahead will be to ensure that the aid and trade and related structural adjustment policies of OECD countries are increasingly seen in their interrelationships and that improved policy coherence is achieved. The development co-operation voice should be sufficiently strong and articulate in the processes of governmental decision-taking and international negotiations in areas which have an impact on development. Areas of actual or potential conflict in development and other aims need to be further investigated and highlighted and brought to the attention of decision-makers. It is important to emphasize in the broader policy context that the "aid system" is an essential instrument not only for poverty alleviation but also for global adjustment and contributing to improved world economic growth.

Attempts to help the weaker members of the world economic system by granting them preferential treatment in some international agreements governing the rules of the game for international trade, investment and technology (e.g., through trade preferences and special provisions in private investment and technology transfer codes and in commodity arrangements) have received less emphasis in recent years — not only because of the difficulty of finding politically acceptable compromises, but also because such approaches are increasingly seen as ineffective if not counterproductive also from the point of view of developing countries themselves. An open multilateral international trade, finance and investment system and effectively working international markets are essential requirements for successful development, accompanied, in the case of the weaker countries, by assistance to increase their capacity for active participation in the world economy.

Developing countries have an important stake in strong international institutions (especially the IMF, World Bank, GATT) capable of preserving a well-functioning multilateral trade, finance and investment system, ensuring effective co-ordination of the economic, financial and structural adjustment policies of the major actors in the world economy and coping with the difficult new issues on the environment front. UN agencies have become the vehicle for international decision-making for a wide spectrum of matters ranging from rules for civil aviation to measures related to trade in toxic chemicals. These functions will be of growing importance in the 1990s. Many of the emerging global issues of the 1990s cannot be solved without developing the co-operation and participation of developing countries in these institutions.

60

IV

DEVELOPMENT CHALLENGES IN MAJOR REGIONS

1. THE BASIC PHENOMENON OF COUNTRY DIVERSITY

Differences in economic, social and other development conditions and the related diverging capacities to cope with economic shocks and structural change, have led to an increasingly pronounced diversity in economic and social performance.   Indeed, the developing countries present a picture of bewildering economic and cultural diversity and complexity, even within quite small geographical regions and, indeed, within countries.   The DAC has recently agreed to look at central aid issues, initially on an experimental basis, increasingly in specific regional contexts.   Some essential trends and factors are sketched below.

2. EAST AND SOUTH-EAST ASIA

East and South-East Asia encompass a wide range of economies at very different levels of income and population.   Although there is still a long way to go in most countries before all development problems are effectively resolved, on the whole this is a region where development progress has been made.   The greatest successes in economic growth, participation in world economic trade and perhaps social development have been in the Asian NIEs (Korea, Taiwan, Hong Kong and Singapore).   Policies emphasizing high investment rates, export promotion and human resources development (including official family planning programmes contributing to a slowing of population growth) are the essential factors behind these achievements.   Although the average per capita incomes of these countries are still only less than a third those of OECD countries, they have become major actors in the world economy.   Informal consultations have begun with the OECD on subjects of mutual interest.

Malaysia and Thailand are among the most dynamic Asian economies, with high growth rates in exports of manufactures.   The rapid take-off in their exports of manufactures was facilitated by investments in human capital and physical infrastructure.   These two ASEAN countries have also successfully developed their agricultural sectors throughout the period of industrialisation. Their record shows the benefits of relatively stable policy orientations, but also flexibility in accommodating external shocks through changes in policy. The important challenge for these countries is to maintain fiscal and monetary stability as the basis for pursuing structural economic policies which increase efficiency and export potential, while reducing the adverse environmental impacts of rapid growth.

Indonesia, a large, low-income oil-exporting country, has carried out the economic management challenges of declining oil prices with skill and determination. Steady improvements in agricultural productivity have underpinned living standards for a large population. Rapid diversification of the sources of public revenues and export earnings has laid the basis for continuing and, if economic policies and political conditions evolve favourably, possibly faster development progress. Indonesia is receiving substantial amounts of external assistance, although with aid flows amounting to less than 2 per cent of GDP Indonesia is by no means an aid-dependent country. In the Philippines, political problems and associated economic management and external debt difficulties have impeded development progress in the 1980s. The current improvement in the situation remains fragile and major economic, social, environmental and political challenges must be confronted in the immediate future.

The most advanced developing countries in the region have effectively graduated from being recipients of aid, and indeed Korea and Taiwan are emerging as aid donors. In the other middle-income countries of the region, Malaysia and Thailand, growing financial strength and institutional capacity have progressively reduced the scale of development assistance requirements, but scope remains for effective help in rehabilitating and upgrading infrastructure, in developing small and medium-size enterprises, in human resource development (including in the areas of research and development) and in narrowing the differences in the development level within countries (between rural and urban areas, and within urban areas, where the absorption of migrants into the cities is a major problem). The terms and nature of such assistance should reflect the financial and institutional capacities of these countries.

In the low-income countries of the region, major adjustment and policy reform-based assistance requirements exist, along with long-run development co-operation tasks in infrastructure development, rural and industrial development (especially with the diversification of exports in view) and poverty-oriented programmes based on income generation. In the Philippines there is a particularly important role for a significant, co-ordinated effort to support economic and social reform programmes.

3. CHINA AND INDIA

India and China are by far the largest low-income countries, accounting together for half of the total population of developing countries. Both countries have been trying to step up development progress by altering major aspects of their development strategies.

India's development policies and financial needs have been discussed in an aid consortium for over thirty years; no similar arrangements for collective discussion with donors exist for China, which did not become a major user of aid until the 1980s.

India is beginning to draw gains from the reforms in its development strategy characterised by greater reliance on market forces and decentralisation. In terms of aggregate growth, allowing for the disruptions in the agriculture sector and in other rural activities caused by severe drought, the rate of progress in the 1980s has shown an upward shift compared to the trend in the 1970s. The successful containment of the disruptive impact of the drought itself is an illustration of a more flexible functioning of the Indian economy and its management than before.

These recent signs of long-awaited acceleration of economic development need to be confirmed with more convincing evidence on trade performance and social progress, although there are now some encouraging trends in these areas. However, there have been some serious deteriorations, which, if unabated, would undermine the gradually emerging private sector optimism — both domestic and foreign; notably, the rapid worsening of public finance deficits and equally rapid deepening of the trade deficit. The government is faced with a challenge of dealing with these major problems without disrupting its new strategy for liberalisation, confidence in which has been increasing. In a still highly regulated economy, such as that of India, the sequence of major reform actions is critical for the avoidance of large macroeconomic imbalances such as balance-of-payments difficulties, large public-sector deficits, inflation and large-scale open unemployment or rapid and sudden elimination of marginal agricultural activities. An external debt constraint is beginning to emerge in this period of historic transition, which is due not so much to the scale of foreign borrowing as to the previous lack of dynamism in export receipts. Sustained foreign borrowing at market terms will require policy orientations which force the pace on the price and quality competitiveness of the Indian economy.

The structure of agricultural production is being reassessed, with account taken, among other things, of international market factors, scarcity of managed water resources and the opportunities for further technological progress. At the same time, however, poverty alleviation in the rural sector through institutional reforms still lacks momentum, and more direct policy actions intended to improve the conditions of the rural poor seem to suffer because of such factors as the traditional complex socio-economic structures at the local level. Certain aspects of India's agricultural policies may need to be reassessed from the point of view of safeguarding environmental resources, since the intensive use of agricultural inputs, in some cases, appears to have become dangerous for soil and safe-water conservation. In sum, India has to tackle a broad development agenda, including both the improvement and extension of basic infrastructure and taking further its policy reforms to upgrade agricultural and industrial productivity, to promote foreign exchange earning capacity and to improve environmental preservation, social services delivery and equitable access to income-generating employment opportunities.

China created a strong momentum of domestic economic reform after 1978, which accelerated noticeably up until serious inflationary pressures and internal political problems emerged in the late 1980s. A number of interrelated institutional changes affecting practically all productive sectors as well as public institutions had been carried through although the reform process was far from complete.

China's uniqueness from the developmental point of view is that it had already achieved major improvements in basic social conditions during the earlier stages of its development efforts. The achievements seen in life expectancy and literacy rates, for instance, have reached levels that go beyond what other low-income countries might hope to attain in the coming decade. Despite this already considerable achievement, China suffers from a lack of educated and trained manpower in its efforts to step up industrial development and expansion and modernisation of the services sector. Together with the improvements in the way in which capital and technology are used throughout the economy, this task of human resource development may constitute one of the key development factors for China to sustain its recent performance in the 1990s.

Led by an extraordinarily fast growth rate of industrial expansion encompassing many sectors, China's aggregate economic growth rate has remained at one of the highest levels observed in the post-war period. In the past few years, some major problems have developed, especially in external balances, because of the very rapid expansion of imports. A related problem has been uncontrolled external borrowing by many entities that had been empowered to borrow on non-concessional terms. While these two problems seem to have been brought under better control in the past year or so, the pace of industrial growth and domestic demand expansion has pushed inflationary pressures to an unprecedented level. China has problems in controlling domestic demand without causing abrupt slowdown of its economic growth. Effective economy-wide monetary policy or fiscal measures need to be developed and implemented. At the same time, it is important to preserve momentum in the move towards market-determined price movements. There is also a need for a more flexible functioning of the labour market — this is only gradually becoming accepted (e.g., detaching housing from the remuneration package). These reforms would help to improve the allocation of resources and to ensure that decisions regarding the major infrastructure investments needed to overcome bottlenecks in the economy are economically sound. In turn the easing of these bottlenecks will help to avoid the inflationary pressures that have been associated with rapid economic reform.

China's population, at 1 billion, is the largest in the world. Rigorous family planning policies, together with successful basic health programmes have lowered the fertility rate considerably. Nevertheless, population pressures remain serious and the social impacts of the changes in family and demographic structures brought about by the population policies have yet to become manifest. Environmental concerns have not been widely recognised during the major reform period. In this area, too, China needs to instal modern capacity to cope with a broad range of hitherto under-emphasized environmental issues, related, for instance, to the agriculture, industry and urban sectors. These new issues are complex and are superimposed on vast requirements to upgrade and expand basic infrastructure in key sectors such as transport and energy.

These are major challenges. Whether China's rapid economic progress will continue in the 1990s — and with it much more interaction with the developing economies of East and South-East Asia, in particular, through trade and investment relationships — will depend on finding effective ways of combining the twin requirements of economic rigour and the stimulating effects of liberalisation and decentralisation. The recent political crisis in China has increased the uncertainties surrounding this critical question.

4. OTHER ASIAN LOW-INCOME COUNTRIES

Several Asian countries are classified as "least developed", with all the characteristics of poverty and institutional backwardness that this classification implies: Afghanistan, Bangladesh, Burma, Nepal, Bhutan and Laos.   Others such as Viet Nam and Kampuchea have much ground to make up after two decades of war and unrest.   Two countries, Pakistan and Sri Lanka, have seen rates of economic progress over the last two decades close to that achieved by well-performing developing countries.   Sri Lanka stands out as a low-income country with relatively high social development, the result of a successful basic human needs focus combined with (until very recently) good rates of growth in per capita incomes.   Both countries have been carrying burdens associated with civil conflicts in their own or neighbouring countries.

Most if not all of these South Asian economies have a large labour force in the rural area, dependent mainly on agriculture.   Given the rapid rate of growth of population in these countries, the rural labour force is growing at a fast rate, even with the rising degree of urbanisation.   Since there are limitations to the speed at which a labour surplus in the agriculture sector can be more gainfully employed in non-agricultural occupations, even if a labour-intensive industrialisation strategy is pursued, these countries have to carry the burden of surplus agricultural labour for at least a few more decades.   In view of the severe land constraints already operating in these countries, it becomes all the more important for them to design agricultural strategies that will be both land-saving and labour-intensive.   The attention given to social development activities is not yet sufficient (apart from the exemplary case of Sri Lanka).   Human resource development should therefore form an important component of development strategies.   As a result of domestic savings constraints and serious institutional weaknesses, these countries have become, together with Africa, major users of external financial and technical assistance (see "Basic Aid Data").   The requirements for development co-operation range widely across basic infrastructure, human resource development, food production, rural development, industrial development for job creation and export promotion, as well as basic needs such as planning and health care.

The aid community will face the challenge and opportunity in the decade ahead of assisting economic reconstruction in Indo-China if and when the conflicts which have ravaged this region in the past are resolved.

5. LATIN AMERICA

Latin America is a highly diverse continent, with incomes per capita ranging from levels near to industrial countries (Venezuela) to the level of the least developed countries (Haiti).   There a number of low and low-middle income countries, especially in Central America and the Caribbean, some of which have aid dependence ratios similar to those prevailing in Sub-Saharan Africa.   Even the advanced economies of the region (Brazil, Mexico, Argentina, Venezuela, Chile, Uruguay, Colombia and Peru) have marked dual economy characteristics, with extensive areas of poverty and underdevelopment.

Following two decades of impressive and generally widespread economic progress when per capita incomes grew on average at about 3 per cent per year, the 1980s have seen serious setbacks in most if not all of the countries of the region due to a combination of policy deficiencies, imprudent borrowing and lending activities and external economic conditions.   Per capita incomes in 1987 were lower in real terms than in 1980 in all but five out of 25 countries in the region and in six countries they were lower than in 1970.

While the situations, problems and economic structures of individual countries vary widely, a common underlying factor in many cases was that the extreme reliance on external debt finance to fund expansion in the 1970s was not matched by a fundamental increase in debt-servicing capacity because of the inward-looking development strategies and generally inefficient resource allocation characterising the region.   Export volumes for the region as a whole expanded by less than 2 per cent per year in the 1970s compared with 11 per cent per year for Asian developing economies.   The world recession plus the major increase in real interest rates and falling terms of trade for primary exports in the early 1980s were thus sufficient to undermine the financial, economic and policy foundations of many Latin American economies.

The very large corrections required involved internal and external adjustments of a magnitude that inevitably affected growth performance and living standards.   They also helped to create political and economic uncertainties that have affected investment confidence.   The region moved from a position of absorbing significant external resources in the 1970s to exporting domestic resources in the 1980s both as debt service and as capital flight.   The effort to increase exports while containing imports and to raise government revenues while cutting back expenditures and subsidies has been accompanied by a major fall in domestic investment and, in many countries, a significant rise in inflation.   The large trade surplus of the Latin American region indicates the large external adjustment that has been accomplished, but inflation and the investment decline indicate that the internal adjustment task has not been resolved.   Indeed, it could be said that there has been over-adjustment externally and under-adjustment internally.

With the recent trend towards democratic government in the region, establishing a political basis for effective and sustainable stabilization and adjustment programmes is a delicate yet essential task for Latin America's leaders.   The adoption of more effective and equitable policies, which is hampered in many cases by severe political, social and institutional constraints, is the key task ahead for Latin America in the 1990s.

Given the severity of Latin America's economic and social problems, and the enormity of the tasks that confront the countries, solutions will imply deep structural change.   Although these efforts will differ from country to country, they will have to incorporate two basic policy themes: stimulating creative market forces through an incentive system that fosters production and efficiency; and comprehensive reform of the public sector to eliminate structural deficits, which erode savings and are at the root of the inflation and debt problem, and to improve public sector efficiency.

Progress to date in individual countries varies widely; indeed this variance in policy reform and adjustment progress produces a new kind of differentiation among the countries of the region.   The most comprehensive policy reforms have perhaps taken place in Chile and Mexico; whereas the former is now on a dynamic growth path, growth in Mexico has stagnated, partly because Mexico had also to absorb the fall in oil prices. But in these countries and in some others, including Uruguay, Bolivia and Jamaica, the policy environment is now radically different from the 1970s and provides a promising basis for renewed development progress in the future. In Brazil and Argentina, there have also been important efforts to reorient economic policies, but they have been less systematic and furthermore the basic domestic stabilization problem remains unresolved despite successive attempts. In Peru, little effort has yet been made to meet the fundamental policy and institutional requirements and there are serious debt issues which are not being approached on the co-operative basis which almost all other countries of the region have adopted; there is a major deterioration not only in the economic situation in Peru but also on the level of civil order.

On the export front, there are already signs of a new dynamism. The export pattern is becoming much less concentrated on major primary export products than in the past, although a few countries remain very dependent on one or two export crops. The growth of non-traditional exports is a focus of policy in many countries (and, in the Caribbean region, of the Caribbean Trade Initiative launched by the United States). There is more attention being given to developing trade within the region, including various kinds of regional integration schemes. But the export competitiveness of Latin American countries will depend fundamentally on the total policy environment and on the recovery of investment, which in turn is linked closely to making progress on resolving debt problems so that the countries of the region have more external and internal resources at their disposal to generate efficient economic and social development.

Latin American countries will also have to confront major issues in the 1990s in the areas of drugs and environmental problems (such as deforestation, especially in Brazil) which have a global dimension. While these economic, political, social and environmental challenges constitute a formidable agenda, against the background of interrupted development progress in the 1980s, political and economic debate and change is under way on a broad scale in the region, which it may be hoped will prepare the ground for a new period of modernisation and growth.

There is as yet no clear strategy in which donors have defined their role for wider development co-operation to help Latin American countries master their current social and economic problems and develop their economic potential. The existence of large areas of poverty and serious policy deficiencies in countries in the middle-income range and with sophisticated infrastructures presents a difficult dilemma for aid donors.

6. MIDDLE EAST AND NORTH AFRICA

The Middle East is an area of high political tension and strategic concern. It is highly diversified, including least developed countries as well as countries with very high per capita incomes. The Gulf countries will remain the largest sources of oil entering world trade. Egypt and Israel are among the largest recipients of external assistance and some other countries in the area are also signficiant users of aid.

In the 1970s high oil prices took many of these countries into an intense phase of modernisation and development. In Iran, the most diversified economy of the region (apart from Israel), this led to a political and cultural eruption, but other countries in the region, such as Saudi Arabia and Jordan, have managed to retain and consolidate the fruits of this burst of progress. In the 1980s, falling oil prices and prolonged conflicts have seriously retarded economic progress in a number of countries. In some countries, debt burdens are now large.

In North Africa the recent difficult economic conditions have stimulated a number of the major economies of the region to adopt more rational economic and development policies. The process of policy reform and economic restructuring will require sustained further efforts.

7.   THE SPECIAL CASE OF SUB-SAHARAN AFRICA

Sub-Saharan Africa suffers from a combination of historical, economic, social, political, institutional and environmental handicaps which have so far largely defied the development efforts of the African countries and the countries trying to assist them. In spite of very substantial aid use (see "Basic Aid Data"), development results have remained limited. Weak institutions, ineffective policies, excessive government controls, absence of a dynamic private business sector, together with political instability and ethnic conflicts, have been major adverse factors. African leaders are only beginning to recognise that rapid population growth causes unsustainable pressures on the natural resource base and puts a brake on per capita growth. In some areas AIDS has become an important problem.

At the same time, it has to be recognised that major strides have been made in laying the human and institutional basis for development in Africa in the relatively short period of time since independence. There are growing cadres of competent and devoted officials, a growing determination to emphasize more self-reliant development styles and more active, self-critical debate. This is something that can be and is being built upon.

Human resources and institutional development, small-farmer agriculture, improved strategies for agricultural research, development of entrepreneurship and small-scale industry, more participatory styles of government and closer regional co-operation (overcoming the problems of small economies and markets) are essential elements for strengthening the development process. The status of women as leaders, farmers, traders and providers as well as consumers of health and other services, and indeed as community leaders, needs to be given much greater recognition.

There is a growing acknowledgement that Africa has to become more cost-effective if it is ever to compete successfully with Asia on world markets. For reasons which go well beyond overvalued exchange rates, unit costs in Africa are much higher than in Asia. Consumption styles in much of the modern sector have been unsustainable, supported indirectly by exploiting rural populations, earlier commodity windfalls and excessive borrowing and certain forms of aid.

Strong corrective action is now being taken. At present, almost 30 African countries have embarked on adjustment programmes with the active support of the donor community. These programmes have involved fundamental shifts in economic policies for many countries, including such essential elements as public sector reform, exchange-rate realignments, restructuring of parastatal enterprises, and changes in agricultural

68

price and marketing systems. These programmes have already produced some results, in Ghana for instance. Other countries, such as Guinea, Tanzania and Uganda, after long periods of decline, have recently experienced, through the adoption of economic recovery programmes, higher growth rates for GNP than for population. Too little time has yet elapsed to assess whether adjustments have been sufficiently deep and broad to generate a sustainable growth process. Progress needs to be consolidated and sustained in the 1990s in order to reverse long-term trends of declining living standards.

Food security and nutrition will remain a primary concern in the 1990s. Even assuming substantial increases in food production, malnutrition will continue to be an important problem because of low purchasing power of poor segments of the population. Substantial emphasis on food production is required in the years ahead. Increasing agricultural production will require support for education and training as well as research. Agricultural research responding to the continent's varied and particular agroclimatic conditions is an important ingredient in a new emphasis on agriculture. Effective use of increased food production will require improved distribution and storage facilities. Environmental aspects will have to be much more seriously integrated into an approach to development which gives much greater weight to the management of natural resources as a pervasive issue.

Investments in health and education are essential for human resource development as well as for improved living standards and poverty alleviation. Attention to these sectors in the 1990s in the Sub-Saharan context should focus on:

— Primary health and education;
— The cost-efficiency of providing these services; the provision of these services has been too costly in the past;
— Greater participation by users and local agencies including NGOs, recognising the important function of women as family health workers.

A major problem in Africa is the falling rate of investment. Higher savings and investment ratios together with open and competitive markets are necessary for a sustained growth process. Returns on investments and savings incentives are low. As the adjustment process proceeds, more attention will have to be given to basic economic infrastructure needs. Roads, railroads and ports to the limited extent that they exist have deteriorated badly in parts of the continent so that communications and trade are severely hindered. But investment in the rehabilitation and construction of the infrastructure needed for development must be accompanied by the strengthening of the human resources and institutions needed for investment decision-making and implementation and maintenance of projects. Sub-Saharan Africa needs continued strong aid support in its difficult development tasks ahead.

8. PACIFIC ISLANDS

The Pacific is characterised by newly independent small island micro-states and territories. All have narrow output and export bases and are very open in the sense of high ratios of imports to GDP. Export earnings fluctuate widely. Isolation and smallness impose heavy costs, reducing competitiveness and the dissemination of technology. Macroeconomic stabilization is particularly problematic. The physical environment is fragile. Some islands are very low-lying. Rising water levels would further impair their economic viability or even habitability. Population growth levels are high by developing-country standards.

Growth during the early 1980s was satisfactory for some, but by the mid-1980s most were experiencing negative growth, hit by falling commodity prices, or heavy cyclone damage, political turmoil, or a combination of all. For others, their economies have been stagnating for some time.

By any standards these states and territories are highly dependent on aid flows and in some cases this dependency is rising. In some instances, the currently known resource base is so limited that aid dependency will be a long-term reality. Aid donors will need to find ways to provide this aid in harmony with the desire for greater sovereignty, and taking account of limits in the capacity to absorb aid. Considerable care will be needed to ensure that aid does not overwhelm the delicate economic and political organisms in the region. The important role of regional institutions must be recognised and effective aid co-ordination will be essential. Donors must work together to promote a larger role for the private sector than is currently the case. Helping these economies with their main resource bottleneck, which is the scarcity of skills, is also a major priority.

POLICIES FOR BROAD-BASED GROWTH, PARTICIPATORY DEVELOPMENT AND ENVIRONMENTAL SUSTAINABILITY

V

WORKING WITH DEVELOPING COUNTRIES TO ACHIEVE BROAD-BASED ECONOMIC GROWTH

It is an essential thesis of this report that broad-based economic growth, participatory development and sustainability are all mutually necessary and reinforcing elements of a successful development process.

Broad-based economic growth is essential for development.   While growth is not synonymous with development, without broad-based economic growth the basic structural transformations which make up the process of development will not occur, developing countries will not generate the number of jobs they must create, they will not produce the resources required to provide adequate social services, and standards of living will remain inadequate.   Broad-based growth, therefore, is an essential basis for equitable development.   At the same time, the requirements of longer-term environmental sustainability should be an integral part of the orientations of economic growth policies set by the central decision-making bodies.

This chapter concentrates on the importance of effective economic policies for broad-based economic growth and frameworks for international co-operation to encourage such policies.   Subsequent chapters will take up other essential ingredients of development co-operation for economic growth such as support for private sector development and basic economic and human infrastructure.

1.   EFFECTIVE POLICIES FOR BROAD-BASED GROWTH: STRUCTURAL ADJUSTMENT IN THE PERSPECTIVE OF THE 1990s

The 1980s have witnessed a recognition by both developing countries and the aid system of the central importance of effective strategies and policies for growth and development.   While development performance is determined by a complex of internal and external factors, policies are fundamental.

Developing countries are responsible for determining their development objectives and the policies to meet them.   It is also clear that many developing countries need international assistance in their efforts at designing and implementing effective policies and programmes.   Effective policies are essential, but, like any investment, they need adequate financing.   Developing effective and mutually acceptable arrangements for international policy support (policy-related aid) is one of the key challenges for development co-operation.

The success of structural adjustment and policy reform efforts by developing countries depends crucially on the external economic environment, which in turn is heavily influenced by the policies of OECD countries.   In fact the core structural adjustment policies identified below apply also very largely to industrial countries.   These interrelationships have been discussed in Chapter III.

The Core Elements of Economic Policy Reform Programmes.   While the specification of effective policies must be related to specific country situations — historical, economic, social and political — a core agenda has emerged in recent years.   These core elements of policy reform programmes which are consistent with longer-term development objectives may be identified as follows:

- Policies and incentive systems — including market-based pricing — which contribute to the fuller and more productive use of national resources and encourage fuller participation of farmers and enterprises;
- Creating the conditions for a larger role for a productive private sector as an essential core element of a strategy for broad-based economic growth (see Chapter VI, Section 2) below);
- Policies and institutions which encourage domestic savings (and the return of flight capital) and their use for productive investment in physical and human capital as the indispensable basis of growth and development;
- Liberalisation of trade regimes to improve the efficiency of resource allocations under the spur of external competition.   There may be cases for careful fostering of "infant industries" but the risks of building up inefficient industries which will become an economic and social burden to the economy needs to be contained by firm rules and disciplines;
- Economic and financial policies which avoid unsustainable fiscal and external imbalances and resulting price, cost and income distortion through inflation;
- Improved fiscal management, with a focus on improving mechanisms for the selection and monitoring of public investments, rationalisation of budget systems and the management and monitoring of the public enterprise sector;
- Improving the efficiency, accessibility and sustainability of public services;
- Effective systems of taxation which strike a balance between effective incentives to work and save and a fair sharing of the gains of economic growth and which produce the revenue required to maintain adequate systems of education, basic health and other essential services;
- Concern with environmental impacts and sustainability.

While there is broad agreement on the desirability of these policy orientations, there are still many difficult issues of pace and substance, including in particular social impacts which have to be confronted in designing and implementing policy reform programmes.   The Development Committee has defined the essential conditions for structural adjustment programmes as follows.

— Programmes should be "owned" by the government to ensure real commitment. There needs also to be sustained political commitment to sound macroeconomic policies.
— Programmes should be well designed and enjoy broad public understanding. They should be drawn up with a realistic time frame taking into account the deep-seated structural problems and the country's social, demographic and political environment.
— Poverty reduction objectives and environmental considerations should be integrated into the design of programmes, along with ways of mitigating the adverse effects on the most vulnerable groups, preferably by income-generating programmes.
— Administrative and institutional capacity adequate for their implementation is a fundamental requirement and could be strengthened where necessary with the assistance of the Bank, the Fund and donors.
— Adequate and timely financing, a supportive external environment, including open markets and structural adjustment in the industrial countries are essential contributions on the side of the OECD community.

Structural adjustment programmes embrace not only short-term stabilization efforts aimed at correcting external and internal payments imbalances. They also address basic structural policy reforms aimed at improving the flexibility and productivity of the economy. They therefore must include sectoral and infrastructure programmes and investments which are the essence of long-term development efforts. There is thus no dichotomy between structural adjustment and policies and efforts for economic and social development or between the short term and the long term. Rather, the objective of structural adjustment programmes is to achieve the economic conditions and policy environment in which sustainable longer-term development efforts can take place and bear fruit.

2. FRAMEWORKS FOR INTERNATIONAL CO-OPERATION FOR ENCOURAGING EFFECTIVE DEVELOPMENT POLICIES

Recent international co-operation in support of structural adjustment efforts in Sub-Saharan Africa sets a new pattern for coherent tripartite co-operation between low-income countries determined to improve their policies and programmes, the World Bank and other international financial institutions and donors.

This new approach implies the commitment of developing countries to adjustment programmes and policy change, donor efforts to ensure an enhanced and more co-ordinated aid effort, the provision of more flexible structural adjustment support by donors, appropriate IMF facilities, and the recognition of the need for substantial concessional debt relief on a case-by-case basis.

A number of key instruments for carrying through this new approach have been put in place over the past two or three years:

— The creation of common frameworks within which donors can work with developing countries towards improved economic policies and management, expressed in a few key strategic documents;

- Policy Framework Papers (PFPs);
- Public Investment Programmes (PIPs);
- Public Expenditure Programmes (PEPs).

— Adjustment-oriented financial mechanisms, including:

- The co-ordinated cofinancing programme within the framework of the Special Programme of Assistance for Africa (SPA) launched by the World Bank, with its associated multi-donor consultation mechanisms;
- Increased bilateral donor provision of quick-disbursing funds, including streamlining of procedure and substantial untying;
- The Enhanced Structural Adjustment Facility, increasing the concessional resources available from the IMF;
- The Paris Club agreement on a set of options for providing significant concessional debt relief.

It has been agreed that the international community should work toward facilitating external financial support to African governments' adjustment efforts in the period beyond 1990. This should include continuation of the collaborative framework for donor action developed under the SPA and co-ordinated by the World Bank as well as the examination of possible additional measures to address the economic and debt problems of these countries. The need to supplement quick-disbursing assistance to support adjustment in Sub-Saharan Africa with adequate investment financing and technical assistance to help deal with the longer-term problems of the region has been underlined.

The key policy documents which are the basis for international support are a matter for negotiation between the developing country and the World Bank and the IMF. To be credible and effective, however, it is important, above all, that the developing country itself have the leading role and final responsibility in specifying the directions and the content of its economic strategy. It is also important that donors be consulted on programmes which they are being asked to support. The aim is to develop a process which generates a continually evolving strategy adjusting to new factors as they arise, and where donor inputs on important questions become part of established practice. This requires a strengthened role for local aid co-ordination arrangements, appropriate staffing and back-up for local aid missions and more active communications between aid agencies and the World Bank and IMF, especially at the local level. (For a broader discussion of aid co-ordination issues see Chapter XII.)

Where developing country authorities lack the necessary policy-making resources and structures to assume in full their responsibility in designing policy programmes and in leading local aid co-ordination, donors should look for opportunities to encourage and support the upgrading of capacities in this central function. This must be a central priority for donor/recipient co-operation, with special responsibilities for the international institutions, especially the UNDP.

The arrangements for internationally co-ordinated support for policy reform efforts outlined above were designed in the specific context of African low-income debt-distressed countries, taking into account their special problems and characteristics. These arrangements put a heavy organisational and administrative burden on the World Bank and IMF as international lead agencies in this process. The degree of involvement of these institutions and the amounts of financial support granted by the aid community reflect the depth of the problems and of the policy reform needs of the developing countries concerned. For developing countries with relatively stronger structures for policy making and management, organisationally lighter arrangements for assisting policy reforms and structural adjustment have been developed. More generalised use of the Policy Framework Paper approach is under discussion.

Large-scale provision of policy-related programme assistance is an essential part of programmes in support of policy reform. But, it poses problems for donors who are accountable to parliaments and public opinion for effective aid use. Adequate safeguards and monitoring and evaluation arrangements to ensure effective implementation of policy reform efforts are in the interest of donors and users alike of policy-related programme aid. As the World Bank concluded in a recent evaluation of experience with adjustment lending, adjustment lending is potentially both a high pay-off and a high-risk instrument.

Support for policy reform efforts necessarily calls for substantial external support in the form of co-ordinated policy-related programme assistance. This does not imply, however, that the new emphasis on policy reform support necessarily means wholesale and permanent shifts in the project/programme assistance mix. There is a continuing need for project and sector-related assistance addressing specific investment and human resources and institution-building requirements. The aim should be to relate *all* types of financial and technical assistance to well designed sector strategies, attempting to achieve clearly defined objectives and addressing specific development bottlenecks.

3. ENCOURAGING REGIONAL ECONOMIC INTEGRATION

A number of developing regions are highly fragmented in economic terms, characterised by small economies with many different barriers to integration: political, ethnic, geographical and economic. Often, economic and communications linkages are stronger between these small economies and the major metropolitan countries than they are either within the country itself or within the region. The implementation of structural adjustment programmes which open the way towards sustainable long-term development will create stronger, more rational economic structures capable of participating competitively and with benefit, in the open world economy. However, even so, many smaller countries may not be able to reach genuine long-term viability except as part of a larger economic region.

While traditional regional integration agreements may provide a model in some cases (with appropriate adaptation to local circumstances), they have often failed to live up to expectations or have become stalled in the face of political obstacles. To the extent that developing countries opt for reduction of trade barriers as part of an economic reform programme, there is already a better prospect of regional integration. However, other obstacles just as important often remain — the absence of appropriate transport and communications infrastructure, tensions arising from ethnic diversity and migration, national rivalries etc. This suggests that less ambitious objectives, adapted to the circumstances of the region and pursued pragmatically, may in practice lead to the most progress. The range of co-operation should extend well beyond trade, to sector projects and programmes, human resources development, scientific and technological development etc. Underpinning such co-operation there would need to be an understanding of why regional economic co-operation is a compelling objective, and a strong political commitment to that objective. The fostering of *processes* of consultation and contact can itself contribute materially to breaking down political obstacles.

There are a number of existing models that might be studied to provide inspiration and guidance. Features that are likely to emerge as necessary or at least desirable in regional co-operation arrangements include strengthened consultation mechanisms on national policies; intensified involvement of the business sector, social sectors and citizens in general in discussion and co-operation processes; attention to small projects as much as large projects (to spread opportunities and involvement) and projects outside the public sector; a strengthening of mechanisms for common evaluation of external developments; and the development of information networks within and between integration groupings. Donors, for their part, need to be ready to adjust their programmes and modalities (including co-ordination arrangements) to match regional integration efforts. There should be a readiness to give support to less advanced states in a regional group to enable them to participate in the benefits of integration.

VI

STIMULATING PRODUCTIVE ENERGIES
THROUGH PARTICIPATORY DEVELOPMENT

1. THE NOTION OF PARTICIPATORY DEVELOPMENT

The history of economically, socially and culturally successful societies is very largely the history of the deployment of individual and collective energies. While there are many complex social, political and cultural forces at work, economic policies and institutions can contribute to the process of stimulating and liberating human energies. It is increasingly realised that excessive centralisation of decision-making and overregulation stifle productive energies. There is an active debate going on in many countries, industrial as well as developing, about the role of the state in economic life and society, about the balance between the market and regulation, decentralisation, regionalisation. There are no ready recipes and certainly no standard recipes to pass on to the diversity of developing countries with their very special political, social and cultural traditions. But there is a growing world-wide consensus on the importance of a series of factors which can be subsumed under the notion of participatory development.

The notion of participatory development emphasizes the relevance for sustainable and equitable development of broad-based participation in the productive and decision-making processes, in access to education, health and other relevant public services and in the benefits of development.

There is a growing recognition that policies need to encourage private-sector initiatives and devolution of authority to the local level within the public sector too. Rather than do the job themselves, governments need to provide a framework which will encourage individuals' private concerns and local communities to provide critical services needed by the population.

In this vein, aid agencies recognise the need to place greater emphasis on ensuring the commitment of recipients' executing agencies through their active involvement in selection, design and implementation. For many types of projects, active involvement of end-users and beneficiaries through communities and other local organisations, ensuring that the project meets actual needs and circumstances, is essential for project success and mobilising local energies. The fuller involvement of women in the planning and implementation of development projects is a basic element of the notion of participatory development (see Chapter IX, Section 5).

77

Emphasis on participatory development also means seeking opportunities in the dialogue with developing countries for using aid to promote conditions for a productive and dynamic enterprise sector and more generally to strengthen the role of individual initiative and the market mechanism. There is a largely convergent policy trend in both industrial and developing countries in this direction. But there are, also, some inherent limits to the extent to which government-to-government aid can foster decentralised and private-sector development. DAC discussions have already identified the need to re-examine effective instruments of financial intermediation with increasing use of local credit institutions as channels of aid. Taking a medium-term perspective, a more determined emphasis on decentralised and private-sector promotion will require less "governmentalised" channels of aid building on national and local non-governmental institutions. New emphasis on participatory development does not imply by-passing developing country governments. It is important to develop forms of development co-operation which promote participatory development through the use of decentralised channels and institutions as part of government-to-government co-operation. In the same vein, there is a growing emphasis on the use of non-governmental organisations (NGOs) in both the North and the South as channels of aid and development co-operation. These two new strands of co-operation are dealt with in greater detail in sections 2 and 3 below.

The promotion of more participatory and decentralised forms of development raises issues of relevance for the development co-operation dialogue. A more equitable orientation of policies and resource allocation is not likely to occur without a minimum of democratic processes and economic and political pluralism through a broader sharing of economic and political responsibilities. There are forms of development co-operation which may contribute to this process. Associating end-users through appropriate organisations with the design and implementation of aid-financed projects, and promoting co-operatives and similar associations can contribute to more participatory development. There is also scope for private sector constituency building, as in business education programmes, chambers of commerce, and employers' and workers' organisations. Similarly, there is room for constructive co-operation in strengthening fair and effective judicial systems and democratic institutions of government at local and central levels. This includes support for institutions to facilitate feedback, accountability and transparency in decision-making. Respect of human rights, justice and equity are legitimate subjects for dialogue among sovereign partners. Fuller mobilisation of human resources and their productive energies will be facilitated when basic human rights are respected.

2.   A LARGER ROLE FOR A PRODUCTIVE PRIVATE SECTOR: THE CONTRIBUTION OF MARKET FORCES AND PRIVATE ENTERPRISE TO DEVELOPMENT

There is now a broad consensus on the need for greater reliance on private enterprises and markets to promote growth in developing countries. In general, countries which have used market opportunities and developed dynamic private sectors have fared better than those that have not. A large number of countries, including some in the low-income bracket, are adapting their development strategies to incorporate a larger role for market forces, so as to raise the efficiency of both public and private enterprises. In a broad range of developing countries, profit-motivated businesses, competing in open markets, have launched broad-based economic development. The private sector has shown its ability to read market signals more rapidly and efficiently than the public sector, to mobilise resources, to create jobs and to generate revenues.

There is a widespread trend towards cutting back overextended public sectors, which have drained public finances and inhibited economic efficiency. It is evident that the massive requirements for productive employment creation can only be met through dynamic expansion of the private sector, including substantial direct foreign investment.

These opportunities, however, are not evenly spread over the developing world. In the poorest countries, some of the fundamental requirements for the emergence of a strong private sector are missing — educational attainment, entrepreneurial spirit and management, basic infrastructure facilities, political commitment to the development of competitive markets and legal protection against monopoly, and legal and financial services.

In their work on strengthening development co-operation for private sector development, including foreign direct investment, DAC Members are proceeding from several common assumptions.

— The private sector, including foreign direct investment, plays a central role in development and can make much greater contributions in most developing countries if properly encouraged to do so.

— A positive and stable policy framework, based on a fair and efficient legal system, is paramount for the development of productive and self-sustaining private enterprise.

— Private sector development depends crucially on an effective public sector, decentralised, capable of providing governance, delivering infrastructure services, both economic and social, including education, and maintaining a policy and economic environment conducive to private investment, competitive markets and rising productivity.

— The private and the public sectors are complementary, but they also compete for the limited human and financial resources. The central issue is how best to use those limited resources to achieve growth and development.

There are many requirements for successful private sector development, principally in the orientation of institution-building and in economic policy-making. Most fundamentally, however, private sector development both implies and requires the emergence of a pluralistic society. In many developing countries, including some of the more advanced, this remains a key challenge. It involves deregulation, enhancing competition and generally ending the privileges currently enjoyed by those who benefit from protection and regulation.

Strong reliance on private sector activities clearly has distributional implications which need to be watched. Building efficient private sectors and deregulation should contribute towards fairer income distribution in a context of effective competition which in turn requires strong and effective governments. Constructive labour relations are an important aspect of private sector development.   Beyond that there remains a need for positive action to ensure equitable development (see Chapter VIII).

The Role of the Aid System in Encouraging Productive Private Sectors

The basic strategy and the setting of priorities for private sector development is the responsibility of developing countries.   Suitable economic conditions and a functioning market mechanism are essential requirements.   However, there is some scope for support by the aid system through a constructive policy dialogue with emphasis on strengthening developing countries' policies, institutions and infrastructure in the widest sense, including training.   The policy dialogue should be based upon analytical study, preferably led by local authorities, and focus on the advantages of competition over monopoly and of a coherent market-based price structure over bureaucratic price control and regulation.

DAC Members have established a broad range of programmes and facilities to encourage private sector development and foreign direct investment.   This will be described in detail in a forthcoming OECD publication *International Co-operation for Private Sector Development in Developing Countries*.   Work is in hand to explore further ways of strengthening these support activities and to establish the appropriate role of official concessional development assistance in private sector development.   Broad consensus exists on assistance for supportive activities, such as training, education, basic infrastructure, in transport and communications and in effective banking services to private enterprise.   Where donors finance private sector projects directly, such projects should be consistent with the broader sectoral priorities and programmes of the recipient country.   Careful project appraisal is required as well as, in many cases, substantial monitoring and technical advice.   In setting terms for end-users, care must be taken to avoid distorting effects on resource allocations and income distribution.   Two-step financing procedures are a useful device to avoid such distortions; i.e., the project is expected to carry domestic market interest rates while the concessionary element accrues to the central government.   This is important in the case of revenue-producing projects and particularly projects producing for competitive markets.   Project appraisal will make it possible to decide whether it may be justified to pass on all or part of the concessionality in terms to end-users on social or infant-industry grounds.   But such practices should be consistent with the recipient's broader sectoral policies; and financial sustainability and equity considerations must be kept in mind.

Enterprises vary in size and nature, and a variety of support approaches may be considered.   The dynamism of small enterprises deserves special recognition and encouragement.   Moreover, medium-sized enterprises require special support, since in many poor developing countries this "missing middle" constitutes the weakest element between a broad informal sector and some large and often government-controlled enterprises. However, the difficulties in assisting the sector are recognised.   NGOs have a special role to play in the area of micro-enterprises.   Promotion of small-scale enterprises also represents a valuable means for supporting the entrepreneurial efforts of women and facilitating their participation in the development process.   In this respect, there is a need to eliminate or offset discrimination against women in private-sector development.

Women's initiatives can be supported by special measures which are adapted to their time constraints and to their levels of training and literacy.

Adequate financing of private sector-development remains a problem in many countries. In designing non-project aid to a structural adjustment or sectoral development programme, donors should seek to expand the supply of long-term investment funds for private enterprise as well as to support the current import needs of the country or a development sector. Structural adjustment programmes and private enterprise development programmes or strategies should address the key regulatory (including legal) constraints to their goals, such as barriers to entry or exit from a field of production, labour laws imposing prohibitive costs on job creation, complex procedures for licensing businesses, and rules which effectively restrict competition and initiative.

Financial intermediaries in developing countries, such as local industrial and agricultural credit institutions, are indispensable to reach — with credit and advice — the large number of small and medium-sized enterprises. It is an important function of development cooperation to strengthen these institutions. The record of the past has been mixed. It is important to ensure that these institutions combine judiciously their development promotion function with financial prudence.

In advising and supporting developing countries in economic stabilization and adjustment programmes, options should be examined for relief of budgetary pressures through privatisation of appropriate services (e.g., training, health or sanitation services) to the public. Whereas local private enterprise may have had no opportunity to demonstrate competence in a service historically monopolised by the state, a contract for a pilot project to produce and deliver such a service may be sufficient to induce a private company to initiate it. Development co-operation agencies, including investment finance and investment guarantee agencies, should consider supporting such pilot projects or providing technical advisers or helping to find foreign partners or contractors who can accelerate the development of local private capacity in such services.

A key need is to rationalise the parastatal (state enterprise) sector which in many developing countries continues to dominate both essential services and the principal industrial and market aspects of their economies. It is important to ensure that the government is committed to pay the price of reform, including loss of control, patronage and sometimes illegal benefits, through the introduction of realistic pricing, competition and accountability. Development assistance institutions can facilitate privatisation through financial and technical support and can provide to enterprises remaining in the public sector expert analytical services, opportunities for exchange of experience with other developing country authorities, technical and management advice, and long-term management reinforcement. Assistance can also be provided to identifying opportunities for exposing parastatals to private competition or for divestment of appropriate functions to private buyers.

Privatisation — while not an end in itself — will in many cases be needed to improve efficiency and reduce burdens on governments. While the process of privatisation is often long and complex and there are serious constraints in some countries, there now exists a body of successful experience whose lessons should be shared. The overriding objective should be effective management in an environment of competition. Some believe that this can be achieved under public ownership while others have concluded that private ownership is essential.

The concern of labour unions and political leaders with the potential short-term unemployment effects of reform of parastatals must be addressed by programmes of redeployment and training of workers who may be displaced.

The World Bank/UNDP sponsored consultative groups and round tables are among the fora to encourage and assist developing countries to plan and carry out strategies and programmes and projects for private enterprise development.

These aid co-ordination bodies should also review the adequacy of manpower-planning systems and manpower development programmes with a view to avoiding manpower constraints on exports or on other critical private enterprise operations and investment. Such reviews should identify requirements for training support needed by industry as well as local education and training institutions. A comprehensive review of the national infrastructure investment programme should be made a regular feature of aid co-ordination group meetings and in-country aid co-ordination arrangements, to consider whether the infrastructure needs of private enterprise and export development are adequately provided for in the public investment programme.

Deregulation, reduced and more transparent systems of state control and more transparent government procurement can contribute to a reduction of corruption, a basic symptom of underdevelopment and poverty and a major source of inefficiency and inequity which industrial countries have experienced during earlier phases of their economic, political and institutional development. It should be recalled in this connection that the OECD Guidelines for Multinational Enterprises call on firms of Member states not to render any bribe or other improper benefit, direct or indirect, to any public servant or holder of public office.

3. BROADENING THE BASE OF DEVELOPMENT CO-OPERATION: WORKING WITH NON-GOVERNMENTAL PARTNERS

NGOs have emerged as prominent partners in the development field. By the early 1980s virtually all DAC Members had adopted some system for cofinancing projects implemented by their national NGOs. Official contributions to NGOs' activities over the decade have been on an upward trend, amounting to $2.2 billion in 1987 and representing some 5 per cent of total ODA. In the same year, NGOs themselves had collected $3.3 billion for development through private fund-raising.

Access to expanded government funding has allowed many NGOs to become more professional, enlarge the scope of their activities and fund more NGOs in developing countries. They have been able thereby to promote the people-to-people dimension of development. Many NGOs are increasingly active in developing education. Although the viewpoints and priorities of governments and NGOs may differ, the broader experience thus acquired by NGOs over the years has reduced the problems found earlier in some cases in relations between the official and voluntary sectors.

In order to preserve the autonomy, integrity and distinctiveness of NGOs, some donors have adjusted their cofinancing procedures, originally based on matching grants, by introducing more flexible and long-term arrangements such as block grants, multi-year funding, revolving funds and credit guarantees. It is generally agreed that in the future donors should proceed in this direction and promote the financing of multi-year programmes which enhance long-term planning and co-ordination rather than rely on the more traditional fragmented project support.

A major evolution is the growing maturity acquired by the NGOs of developing countries. They increasingly tend to play a major role in articulating the needs of the poor in their communities. The growth of indigenous NGOs has introduced a new dimension into the discussion on the role of NGOs. The funding of these organisations becomes more complex and compels the aid system to consider the political ramifications, funding procedures, absorptive capacity, vulnerability and dependency of these organisations on external sources of funds.

If self-reliant, sustained and equitable development is the ultimate goal of development activities, then the role of the aid system is to support and strengthen the institutional capabilities of indigenous NGOs, particularly those which hold special potential for poverty reduction and socio-economic development, such as women's organisations and rural associations. Experience demonstrates that it is not merely the quantity of financial flows but the conditions under which funding is provided which determine its effectiveness as a tool for institution-building.

A primary goal in supporting indigenous NGOs is to enable them to define their own objectives, to carry out development activities, to gain access to resources and to make them recognised by their own authorities as partners in development. Donors should therefore encourage steps towards a policy setting that facilitates the expansion of a dynamic and independent voluntary sector with less restrictions on registration and access to funds.

In the future donors should contribute funds to technical and managerial training, self-evaluation, overhead administrative costs, and emerging NGO networking systems. They should also facilitate information flows, encourage NGOs' understanding of macro-economic issues and foster their participation in the formulation of development policies and programmes.

There is agreement that differing requirements with respect to project activities, reporting, monitoring and evaluation by a multiplicity of donors create serious difficulties for NGOs of developing countries. Although donor governments have to meet legitimate demands for accountability which may constrain radical changes in approach, they should reduce the administrative burden on NGOs.

VII

LAYING THE BASIS FOR BROAD-BASED GROWTH
IN KEY SECTORS

1. ECONOMIC INFRASTRUCTURE

Economic growth requires adequate economic infrastructure — transport and communication facilities, energy — and the build-up of productive capacity in agriculture, industry and other productive sectors. In poorer developing countries in particular, with insufficient domestic financing and limited external debt-servicing capacities, official development assistance has an important role to play in infrastructure support. More than one-third of total bilateral official development assistance from DAC Members together is used for these purposes, the proportion being considerably larger for multilateral development financing ("Basic Aid Data").

DAC Members have agreed on Principles for Project Appraisal (see Chapter XII, Section 6 below), which apply particularly to the selection and design of infrastructure investment projects. Indeed, the judicious and conscientious application of sound project appraisal principles is essential to ensure that development assistance for infrastructure makes a positive contribution to the development process, avoiding distortion and waste in the allocation of resources, perverse effects on income distribution and unsustainable financial and maintenance burdens. Moreover, infrastructure development projects need to be treated as an integral part of development plans (and Public Investment Programmes where these exist), and to provide for institutional strengthening to ensure adequate management and maintenance capacities where necessary.

2. THE ENERGY SECTOR IN A DEVELOPMENT PERSPECTIVE

Among the economic infrastructure sectors, the DAC has paid particular attention to energy. The expanded production and application of energy is essential for development and the promotion of a higher quality of life for both rural and urban populations in developing countries. While oil prices have declined drastically from the levels which

85

put the spotlight on the "energy crisis", the longer-term outlook requires continued efforts to develop economic local energy supplies and ensure more efficient use of energy. Moreover, more efficient use of energy has become an important environmental concern.

There are major institutional, policy and management shortcomings in energy sector operations in developing countries. Energy pricing policies are often far from optimal and undermine the financial integrity of energy investments. Expensive plant is often out of service because of inadequate maintenance systems. Energy planning, in addition to its present strong focus on providing new power facilities, needs to give greater emphasis to identifying energy needs and conservation possibilities. Aid agencies can assist in orchestrating actions directed at these problems, which would significantly raise energy output from existing facilities, thus conserving energy resources through conservation and more efficient use.

Potential gains for a developing country through such assistance can be the equivalent of investment in several new plants. The reduction in energy costs and energy investment needs would bring benefits felt across the whole economy. Among the major economic sectors, therefore, the energy sector offers perhaps the greatest opportunities for aid practitioners to make a discernible and relatively quick impact not only on sector performance, but also on national economic performance.

Many opportunities exist for developing smaller decentralised power systems, with relatively low investment requirements (and therefore low annual capital charges), based on indigenous and often renewable energy resources. Such systems can be put on stream quickly to meet specific power needs for rural development, irrigation, agricultural processing and household electrification (which constitutes one of the single most important steps towards better living conditions for masses of poor people).

Since it is essential that the construction, maintenance, operation and output of decentralised energy systems be integrated into the local economy, such systems offer large scope for stimulating local enterprise and widening and deepening local economies. They constitute a development tool that could be much more widely applied.

The fuelwood crisis is having an impact on hundreds of millions of poor people in many different regions, who are largely disconnnected from the oil economy, and face a future of increasing scarcity of a resource which is central to their daily existence. Commercialisation of household fuels, and the spread of decentralised energy systems, can ultimately provide a solution, but this will take time.

The single most important priority in meeting the fuelwood crisis is to persuade developing-country governments that there is a real crisis situation demanding urgent action on a major scale. A first requirement is for each developing country to design and implement forestry strategies, which involves solving land tenure problems, creating incentives, and identifying and selecting appropriate tree types and planting and management techniques.

Comprehensive efforts to improve and develop the energy sector in a developing country will require donor/recipient agreement on the policy framework and on the specification of tasks in such areas as management and institutional improvement as well as system development projects. Such agreements could constitute the basis for co-ordinated multi-donor programmes which are coherent and effective, as a number of cases already demonstrate.

Energy sector development and efficiency can benefit substantially from expanded participation by the private sector and, more generally, entrepreneurial initiative. Opportunities arise in the areas of management and operational contracting, private ownership of plants feeding into national grids and the setting up and operation of decentralised energy systems, where the stimulation of local enterprise and new economic activities has important developmental potential. A role exists for aid agencies to promote and assist programmes directed towards increasing the role of the private sector and enterprise development.

3. THE CENTRAL ROLE OF PRODUCTIVE AGRICULTURE

The experience of many of the successful developing countries and indeed that of industrial countries during earlier phases of their economic history demonstrate the central role of a productive agriculture for development. Increased agricultural and food production leads to increased rural incomes, which in turn provide effective demand for goods and services from the agricultural as well as the non-agricultural sectors. Production of these commodities generates employment opportunities. On the other hand, a productive agriculture requires a conducive general policy, institutional and economic environment, including in particular effective price incentives and adequate priorities in allocation of public investment and services. Effective systems of rural education are essential not only to facilitate the institutional requirements of technological change, but for educating farmers and their families to help them make use of increasingly complex technology. Extensive physical investment is required to allow broad diffusion of and participation in agricultural development over the full extent of the country's geographic area. This includes roads, electric power, irrigation, and communications to facilitate the commercialisation of agriculture and its increasing input intensity.

Technological progress which increases factor productivity in agriculture is central. The rate of growth in factor productivity has slowed in many developing countries in the 1980s from the pace of the late 1960s and 1970s. The Green Revolution has tended to have its greatest impact under conditions already favourable to agriculture. The remaining rural poverty problem will be more intractable in the 1990s. Poverty in middle-income countries is concentrated in areas which are still rural but with low potential, where returns to investments are lower and risks higher.

Too many developing countries have badly neglected their agriculture and rural areas. There are many signs that this is changing. Donors can assist developing countries to improve agricultural and rural development in many ways.

— Broaden the emphasis in their policy dialogue with developing countries towards raising the priorities for rural and agricultural development in the allocation of national and aid resources and in the effectiveness of their uses.

— Assist the governments of low-income countries in designing feasible national programmes of agricultural development which comprehensively deal with the policy, programme and institutional framework of the sector, including concrete and economically practicable measures to improve the efficiency and sustainability not only of supply but also of marketing services, and to address more explicitly demand and employment aspects.

- Help improve national food information systems of low-income countries to collect, process and use for policy-making purposes reasonably timely and reliable data on the production, marketing and consumption of main food crops.
- Ensure effective farmer responses through desirable pricing and marketing reforms for both export and food crops.
- Screen farm policies and projects for their impact in economising and increasing the supply, quality and "rurality" of scarce skills and institutional capacity, and give increased emphasis to more systematic investigation of land tenure issues.
- Increase support for agricultural credit projects and inputs delivery systems aimed at small-farmer development.
- Give more attention to research; in particular ensure that agricultural research assistance activities initiated by international and national consultative arrangements allocate sufficient resources towards raising small-holder productivity and promoting agriculture in areas under unfavourable climatic and soil conditions.
- Encourage and support improvements of co-ordination of aid and national efforts in the agriculture sector at the country level, and take steps to initiate effective operational co-ordination in the sector, using existing local aid co-ordination arrangements.

Sustainable agricultural and rural development has notably been effective when prospective small-holder beneficiaries of government and aid-supported projects, and particularly women (who play important roles in agricultural production), have participated in project identification, design and implementation. Since such cases have been rare, greater efforts should be made to provide for these groups in the project cycle.

Land-tenure arrangements are critical to the success of a small-farmer based development strategy. This is not simply a question of determining ownership but also of providing credible titles. Land reform must be combined with a whole range of measures ensuring effective land use and agricultural production. In some countries, successful land reforms have proved to be the springboard for rural development, which subsequently has provided a firm basis for industrialisation. Where land reform has not been successful or sufficient, rural poverty can persist into the later stages of development and constitute a point of social and economic vulnerability for developing countries (as some of the Latin American countries bear witness). While the role of aid in land reform has been limited in the past, there have been occasions where donors played a significant role at the level of persuasion and finance. Others have helped with assistance in land surveying and titling, and in formalizing land use rights. On the whole, however, this admittedly difficult area seems to have been neglected by donors, a deficiency which should be made good.

During the 1990s, the agricultural production potential will increasingly be affected by environmental conditions and natural resources constraints. Prominent among these are the continued loss of top soil from croplands, the conversion of croplands to non-farm uses and the precarious water situation. There is growing awareness of the linkages between water and food. Supply constraints are increasing, aggravated by droughts, depletion of aquifers and deforestation, while the demand for water for irrigation is rising rapidly. Salination caused by irrigation may now be removing as much land from production as is added by irrigation, and inappropriate irrigation has wasted water, polluted ground water and damaged millions of hectares. Hydrologists have pointed out that population pressure on water is systematically neglected by always referring population to land area, i.e., inhabitants per square kilometre. For arid and semi-arid regions, where water is the most scarce and uncertain resource, it would be appropriate to relate population to units of water flow as a supplementary characteristic; livestock needs should be added for man/water ratios.

Environmentally sound land-use planning and natural resources management will have to be given far more attention in the following decade if agricultural productivity is going to be increased without land degradation. Far more attention will also have to be paid to forestry and more specifically reforestation by aid agencies.

There is a potential in several developing countries for increasing agricultural exports in particular in labour-intensive commodities like fruit, vegetables and certain types of livestock for which demand is growing. Production in these areas is important to increase rural income, employment and foreign exchange earnings. A strong research effort is needed both in production to reduce costs and in marketing if new exports are to develop.

To permit developing countries to take full advantage of export opportunities, the OECD countries will have to do everything possible to ensure open markets for the exports of developing countries. There is a need for them to impart a decisive momentum to multilateral trade negotiations especially in the areas of agriculture and tropical products by strictly adhering to standstill undertakings and intensifying efforts to roll back protectionist measures. The Uruguay Round of GATT negotiations will be of decisive importance in this context. It should take duly into account the growing and differentiated role of developing countries in the world economy.

The *future role of food aid* in improving agricultural development and food security requires critical re-examination. Significant amounts of food aid will continue to be delivered in the 1990s. The role of food aid for emergencies is undisputed but raises difficult organisational problems. Its effectiveness will be greatly enhanced through measures aimed at timely, orderly and well targeted deliveries. Improved stockpiling and transport facilities are also of critical importance. Food aid is also used in food-for-work and nutritional projects. Such projects are not easy. The inherent design and implementation requirements are often beyond the capacity of recipient governments. Food-for-work projects could become more effective when better integrated with recipient governments' rural development programmes, thus focusing on priority needs for infrastructure and leading to the generation of permanent employment opportunities. Much greater attention will also need to be given to programmes targeted to the malnourished.

Most criticism on food aid, however, relates to commodity food aid. A basic criticism has been that the nature and modalities of this kind of food aid have often been driven by food-surplus disposal motives on the part of the food donors. Such pressures have been diminishing, however, as food surpluses have decreased. Concerns have also been expressed about food aid potential disincentives to agricultural development, undesirable changes in local consumption patterns and the risk of perpetuating dependency on food imports.

There remains a need to put food aid more explicitly into a developmental framework, case by case, according to recipient needs and conditions in order to avoid these disincentives, dependencies and distortions. Macroeconomic use of food aid for countries following appropriate policies and programmes is an important alternative to the delivery of food aid commodities directly to the target groups. It may be cost-effective to sell food aid in urban areas to generate budgetary resources which can be used to support needed policy reforms and local purchases. These purchases in surplus areas of the country or in neighbouring countries should be encouraged. Such food aid sales can also save foreign exchange if they substitute for commercial food imports. Much greater aid co-ordination with recipient countries' development plans and integration of food aid into development assistance as a whole are required if this approach is to be pursued.

4. SCIENCE AND TECHNOLOGY IN THE SERVICE OF DEVELOPMENT

Scientific research and technological innovation are essential for sustaining and accelerating development. The capacity of many developing countries to absorb, develop and apply modern science and technology is very limited and needs to be strengthened. Agriculture, including forestry, health, and environmental degradation are key areas requiring more attention from the scientific community of both the North and the South. Scientific research and technological development (R & D) are successful if two conditions are met: first, a major discovery; and then, its application to solving major problems. This happened in agriculture: the development of new, high-yield hybrid varieties of maize, wheat, rice and other cereals allowed farmers in developing countries — after careful training and demonstration — to achieve the "green revolution".

While in most developing countries the capacity for R & D is still underdeveloped and underfunded, OECD countries also devote only a small fraction of their R & D efforts to problems that are Third World-specific. To harness the potential of modern science and technology for the support of development future action should aim at four central objectives:

   i) Helping developing countries to promote indigenous research at basic and applied levels (the research "infrastructure"), in particular by strengthening or establishing appropriate institutions;

   ii) Establishing more effective ways for identifying research needs in line with the priorities spelled out by developing countries [example: the Consultative Group on International Agricultural Research (CGIAR), in which the World Bank, FAO, UNDP and bilateral public and private donors co-operate];

   iii) Devising efficient ways, compatible with the protection of intellectual property, of transferring relevant results of scientific research and technological development from OECD to developing countries, including measures that would lead to an increase of Third World-specific research in the "North";

   iv) Involving the research institutions of developed countries or the international research institutes in the field of upstream research for developing countries.

Training of scientists and technicians from developing countries in their home countries, but also in developed countries, contributes to building research "infrastructure" and to transferring appropriate knowledge from the North to the South. The personnel trained must, of course, be motivated to stay in their country to avoid adverse "brain drain" effects.

External assistance for research, establishment of research institutions and training of scientists cannot be carried by aid agencies alone. Collaboration with specialised institutions in DAC Member countries is required. Similarly, in developing countries not only official institutions responsible for economic planning and finance must be involved, but also those concerned with education, R & D, enterprise development, health, agriculture and social research.

Areas of R & D where improved international co-operation would be desirable comprise chemical and biological research (tropical diseases, pest control), protection of the physical environment (purification of drinking water, reduction of soil pollution, fight against desertification and deforestation), geology (surveys of mineral resources, earthquake prevention), and forestry and agro-forestry research. Concerning micro-electronics and information technologies, no particular effort seems to be made presently by the — mainly private — research laboratories in OECD countries to direct efforts also toward developing-country application. The same is largely true for biotechnology. More R & D should be directed to improving production levels of crops important for rainfed agriculture. A recent step in this direction was the establishment of the UN International Centre for Genetic Engineering and Biotechnology. The work of the CGIAR research network and of the UN Centre [carried out at its branches in Trieste (Italy) and New Delhi (India)], will benefit agriculture and health in developing countries.

5. THE CHALLENGES AND OPPORTUNITIES OF URBANISATION

In the 1990s, increasing numbers and shares of the population of developing countries, including low-income countries, will be living in urban areas. The numbers are staggering (see Table 2-3).

The rapid process of urbanisation in the developing world has led to a situation where the populations of the so called "megacities" are rapidly surpassing the size of the largest cities in the industrialised countries. The rate of growth of cities with more than 2 million people in developing countries is on the average ten times the rate in the developed countries.

While rapid urbanisation, especially in megacities, poses enormous problems, it must also be emphasized that cities and towns play a vital and increasingly central role in the economic development process. Urban areas can be engines of growth and of informal and private sector development, and dynamic creators of employment opportunities. A substantial and increasing proportion of GNP in developing countries is produced in cities and towns. Greater economic and social efficiency of cities is essential for development.

Growing urbanisation also implies enormous organisational challenges and huge

Table 2-3. POPULATION IN URBAN AREAS, 1950-2000

Region	1950	1985	2000
	Per cent		
World total	29.1	41.2	46.7
More developed regions	53.8	71.5	74.8
Less developed regions	16.9	31.5	39.5
Africa	14.5	31.1	41.3
Latin America	41.5	69.2	77.2
Asia	16.4	28.1	35.0
China	11.0	20.6	25.1
India	17.3	25.5	34.2
	Millions		
World total	733	1 998	2 917
More developed regions	448	840	945
Less developed regions	285	1 158	1 972
Africa	33	174	361
Latin America	69	279	417
Asia	226	797	1 292

Source: Department of International Economic and Social Affairs (1988 estimates), United Nations, New York.

Table 2-4. MEGACITIES IN DEVELOPING COUNTRIES

In millions

City	1950		Most recent figures		UN projection for 2000
Mexico City	3.1		17.3	(1985)	25.8
Sao Paulo	2.7		15.9	(1985)	24.0
Bombay	3.0	(1951)	10.1	(1985)	16.0
Calcutta	5.4	(1951)	10.3	(1981)	14.2
Jakarta	1.5		7.9	(1985)	13.2
Cairo	2.5		7.7	(1985)	11.1
Delhi	1.4	(1951)	7.4	(1985)	13.2
Manila	1.8		7.0	(1985)	11.1
Lagos	0.3	(1952)	3.6	(1985)	8.3
Bogota	0.6		4.5	(1985)	6.5
Nairobi	0.1		0.83	(1979)	5.3
Dar es Salaam	0.2	(1960)	0.9	(1981)	4.6
Gter. Khartoum	0.2		1.05	(1978)	4.1

Source: *The State of World Population 1988*, UNFPA, New York.

investment and maintenance requirements, in particular in terms of water supplies, waste disposal, transport, energy, and housing, as well as provision of health and educational facilities. Urban pollution causes serious problems, difficult to cope with. Shanty-towns with primitive sanitary facilities, overcrowding and, in addition, often hazardous locations constitute a major environmental problem. The dumping of industrial waste into rivers has serious implications since the same water often is used for drinking, cooking and washing. The emergence of millions of street children, particularly in Latin America, is a major social and humanitarian problem.

In order to provide adequate responses to the growing urban challenges it must be realised, first, that — although the process of urban population increase is diverse among countries — large cities usually grow mostly from natural population increase, while cities in earlier stages of development grow mostly from migration. Secondly, cities have been growing fast because development inevitably involves urbanisation.

Donors need to strengthen their capacity to assist developing countries to cope with urban development challenges and opportunities. The urban-rural balance in aid allocations needs to be reviewed. Greater emphasis should be placed on urban management in the broadest sense, encompassing the effectiveness of local public institutions, the balance between new investments and the maintenance of existing assets, and plans for mobilising resources for both capital and recurrent expenditure. More attention needs to be given to the development of appropriate urban infrastructure and more research is needed on low-cost urban facilities. At the same time, it is important to slow down migration towards the cities through the development of rural areas, changing the often distorted economic incentives of migration and providing improved employment opportunities and amenities.

More work is required on the role of medium-sized cities which may absorb more of the inevitable urban growth. Carefully designed urban development policies can have a substantial impact on the living conditions of the poor by improving their access to affordable urban services and housing. Shelter problems are largely the result of misguided economic and social policies which produce a bias towards the supply of high-cost housing for only a few. New housing policies are required, encouraging the informal sector to provide shelter production with a disengagement of the public sector from direct provision of housing, concentrating instead on providing off-site infrastructure, land registration and credit. More research and analysis are necessary on the roles of the informal and public sectors in the provision of housing. Appropriate public sector measures affecting land entitlement and land markets are of decisive importance to unleash the potential of the private sector — including the savings potential of low-income groups — in providing housing finance. Barriers must be removed to allow a smoother functioning of land markets, and community participation in project planning and exccution must be expanded instead. Moreover, donors need to support recipients' efforts to improve urban management capacities.

VIII

STRATEGIES FOR EQUITABLE DEVELOPMENT

1. ACHIEVING EQUITABLE DEVELOPMENT THROUGH EFFICIENT AND BROAD-BASED GROWTH, PARTICIPATORY DEVELOPMENT, PRODUCTIVE EMPLOYMENT AND INVESTING IN PEOPLE

Broad-based sustainable growth is an essential requirement for equitable development. At the same time, sustained growth cannot be maintained unless there is participatory and equitable development in which the masses of the people are involved in the productive processes and in the sharing of its benefits. Beyond broad-based participatory development, nations must be concerned with the fate of the poorest and most vulnerable segments of the population. The poor have productive potential which is not being realised. They have shown an extraordinary degree of creativity and ability to help themselves in situations of utmost difficulty.

Market and efficiency-oriented growth policies and their effective implementation by governments will go a long way to generate broad-based equitable growth and help alleviate the poverty problem. Market-based efficiency-oriented policies contribute to greater equity by involving the masses of people in productive processes and strengthening the employment content of economic growth. Enhanced competition contributes to efficiency and a broader sharing of the economic benefits of growth. This is an essential lesson from the experience of the "newly industrialising economies" (NIEs) and some other successful developing countries.

It is clear also that for markets and competition to co-operate effectively, strong and competent governments are required.

Beyond effective growth and competition policies, there is need for special pro-equity policies and programmes, in order to correct the existing maldistribution of income and access to productive resources and services.

2. CREATING PRODUCTIVE JOBS: THE BASIS OF EQUITABLE DEVELOPMENT

Because of demographic growth, the demand for new jobs will increase by very large numbers in the 1990s. An increase of some 360 million job-seekers is foreseen

Table 2-5.   GROWTH OF LABOUR FORCE IN DEVELOPING COUNTRIES, 1990-2000

	1990	1990-2000 Annual growth	2000
	Millions	%	Millions
North Africa	32	3.0	43
Sub-Saharan Africa	198	2.7	259
South and East Asia	591	2.0	720
China and Asian planned economies	724	1.2	818
West Asia.	35	3.5	48
Mediterranean	35	1.6	41
Western hemisphere	158	2.5	199
LLDCs	162	2.5	208
Developed market economies	381	0.5	401

Source: Department of International Economic and Social Affairs of the United Nations Secretariat, based on country population data in *World Population Prospects - Estimates and Projections as Assessed in 1984* (United Nations publication, Sales No. E.86.XIII.3), and labour force participation rates from the International Labour Organisation (ILO), *Economically Active Population, 1950-2025,* Geneva, 1986. The projections for 1990 and 2000 are based on the "medium variant" population projections.

during this period (see Table 2-5).   Asia will experience the greatest increase, followed by Africa and Latin America.   This comes in addition to the several hundred million currently unemployed and underemployed.   Creating jobs for these people will require extraordinary investments.   While domestic markets will and must expand, there will also be a strong push for finding market outlets abroad, with a consequential need for adjustment in OECD countries.   Migration pressures, both internal and external, will grow.

The employment challenge facing the developing world is increasingly an urban challenge.   Natural growth in urban areas will continue to expand cities rapidly. Although more effective agricultural policies may create rural employment, it is likely that the urban growth will be augmented by a sizeable influx of largely untrained labour from rural areas in search of income opportunities.   In many countries, particularly in Africa, a large group of young educated people will find it increasingly difficult to find jobs corresponding to their qualifications, partly because of incompatibilities between education and training opportunities and labour market needs.   For both these groups the "expectations gap" is likely to widen, with potentially serious and disruptive socio-political consequences.

Anti-employment biases in policies should be avoided, notably in the form of policies that make labour expensive relative to capital through unrealistic wage structures or negative real interest rates.   Besides the removal of distortions, rigidities in labour markets should be relaxed so as to promote the flexibility and adjustment capability of the economy.   Investments in human capital should be encouraged and supported. Price and regulatory policies should not create biases in favour of capital-intensive modern sectors and against labour-intensive informal sectors.

More attention needs to be given to promoting employment potential in the rural sector and the linkages between small and medium-sized agriculture and agro-based

96

industry. This would diversify economies and bring productive employment to rural growth centres and mitigate migration to megacities.

Small and medium-scale enterprises and the "informal sector" in both urban and rural areas have shown much dynamism in many developing countries, despite, in some cases, rather discouraging official policies. In the 1990s, policies must be more supportive of the development of the sector, fostering entrepreneurship and encouraging small-scale activities. Training, credit schemes and equal opportunities for competition between private and public sector activities are important components of such development.

The aid system should pay more regard to supporting developing country efforts to adopt policy frameworks which enhance opportunities for productive employment. Donors also need to appraise carefully individual development projects with respect to their employment implications.

The newly industrialising economies and also some other developing economies have shown the very large employment creation potential of outward-oriented development strategies. Continuous adjustment and flexibility are needed for successful export strategies. Industrial countries need to ensure market access in order to facilitate employment-intensive imports (see Chapter III above).

International Migration. The industrial countries of Europe and North America have, during the past two or three decades, shown an extraordinary permeability for migration from developing countries to the extent that they have largely become multiracial and multicultural societies. Migration has provided benefits to the migrants themselves, to countries of origin (reduced labour market pressure, earnings from remittances (in some cases "brain drain" has also caused problems) and to host countries (increased labour supply often in jobs which nationals are increasingly unwilling to accept). Migration pressure is likely to increase with continued rapid population growth and unemployment in developing countries. As a recent SOPEMI Report (the OECD Continuous Reporting System on Migration) states, "since the 1970-74 period, most Member countries have sought to curb illegal entry and residency while stopping or significantly reducing foreign labour recruitment".

3. IMPROVED FOOD SECURITY AS AN ELEMENTARY OBJECTIVE OF DEVELOPMENT

According to the International Food Policy Research Institute (IFPRI) between 700 million and 1 billion people suffer from chronic food shortages. Vagaries of weather, natural disasters and civil strife cause periodic famines and human suffering. Among the undernourished, 350 million live in South Asia and 140 million in Sub-Saharan Africa, mostly in rural areas. Women and children are most vulnerable to malnutrition. There is a real risk that in the 1990s the number of malnourished will continue to grow substantially.

The reasons for malnutrition are manifold. Many developing countries have badly neglected their agriculture and rural areas, and have paid inadequate attention to the food security of the vulnerable groups of their populations. Malnutrition, however, is not primarily a matter of inadequate total food supplies.   Food security for some people, e.g. urban poor, will not be achieved through agricultural and rural development. National food self-sufficiency is neither necessary nor sufficient to ensure that everyone is adequately fed.   A basic reason for malnutrition is the low purchasing power of some categories of the population.   Adequate nutrition can only be attained through a broad-based poverty alleviation strategy with emphasis on employment and income generation in and outside agriculture.   This usually means, within agriculture, a careful weighting of prospects for food and export-based agriculture as well as policy and programme support for a whole range of activities including small-farmer agricultural growth, and food production, distribution, transportation, food processing and support services (see Chapter VII, Section 2).   For some groups, both urban and rural, unable to earn a living wage, selective targeted subsidy programmes may be required.

National policies and programmes aimed at improved food security ("food strategies") can be strengthened by increased local food production, improved storage and the inclusion of strategies for nutritional improvement.   The main thrust of these strategies should be nutrition and health education directed at both men and women. They should be taught good nutritional practices, particularly in respect of children, and simple techniques for the prevention and treatment of malnutrition and control of diarrhoea.   Women should be encouraged to breast-feed their children as long as possible and to use improved food preparation methods.   Nutritional improvement strategies which include direct feeding programmes should include nutrition education.

Interregional income disparity can also be a major factor contributing to chronic food insecurity.   The benefits of new seed-fertilizer technology have been concentrated in lowland irrigated areas whereas upland hilly and mountainous areas have been largely bypassed.   In order to upgrade the nutritional status (and the general living standards) in such unfavoured areas, it is vital to make efforts to develop profitable yet soil-conserving farming practices such as agro-forestry farming systems, combining perennial crops and livestock with annual crops.

National food information systems can play a useful role.   They should include early warning systems for the detection of an impending famine, including levels of food stores, and nutritional surveillance systems.

4.   IMPROVING ACCESS AND AFFORDABILITY OF ESSENTIAL ECONOMIC AND SOCIAL SERVICES

Improving the access of the broad masses of people, including the poor and vulnerable groups, to essential economic and social services is a central element of pro-equity and poverty alleviation strategies.   The central objective is investing in people to enhance their chances for fuller participation in productive income-generating processes.   The following orientations are offered as a basis for policy dialogue with developing countries and as indications of opportunities for donor assistance.

— There should be more effective treatment of equity and poverty considerations in the orientation and design of the whole range of development policies and programmes, in combination with specifically anti-poverty programmes.

— Critical tests of all government-provided services should be (in addition to quality) accessibility and affordability for the masses of the population, including the poor.

— Financial sustainability of government-provided services is essential for sustained and broad-based accessibility. In the DAC Project Appraisal Principles Members have concluded that user charges ensuring cost-recovery are the best safeguard of the financial viability of a project and consequently of its sustained ability to provide continuing benefits to recipients. Where cost-recovery through user charges is not feasible or socially acceptable, it is essential that realistic provisions for financing be made. User charges and public price policies, giving appropriate weight to overall financial viability and repercussions on vulnerable groups, are an important subject for aid co-ordination betweeen recipients and donors.

— Within public investment programmes, more resources should be directed at expanding rural infrastructure, particularly rural roads, small-scale irrigation works, rural electrification and communication, and rural water and sanitation facilities. Similarly, there is an urgent need for programmes designed to provide up-grade public facilities servicing low-income urban areas.

— Fuller access to development-relevant primary education is critical for development strategies oriented towards growth, sustainability and equity. It prepares people for employment, improves health, affects population growth rates and improves conditions for more participatory development.

— Access to affordable quality health services for all is essential for the full development of human potential and productivity. Primary health care holds particular promise as a cost-effective means of providing a combination of preventive and curative services.

— Family planning programmes will lower child and mother mortality and will help developing countries to achieve more sustainable rates of population growth.

— More active participation of women in the process of development at all levels is an essential element of equitable development, with important implications for production, improved family welfare and social standards.

— NGOs should be encouraged to expand services, since they have proved to be effective in reaching the poor in such areas as health, family planning and nutrition.

Key issues in the central human resources development areas of education, health, women in development, and the population sector are pursued in the following chapter.

5. IMPLICATIONS FOR AID

In the eyes of large segments of aid-supporting public opinion in donor countries helping poor people in poor countries to live more decent lives is the essential rationale of development assistance. While governments have to take a complex range of objectives and foreign policy aims into account in the use of official development assistance, aid effectiveness must in the end be assessed against this standard. Aid critics have a legitimate function in reminding governments of it as the core of aid. But they also have a responsibility to give due recognition to the complexity of the task.

Aid agencies will have to explain to their concerned public opinion that a balanced approach to equitable development and poverty alleviation requires, in addition to specific social programmes, broad-based assistance efforts covering the whole range of economic and social infrastructure, technology, and finance needed for development. Public opinion needs to understand better the linkages between aid, effective market-based policies and incentive structures and equitable development.

It is also important to bear in mind the many difficult issues developing countries will have to face in implementing poverty alleviation strategies. They relate to the immense technical and organisational complexity of the task of reaching the masses of the poor. They also relate to the intense political and social sensitivity of the policy choices and distributional issues involved.

The aim must be to develop programmes with broad and sustained impacts. In each field there are relatively low-cost interventions which will help. Where recipients would welcome the help, donors can work with them on sectoral and subsectoral strategies which give the cost-effective interventions priority.

In terms of aid modalities, there needs to be more programme support, a greater willingness to use foreign exchange for local-currency requirements, less support for discrete projects unless part of a sectoral or subsectoral plan, and a more institution-building approach to technical assistance. Beneficiaries within developing countries should more often be involved in the identification of needs and methods as well as in implementation. This suggests more involvement of the wide variety of local groups which exist in developing countries and greater use of donor-country non-governmental organisations. Timeframes for support should often be extended to stretch over ten to fifteen years. Donors working in the same field should work with the recipient government to co-ordinate policies and procedures, being sure each effort supports the sector strategy.

High priority for achieving more equitable development and poverty alleviation on a global scale has implications for geographic aid priorities. The bulk of the world's poor live in the low-income countries. They clearly deserve priority in international aid efforts. (Current geographical aid patterns are shown in Table 33-34 in the Statistical Annex.) There are serious problems of poverty and social imbalances also in many middle-income countries. The appropriate role for aid here needs further attention.

IX

A NEW EMPHASIS ON INVESTING IN PEOPLE

1. HUMAN RESOURCES: A STRATEGIC DEVELOPMENT INVESTMENT

Human resources need to be given stronger emphasis in development strategies and development co-operation. Investments in education, health and other social services have tended to be looked upon as software, often classified as humanitarian concerns rather than productive investments. Investing in people is critical to development. This is one of the central lessons of the experience of the successful countries. Improvements in health care, water and sanitation, family planning services, and especially education not only contribute to an improved quality of life; they are also indispensable for longer-term development. Paying special attention to the key role of women in development is particularly important.

2. EDUCATION

Education is a major public policy and resource management issue. The crucial importance for economic development of high quality education and technical and vocational training accessible to the masses of young people has been demonstrated by the experience of the successful developing countries. More than forty years ago the Universal Declaration of Human Rights states that "everyone has a right to education". In the 1960s and 1970s developing countries achieved remarkable expansions of education at all levels, including countries in Sub-Saharan Africa, but often at the expense of qualitative improvement. They devoted large shares of their resources (up to 30 per cent of recurrent budgets in some cases) to a substantial increase in enrolment ratios, with an increasing share going to higher education. The tremendous remaining disparities in public per capita education expenditures (see Table 2-6) are largely a reflection of similar discrepancies in general standards of living; they also show rather dramatically the cruel differences in opportunities for young people in poor countries.

Educational development slowed in many cases by the mid-1980s, because of resource scarcities and population growth. Moreover, the outlook for the 1990s is poor given the expected growth of school-age populations. The numbers of young people

101

Table 2-6. PUBLIC EDUCATIONAL EXPENDITURE

US$ per capita

Country group	1985
North Africa	87
Sub-Saharan Africa[a]	21
South Asia	9
China	10
East Asia newly industrialised countries	126
Other East Asia	22
West Asia	192
Mediterranean	75
Western hemisphere	78
Least developed countries	7
Developed market economies	660
Centrally planned economies of Europe	188

a) Excluding Nigeria, because available data do not include large non-federal expenditures.
Source: Department of International Economic and Social Affairs of the United Nations Secretariat.

out of school at primary and secondary levels will increase substantially in Sub-Saharan Africa and in the group of least developed countries as a whole.

In spite of a remarkable rise in girls' school enrolment over the post-war period, in developing countries over 40 per cent of girls do not complete primary education. In rural areas especially, the immediate advantages to the family of girls' work at home can often override what benefits are seen in female education. In the absence of equitable educational expansion, factors thwarting girls' access to education will persist.

Apart from problems of access and equity in a number of Latin American and Caribbean countries, South Asia and Sub-Saharan Africa face the most challenging problems. In terms of their education and training needs and policies to address them, there are some common elements but also significant regional and national differences. India and Pakistan and to a lesser extent Bangladesh have well established formal education structures: but their emphasis on higher education and remarkable achievements at that level led to unemployment and emigration amongst university graduates, and deficient primary schooling. They, and other countries in similar situations, could well reorient and rationalise their resource use and improve and extend primary schooling as well as other elements of basic education, particularly adult literacy programmes.

Sub-Saharan Africa faces a unique situation. Its economic crisis has caused a general deterioration marked by enrolment stagnation; acute shortages of didactic materials; worsening internal efficiency and learning quality; poor external productivity at secondary and tertiary levels, which has absorbed the bulk of educational resources in the past, due to their mismatch with manpower needs; the collapse of training to provide skills for economic growth.

Many Sub-Saharan Africa countries need to pursue systematic reform geared firstly towards improving primary education as well as skill-training. Qualitative improvements leading to better efficiency and higher completion rates are as vital as equitable quantitative expansions.   The post-primary levels need to be reviewed, including, in particular, realignment of curricula with trained manpower requirements and cost containment through recovery and other measures.   Unit costs per student year at the tertiary level are 50-100 times those at the primary one, although rates of return on primary education investments are substantially higher.

A number of interrelated key areas can be identified to guide donors in their joint efforts with recipients to assist particularly South Asian and Sub-Saharan African countries.

— Assisting interested developing countries in formulating national education strategies is an essential prerequisite for effective educational progress and external assistance.   In turn, educational assistance should increasingly be given in support of well-designed educational sector strategies and programmes.

— Formulation and implementation of education strategies will require development of indigenous analytic and planning capacities as well as a sound data base of educational statistics and indicators, which are at present inadequate in many developing countries.   In recipient countries pursuing structural adjustment, education strategies should be linked to adjustment programmes.

— Notwithstanding the importance of quantitative expansion, strategies should give priority to reversing declines in the quality and outcomes of the learning process at all educational levels.   This is vital for primary schooling, which is the base of formal education, and the vehicle for providing sustainable cognitive knowledge to the majority of people as a matter of equitable development. It is also vital for post-primary levels including higher education, which becomes increasingly important in order to narrow the widening technological gap between the industrialised countries and virtually all developing countries.

— It is important to achieve an appropriate balance between the various levels in the education sector consistent with national needs and available budgetary resources.   This may require some rationalisation by recipients and donors of resource deployment and use.   External aid is most urgently needed for primary and basic education, as well as for technical vocational education, both formal and non-formal.   In extending aid for tertiary education, donors should ensure that such assistance does not shift local funds away from primary education or retard attempts to reform higher-education.

— Education influences womens' economic participation and earning power and it lowers fertility rates and enhances children's health.   Highest priority should therefore be given to female education as an essential means to achieve development and human well-being.

— Educational development should be pursued flexibly if it is to adapt to major changes in the next decade such as the revolutionary advances in communications and information technologies.

— Given the high share of recurrent outlays in educational expenditures, especially for primary schooling, donors may need to help finance recurrent costs for clearly specified priority purposes.

— Donors should help recipient countries develop more effective education management capabilities.   This is critical to maximising resource allocation and utilisation in education and training systems.

103

— Donors need to shift from extending mostly project aid to programme assistance for supporting sound, national strategies of systematic reform and development.
— Policy-based programme aid will necessitate close inter-donor and donor-recipient co-ordination, especially at the central and sectoral levels in the recipient countries. Donors need to agree not only on policies but on a division of labour amongst themselves, by which each could contribute to subsectors of education and training in which it has specialised advantage. Recipient governments have to make their own policy and implementation decisions and lead the co-ordination process. But these endeavours need closely co-ordinated external aid.

3. MEETING BASIC HEALTH NEEDS

While good health depends on economic and social standards, it is also a prerequisite of development. Health is an important economic factor through its critical influence on productivity and on demographic developments. Health policies therefore need full attention in the formulation of a country's general development strategy.

Although considerable progress has been made in the health situation in developing countries over the past decades, malnutrition and diseases still prevent the development and full use of physical and intellectual potentials in many developing countries. The emergence of AIDS poses serious additional problems in several countries. Health-care systems have often been unresponsive to the needs of the majority of the population. A reorientation towards primary health care is therefore a condition for achieving greater equity.

The relatively low priority given to health in general and to primary health care in particular is reflected in recipients' own allocations. Health rarely claims a significant proportion of developing-country budgets, which often leads to problems of sustainability. Such economic constraints reinforce the importance of primary health care as a cost-effective way of achieving broad-based and general health improvements.

The key to future progress is the strengthening of recipient countries' capacity to formulate and execute adequate health policies and strategies including plans for primary health care and provision of family planning services. This implies support to national operational research and the development and appropriate use of information and indicators on health needs and problems, in particular as perceived and experienced by the people. Sector plans facilitate co-ordination and ensure coherence of national efforts and donor assistance.

In spite of their stated commitment to primary health care, relatively large resources are devoted by donors and recipients to sophisticated urban-based facilities including hospitals and specialist clinics. Political, commercial and other considerations may come into the picture. There is a need for a better balance between different levels of health care, primary/specialist, preventive/curative, and vertical/horizontal.

The policy dialogue in the health sector will have to address the critical issue of the appropriate "health balance". Greater emphasis on deprived groups in both urban and rural areas and on preventive care is required, and may involve limiting allocations for disproportionally expensive specialised services used mainly by the better-off segments of the population.

Cost recovery and increased efficiency are likely to be major issues in the health field all through the 1990s, and recipients must be assisted in improving the efficiency and quality of their health services and identifying alternative and/or additional sources of funds. Experience of existing schemes of cost recovery must be given particular attention, especially with respect to the equity issue.

The likelihood of long-term sustainability of primary health care will depend on the efficiency and effectiveness of the health system. It can be increased if full use is made of the private sector, local communities, NGOs, women's groups and similar organisations to extend information and services.

While people's participation in health activities is one of the fundamental principles of primary health care, the role of women is particularly important. Women act both as protectors of health in the household and as members of health-care teams, thus contributing to others' health; but they also constitute a vulnerable group with high maternal mortality and morbidity. Primary health care has the potential both to enable women to participate fully in health activities and to improve their own health considerably. Birth spacing is an important health issue and family planning forms an integral part of the strategy to improve people's health.

The urgency of particular health problems faced by developing countries has sometimes prompted governments and donors to initiate vertical programmes specifically designed to tackle these special problems. Technological opportunities such as immunisation and oral rehydration can have significant health impacts. With recognition of a continuing need for such vertical initiatives in certain cases, it becomes critical to evolve health systems that are strong enough to sustain primary health care in accordance with the Alma Ata principles and, at the same time, to operate temporarily in vertical fashion whenever necessary.

4. THE NEED FOR DRUG ABUSE CONTROL

Drug abuse (production, trafficking and consumption) is increasing at an alarming pace in developing countries and has become a crucial problem in many of them. Drug abuse not only has adverse effects on agricultural production, national budgets, the balance of payments, health and human resources, but also undermines national institutions, weakens governmental authority and encourages corruption. At the same time, it should be recognised that drug abuse is often as much a consequence of underdevelopment as a cause. It is progressing most rapidly in countries with deteriorating economic and financial conditions. Narcotics crops are often grown by the poorest people in the poorest areas where government control and services are weakest.

More attention needs to be paid to the drug issue in bilateral and multilateral development assistance programmes. On the production side, comprehensive development strategies in narcotics-producing areas seem to offer some promise. These strategies rely on a wide range of measures, from the selection of a suitable mix of crops with production outlets to the adoption of appropriate pricing and marketing policies, providing needed infrastructure, supporting the development of rural industries and assisting the host country's rural health care delivery, and vocational and educational activities.   The main objective of such measures is to provide subsistence farmers with alternative sources of income or employment on and off farm, and the rural communities with improved social services.   Public information and education programmes to reduce demand are essential as are law enforcement activities to ensure farmers' security and curb illicit trafficking.   It should be recognised that the problem cannot be solved unless decisive measures are also taken in developed countries to reduce drug use.

5.   ENHANCING THE ROLE OF WOMEN IN DEVELOPMENT

In the 1980s the role of women in development (WID) became a new priority in development co-operation.   The Guiding Principles to Aid Agencies for Supporting the Role of Women in Development adopted by the DAC in 1983 bear witness to this as well as the subsequent policy declarations, plans of action, sector guidelines, and check-lists issued by donors individually to ensure that women participate in and benefit from development assistance programmes.   There has been some progress over the past ten years in such areas as legislation, education and employment, health and family planning.   In general, however, the status of women and especially poorer women cannot be said to have greatly improved.   The growing recognition of women's critical role in development has yet to be translated into action.   The Forward Looking Strategies for the Advancement of Women adopted by all governments in 1985 at the end of the UN Decade for Women will remain the blueprint for action in the 1990s.

The role of the aid system is not primarily to plead for more resources for a disadvantaged section of the population but to demonstrate how structural and policy changes could enable women to become increasingly effective agents and indeed leaders in the process of development.

Women produce more than half the food in developing countries, and as much as 80 per cent in Africa.   In spite of their predominant role in agriculture, women's production and productivity are constrained by restrictions on their access to fertile land, commercial fertilizers, credit, education, extension services and technological improvements.   Their productivity is also limited by the extra time required for their additional domestic workload.   In recognising that the use and expansion of women's productive capacities is a necessary condition for social and economic progress, donors should help reduce these constraints as a means to tap women's productivity for development. Projects, programmes and policies should be analysed with a gender perspective and should be adapted to overcome special constraints on women's productivity, participation, and access to benefits.   It has been argued, in particular, that in Africa attention to women's farming skills and constraints could be the single most cost-effective approach to alleviating the food security problems.

In supporting private sector initiatives donors should ensure that women's access to the market and their dynamism in creating microenterprises are not impeded by discriminatory allocation of relevant inputs such as credit, training and technology.

The education of women contributes to lower fertility, better family health and nutrition, reduced infant and child mortality, greater participation in the formal sector labour force, higher earnings and increased economic growth.   Even though education is the area where women have made the most progress, as shown by the increase in the enrolment of females in school from about 100 million in 1950 to almost 400 million in 1985, the gap in the numbers of girls in school, compared with boys, is growing, as are the numbers of female illiterates and school-age girls not in school.   In the 1990s, the aid community should give higher priority to female education.

During the past decade it has become increasingly apparent that women are the major primary health workers, since they have the greatest influence on the health of their families.   Women themselves do not enjoy good health, however, owing to frequent pregnancies, abortions and substandard nutrition.   Generally prevailing life expectancy differentials between women and men are lower in low-income countries.   Malnutrition is more prevalent among girls than boys, since girls are proportionately given less food.

Falling fertility rates are closely related to better education and higher incomes for women.   Knowledge of family planning methods and their availability affect the family size preferred by women.   Lack of modern family planning facilities has led many women to use less reliable methods.   WHO estimates that 20 per cent to 35 per cent of pregnancies are currently aborted.

As food producers, wood and water gatherers, women are the main natural-resource managers over much of the developing world, especially where they account for most of the subsistence food production.   In sectors which affect the environment, however, especially water supply, forestry, energy, and human settlements, women are frequently excluded from the planning and implementation of projects, and their concerns, needs and special knowledge are often ignored.   Aid agencies need to recognise the connection between women and the environment in strategic policy-making, project design and training.

Considering the short period that has elapsed since the formal adoption of WID policies, progress made in their implementation has not been insignificant.   But, major efforts are needed in the coming decade to fill the gap between policy and implementation and achieve the ultimate aim of integrating WID considerations systematically in development co-operation.   In this respect, a major challenge for aid agencies will be to ensure that an awareness of gender implications permeates the whole staff both at headquarters and in the field.   Major efforts will also have to be made to collect and analyse gender-disaggregated data to identify female constraints, inputs and outcomes relevant to particular projects and policies.

6.   INSTITUTION-BUILDING:
A KEY PRIORITY FOR DEVELOPMENT CO-OPERATION

Sustained and self-reliant development depends upon the strength and quality of a country's institutions.   Institution-building, including human resource development, should therefore be given priority in the forthcoming decade.   Government institutions, including the legal system, need to be strong and effective but so should be the educational system, financial institutions, businesses, local communities and voluntary organisations — they are all part of the fabric of a society through which ideas and skills and new technologies are carried, and individual energies deployed.

Helping developing countries in institution-building is one of the most important aims of development co-operation. This is a difficult task. It is necessary to reconcile the requirements of efficient and dynamic modern societies and traditional structures and values. The diversity between countries is considerable. Successes in India, Pakistan, Korea and Taiwan have left those countries with strong institutional infrastructures. In Sub-Saharan African countries, institutional and related human resource capacities are usually weak in the public and private sectors. Each country should appraise its specific capacities and identify key weaknesses to be addressed. It should specify long-term and short-term institution-building objectives; and integrate them along with plans to attain them into its development planning, budgeting, and macro-level, sectoral and subsectoral strategies.

Although the importance of human and institutional development has been reaffirmed repeatedly, more needs to be done by donors and recipients together to address this central objective more effectively. Institution-building should be an integral element of *all* aid activities. Indeed, an aid activity cannot be regarded as successful unless it has contributed to strengthen the local institutions through which and for which it works. Technical Co-operation (TC) has a particularly important role to play in this perspective. Experience shows that in order to be efficient and effective, TC must meet genuine local needs and be demand-driven. TC interventions should complement, strengthen and whenever possible build on local know-how.

Recent DAC work on technical assistance for institution-building provided the following orientations.

— Each national or local situation is unique and generalisations must be handled with care, but some major trends concerning technical co-operation objectives emerge.

— The development of institutional capacities is a major objective of TC. It should be aimed in particular at strengthening the policy-making and managerial capacity of government institutions. More emphasis should be given to institution-building and to the institutional framework of projects and programmes from the outset of activities. This implies an assessment of the implementing or operating agency's capacity to execute a project effectively as well as an assessment of the institutional environment in which the project will operate.

— Human resources development is a prerequisite for institution-building as well as for successful and sustainable capital projects. Education and training at all levels are key areas for external support.

— Long-term institutional objectives should take priority over short-term specific project goals. In some cases, however, short-term operational objectives, such as direct support and transfer of technology, can be legitimate.

— In the years ahead, one of the major challenges will be to maintain and enhance the management capacity of recipient governments. An efficient public sector is vital for development.

108

— TC should also contribute to strengthening private sector management since effective involvement of the private sector is essential to the development process.

— TC needs should be clearly identified and related to macro-level, sectoral and subsectoral strategies. They should be included in recipients' plans and budgets in order to maximise efficiency and avoid supply-driven TC. Recipient governments should be encouraged and, if necessary, supported to undertake a comprehensive assessment of TC requirements with the participation of beneficiaries, including representatives from the private sector and grass-root organisations.

— The design of TC should be based on a thorough analysis of the availability of local manpower. Project design should specify financial, personnel and management responsibilities and address the institutional aspects of TC activities. TC should build on existing structures and capacities, public as well as private, and avoid the creation of parallel structures.

— National remuneration issues are most effectively addressed by assisting developing countries to effect required policy changes (for instance civil service reforms). Salary supplements by individual donors can have distorting effects. In exceptional cases and where the recipient government feels it is essential, salary supplements (or fringe benefits provided for similar purposes) may be considered, provided that it is on a short-term basis and in consultation with other donors, that it follows explicit rules, and that donor practices are harmonized.

— Donors should make fuller use of local experts and consultants, especially, but not exclusively, when activities require a deep understanding of national and cultural factors. This could be fostered by better information on available local experts, flexibility in recruitment of experts and in the procurement of goods and services, decentralisation of authority to field staff, and measures to encourage foreign consultancy firms to work with local consultancy firms.

— Inherent pressures to use expatriate TC financed experts rather than locally available manpower mainly for budgtetary reasons should be resisted.   This may imply greater flexibility in recurrent cost financing.

— Twinning arrangements have proved useful in achieving institutional development and transferring skills. Such arrangements may be promoted between various kinds of institutions, provided there is a match of goals and tasks, flexibility to meet changing needs, long-term commitment, mutual trust, and a willingness to adjust to local circumstances.

7. HELPING DEVELOPING COUNTRIES
TO ABATE UNSUSTAINABLE POPULATION PRESSURES

Continued rapid population growth in developing countries involving ever larger increases in absolute numbers will pose enormous problems in the 1990s. Earlier parts of this report have drawn attention to the implications for resource requirements in productive capacities for massive increases in job-searching, in economic and social infrastructure, urban facilities and environmental resource pressures more generally.

It is vital that people understand the imperative need to curb population growth rates in those many countries where these rates are too high to permit sustainable development. Offering people in developing countries the opportunity to plan the size of their families, a human right now taken for granted in the industrialised countries, can help to avoid an aggravation of already difficult social, economic and environmental problems. Development co-operation can help governments assess their demographic problems and establish effective strategies and programmes. While considerable educational efforts will be required, there is clear evidence that existing demand for family planning services is unmet.

The WHO estimates that about 300 million couples who do not want more children are not using any method of birth control. An analysis covering 18 developing countries shows that if those women who stated that their last birth was unwanted had had the means to prevent it, the natural population increase in those sample countries would on average have been only 1.3 per cent instead of 2.2 per cent (World Fertility Survey).

Developing countries will thus grow by at least 850 million people in the next decade. Satisfying the unmet need for family planning information and services will have immediate effects in terms of improved individual well-being, particularly among women and children; there will be a slower increase in the demand for water, food, shelter, schools, health care and other public services with correspondingly lower pressures on resources which would be available for productive investments and quality improvements. Over time the pressures to create additional jobs will be lessened and the explosive growth of cities and shanty-towns will be modified. The effects on migration, resource consumption and the environment will be considerable. There is hope that people at the grass-roots level will increasingly come to understand that their self-interest lies in family planning and curtailing the number of their children. Otherwise, many people will be deprived of welfare gains in the immediate future, and the welfare if not the survival of large numbers of people in the coming generation will be jeopardised.

In the early years, development was discussed and planned with little reference to demographic factors. Census work and vital registration were seldom carried out and thus the size and composition of the populations, supposedly the beneficiaries of development, were largely unknown. Attitudes to family size and child-bearing were poorly understood and family planning was considered highly sensitive. It was left to non-governmental organisations, notably women's groups, to worry about the rapidly growing number of illegal abortions and to interpret their implications in health, attitudes and costs.

The 1974 World Population Conference in Bucharest constituted the first recognition by the world community that population factors are essential determinants of development. People, their numbers, needs and aspirations will decide what direction development will take; sustainable development requires well co-ordinated action in which humane and effective family planning forms a central part.

Recent progress has been impressive. Ignorance and unfounded assumptions have been replaced by encouraging experience. Official family planning programmes have grown considerably during the 1980s and have achieved historically unique declines in birth rates — Barbados, China, Costa Rica, Cuba, Hong Kong, Indonesia, Korea, Mexico, Singapore, Sri Lanka, Taiwan, Thailand are countries well on their way towards demographic transition. "The steadily rising trend in contraceptive practice in developing countries in recent years has provided crucial empirical evidence that programme efforts in providing family planning service and information can change people's fertility behaviour" (UNFPA 1989). In Brazil and Colombia, NGO programmes have had similar success. According to UNFPA, contraceptive practice in developing countries had risen to 49 per cent in 1987. (Excluding China the figure drops to 35 per cent.) The population of developing countries would probably have been several hundred million larger without population policies and family planning programmes.

The countries which have been most successful in lowering national birth rates have several features in common. Many have explicitly tried to provide for growth with equity. They have given priority to the development of human resources. They have invested in social services, including health and education, paying special attention to the status of women, female employment and improving maternal and child health care. Above all: they have given strong support to family planning information and to contraceptive services, in which community participation, decentralisation and training have proved to be the keys to success. A number of governments have also introduced incentive and disincentive schemes to discourage high fertility and encourage the use of family planning. The experience of these well documented successful national population policies and programmes provides good guidance for national and donor strategies in the 1990s.

Africa stands in stark contrast to Asia and Latin America, where efforts to reduce fertility have seen impressive results in a considerable number of countries. In Sub-Saharan Africa in particular, only a few governments have been really committed to family planning (e.g., Cape Verde, Kenya, Mauritius and Zimbabwe). The social and economic conditions also differ considerably from those of other continents. Donors can promote awareness, in countries where the understanding of demographic impact on development is poor, of successful public and private population policies and programmes elsewhere, and their beneficial effects on development.

In the early days of development co-operation, foreign assistance stood for some 80 per cent of total investment in population and family planning programmes in the developing world, and national governments provided only 20 per cent. Today the ratio has been reversed. Despite this significant increase in the commitment of developing countries themselves, in most of them family planning still accounts for less than 0.5 per cent of national budgets. Less than 2 per cent of ODA is spent on population and family planning.

Massive increases are needed in funding of expanded population programmes. The World Bank has estimated that to achieve the extent of contraceptive use necessary for further improvement in women's health and for a more rapid decline in population growth, total family planning expenditures in the developing world would have to reach more than US$9.5 billion (in 1988 US$) annually by the year 2000. This is three to four times current domestic and foreign expenditures.

This figure only covers *direct* expenditures on family planning and contraceptive services. In addition, major investments will be needed in multi-purpose delivery systems, including information, education and communication channels, in which family planning information and services should also be integrated. Primary health care, including maternal and child health services, broad support for WID programmes, social science and biomedical research to improve contraceptive technology and practices and national census work are examples of areas in need of major increases in external assistance, both in their own right and as facilitating mechanisms for the implementation of national population policies. Female education is particularly important as a way of reaching women with information, but also to mobilise women as extension workers in the field. There is also a need to increase and broaden their economic opportunities and to give them a greater say in decisions concerning family size. Men's often negative attitudes towards family planning must be changed through major educational efforts.

The efficiency and effectiveness of population policies and programmes need improving. Lessons from successes and failures have been underutilised; co-ordination of scarce resources needs improving, particularly at the country level; there has to be a move away from projects towards programme support, including longer-term commitments; governments must begin to implement their rhetoric and make real efforts to increase women's roles in productive and reproductive decision-making; institution-building, including training and management upgrading, remain cross-cutting needs at all levels and in most national programmes particularly in Sub-Saharan Africa; support for grass-roots organisations which play important roles in advocacy, education and the provision of services must be provided; commercial distribution networks can make major contributions; last, but not least, national programmes must be developed in response to the specific socio-cultural forces at play.

To make available the opportunity to regulate fertility will enhance the health of mothers and children and also lighten the burdens of rapid population growth. Where family planning services are widespread and affordable, fertility has declined more rapidly than social and economic progress alone would predict. There is scope for substantial increases in external assistance to direct and indirect measures to reinforce this trend in the 1990s.

X

BUILDING CONSENSUS ON ENVIRONMENTAL ISSUES

1. THE NEW AWARENESS OF ENVIRONMENT AS A CRITICAL PROBLEM FOR DEVELOPMENT

There is a growing awareness among all countries, both developed and developing, that to be economically sustainable development must be environmentally sustainable. Contributing to environmentally sustainable development is a major new challenge for development co-operation in the 1990s. Without major national and international efforts in this period, irreparable damage could be done to developing countries' resource base and natural environment, and the problems could become increasingly intractable and expensive.

The notion of "sustainable development" that has come to prominence recently introduces an essential emphasis on the need to be concerned with longer-term impacts of policies and in particular on the need to develop forms of economic growth and natural-resource use which are sustainable in the long run.

Much of the population increase in the 1990s will take place in environmentally fragile regions of the developing world. Desertification, deforestation, soil depletion through over-use of fragile land, acute water shortages, loss of bio-diversity and pollution in its many forms are areas of growing concern. It will have a serious impact on the livelihood of the urban and rural poor, and there are indications that women will be particularly affected.

Poverty and in particular the growth in the number of poor people contribute to environmental degradation. Poverty pushes towards over-grazing, over-cutting, over-farming, destroying the very basis on which future development depends. Ultimately, such over-use contributes to famine (as in Ethiopia) and to devastating floods (as in Bangladesh and Sudan).

The causes of deforestation are inseparable from developing countries' major development problems. Population pressures, poverty, inadequate systems of land tenure, inappropriate fiscal policies, all contribute to environmental degradation, including the clearing of new land and cutting and burning of forests, which is to a large extent due to the ever-increasing need for fuelwood, in particular in Africa and Asia, the opportunities for diversification of fuel resources being very limited. Slow growth in other sectors reduces alternative income-generating possibilities. Pressures to generate foreign exchange push towards the mining of forests and converting forested land to cash crops and cattle ranches. Deforestation is increasingly seen as a problem of global dimensions because of its effects on the global climate, with potential far-reaching effects on all countries. Apart from this environment-related aspect, forest development remains a major economic activity in several countries.

There are serious and growing natural resources constraints on the agricultural production potential in many developing countries arising from losses in cropland and increasing scarcity of water, as pointed out in Chapter VII, Section 3 above.

Women have a unique relationship with the environment and natural resources, primarily because of the daily tasks they perform (growing food, and collecting fuel, fodder and water) for the survival of themselves and their families and to sustain livelihoods. They are often the main environmental managers in an area. Moreover, because of their traditional knowledge and experience of natural resources, they are the main environmental educators of children. These concerns are central to the work of the DAC Expert Group on Women in Development.

Problems of pollution have become especially critical in the urban/industrial agglomerations. They lead to acute problems for water supply, waste disposal, health risk through air pollution and deteriorated living conditions more generally.

Another problem area that requires fuller attention stems from natural disasters which, when they befall developing countries, destroy the fruits of long-term development. Such disasters include earthquakes, hurricanes, locusts, unprecedented floods and dry spells. To a certain degree, methods exist or are being developed to prevent or attenuate the devastating effects of natural disasters, and enhanced development co-operation towards this objective should be given high priority.

Rapid and environmentally sustainable economic growth is a shared global objective and must remain a central objective of development co-operation. At the same time, rapid population growth will continue throughout the 1990s, even though determined action can contribute to a slowing down. These trends will produce increasing pressures on the environment and natural resources. Improved policies and resource management practices as well as slower population growth, however, can lead to a type of growth and development and consumption patterns in which natural resources are used more rationally, and in which additional financial resources are available for conservation. Improved technologies backed by targeted scientific research can contribute to more efficient resource use.

Developed and developing countries, in UNEP, have recently identified key concerns as crucial for achieving an environmentally sound and sustainable development in all countries:

— Protection of the atmosphere by combating climate change and global warming, depletion of the ozone layer, and transboundary air pollution;
— Protection of the quality of freshwater resources;
— Protection of ocean and coastal areas and resources;
— Protection of land resources by combating deforestation and desertification;
— Conservation of biological diversity;
— Environmentally sound management of biotechnology;

114

— Environmentally sound management of hazardous wastes and toxic chemicals;
— Protection of human health conditions and quality of life, especially the living and working environment of poor people, from degradation of the environment.

2. STRATEGIES AND PROGRAMMES
FOR SUSTAINABLE NATURAL RESOURCE USE: AN URGENT NEED

The first priority is to help developing countries integrate sustainable resource management into their development strategies. This implies at the country level the launching of national assessments of the state of the environment, with strategies and action plans for the sustainable use of natural resources. For environmentally sensitive projects and programmes as well as in structural adjustment, environmental impact assessments are an indispensable management tool. In some cases, regional co-operation is required to ensure effective action.

The programmes for resource management and environmental protection may take many forms and occur under different names. Nepal, Botswana and Zambia are well advanced in developing natural-resource planning processes in the form of national conservation strategies. They have been helped by the International Union for the Conservation of Nature and Natural Resources (IUCN), working with bilateral donors. Mauritius and Madagascar have recently worked out a comprehensive environment action programme, covering political, institutional, legal and infrastructural aspects as well as investment requirements. A number of donors, together with the World Bank, IUCN and other agencies, are prepared to support this programme financially and to use it as a basis for the orientation of their aid.

In implementing conservation strategies or action plans, a primary objective should be to build the permanent institutional capacity of developing countries to collect facts, analyse issues, and make natural resource planning a part of their development processes. Environment planning needs to be associated with political decision-making. Environmental monitoring and inspection services should be strengthened by personnel and technical equipment in order to ensure conformity with the applicable national standards.

Environmental concerns must be integrated into the development policy planning process. Environmental planning and management capacity should be developed in the developing-country institutions, such as planning commissions, where key priority setting and strategy articulation takes place. The established processes of international aid co-ordination at the country level (consortia, consultative groups, round tables, local co-ordination groups) provide opportunities for working towards a donor/recipient consensus on strategic issues.

Environmental concerns must be fully taken into account also at individual project level. Projects with significant environmental impacts financed with or in association with aid should be the subject of an environmental impact assessment (EIA). In accordance with the OECD Recommendations on environmental assessment and development assistance for donors, the first tasks are to encourage developing-country interest in this process and to help develop institutional capacity. Donors should also encourage developing countries to submit their own projects and programmes to an environmental impact assessment. Local environmental NGOs should be actively involved in this process.

A judicious balance must be struck between market-oriented instruments, government regulations and special government-financed programmes to enhance environmental protection. This is essential both for efficiency and because of limited public financial resources. It is essential in particular to ensure realistic pricing of environmental costs and benefits in policy-making and programme and project design. Environment-efficient regulations and land and tree tenure systems are essential components of effective environment preservation policies. Integration of resource accounting into national-income accounting can contribute to more rational policy making. As a minimum, subsidies for activities which imply wasteful and environmentally negative practices should be abolished.

OECD countries have adopted the "Polluter-Pays Principle" for private sector activities with environmental impacts: the polluter — rather than the tax-payer — should bear the expenses which are necessary to ensure that the environment remains in an acceptable state. The cost of these measures of environmental protection should be reflected in the cost of goods and services which cause pollution in production and/or consumption. Uniform application of this principle is designed to encourage the rational use and the better allocation of scarce environmental resources and prevent the appearance of distortions in international trade and investment.

3. INTERNATIONAL ACTIONS IN SPECIFIC AREAS

The *Tropical Forestry Action Plan* (TFAP) developed by the World Bank, the United Nations Development Programme, the Food and Agriculture Organisation and others to reduce deforestation and promote the sustainable use of tropical forest resources in a range of developing countries concerned is a major new initiative. Implementation of the plan has twice been discussed at the "Bellagio Meetings", convened by the Rockefeller Foundation, the UNDP, the World Bank and the FAO. The objectives of the TFAP are to protect and rehabilitate tropical forests to combat desertification, improve land use and promote agro-forestry, in particular fuelwood production. An effective TFAP must also lead to a planning of land use, delimiting the areas reserved for natural forests, managed forests of various types and agriculture; ultimately these plans must be co-ordinated with the conservation strategies mentioned above. Thus far, forestry sector reviews have been completed in 20 countries and are continuing in 34 others. These include Congo, Zaire, Colombia and Ecuador. Inquiries and requests for assistance have been received from a further 14 countries. It is important that the TFAP lead as quickly as possible to specific action plans and fundable projects and that adequate financing be forthcoming. It is noteworthy that the TFAP, in its strategy for translating plans into action, puts special emphasis on institution-building. Specific relevant research support activities have been launched in recent meetings of the Consultative Group on International Agricultural Research (CGIAR). Reference has been made above to the manifold causes of deforestation, including population pressure, poverty and ill-adapted land tenure systems. All these causes need to be addressed in an integrated fashion.

The *International Tropical Timber Organisation* (ITTO), set up in 1985 and comprising producer and consumer countries, encourages the development of national policies aimed at sustainable utilisation and conservation of tropical forests and maintaining an ecological balance in the regions concerned.

Technical solutions to *combating desertification* and *soil degradation* more generally have often been successfully applied to reforestation, control of surface water run-off, the planting of windbreaks, and the stabilization of sand dunes. Yet progress in this area has been disappointing and should receive greater attention from aid agencies. UNEP co-ordinates the UN Plan of Action to Combat Desertification. The Sahel Club supports the CILSS and works with bilateral and multilateral aid agencies on the improvement of land protection to combat the disastrous effects of the dry spells and the overexploitation of natural resources. The Sahel countries have elaborated plans which form the framework for these actions. The UNDP and UNEP jointly support the UN Sudano-Sahelian Office (UNSO). The EEC has put together an action plan to fight desertification and to preserve, re-establish or improve fundamental socio-ecologic equilibria.

Shipments of *hazardous waste* to developing countries have recently made headlines. These shipments seem to offer considerable commercial advantages and avoid political resistance in the source countries. At the end of March 1989, 104 countries and the EEC signed the final act of a conference in Basle, Switzerland on the control of toxic waste exports. The final act refers to a convention, which a considerable number of countries have now signed. The key feature of this agreement is that exporting-country governments must obtain permission from the government of the country to which dangerous residue is to be shipped. Recent collective efforts among OECD countries aim at endorsing global toxic waste rules within the framework of UNEP. Emphasis is also placed on minimising waste at the production stage, on encouraging recycling, and on requiring informed prior consent of all countries concerned. It will be the task primarily of the OECD Member countries to implement the Basle Convention by domestic legal instruments and adequate personnel.

The issue of *biological diversity* has come increasingly to the fore. The Governing Council of UNEP has authorised the Director-General to convene an ad hoc working group to negotiate an international legal instrument and other measures for the conservation of the biological diversity of the planet.

4. THE ENERGY-ENVIRONMENT DILEMMA

Particularly difficult policy challenges arise in reconciling energy needs and environment concerns. Availability of sufficient and low-cost energy is indispensable for growth and development in developing countries. Development of energy sources, however, often has serious environment implications. This is true in particular for

117

large-scale coal development projects. Even hydro-energy projects, a renewable source of energy, can cause environmental problems unless the projects are carefully designed.

Technologies and practices which ensure a more efficient use and conversion of energy deserve high-priority attention. Examples are a larger use of natural gas, environmentally acceptable methods of burning coal, district heating and waste heat utilisation, less polluting motor vehicles and more efficient public transportation. The more efficient use of wood as a fuel for heating and cooking should be encouraged. The replacement of wood by other fuels (natural gas) or electricity can lessen local pollution and reduce the often environmentally detrimental over-utilisation of trees.

A major issue for developing countries is the future of nuclear power. (The following countries have nuclear capacity which accounts for, or is planned to cover, a significant part of their electricity production: Argentina, Brazil, India, Pakistan, South Korea.) Nuclear power does not generate the mass polluants and the greenhouse gas emissions known from other thermal power plants but produces dangerous radioactive residues and is beset with safety risks. This has provoked serious public resistance in many countries. It is important to develop safer waste disposal and reactor designs. The present prospects are that for developing countries as a whole nuclear power will still be making an insignificant contribution to energy requirements well beyond the year 2000.

More needs to be done also to develop environmentally acceptable and competitive renewable energy sources — rather than to relax these efforts in what might well be a temporary period of low oil prices. Chapter VII contains the conclusions of the DAC work on energy which is relevant for environmental concerns.

5. THE GLOBAL DIMENSION OF ENVIRONMENT: LONGER-TERM CHALLENGES AND RISKS

There is a growing concern about a number of environmental deteriorations of global dimension. The build-up of greenhouse gases, creating a one-way thermal barrier with the risk of global climate changes, is one of the most serious potential threats. It is largely related to the use of fossil fuels, which now account for 80 per cent of the world's drastically increased energy consumption. But the cutting and burning of tropical forests also add substantially to the build-up of carbon-dioxide.

Industrial countries have been a major source of greenhouse gases. They must get their own environmental house in order, including the adoption of more rational energy policies. But developing countries are also concerned, both as sources and as potential victims of global environmental degradation. Coping with these issues is a joint global responsibility and will be a major challenge for international co-operation. (Table 2-7 provides data on comparative energy uses and carbon dioxide emissions.) Carbon dioxide emissions originate not only from fossil energy use. Forest burning and deforestation and changing land use more generally are other sources of CO_2 emissions. Forest burning not only produces CO_2 — a one-time effect — but burnt forests stop playing the role of the Earth's lungs by not absorbing CO_2.

118

Table 2-7. GLOBAL PRIMARY ENERGY CONSUMPTION AND CARBON DIOXIDE EMISSION, 1986

Countries by income groups	GNP	Energy consumption	Population	Total energy consumption	Growth rate of energy consumption 1980-86	Percentage share of global:			
						Energy consumption	CO_2 emissions industrial 1985	biotic 1980	Total
	$ per capita	Kg oil equivalent per capita	Million	Million tonnes of oil equivalent	Per cent/p.a.				
LICs	270	314	2 493	783	5.6	11	13	..	..
of which:									
China/India	300	394	1 835	722	5.8	10	12	..	..
Other LICs	200	93	657	61	3.8	1	1	..	..
LMICs	750	346	691	239	4.1	3	3	..	..
UMICs	1 890	1 527	577	881	2.4	12	12	..	..
Total LDCs	*641*	*520*	*3 780*	*1 966*	*4.0*	*27*	*27*	*92*	*43*
Centrally planned economies	*..*	*4 552*	*367*	*1 711*	*2.9*	*23*	*26*	*5*	*21*
OECD countries	*12 960*	*4 952*	*742*	*3 674*	*0.4*	*50*	*47*	*3*	*36*
of which:									
North America	17 170	7 363	267	1 965	0.0	27	25	1	19
Europe	9 628	3 667	333	1 221	0.7	17	15	..	11
Japan and Pacific...	12 840	3 186	122	389	1.5	5	6	2	5
OVERALL TOTAL.........	(2 662)	1 500	4 898	7 351	1.9	100	100	100	100

Source: World Bank, World Development Report 1988; CO_2 emissions: World Resources 1988-89 by World Resources Institute and International Institute for Environment and Development in collaboration with UNEP 1988. Estimates by University of New Orleans and Woods Hole Research Center. Data on biotic CO_2 emissions apply to 1980. For lists of countries in each group, see Statistical Annex, Table 62.

Chart 7. COMPARATIVE ENERGY CONSUMPTION IN 1986

(Kg.oil equivalent per capita)

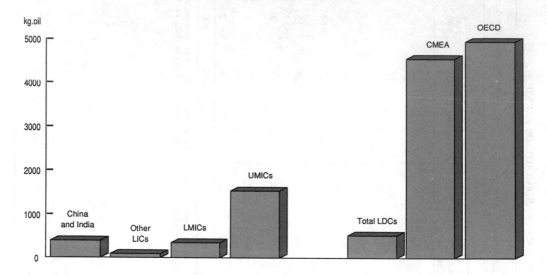

World total = 7351 million tonnes of oil equivalent

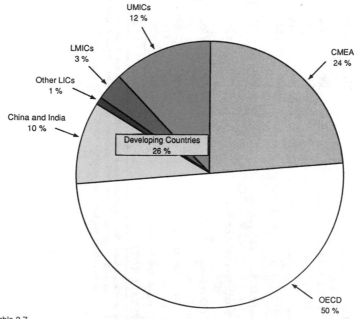

Note: See table 2.7.

Although it must be recognised that the causes and impacts of the greenhouse effect are not yet fully understood, as they are of a highly complex nature, and must be studied with intensity, the risks are sufficiently serious and there is sufficient knowledge to justify immediate environmental action in a number of areas, especially in more rational fossil energy use and preservation and restoration of tropical forests.

A related problem concerns the protective ozone layer, whose depletion produces serious health hazards (skin cancer and eye diseases). The Montreal Protocol of 1987 has been strengthened by the agreement supported by 80 countries at the UNEP Conference at Helsinki in May 1989, to end all production and consumption of CFCs by the year 2000. The Protocol invites the industrialised countries to assist developing countries in finding alternatives to CFCs. By June 1989, 39 states and the EEC had ratified or approved the Protocol.

Major national and international actions and initiatives have been launched to address global environmental issues, to improve scientific knowledge and technological responses and to develop national policies and international agreements and institutional arrangements. The United Nations Environment Programme, together with other international institutions, have an important role to play in organising this effort. Numerous initiatives have already been taken to promote closer co-operation, for instance in the management of oceans, regional seas and coastal zones. Where agreements have been established efforts are needed to put together funding packages for the developing countries concerned. (Efforts in this direction have already been initiated by the World Bank and UNEP, for instance, working together on the Mediterranean Action Plan.) More broadly, the 1992 UN Conference on Environment and Development will give additional momentum to the problem of the global environment in all its complexity, and will provide an opportunity to review the many initiatives already taken in the context of global strategy.

6. OECD/DAC ACTION

An important new impetus to OECD work on environmental issues was given by the 1989 OECD Ministerial Council and subsequently by the Economic Summit in Paris. The Summit participants agreed that "to help developing countries deal with past damage and to encourage them to take environmentally desirable action, economic incentives may include the use of aid mechanisms and specific transfer of technology. In special cases, ODA debt forgiveness and debt for nature swaps can play a useful role in environmental protection." The major thrust of OECD approaches and recent DAC initiatives are summarised below.

There is full awareness by OECD countries that continuing environmental deterioration will threaten the achievement of sustainable economic development and an improved quality of life for all. It is therefore essential that all countries actively participate in confronting the range of environmental problems, including those of a global nature. The OECD countries bear a special responsibility in this respect. The recent series of high-level conferences and meetings make an important contribution to the process of international co-operation.

Given the magnitude, urgency and potential economic, social and ecological implications of environmental problems, all relevant national, regional and international organisations will have to be mobilised in the most effective and efficient way. The OECD will co-operate fully in this process and, building upon the work on environmental problems it has carried out over twenty years, will focus on those aspects where, by nature of its membership and structure, it can make a particular contribution.

It is of critical importance to integrate more systematically and effectively environment and economic decision making, as a means of contributing to sustainable economic development. Taking advantage of its capacity in the field of economic analysis, the OECD will work to place environmental decision-making on firm analytical ground with respect to costs, benefits and resource implications of environmental proposals and initiatives, selection among policy options and, where appropriate, to develop methods to ensure that environmental considerations become an integral part of economic policy-making. Particular attention will be paid to breaking new ground in such areas as: integrating environmental considerations into economic growth models; analysing environment-trade relationships; determining how price and other mechanisms can be used to achieve environmental objectives; assessing the economic costs and benefits of possible responses, including technologies, to cope with atmospheric, climatic, marine and other global environmental problems (in co-ordination with the work carried out in other competent bodies); and elaborating in economic terms the "sustainable development" concept.

In this respect intensified efforts for technological breakthrough are important to reconcile economic growth and environmental protection. The OECD will examine incentives and barriers to the innovation and diffusion of environmental technologies. It will also promote expanded information exchange on technological options.

Industry also has a central role in confronting the environmental challenges of the 1990s, especially in incorporating environmental concerns into their economic decisions. The OECD will continue to stimulate and support closer co-operation between governments and industry to meet these challenges. Progress is beginning to be made in fields such as waste minimisation, industrial processes that conserve energy and raw materials, the design and marketing of cost-effective "clean technologies", and the development of an economically viable pollution control and environmental management industry. There will be an expanded effort to analyse the economic dimensions of these activities and trends and promote information exchange on technological innovation and options.

Integrated policies which further energy security, environmental protection and economic growth are required. In view of increasing evidence of the risk of global warming and climate change and the necessity to respond to this issue, there is a need for vigilant, serious and realistic assessment on a global basis of what energy policies can contribute to meeting these challenges, and of their economic and social impacts. Member governments should contribute in their energy policies to the solution of international and domestic environmental problems. They pledge to pursue in their respective energy policies greatly improved energy efficiency and conservation, new technologies and, where national decisions so contemplate, the use of nuclear power with maintained and improved safety in construction, operation and waste disposal. The transport sector also has a particular significance for the environment.

Co-operation with developing countries is essential for the solution of global environmental problems. The OECD will evaluate relevant policy experience in Member countries. On the basis of this information the Organisation will seek to co-ordinate policies among Member countries with a view to promoting mechanisms for technology transfer to developing countries; the balancing of long-term environmental costs and benefits against near-term economic growth objectives; the design of innovative approaches by development assistance institutions to environmental protection and natural resources management; and the integration of environmental considerations into development programmes, taking into account the legitimate interests and needs of developing countries in sustaining the growth of their economies and the financial and technological requirements to meet environmental challenges. The development of appropriate environmental appraisal procedures for specific developmental projects and programmes financed directly or indirectly by Member governments should be encouraged. Public awareness of the environmental impact of potential projects is essential.

In addition to the Recommendations on environmental assessment and development assistance referred to above, the OECD has recently adopted an "Environmental Checklist" developed by the DAC and the Environment Committee to induce policy-makers in both bilateral and multilateral development assistance to take into account environmental aspects in the identification, planning, implementation and evaluation of development projects which are proposed for funding.

In virtually all DAC countries, aid agencies now recognise the need to accord environmental issues an important place in the policy and decision-making process. A growing number of aid agencies have set up environmental assessment policies and procedures for their aid activities. Increasingly, donors also assist developing countries in strengthening their capability to deal with environmental issues. Specific aid projects and programmes to upgrade and rehabilitate environmental conditions in developing countries gain in importance.

DAC Members have agreed to review progress they are making in enhancing their capacity to inject a sound environmental dimension into their aid activities and to assist developing countries in coping with environmental problems.

The DAC will step up further its efforts to address aid-related problems of the environment. Its policy orientations for the immediate future include the following.

    a)   Exchanging information and experience among Members.

    b)   Developing, based on a synthesis of experience of both developed and developing countries, agreed policies and approaches covering such elements as:

       — Assisting developing countries to strengthen their environmental assessments, policies and programmes and their environmental planning and management institutions;

       — Improving and, as far as possible, harmonizing environmental impact assessments and standards of aid-supported projects and programmes;

       — Identifying key elements for strategies and programmes specifically designed to protect and rehabilitate the environment and natural resources in developing countries;

— Addressing issues of economic cost and benefits of environment concerns and responses and related financial questions.

c) Considering the contribution of the aid system to addressing global environmental concerns, including preparations for relevant international conferences and assisting developing countries in the preparation and implementation of international environmental treaties.

IMPLICATIONS FOR RESOURCE MOBILISATION AND THE AID SYSTEM

XI

THE FINANCIAL CHALLENGES AHEAD

1. CURRENT REALITIES: INTERNATIONAL CAPITAL FLOWS, THE DIVERSITY OF COUNTRY SITUATIONS AND THE WORLD ECONOMIC ENVIRONMENT

The expectation that capital should move from developed countries to developing countries is grounded in both economic logic (rates of return on investment will in principle be higher in developing regions with large under-used economic potential than in developed regions) and generally agreed international economic policy objectives. In the 1980s, the pattern and scale of international capital flows shifted, in aggregate, the other way. OECD countries moved as a group into substantial current account deficit, while non-oil developing countries as a group moved from a large deficit nearly to current account balance (actually with a small surplus in 1987 and 1988). This result, however, is composed of a complex differentiated set of situations in the developing countries and a similarly complex differentiated set of situations in the developed countries. It was no longer possible, at the end of the 1980s, to think in terms of a simple global development-financing scenario, with a world made up of a set of capital-exporting developed countries and a set of capital-importing developing countries. The pattern of overall capital flows in the world economy is in principle reflected in the pattern of current account balances. Table 2-8 shows the broad trends over the 1980s.

Among the *OECD countries*:

— The United States has become the world's largest importer of capital by far, financing a current account deficit in the late 1980s several times larger than that of all developing countries combined;
— Japan has emerged as a major structural capital exporter;
— Germany is also generating continuing large surpluses, but Europe as a whole is moving towards rough current account balance, owing in particular to the emergence of a large deficit in the United Kingdom.

Among the *developing countries*, the trends are as follows.

— South Korea and Taiwan have both generated substantial current account surpluses, although these are now being adjusted.

Table 2-8. BALANCE OF PAYMENTS ON CURRENT ACCOUNT

US dollars

	1981	1982	1983	1984	1985	1986	1987	1988	1989	1990
					Current account					
Global balances										
OECD	-23	-26	-23	-64	-54	-20	-48	-61	-67	-59
OPEC	48	-7	-21	-6	-2	-28	-6	-16	-11	-10
Non-OPEC developing countries	-84	-69	-36	-23	-25	-13	7	-2	-5	-18
USSR and Eastern European countries	1	10	13	14	8	12	17	11	10	9
Total	-58	-92	-66	-78	-69	-49	-30	-63	-73	-78
OECD balances										
United States						-139	-154	-135	-123	-106
Japan						86	87	80	82	83
Germany						39	45	48	45	47
United Kingdom						0	-4	-26	-30	-32
OECD Europe						52	37	16	-5	-11
LDC balances										
Four major Asian NIEs						23	31	26	21	14
Other non-OPEC Asia						-15	-9	-9	-9	-12
Latin America, excluding OPEC						-15	-9	-8	-8	-8
Africa, excluding OPEC						-6	-5	-7	-8	-8
Non-OPEC LDCs less Asian NIEs						-35	-23	-24	-26	-32
								Trade balances		
Four major Asian NIEs						19	25	18	12	3
Other non-OPEC Asia						-29	-20	-19	-19	-20
Latin America, excluding OPEC						15	18	23	26	26
Africa, excluding OPEC						-3	-4	-8	-8	-8
Interest rates[a]										
LIBOR	16.7	13.6	9.9	11.3	8.6	6.8	7.3	8.1	9.9	9.2
GNP deflator (industrial countries)	8.7	7.2	5.0	4.4	3.5	3.4	2.9	3.1	3.8	3.5
Real interest rate	8.0	6.4	4.9	6.9	5.1	3.4	4.6	5.0	6.1	5.7

a) IMF, *World Economic Outlook*, April 1989.

Note: The large world current account discrepancy means that the global capital flows picture is not entirely clear. Although the OECD countries appear to be importing capital, there is not a counterpart export of capital by the rest of the world. However, there has been a definite change from the 1960s, when the OECD countries were clearly a net exporter of capital, mainly to the developing countries. The bulk of the world current account discrepancy is thought to reflect discrepancies on investment income and receipts, and to involve mainly OECD countries (though there may be under-reporting of developing country receipts of investment income associated with capital flight).

Source: OECD.

— The major middle-income debtor countries have effected a huge external adjustment and are now running only a modest current account deficit. This adjustment has involved the creation of very large trade *surpluses*, particularly in Latin America, in order to meet interest obligations in a situation where new financial inflows remain low. These trade surpluses, for the most part resulting from cuts in import levels, constitute a transfer of real resources from the major debtor countries to the rest of the world which is the counterpart of their negative net financial transfers position (i.e., interest payments in excess of net financial inflows).

— Low-income countries in Africa have also had to adjust their external positions in the face of rising debt service obligations and falling export revenues and private financial flows. Increasing concessional flows, however, and the relative concessionality of their debt stock, have helped to avoid the emergence of negative net transfers and associated trade surpluses.

— India and China have emerged as significant users of non-concessional finance, in addition to aid, with China becoming a major absorber of foreign direct investment as well as bank loans. Indeed, the only major expansion of non-concessional financial flows to developing countries in the 1980s was to these two large low-income countries. Their debt service burdens are now increasing quite sharply (with the debt service/exports ratio much higher in India than in China, owing mainly to the dynamic export growth in the latter). Although in neither case is any major problem imminent, there is a clear need to follow policies which will maintain and increase debt-servicing capacity in the future.

— Other countries in Asia have sharply reduced their recourse to external finance, but for reasons which vary from the debt problem in the Philippines to decisive adjustment policies in Indonesia, to general prudence combined with strong savings and export performance in Malaysia and Thailand. Recently, foreign direct investment flows within the Asian region have shown a marked expansion, with Japan, Korea and Taiwan, the major source countries.

— The oil-exporting countries all moved into substantial deficit with the fall in oil prices and have had to adjust to more sustainable current account positions.

The current pattern of international capital flows described here cannot be regarded as optimal in development terms. How a more favourable situation might be engendered in the 1990s is addressed in the following sections.

The starting point for the 1990s is characterised by the still incomplete efforts to resolve debt problems and by the sustained but now maturing economic recovery in the OECD area. Buoyant investment in OECD countries induced by the need to expand production capacity has over the past year finally produced a marked recovery in the prices of primary materials. The terms of trade for the non-fuel primary exports of developing countries, however, remain on a declining historical trend. The appearance of inflationary tensions in a number of OECD countries and the persistence of major current account imbalances constitute a potential threat to continued world growth. Nevertheless, the medium-term growth prospects for OECD countries have improved, reflecting in part the spreading application of new technologies and efforts to improve the functioning and flexibility of OECD economies. The broad policy orientations through which OECD countries could strengthen the medium-term outlook for the world economy, and hence help to lay the basis for a healthy flow of resources to developing countries, have been set out in Chapter III Section 2).

2. SUSTAINABLE AND EQUITABLE DEVELOPMENT IN THE 1990s: THE FINANCIAL DIMENSION

It is clear from the experience of the 1970s that large inflows of external finance may engender growth patterns which are neither sustainable nor equitable. They may also be accompanied by domestic capital flight, resulting in the financial and social degradation evident in many of the debt-problem countries today. The only effective defence against this kind of outcome is an economically rational policy framework (with a broadly "correct" exchange rate as a central component), strong fiscal and financial disciplines and effective private and public sector institutions, as outlined in Chapter V. The link between policy reform, economic efficiency and external financing is at the heart of the growth-oriented strategy for resolving debt problems (and is a sine qua non in cases where reduction of debt and debt service is indicated).

Furthermore, the conditions under which external financing can contribute to sustainable and equitable development are also conditions which will promote domestic resource mobilisation. The promotion and effective use of domestic savings is indeed central to sustainable and equitable development progress.

Financial sector development and reform, which requires both an appropriate policy framework and appropriate institution-building efforts, must therefore be a fundamental priority in those developing countries where domestic resource mobilisation is low or where the allocation and use of financial resources is inefficient and financial institutions encumbered by low or non-performing assets (often because of politically imposed constraints or directives). A well-functioning financial sector is critical to the evolution of the private sector, whether at the level of large or medium-sized enterprises or at the microenterprise level. It is also critical to the promotion of equity. Positive real interest rates on bank deposits, which help to bring savings and investment into better equilibrium, together with the avoidance of subsidised credit policies, which often result in redistributing income to the rich and encourage the use of capital at the expense of employment, are key ingredients of sustainable and equitable development strategies. In other words, soundly based financial sector development is central to the promotion of participatory development, harnessing and stimulating productive energies broadly throughout the population, as set out in Chapter VII above.

Finally, while external capital and aid have an important role to play, it is clear that the huge financial resource requirements deriving from the development challenges ahead must be generated very largely in the developing countries themselves. There is great potential for increasing savings ratios in the many developing countries where domestic resource mobilisation is still low. The development experience of the past thirty years shows that there is no basis for savings pessimism. (At the beginning of the 1960s, savings ratios in Singapore and Korea were lower than in most African countries today.   India, with a per capita income lower than the average in Africa, has a domestic savings ratio higher than the OECD average.) Growing domestic resource mobilisation, and the policy and institutional framework that this implies, must be the fundamental basis for real development progress.

The objective to be aimed for in the 1990s, is to stimulate a greater range and depth of financial resources and intermediation, both domestic and external.   Aid donors can do much to help in this area.   The current discussion on using aid as a catalyst for foreign direct investment is one example.   (See Section 5 below.) More generally, aid agencies should encourage and assist developing-country authorities to design and secure the adoption of multi-year national strategies for financial market development including specific measures and action plans.   Technical assistance for financial market development should be supported by research which clarifies all of the major features of the country's financial markets, including the informal sector's sources of funds and credit extensions.

3.   IMPROVING THE SUPPLY AND ALLOCATION OF CAPITAL AT THE GLOBAL LEVEL IN THE 1990s

While developing countries' own savings can and should provide most of the resources needed for accelerated development progress in the 1990s, it is also important that the size and pattern of international capital flows should be optimised in a global development perspective with an appropriate role for aid in countries with low savings potentials and severe structural and institutional development bottlenecks.

Two main problems are at the centre of the present non-optimal situation: *first*, the lack of creditworthiness in many developing countries, notably in the major debt-problem countries, and *second*, the problem of the investment-savings gap within the OECD area.   Only when these sets of problems have been effectively resolved will it be possible for the underlying logic of capital flowing from developed to developing countries in significant volume to prevail in the world capital markets.   Even major increases in financing from official sources are unlikely to result in a higher *total* net flow of capital to developing countries if the fundamental economic conditions in both developed and developing countries are not right.

Savings levels in OECD countries which do not match OECD investment demand result in higher world real interest rates and will tend to "crowd out" capital flows to developing countries.   The emerging recognition of savings behaviour and national savings performance as an important policy issue in the OECD area is therefore to be welcomed.

National savings performance in OECD countries has been affected by excessive fiscal deficits and falling household savings.   While there has been a general effort to consolidate fiscal positions and halt the build up of public debt, this has still not gone far enough in some countries, including the United States where this is a major policy goal.   Improved fiscal positions have also been offset in some countries, again including the United States, by a decline in household savings.   It is difficult to identify with

129

certainty the explanation for the evolution in household savings behaviour. The de-regulation of financial markets and the technical and institutional innovations in the consumer credit industry in the 1980s are probably a factor. Another important influence could be demographic in nature — the transition in many OECD countries of the large "baby boom" generation through a low-saving period in its life-cycle during the 1980s. As this generation moves into the high-saving pre-retirement stage, household savings levels in OECD countries could well rise significantly, with an impact on total savings performance.

In summary, in a longer-term perspective adequate levels of saving in the OECD area as a whole, exceeding investment demand, is a basic requirement for sustained capital flows to developing countries.

4. DEALING WITH DEBT OVERHANGS

On the other side of the equation, it is equally necessary to restore creditworthiness in developing countries with debt problems. This is first and foremost a question of macroeconomic adjustment and economic policy reform by the debtor countries. How-ever, although countries implementing consistent policy reforms have made progress, growth has not been sufficient in many debtor nations, debt burdens have increased and inflation has worsened in some countries. It is increasingly recognised that the essential political basis for adjustment and policy reform is not likely to be sustainable where the magnitude of the debt burden itself prevents these efforts from being translated into renewed growth and development. Various options for addressing the financial needs of these countries have been emerging. In particular the expansion of voluntary debt and debt service reduction by private banks has been proposed as a way forward which would serve both creditor and debtor interests.

Following the agreement in 1988 to provide concessional terms for rescheduling the official debt of low-income countries, it has now been agreed that the World Bank and the IMF provide direct financial support for voluntary debt and debt service reduction operations by countries with an overhang of private bank debt which are willing to negotiate IMF/World Bank programmes.

The aim of this approach is to restore creditworthiness, so that new finance can flow alongside debt and debt service reduction. If official financing can play an important role in facilitating debt and debt service reduction operations then the commitment of public money can be justified on development grounds. Furthermore, as things stand, in the absence of progress in clearing up debt problems, there are limits on how much more the IMF and World Bank can increase their exposure to debt-problem countries while private banks are withdrawing funds. Effective debt and debt service reduction operations hold the potential for enhancing the value of outstanding claims of private banks following debt reduction operations, thus facilitating the eventual restoration of normal access to international capital markets.

A first agreement on these lines has been reached in the case of Mexico, with financial support from the IMF and the World Bank, with parallel support from Japan. The success of this approach will depend on the scale of debt and debt service reduction achieved in each case and on the ability and willingness of each country benefitting from the scheme to create and maintain a sustained commitment to appropriate economic policies and reforms.   Adjustment efforts should focus particularly on policies to mobilise increased domestic savings and foreign direct investment, to create a sound fiscal position, and to promote the return of flight capital.

For debtor countries, their creditors and the world economy, the potential benefits of success in this approach are considerable.   Increased consumption and investment in the heavily indebted countries would lead to higher growth, help alleviate poverty, and stimulate world demand for imports, including both manufactures and commodities.

In the low-income countries with debt overhangs, there may also be a case for considering whether, and through what modalities, debt and debt service reduction operations might be a justified use of scarce concessional finance in some cases, clearing the way for the resumption of non-concessional financing, both public and private, later in the decade, as the policy and institutional framework and debt-servicing capacity gain strength.   Donors have already provided finance for a substantial buy-back of private bank debt by Bolivia.   But most of the external obligations of debt distressed low-income countries are held by official creditors.   The new Paris Club rescheduling options for low-income countries decided in 1988 constitute a departure from the rule that bilateral official debt is rescheduled at market terms, and represent an important step. The scheme will slow the unrealistic build-up of non-concessional official debt, but seems unlikely to remove the debt overhang in the foreseeable future.

There is, in other words, a series of outstanding challenges to be faced in dealing with debt overhangs in some low-income countries.   In a number of low-income countries the burden of multilateral debt obligations is quite large.   Efforts to address these problems must be predicated on sustained, comprehensive macroeconomic structural adjustment efforts, on donors giving priority to supporting these efforts with concerted concessional financing, and on the full utilisation of the policies of the multilateral institutions to provide appropriately strong financial support.   Several low-income countries are in arrears to the Fund and the World Bank and do not qualify for further multilateral financing.   The enhanced collaborative approach to overdue obligations endorsed by the IMF Interim Committee provides a framework for addressing the arrears problem, although it is premature to judge its ultimate effectiveness.

5.   FOREIGN DIRECT INVESTMENT

Within total capital flows, foreign direct investment plays a particularly important role in the development process.   In a development perspective, the role of foreign direct investment goes well beyond its contribution in the form of equity capital, important as that may be to those countries which have difficulty in raising new loan capital.   The more fundamental development contributions of foreign direct investment are the transfer of management and marketing skills and technologies to the local economy, in a variety of ways, including training of local managers and technicians and the nurturing of local suppliers who can meet international standards.

There has been a swing in developing-country attitudes towards foreign direct investment, but their policies are often still characterised by inconsistent mixtures of incentives and performance requirements. Financial constraints and debt burdens in Africa and Latin America present operating difficulties for foreign companies, not only through their impact on market prospects, but also through shortages of basic inputs and spare parts.

Foreign direct investment is tending to bypass many of the low-income developing countries. Many of these countries cannot offer what potential investors consider a favourable investment climate or large effective domestic markets, and their low-cost labour has declined in importance, especially where labour productivity is low and a contemplated investment requires sophisticated production techniques using skilled labour.

It is important to underline the irreplaceable value of an effective policy, economic and regulatory environment ("investment climate") to encourage foreign direct investment. Government attitudes and policies for enterprise development usually govern the activities of both domestic and foreign investors. An important indicator to a foreign investor of the investment climate is therefore the attitude of local capital toward investment in productive domestic enterprises — as opposed to placing capital abroad or real estate speculation.

Supportive action for expanding productive foreign direct investment put in place by a number of DAC countries includes a widened network of investment protection and double taxation agreements, improved investment guarantee schemes, strengthened information and promotion services, technical assistance, incentives for joint ventures and special attention to encouraging investment from middle-level enterprises.

XII

IMPLICATIONS FOR THE FUTURE ORIENTATION
OF THE AID SYSTEM

1. THE CAPACITY OF THE AID SYSTEM
TO RESPOND TO THE EMERGING CHALLENGES

Developing countries will need the support of an effective international aid system to meet the challenges of the 1990s. This survey has underlined the enormous dimensions of the development tasks ahead and the complexities of the policies and actions required to contribute to better progress towards sustainable and equitable development.

Substantial additional aid efforts will be required not only quantitatively but also qualitatively. The development co-operation process is becoming increasingly demanding in terms of expertise and organisational effort. The growing diversity of developing countries calls for increased efforts by donors to adapt and differentiate their aid policies and modalities according to specific highly varied country needs and circumstances.

Donor countries will be able to assist developing countries effectively only if they relate their national aid activities to concerted action in support of effective programmes and policies of the assisted countries. National development assistance efforts must be seen as part of a larger international effort. No individual donor country has an aid programme large enough in any single developing country to achieve significant development objectives on its own. Staff constraints are such that effective aid management imperatively calls for increased donor co-operation based on some specialisation. The primary performance measure of the individual national aid programme — and indeed of the individual aid manager — must be its contribution to the larger development effort.

Effective development co-operation requires a reconciliation of the range of national policy interests with the underlying objectives of development and measures to ensure that the sum of individual donor efforts adds up to a coherent whole. Greater efforts need to be made to explain to national public opinion that national development assistance efforts are part of a larger international effort.

2. THE CONTRIBUTION OF AID

Aid agencies are confident of their capacity to make a positive contribution to development. When DAC Members reviewed the record of "Twenty-Five Years of Development Co-operation" in 1985, they assessed the contribution of aid as follows: Development achievements have been mainly attributable to the efforts of developing countries themselves. Access to the markets, private capital and technology of OECD countries has been an important factor. However, financial and technical assistance have also made crucial contributions. Aid has been most successful where it has reinforced strong commitments to development on the part of developing countries, helping them to adopt and implement consistent policies and programmes. Aid has saved lives and mitigated suffering in situations of natural and economic emergency. Basic infrastructure, institutions and administrative and technical manpower have been developed and strengthened with the help of foreign assistance. Through research, technical advice, training and financial support, aid has made important contributions to the achievement of self-sufficiency in staple food production by most of Asia, reversing the chronic threat of famine.

Aid agencies realise that aid is only one of many factors operating in the development process. Many factors account for the divergent development records of developing countries. The external world economic environment — to a large extent influenced by OECD country economic performance and policies — and the ability of developing countries to adapt to it and use its opportunities is a central factor. Most important has been the progressive improvement of national policies and key institutions in many of them, encouraging better mobilisation and use of domestic resources. Development assistance has stimulated and accelerated such crucial changes in many ways, but most effectively by the timely support given to key change-makers in these countries in the form of technical and financial resources. Aid has been crucial in many cases, both macroeconomically in terms of the resources contributed and microeconomically through vital contributions to the breaking of development bottlenecks.

Official development assistance is not investment banking. It is not its purpose to seek the highest financial investment returns. It is intended to help developing countries to meet critical development bottlenecks. Aid agencies have also been called to help developing countries to cope with acute emergency situations arising from natural calamities such as droughts and floods, refugee influxes or political-ethnic strife. Countries in conditions of underdevelopment tend to suffer more from such calamities than economically more advanced countries. Development and development assistance are, in a sense, longer-term efforts at disaster prevention.

Operating in difficult economic, social, political and environmental contexts requires patience and persistence and is bound to produce mixed results. It is not surprising, therefore, that many aid recipients are not among the fast-growing countries. Almost all have been helped significantly by aid to accelerate social development and to lay at least some of the foundations for rapid economic progress.

Aid evaluation work in aid agencies and under DAC auspices has strongly emphasized the "learning function", and it can be said that considerable progress has been made in recent years. Securing stronger feedback of the findings of aid evaluation work into aid decision-making would enable further improvement in developmental aid effectiveness. The increasing use of policy-related programme aid is an area calling for careful evaluation.

At the microeconomic level of operation, there is now a solid body of knowledge on the design and implementation of projects, which is reflected in the DAC's recently adopted Principles for Project Appraisal. Many reviews of a wide range of completed projects reveal, unsurprisingly, a mixed record, but nevertheless with a significant success rate in what is an inherently risky business. Beyond often very difficult operating conditions in developing countries, problems have arisen from pressures to meet spending targets and from non-developmental considerations.

Aid agencies have begun to give operational reality to the long-established proposition that aid cannot be more effective than the policies and programmes that it supports. The experience with the recent emphasis on policy-related aid will have important implications for the future orientation of aid. It is particularly important to ensure that aid is not used to put off essential policy reform and structural adjustment.

The policy analysis and orientations set out in this report should help to demonstrate the seriousness and professionalism with which the complex issues of helping other countries in their development process are addressed by aid agencies.

3. AID VOLUME REQUIREMENTS AND THE OUTLOOK FOR AID

For the developing countries to be able to cope with the challenges of the 1990s, they will require substantial additional aid and other financial resources. This review has demonstrated the vast range of the needs and opportunities for effective uses of additional aid. ODA volume alone, of course, is not a sufficient basis to assess aid requirements; aid quality and recipient country performance also have to be taken into account.

The Aid Record. Aggregate ODA from DAC Members has increased regularly. Contrary to private flows, which have shown sharp fluctuations, ODA has been a stable and reliable source of external financing.

During the last ten years DAC ODA has increased by roughly 40 per cent, from $30 billion in 1977-78 to $45 billion in 1988 (at 1987 prices and exchange rates), i.e., at an average annual rate of just over 3 per cent, roughly in line with aggregate DAC GNP growth.

DAC Members collectively have not been able to improve the average ODA/GNP ratio, which has fluctuated around 0.35 per cent since 1975. The unweighted DAC ODA/GNP ratio stands at 0.50 (1987-88) and has significantly increased from 0.46 in 1980-81. (The comparative aid record of DAC Members is documented in the Statistical Annex.)

The DAC average performance conceals large differences among individual DAC countries. Burden-sharing remains a sore issue in DAC discussions. Sweden, the Netherlands, Norway and Denmark remain the only countries which have reached and indeed exceed the 0.7 per cent target. The following countries have substantially increased their ODA/GNP ratios during the past decade: Finland (soon to reach 0.7 per cent), Italy, France and Switzerland. By contrast, between 1977-78 and 1987-88 the ODA/GNP ratio declined in the case of New Zealand, Australia, the United Kingdom, Belgium and the United States.

As a result mainly of declining aid from Arab countries (from exceptionally high levels in the 1970s), total aid from all sources (DAC, CMEA, Arab aid) has remained approximately stable since the beginning of the 1980s.

Outlook for Aid Volume. DAC Members fully recognise the crucial role of official development assistance in the years to come. At their High-Level Meeting in December 1988, DAC Members reaffirmed that "in view of the huge development tasks ahead, they consider it important to increase so far as possible official development assistance and further promote other financial flows. They recall the target already established by international organisations (0.7 per cent) for the future level of official development assistance."

Present indications for the aid outlook are as follows.

— Countries which have set themselves ODA/GNP ratios as targets (Denmark, Finland, the Netherlands, Norway and Sweden) can probably be expected to maintain them with further regular increases in the medium term at least in line with GNP growth.

— Following a one-time cut made in FY 1989/90 as part of an effort to reduce the budget deficit, the growth of Canada's aid will resume during the first half of the next decade. ODA will expand more rapidly than GNP but more slowly than foreseen in the past and aid appropriations are expected to represent 0.47 per cent of GNP in FY 1993/94, the end of the present planning period.

— France's aid will increase from the present level of 0.51 per cent of GNP until the 0.7 per cent target for independent countries is met. No date has been set for achievement of this target.

— Aid from Japan can be expected to increase. Under current plans, which extend to 1992, major increases are envisaged raising Japan's aid to the DAC average ODA/GNP ratio. Annual rates of increase during recent years were close to 6 per cent in real terms.

— Prospects for the other donors, including some of the larger ones, such as Germany, Italy and the United Kingdom, are difficult to assess. It is to be hoped that future levels of aid of these countries will progress as a share of GNP, implying increases in absolute terms somewhat higher than their GNP growth. The global outcome will be substantially influenced by the evolution of the United States aid programme, which is currently under review.

Taking these indications together, further increases in the level of total DAC aid in the 1990s can be expected. But substantial additional efforts would have to be made by at least some countries beyond present plans if the aggregate DAC ODA/GNP ratio were to be significantly increased.

Continuing highly differential aid growth paths among DAC Members will further change the relative weight of individual countries as sources of aid. This could well have an impact on the overall geographical and sectoral distribution of aid.

Aid volume will remain a major issue during the 1990s. There is a range of fundamental questions which DAC Members will need to discuss among themselves and with their developing country partners.

— Do the improvements in economic conditions in Member countries enhance the climate for more positive aid-volume decisions?
— Could fuller awareness in donor countries of the interrelated problems of population growth, poverty and environmental risks *and* the existence of effective programmes and policies on the part of developing countries to address these issues contribute to more positive volume responses?
— Would it be useful and feasible to work with the competent international institutions and developing countries in identifying priority areas which require increased financial resources?
— Are more countries ready to make firmer time-bound commitments to reaching the 0.7 per cent target during the 1990s?
— Should donors give priority to making progress towards the aid target for least developed countries (0.15 per cent of GNP)?

Donors and recipients confront the dilemma that in the face of enormous unmet needs there are often absorptive capacity constraints, particularly in the administratively weaker low-income countries, which need to be addressed.

It is one of the fundamental dilemmas of development co-operation that poverty and low levels of institutional development put constraints on the effective use of aid. A poor public sector coping with chronic severe financial constraints, with low-paid and consequently often unmotivated officials, and lack of basic facilities, which is characteristic of most least developed countries, hardly offers a propitious receiving structure for massive external assistance, including even technical assistance.

This, once again, underlines the need, so often emphasized during this review, to redouble efforts to strengthen with patience and persistence the aid-implementing institutional structures in administratively weaker low-income countries.

It is also important, on the other hand, to ensure that high levels of assistance, especially in combination with high dependency ratios, do not impair self-reliance and effective policy reforms.

Opportunities for effective use of substantial additional aid also depend on the extent to which some of the large low-income countries with stronger administrative capacity will be increasing recipients of aid. While these countries are receiving substantial aid in absolute terms, aid receipts in relation to their GNP are generally relatively low and have tended to decline. In the same vein, the question arises under what circumstances substantially increased aid is to be used in some of the middle-income developing countries with difficult development problems (see below).

Donors have in recent years made considerable efforts in adapting aid procedures to permit flexible aid use in low-income countries, for instance in relation to policy-related programme assistance. Increasing amounts of aid are available for local and recurrent cost financing rather than, as used to be the case often in earlier years, mainly for investment projects and import requirements. It is an important question to determine how much further it is feasible and useful, also from the point of view of recipient countries themselves, to go in this direction.

4.   IMPROVING PROSPECTS FOR SELF-RELIANCE

Creating conditions for self-reliance is an important ultimate objective of aid.   Some developing countries have indeed been able to reduce or even phase out aid reliance. In the least developed countries, however, and in some other, generally smaller, low-income countries, the use of aid in relation to GNP has become very high.   Donors recognise that heavy aid use, together with the large-scale presence of expatriates, particularly in smaller and sometimes administratively weak countries, can lead to "aid intrusiveness", with donors unintentionally exerting major influence on resource use patterns and styles.

Donors and recipients will have to work together to improve the conditions for effective aid use, to reduce aid intrusiveness and to preserve prospects for self-reliance. Particular care must be taken with forms of aid which tend to prolong aid dependence. Forms of aid which carry that risk and which should be limited include in particular certain forms of prolonged food aid, open-ended budget support and other prolonged recurrent-cost financing, and major reliance on expatriate experts for regular operational tasks.

Forms of aid which contribute to self-reliance should be encouraged.   This applies to the whole range of financial and technical assistance for human resources development and institution-building.   Developing countries' own institutions should increasingly be used in the analytical design and implementation phases of aid-financed activities. Demonstrated greater administrative ability to use aid effectively should be rewarded by granting forms of aid which leave increasing responsibility for design and implementation to recipient countries and their executive agencies.   Donors should, to a reasonable degree, be prepared to accept some risk of delays and reduced efficiency as an investment in the learning process contributing to self-reliance.

5.   CO-ORDINATION: WORKING TOWARDS CONCERTED DONOR AND RECIPIENT EFFORTS

The number of development assistance institutions operating in developing countries is large.   There remain considerable differences among donors in aid policies and procedures, such as the availability of aid for particular purposes, criteria and procedures for project and programme selection, procurement regulations, end-use controls and more generally the degree of involvement in managing the aid delivery process.   Some donors maintain full-time specialised field staff in recipient countries; others work mainly through diplomatic missions and visiting development specialists.

To ensure that aid, involving various sources and diverse activities, interrelates effectively with the recipient country's own resources and programming processes requires an extraordinary organisational effort.   Frequent donor-recipient consultations on policy and procedural issues are required to establish agreed purposes, approaches, administrative systems and supporting measures.   Chapter V above has given a detailed description of current international efforts at co-ordinated structural adjustment support.

Working towards effective concertation and integration of donor and recipient efforts will become even more important in the 1990s as the dimensions and complexities of the development task increase.

For aid to make a lasting contribution to the economic and social well-being of developing countries, it must be concerned not only with the proper selection, design and implementation of individual projects and their economic and institutional sustainability but also with the support of broader sectoral and national efforts and policies. This requires closely co-ordinated efforts. To avoid the problems that have arisen over developing countries' receiving conflicting policy advice from a variety of bilateral and multilateral donors, policy dialogue should take place primarily in a multilateral framework. Bilateral donors could also promote further bilateral policy dialogues in areas in which they are particularly active, but these should be consistent with policy recommendations which have been developed in a multilateral framework.

The concept of aid co-ordination evolved by the DAC centres on the principles set out below. These principles reflect a firm resolve by DAC Members to work with other donors and recipient countries to relate their individual aid activities more closely to the carefully appraised and jointly reviewed programmes and policies of developing countries.

— Developing countries themselves are responsible for setting their policies and priorities and central responsibility for aid co-ordination lies with each recipient government. Recipient governments could benefit from the role played by the World Bank, IMF and UNDP in stimulating and assisting the aid co-ordination process.
— Aid co-ordination arrangements must be used flexibly to meet the diversity of specific situations; they are required mainly in developing countries which depend heavily on external assistance and need the support of international aid co-ordination arrangements to ensure effective use of resources.
— Stronger collective efforts by recipient countries, donors, and international institutions are required to establish and implement well designed policies and carefully appraised investment and expenditure programmes.
— It is essential for effective use of resources that donors adhere to such carefully appraised programmes, when they have been the subject of consultations and consensus in the international aid co-ordination arrangements.
— Fuller exchange of pertinent information on continuing and planned activities among donors and between donors and recipients is essential for successful co-ordination and effective use of aid.
— DAC Members acknowledge the desirability of providing adequate financing to developing countries that are undertaking effective policy reform efforts.
— Donors stand ready to help recipient governments strengthen their capacity to plan and manage policies, programmes and projects and will seek wherever possible to harmonize and simplify aid procedures.

DAC Members have reaffirmed their determination to co-operate closely with recipient countries, international institutions and other donors in the international aid co-ordination arrangements.

The system of Consortia, Consultative Groups and Round Tables, usually working

139

under the leadership of the World Bank or UNDP, will remain important focal points for multilateral policy dialogues giving guidance and direction for the implementation of coherent development policies and programmes. DAC Members have made suggestions for improving the working of these arrangements, which they will keep under review. These suggestions include encouraging greater participation by bilateral donors in consultations preceding consultative group and round table meetings, facilitating more frank and substantive exchanges of views on key policy issues and problems at these meetings and greater efforts at arriving at operationally relevant conclusions and consensus-building.

There is also a need to strengthen aid co-ordination at the local (i.e. recipient country capital) level, coping as effectively as possible with donors' differences in their administrative structures, field staffs and delegation of authority. There has been considerable expansion of local co-ordination activities recently. Progress has been made at the level of exchange of information, avoiding project duplication and promoting joint activities; but much more needs to be done, especially relating aid to carefully appraised and reviewed investment programmes, and developing and implementing sector policies and programmes.

While progress in aid co-ordination is being made, serious constraints remain both for recipients and for bilateral and multilateral donors. There is a great diversity of country situations as attitudes differ among both donors and recipients. There is also considerable diversity in institutional capacities among recipients and donors. Co-ordination is a lengthy and complex endeavour which requires not only operational and institutional adjustments but also firm political determination on all sides.

6. WORKING WITH DEVELOPING COUNTRIES TOWARDS EFFECTIVE PROJECT SELECTION AND DESIGN

As part of their effort to improve aid quality, DAC Members have worked together on a set of principles for project appraisal, covering the whole process from initial project identification to preparation, appraisal, selection and design and to subsequent monitoring and evaluation (cf. DAC Principles for Project Appraisal, Paris 1988; also reproduced in the DAC Chairman's Report of 1988). In addition to careful economic, financial and technical appraisal, stress is laid on assessments of managerial and institutional capacity, social and distributional effects and environmental impact. This work on individual projects and action to improve developing countries' development policies and programmes are two essential and mutually reinforcing prerequisites for more effective use of external aid and domestic resources.

DAC Members have agreed to review their project appraisal and selection criteria and procedures in the light of these principles and to make adjustments where necessary. They are ready to work together with the recipients of their aid to ensure acceptable standards of rigour and developmental effectiveness in project selection and preparation. The Principles incorporate the following essential elements.

— Better investment management and resource use in developing countries are essential for more satisfactory economic and social development. Project survival and viability can be improved through greater rigour in project selection, clearer and more realistic setting of objectives, greater care in design and preparation, fuller involvement of target groups in design and implementation and quicker adjustment when problems are identified.

— The initial selection of projects should be consistent with well conceived sectoral programmes and strategies of the recipient countries. The broader policy framework in which projects operate must be such as to facilitate their success.

— Close consultation between donor, recipient government and affected communities in the formulation of objectives and the appraisal of projects is necessary to ensure that the project responds to the recipient community's needs and that relevant managerial, social and environmental requirements are taken into account in project design.

— The sustainability of projects is determined by a range of factors — including economic soundness, project design corresponding to the managerial, technical and financial capacity of recipients, compatibility with socio-cultural conditions and, last but not least, environmental sustainability — all of which must be considered at the appraisal and design stage to ensure project success. It is not in the recipient's interest to proceed with projects which are likely to produce minimal benefits in the short run and to be non-sustainable or non-replicable in the long run.

— Strengthening the capacity of recipient countries through training and institutional development for project appraisal, design and management including budgeting and auditing is an important objective for donor/recipient technical co-operation.

— Efficient procurement can yield substantial benefits to recipients in terms of project price and subsequent operation and maintenance. Where procurement is tied, it should be flexibly administered, including careful choice of supplies in which the donor is competent and competitive. There must be effective price and quality controls, and waivers especially for situations where local-cost financing or third-country procurement is essential.

Most donors feel obliged, largely with a view to securing public support, to tie a substantial part of their aid to procurement from domestic suppliers. A broader move to untying would contribute to obtaining better value for aid money. Perhaps even more importantly, it would improve the climate for aid co-ordination and constructive donor co-operation.

7. THE NEED FOR A STRONG MULTILATERAL SYSTEM

The establishment and rapid evolution of a network of multilateral development institutions — institutions in which policies and operations are determined by the collective decisions of contributors and recipients — has been a central element in the process of promoting development. The way in which this network has been developed and refined can be regarded as one of the important achievements of international co-operation. The multilateral institutions are major channels of financial and technical assistance to low-income countries and intermediaries in the flow of market capital to middle-income countries. In addition to their role as channels of development finance, they are central sources of policy advice, technical services and development research, and focal points for aid co-ordination. United Nations agencies have become the vehicle for international decision-making for a wide spectrum of matters ranging from rules for civil aviation to measures related to trade in toxic chemicals. These functions will be of growing importance in the 1990s.

In the 1980s, multilateral funding levels consolidated at about 25 per cent of DAC Members' total ODA (30 per cent including contributions to the EEC) with considerable variations among individual donors (scc Tables 3-12 of the Statistical Annex). It is striking that governments make available major parts of their aid budgets to international institutions, thus giving up direct control over the use of these resources. Understandably, the periodic replenishment of the funds of these institutions and discussions concerning the level and orientation of their operations have given rise to complicated international negotiations.

There is continuing strong support for multilateral aid. Donors' assessments of multilateral agencies, however, are increasingly based on the their degree of perceived effectiveness in the performance of defined tasks, rather than on any general assumption of the superiority of multilateral over bilateral aid. By this standard, some agencies are widely judged to fall short. Consequently, the immediate task for most agencies is to improve their operational capacity and project quality, within a clearer common understanding of objectives.

With the growing complexity of the development and development co-operation task in the 1990s strong multilateral institutions as focal points for coherent efforts are essential. The World Bank, IMF and UNDP are the central bodies for providing the lead in assisting developing countries in aid co-ordination and policy planning, but they could make better use of the expertise of the sectoral UN agencies when they advise governments at the country level. The World Bank has already considerably reinforced its co-operation with other UN agencies. But the sectoral agencies need to reshape themselves in the light of changing needs, and in particular, within the general framework provided by the UNDP, to strengthen their analytical capacity at the country level.

Strengthening the UNDP's position as the central funding agency for UN technical co-operation programmes remains a crucial concern. The UNDP's performance of its central funding role is a prerequisite for bringing coherence to UN programmes as a whole. At the same time, the UNDP increasingly sees itself as having a comparative advantage, and therefore a role of leadership, in the provision of services to support national capability in decision-taking and programme management. It sees itself as doing so especially within the central ministries of development policy, such as finance and planning, but also, in co-operation with the specialised UN agencies, at the sectoral and multisectoral levels. By and large, donors have supported the UNDP in this sharpening of focus.

Some lines of further development are clear. The sectoral UN agencies should be encouraged to strengthen their capacity and responsiveness to go beyond the shopping-list approach, based on individual projects, to make their contribution to a more strategic country-oriented approach, centred on the three essential elements:

142

— Policy improvement;
— Development of programmes within agreed public investment and expenditure priorities;
— Support for institution-building.

There is now general agreement that the regional development banks, while remaining primarily project-oriented, should also to some extent develop policy-based programme lending instruments, working alongside and with the World Bank and IMF. The regional banks still have to strengthen considerably their policy advisory capacity before they can play a more active role.   There is scope for policy-related lending at the sectoral level within an agreed macroeconomic policy framework.   The regional development banks should try to move in that direction, in conjunction with World Bank sector programmes where relevant.

The multilateral development banks have become mature lending institutions with major repayment receipts from earlier lending.   While new lending is substantial and growing, total net financial transfers from their ordinary resources are in most cases diminishing.   This poses problems.   However, the role and impact of these institutions must not be judged only by the size of their net resource transfers.   What is required, rather, is a continuing critical scrutiny of their efficiency and effectiveness in support of specificd useful programmes and projects as well as the availability of adequate funding to finance these activities.

The multilateral institutions will remain central pillars of the development co-operation effort during the 1990s.   A key issue is that of funding.   1990 will see major funding exercises across the whole multilateral system, including replenishments of IDA and the regional development banks.   For EEC members the reconstitution of the European Development Fund as part of the next Convention will be an important factor. Funding exercises consist of three main elements — an argument about the total figures, a debate about burden-sharing and, increasingly, a discussion of the policy and organisational changes needed to ensure maximum impact from the funds provided.   Particularly with respect to the global institutions the challenge is how to preserve both genuine multilateralism through broad-based participation in funding *and* adequate expansion in the total volume of support.

8.   CO-OPERATION WITH MORE ADVANCED DEVELOPING COUNTRIES

While the problems of poverty and under-development are severest in the lower-income countries, there is a range of more advanced developing countries which face serious economic and social imbalances, a pronounced dual structure of urban and rural societies, acute localised urban and rural poverty and problems of environmental sustainability.   There are major continuing requirements for economic and social infrastructure and human resources development.   Some countries are striving to achieve more democratic forms of government in difficult economic, social and financial conditions.   In many cases, economic, social, political and institutional structures are only gradually adapting to the challenges of rapid population growth, the requirements of modernisation of the economy and government and the difficult international economic environment. The continued heavy debt burdens in many more advanced countries are both a manifestation of the deep-seated structural problems and policy deficiencies and a serious impediment to a satisfactory solution of these problems. Restoring the economic vitality of these countries is an important issue for the entire world economy. Although success depends essentially on their own efforts, it is important that the developed countries express their solidarity with these efforts and their readiness to be constructively engaged in the process of recovery and advance.

The key elements of an approach to helping more advanced developing countries master their economic and social problems involve a healthy world economic environment, a strong system of open multilateral trade and access to capital and technology.

There is also, however, scope for strengthening a range of development co-operation activities with more advanced developing countries addressing specific needs in policy improvement and institution-building; poverty alleviation, environmental protection and essential infrastructure development. The specific modalities and terms of such co-operation will depend on specific country situations which vary widely. Indeed, these types of co-operation are also appropriate in lower-income countries depending on their circumstances and opportunities.

There is a major role in more advanced developing countries for the World Bank and the regional development banks as sources of both financing, through their ordinary capital windows, and policy advice. As mentioned above, the World Bank and the IMF have now been asked to provide support for voluntary, market-based debt reduction transactions as part of the assistance they can offer for adjustment programmes.

There are also major needs and opportunities, both through development assistance agencies and a range of other public and private institutions, for industrial and technological co-operation, improvement of public sector management, private investment promotion and scientific and cultural exchanges. Some countries have been experimenting with an integrated approach combining ODA, policy dialogue, investment and trade. (A specific case is the Caribbean Basin initiative.)

9. CO-OPERATION WITH NON-DAC DONORS

The 1990s are likely to see some significant shifts in the orientation of aid from non-DAC donors, mainly a change in the character of USSR aid and the emergence of some new donors among the more advanced developing countries in addition to the Arab donors. (See the Statistical Annex.)

The political and economic changes now under way in the USSR, the largest non-DAC source of aid, is resulting in a reassessment of the Soviet Union's relations with developing countries, including its aid programme. A major expansion in the volume of USSR aid is unlikely and there may even be some reductions in view of the economic and financial circumstances of the Soviet Union. It is to be hoped, however, that its aid programme may be more directly related to development objectives and become more effective from a developmental point of view. The USSR may become more interested in participating in aid co-ordination arrangements, both locally in the recipient countries and in Consultative Groups and Round Tables, and perhaps in the cofinancing of projects with other donors. There is also a new attitude towards multilateral institutions.

Arab aid, mainly from Saudi Arabia and Kuwait, can be expected to remain significant. It is likely to remain concentrated on the Middle East and North Africa. DAC Members consult on an informal basis with the Arab aid agencies which have developed aid approaches and procedures rather similar to those of the DAC countries.

China and India are significant sources of development assistance for some developing countries. Korea and Taiwan may emerge as significant new donors. Korea established a development co-operation fund in 1987 and Taiwan is in the process of doing so. The NIEs have useful experience to offer to other developing countries. While their aid programmes are still modest in volume, it must be hoped that arrangements can be found to make full use of their development experience and expertise.

Spain, the largest source of aid among the non-DAC OECD Members, is likely to expand its aid activities in the 1990s and may join the DAC in the next few years. Portugal has expressed similar intentions. Luxembourg has significantly expanded its aid effort in recent years to a current level of 0.29 per cent of GNP.

Part 3

TRENDS IN RESOURCE FLOWS FOR DEVELOPMENT

I

FINANCIAL RESOURCES FOR DEVELOPING COUNTRIES: 1988 AND RECENT TRENDS

1. TOTAL NET FINANCIAL RESOURCE FLOWS TO DEVELOPING COUNTRIES

There is now a great diversity in the financial situations and trends of developing countries. This fact of life gives rise to an increasing need to analyse and interpret trends in total financial resource flows to developing countries on a disaggregated basis, both by region and by income level, as has been stressed in this report over the past several years, and particularly in last year's Report. The point is re-emphasized in Chapter XI of Part 2 of this Report. A comprehensive "financial geography" of the developing countries can be found in *Financial and External Debt of Developing Countries: 1988 Survey*, OECD, 1989. In this section of this Report, a very broad picture of trends during 1988 in the main aggregates only is presented.

It is helpful to recall the main features of the recent financial resource flow situation, in which the 1988 out-turn should be situated:

— the sharp fall in private financial resource flows, and in particular in private bank lending, after the debt crisis erupted in 1982 was more or less arrested in 1986-87, allowing a return to a rough stability in total financial resource flows;

— the stability of official flows over this period has meant that Official Development Finance now provides some two-thirds of the total financial flow to developing countries, compared with only one-third at the beginning of the 1980s;

— the precipitous decline in net export credits following 1982, with the lack of big new projects in debt-problem countries combining with a high level of repayments, also appears to have bottomed out, but at a level near zero.

Against this background, it is estimated that in nominal terms the total net flow of resources to developing countries from all sources in 1988, after the recovery initiated in 1987, rose by 6 per cent to $103 billion. Net disbursements of official funds were 8 per cent higher in nominal terms, while net private flows fell by 8 per cent. In constant prices and exchange rates, there was a small decrease of total resource flows (See Table 3-1).

Table 3-1. TOTAL NET RESOURCE FLOWS TO DEVELOPING COUNTRIES[a]

	1980	1981	1982	1983	1984	1985	1986	1987	1988	1980	1985	1988
	Current $ billion									Per cent of total		
I. OFFICIAL DEVELOPMENT FINANCE (ODF)	45.6	45.6	44.3	42.4	47.7	49.0	56.1	61.7	65.7	35.5	58.5	64.7
1. Official Development Assistance (ODA)	37.8	36.9	34.0	33.9	35.0	37.4	44.3	48.4	51.3	29.5	44.6	50.5
of which: Bilateral disbursements	30.0	29.0	26.4	26.3	27.2	28.9	34.8	38.3	40.0	23.4	34.5	39.4
Multilateral disbursements	7.8	7.9	7.6	7.6	7.8	8.5	9.5	10.1	11.3	6.1	10.1	11.1
2. Other ODF	7.8	8.7	10.3	8.5	12.7	11.6	11.8	13.3	14.4	6.1	13.8	14.2
of which: Bilateral disbursements	3.0	3.0	3.7	1.3	4.5	3.7	4.0	6.6	8.0	2.3	4.4	7.9
Multilateral disbursements	4.8	5.7	6.6	7.2	8.2	7.9	7.8	6.7	6.4	3.7	9.4	6.3
II. TOTAL EXPORT CREDITS	16.5	17.6	13.7	4.6	6.2	4.0	−0.6	−0.7	3.0	12.9	4.8	2.9
1. DAC countries	15.4	16.2	12.7	3.9	5.2	3.4	−0.8	−1.0	2.6	12.0	4.1	2.6
of which: Medium and long-term	13.6	13.3	9.7	7.4	4.9	0.2	−3.8	−5.1	−1.0			
Short-term	1.8	2.9	3.0	−3.5	0.3	3.2	3.0	4.1	3.6			
2. Other countries	1.1	1.4	1.0	0.7	1.0	0.6	0.2	0.3	0.4	0.9	0.7	0.4
III. PRIVATE FLOWS	66.2	74.5	58.3	48.1	31.7	30.8	28.2	35.6	32.9	51.6	36.8	32.4
1. Direct investment (OECD)	11.2	17.2	12.8	9.3	11.3	6.6	11.3	20.2	19.0	8.7	7.9	18.7
of which: Offshore Centres	3.0	4.1	4.1	3.7	3.8	3.7	6.8	12.0	..			
2. International bank lending	49.0	52.0	37.6	34.7	16.4	13.6	5.0	5.6	4.7	38.2	16.2	4.6
of which: Short-term	26.0	22.0	15.0	−25.0	−6.0	12.0	−4.0	5.0	..			
3. Total bond lending	1.6	1.5	5.0	1.2	0.3	4.8	3.3	1.0	1.6	1.2	5.7	1.6
4. Other private	2.0	1.8	0.6	0.6	1.1	2.9	5.3	5.5	4.0	1.6	3.5	3.9
5. Grants by non-governmental organisations	2.4	2.0	2.3	2.3	2.6	2.9	3.3	3.3	3.6	1.9	3.5	3.5
TOTAL NET RESOURCE FLOWS (I+II+III)	128.3	137.7	116.3	95.1	85.6	83.8	83.7	96.6	101.6	100.0	100.0	100.0
Related data:												
Use of IMF credit, net	2.6	6.1	6.3	12.5	5.4	0.8	−1.4	−4.7	−4.3			
Interest and dividends paid by LDCs, gross	63.6	86.4	94.0	80.6	86.8	88.7	76.2	74.7	86.0			
	At 1987 prices and exchange rates											
Total net resource flows	169.4	188.9	163.5	134.1	123.4	119.4	96.3	96.6	94.8			
Total official development finance	60.2	62.6	62.3	59.8	68.8	69.8	64.5	61.7	61.3			
Total ODA receipts from all sources	49.9	50.6	47.8	47.8	50.4	53.3	51.0	48.4	47.6			
Private flows	87.4	102.2	82.0	67.8	45.7	43.9	32.4	35.6	30.7			
Total DAC ODA (bilateral and multilateral)	36.0	35.1	39.1	38.9	41.4	41.9	42.2	41.5	44.8			

a) Excluding Taiwan. Flows from all sources, i.e. including DAC, CMEA, Arab and other LDC donors.

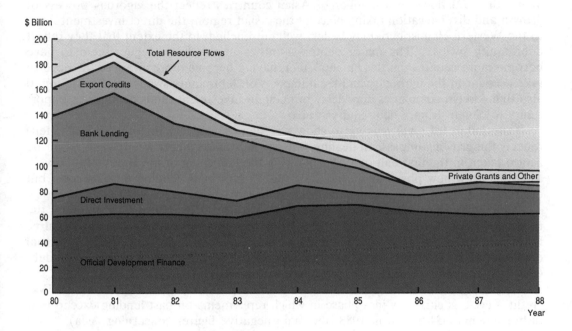

Net *Official Development Finance* ODF (which includes not only ODA but also less concessional multilateral flows and certain bilateral flows) reached an estimated $66 billion in 1988, roughly the same figure as in 1987 at constant prices and exchange rates. Bilateral ODA from all sources further declined in constant terms because of a further drop of the outflow from Arab countries. There was a recovery, however, of non-concessional multilateral net disbursements, notwithstanding higher amortization payments by borrowing countries, a marked increase in non-concessional disbursements from bilateral official sources (in particular disbursements of untied non-concessional loans by the Japanese Export-Import Bank under Japan's recycling programme), and the capitalisation of substantial amounts of interest arrears in debt consolidations, in particular of export credits, as a result of action in the Paris Club.

There was a positive flow of *export credits* for the first time since 1985, although this partly reflected a build-up of arrears which reduced the amount of amortization recorded and inflated the volume of short-term export credits, which as measured include arrears of interest. As in 1987, medium and long-term *export credit* disbursements amounted to some $20 billion on a gross basis.

The marked recovery of *foreign direct investment* (FDI) in 1987 and 1988 requires some comment. It is concentrated on two particular regions - the "Rest of Asia" (including countries such as Thailand, South Korea, Malaysia, Singapore) and the Western Hemisphere (where debt-equity swaps may have been an important factor).

FDI is currently accounting for about a quarter of total flows to Asia and the Western Hemisphere, and nearly 50 per cent of total flows to Upper Middle-Income countries. While the FDI flows to a number of Asian countries reflect the vigorous process of growth and diversification taking place in the Asian region, the direct investment flows to the Western Hemisphere may be less well entrenched, to the extent that they reflect debt-equity swaps. The major debtor countries in this latter region seem to have become more cautious on this "menu" item, having become more aware of the need to take account of the monetary and fiscal impacts of debt-equity swaps and having found also that foreign companies may delay bringing in investment funds pending an opportunity to benefit from a debt-equity swap.

The failure of *bank lending* to show any sign of recovery in 1988 (in fact it fell) reflects the growing impasse in dealing with the debt crisis which was recognised in the action taken in the first half of 1989, following the launching of the Brady "Initiative", to shift into a new phase of the debt strategy. Net bank lending to Asia rose, but declined slightly to Latin America and Sub-Saharan Africa.

Official and private reschedulings, together with private creditors' action under the menu approach, were a significant factor in maintaining the buoyancy of net resource flows in 1988. An estimated $2 billion of *interest arrears was capitalised* by official creditors, and ODA debt owed by certain poorer countries and some export credit debt owed by these and other debtor countries was forgiven.

Following substantial net disbursements during 1981-84, the IMF ("use of IMF credit") cycle is currently in a phase in which repayments on past lending exceed new disbursements (-$4 billion in 1988, the main negative figures concerning Asia). Net disbursements under the Structural Adjustment Facility (SAF) and the Enhanced Structural Adjustment Facility (ESAF) amounted to $0.5 billion in 1987 and 1988 respectively and are expected to rise to over $3 billion by 1990.

International interest rates rose markedly during 1988. This, together with repayment of interest arrears to banks by Brazil explains the large rise (15 per cent in current dollars) in interest payments in 1988.

Prospects for financial resource flows to developing countries in the next few years will be heavily influenced by actions to deal with debt problems. As has been mentioned above, the 1989 out-turn will probably reflect the first full year of disbursements from the IMF's Enhanced Structural Adjustment Facility, which could be running at the $3 billion level in 1990 and 1991, falling off thereafter as planned. Debt relief and debt reduction actions seem also set to gain momentum over the next few years. This will pose considerable problems for the measurement and interpretation of financial flow data. Such measures produce cash flow benefits for developing countries which will not show up always as increased financial flows on current definitions. They may, however, stimulate new financial flows and, it may be hoped, the return of flight capital. If the strategy works, then within a few years there should, in principle, be a much healthier level and pattern of developing-country financing. Other factors which will influence the future evolution of flows are the second Japanese "recycling" plan announced in July 1989 and the impact of the political crisis in China on financial flows to that country, which in recent years has emerged as a major importer of capital. (A fuller analysis of longer-term prospects for financial flows is contained in Chapter XI of Part 2 of this Report.)

2. AID VOLUME TRENDS AND PROSPECTS FOR DAC MEMBERS

1988 Aid Volume

Net official development assistance (ODA) from DAC Members rose by 16.1 per cent from $41.4 billion in 1987 to $48.1 billion in 1988. Adjusted for exchange-rate changes against the US dollar (4 per cent) and inflation (3 per cent) ODA measured at constant prices and exchange rates was 8.2 per cent above the 1987 level. The ODA/GNP ratio for DAC countries combined rose to 0.36 per cent, after the slight decline to 0.34 per cent in 1987. Bilateral aid from non-DAC sources declined again in 1988, mainly because of a further drop in real terms of flows from Arab countries. This led to a decrease in ODA from all sources of about 2 per cent.

The substantial growth of DAC ODA in 1988 was in contrast with the slight decline (1.6 per cent) in real terms which took place in 1987 and was well above the average

Table 3-2. KEY TOTALS FOR ODA FLOWS FROM DAC COUNTRIES

Net disbursements

	1970-75[a]	1975-80[a]	1980-85[a]	1985	1986	1987	1988
	a) $ billion, current prices and exchange rates						
Total ODA	9.7	18.9	27.7	29.4	36.7	41.4	48.1
of which:							
1. Bilateral	7.3	12.8	19.2	21.9	26.2	29.9	33.2
2. To multilateral agencies	2.4	6.1	8.5	7.5	10.5	11.5	14.9
	b1) $ billion, 1987 prices and exchange rates						
Total ODA	26.9	31.2	38.7	41.9	42.2	41.4	44.9
of which:							
1. Bilateral	21.6	21.2	27.0	31.2	30.1	29.9	31.0
2. To multilateral agencies	5.3	10.0	11.7	10.7	12.1	11.5	13.9
	b2) Percentage change over previous year						
Total ODA	2.4	4.4	3.1	1.2	0.7	− 1.9	8.2
of which:							
1. Bilateral	− 0.4	− 3.1	5.5	9.9	− 3.5	− 0.7	3.3
2. To multilateral agencies	12.3	7.4	− 2.4	− 17.7	13.1	− 5.0	20.9
	c) As percentage of GNP						
Total ODA	0.33	0.35	0.36	0.35	0.35	0.34	0.36
of which:							
1. Bilateral	0.25	0.24	0.25	0.26	0.25	0.25	0.25
2. To multilateral agencies	0.08	0.11	0.11	0.09	0.10	0.09	0.11
For further information:							
Grants by private voluntary agencies							
$ billion, current prices and exchange rates .	1.1	1.7	2.4	2.9	3.3	3.5	(4.2)
$ billion, 1987 prices and exchange rates ...	3.2	2.9	3.3	4.1	3.8	3.5	(3.9)
As percentage of GNP	0.04	0.03	0.03	0.03	0.03	0.03	0.03

a) Annual averages except *b2)*, where figures are for percentage change during period.

annual increase in real terms of about 2 per cent over the recent five-year period. The increase cannot be taken as an indication of a change in long-term trends since, as has often been noted in these reports, annual changes in net disbursements more frequently reflect accidents in the timing of aid disbursements rather than changes in underlying policies. Although, as will be seen below, the aid programmes of a number of DAC Members are on a rising trend, there was a concentration in calendar year 1988 of disbursement of funds available for the two fiscal years 1987/88 and 1988/89. This had depressed the 1987 figures while at the same time bringing forward some disbursements that would otherwise have been recorded in 1989, to the probable detriment of the 1989 figures.

The bunching of disbursements in 1988 was again especially noticeable in contributions to multilateral organisations, which rose by 19.8 per cent in real terms (compared with a real increase of 3.7 per cent for bilateral ODA) and accounted for 67 per cent of the $3.4 billion real increase in ODA from 1987 to 1988. It may be recalled in this connection that the fall in contributions to multilateral institutions in 1987 had accounted for more than 80 per cent of the decline in ODA between 1986 and 1987.

Table 3-3. CHANGES IN REAL TERMS IN DAC ODA AND CAPITAL
SUBSCRIPTION PAYMENTS, 1986-88

Net disbursements at 1987 prices and exchange rates

$ million

	1986-87		1987-88	
	Total ODA	Capital subscriptions	Total ODA	Capital subscriptions
Australia.................................	− 222	− 131	264	266
Austria	− 44	− 22	89	91
Belgium	21	2	− 106	− 94
Canada..............................	32	− 89	202	98
Denmark	− 5	3	9	8
Finland..............................	53	− 1	111	− 6
France...............................	497	152	94	− 174
Germany..............................	− 331	− 91	166	− 7
Ireland	− 20	− 15	3	5
Italy................................	− 301	− 357	422	− 115
Japan	790	173	716	243
Netherlands	11	18	48	− 40
New Zealand	− 12	3	2	− 9
Norway..............................	− 38	− 13	33	13
Sweden	85	85	11	− 29
Switzerland	26	9	41	7
United Kingdom	− 277	− 14	412	114
United States........................	− 935	47	863	1 165
Total DAC..........................	− 671	− 242	3 388	1 534

154

These data are strongly affected by the practice of recording subscriptions to major concessional multilateral funds (i.e., the soft windows of the multilateral development banks and IFAD) on a "deposit" rather than on an "encashment" basis. The timing of note deposits is notoriously irregular, and in 1988 data were influenced by a large concentration of note deposits made in connection with the 8th IDA Replenishment.

Table 3-3 shows that the timing of note deposits was a major factor behind the improved volume performances of some individual DAC countries. In the case of Australia and Austria, and even more so in that of Ireland and the United States, increased multilateral contributions offset declines in other ODA flows. They accounted for the bulk of the growth of Denmark's aid and for about half of that from Canada. Even in the case of Japan, whose total programme is on a strongly rising trend, increased contributions to multilateral programmes were responsible for some 34 per cent of the rise in real ODA. Conversely, the bulk of the decrease in Belgium's ODA in 1988 was accounted for by a decline in multilateral subscriptions.

All DAC countries (except Belgium) contributed to the exceptional 1988 ODA volume performance, although to varying degrees. The major increases in absolute amounts (in constant prices and exchange rates) came from the United States (about $860 million); Japan (about $720 million); Italy (about $420 million, a fall in contributions to IFIs notwithstanding); the United Kingdom (about $410 million); and Australia (about $270 million). Canada expanded its real ODA by some $200 million. Smaller but nonetheless significant increases were also recorded by France, Germany and Finland.

Norway, the Netherlands, Denmark and Sweden continue to stand out as the countries with the highest ODA/GNP ratios, with Norway in front at 1.10 per cent of GNP. Seven countries, however, remained below the DAC weighted average ODA/GNP ratio of 0.36 per cent. Increased ODA/GNP ratios on the part of some countries did not result in better burden-sharing. Only six DAC Members (the four named above and France and Finland) recorded ODA/GNP ratios higher than or equal to the unweighted average ratio.

ODA Volume Prospects for the Next Few Years

Against this background, the exceptional 1988 ODA growth should not be seen as the beginning of a period of rapid aid growth but rather as a result of special factors, just as in last year's report the 1987 ODA decline was explained as a combination of special factors which did not establish a new trend. Considering 1987 and 1988 to have been "off trend" years, and (with an expectation that the figures for 1989, too, will probably reflect some of these disturbances of timing) ODA still seems likely to continue to grow over the next few years at a rate close to that which has prevailed in recent years (roughly 2 per cent per annum in real terms).

This assessment is based on indications concerning the aid volume prospects of individual DAC countries. Since these indications have already been noted in Chapter XII of Part 2 and are described in greater detail in Section 3 below, they can be stated briefly.

ODA can still be expected to grow more rapidly than GNP in those countries which are aiming at ODA/GNP ratios higher than current ones. The largest contributor to

ODA growth will be Japan, which is aiming to reach the DAC average ODA/GNP ratio in 1992 (and can be expected to become the largest donor in absolute terms before then). France, which aims at 0.7 per cent of GNP at an unspecified date, and Italy, which intends to regain an ODA/GNP ratio of 0.40 per cent, should also make substantial contributions. Smaller increases in absolute terms should be forthcoming from Denmark (1 per cent of GNP in 1992), Finland (0.7 per cent of GNP by the end of the 1980s), Belgium (which hopes to achieve 0.7 per cent in 1993), and possibly from New Zealand, Switzerland and Austria, who have announced their intention to increase their ODA/ GNP ratios.

ODA growth in real terms roughly equal to GNP growth can be expected from the Netherlands, Norway and Sweden, which all achieved their volume targets in the 1970s, and whose aid should remain stable as a share of GNP in the years ahead. Aid from Denmark and Finland may be expected to follow the same pattern when these countries reach their volume targets.

Aid from Germany and the United Kingdom is, on present indications, likely to continue to expand in real terms but possibly not as fast as GNP. The case of Canada is somewhat complex. On recently announced plans ODA will grow more rapidly than GNP between fiscal years 1990/91 and 1993/94. Growth will start from a lower base, however, than that achieved in 1989 (ODA is to be subject to a one-time cutback in FY 1989/90) and the ODA/GNP ratio aimed at for 1993/94 is lower than the current one. Aid should nevertheless expand moderately in real terms between 1988 and 1993/94. No indications are currently available concerning the evolution of Australia's ODA for the next few years.

The outlook for aid from the United States continues to be heavily influenced by the need to reduce the deficit of the federal government. On currently available indications, the most likely outcome for the next few years is one of rough stability of aid flows in current prices. This in turn implies some decrease in ODA both in real terms and as a share of GNP. Ireland's aid will also probably be affected over the next few years by the effect on aid budgets of policies aiming at reducing the budget deficit.

3. TRENDS IN AID PATTERNS FOR INDIVIDUAL DAC MEMBERS

Australia

The evolution of Australia's aid in recent years has been characterised by sharp annual fluctuations reflecting mainly the difference between its fiscal and calendar years and the timing of contributions to international financial institutions. Thus, Australian aid disbursements (on a calendar year basis), after registering a drop in the ODA/GNP ratio from 0.47 per cent in 1986 to 0.34 per cent in 1987, rose sharply in 1988, increasing by 44 per cent in real terms to the equivalent of US$1 101 million, or 0.47 per cent of GNP. This increase was brought about by significantly higher contributions, measured on a deposit basis, to international financial institutions (which were exceptionally low in 1987). Bilateral disbursements continued to decline in real terms. The Australian

Net disbursements

Table 3-4. ODA PERFORMANCE OF DAC COUNTRIES IN 1988 AND RECENT YEARS

	$ million			Per cent of GNP						Per cent change 1988/87			Annual average % change in volume[b] 1982/83-1987/88
	1988 actual[a]	1987 actual[a]	1988 at 1987 prices and exchange rates	1975/79 average	1980/84 average	1987/88 average	1986	1987	1988	In national currency	In $	In volume terms[b]	
	(1)	(2)	(3)	(4)	(5)	(6)	(7)	(8)	(9)	(10)	(11)	(12)	(13)
Australia	1 101	627	901	0.51	0.48	0.41	0.47	0.34	0.47	56.8	75.5	43.6	−1.5
Austria	302	201	290	0.22	0.29	0.21	0.21	0.17	0.24	45.5	50.3	44.4	−5.1
Belgium	597	687	581	0.54	0.56	0.44	0.48	0.48	0.40	−14.5	−13.1	−15.4	−3.7
Canada	2 342	1 885	2 087	0.50	0.45	0.48	0.48	0.47	0.49	15.3	24.2	10.7	6.9
Denmark	922	859	868	0.72	0.76	0.88	0.89	0.88	0.89	5.6	7.3	1.0	5.8
Finland	608	433	544	0.18	0.29	0.55	0.45	0.49	0.59	33.6	40.4	25.7	16.4
France incl. DOM/TOM	6 865	6 525	6 618	0.59	0.72	0.73	0.70	0.74	0.72	4.3	5.2	1.4	2.3
France excl. DOM/TOM	4 777	4 489	4 605	0.32	0.46	0.51	0.44	0.51	0.50	5.5	6.4	2.6	3.5
Germany	4 731	4 391	4 556	0.39	0.46	0.39	0.43	0.39	0.39	5.4	7.8	3.8	−1.7
Ireland	57	51	54	0.15	0.20	0.20	0.28	0.19	0.20	7.6	10.3	5.3	−1.6
Italy	3 183	2 615	3 038	0.11	0.20	0.37	0.40	0.35	0.39	22.2	21.7	16.1	16.1
Japan	9 134	7 342	8 058	0.23	0.31	0.31	0.29	0.31	0.32	10.2	24.4	9.8	5.4
Netherlands	2 231	2 094	2 142	1.03	1.01	0.98	1.01	0.98	0.98	4.0	6.5	2.3	2.1
New Zealand	105	87	88	0.39	0.28	0.27	0.30	0.26	0.27	9.5	21.3	1.5	−0.2
Norway	985	890	923	0.83	0.97	1.10	1.17	1.09	1.10	7.0	10.6	3.6	4.9
Sweden	1 529	1 375	1 386	0.86	0.85	0.88	0.85	0.88	0.87	7.5	11.2	0.8	1.4
Switzerland	617	547	588	0.20	0.27	0.32	0.30	0.31	0.32	10.7	12.9	7.5	4.7
United Kingdom	2 645	1 871	2 283	0.45	0.37	0.30	0.31	0.28	0.32	30.0	41.3	22.0	−1.3
United States	10 141	8 945	9 808	0.24	0.24	0.20	0.23	0.20	0.21	13.4	13.4	9.6	−0.1
Total DAC	48 094	41 426	44 813	0.34	0.36	0.35	0.35	0.34	0.36	13.5	16.1	8.2	2.3
Memo:													
Unweighted average	—	—	—	0.45	0.48	0.50	0.51	0.49	0.51	—	—	—	—

a) At current prices and dollar exchange rates.
b) At 1987 prices and exchange rates.
Note: For additional comparative statistical data on essential aspects of the volume, terms and composition of the aid programme of individual DAC Members see "Basic Aid Data" in the Statistical Annex.

Government's aid volume intentions, however, are more accurately reflected by fiscal year aid budget data. As part of a general policy of budget restraint these were reduced in real terms by 11.9 per cent in the FY 1986/87 budget and by 3.1 per cent in FY 1987/88, resulting in a drop in the ODA/GNP ratio on a fiscal year basis from 0.45 per cent in 1985/86 to 0.36 per cent in 1987/88. The current 1989/90 aid budget allocation is estimated to correspond to 0.33 per cent of GNP compared to 0.37 per cent in FY 1988/89. Levels in FY 1988/89 and 1989/90, however, have been distorted by a decision to bring forward payments to the World Bank and the Asian Development Bank from 1989/90 to 1988/89. This had the effect of increasing aid expenditure in FY 1988/89 but decreasing expenditure in FY 1989/90. It remains the Australian Government's objective to bring the ODA/GNP ratio of budgetary aid expenditure up to a level of 0.4 per cent as soon as possible, but there will continue to be difficulties in making major gains given the economic and budgetary constraints faced by the Government.

Australian aid is provided entirely in grant form. In 1987-88 about one-third of total ODA was channelled through multilateral institutions. Bilateral aid remains significantly oriented towards recipients in the Asian and Pacific regions. In 1987-88 about 43 per cent of allocable bilateral ODA disbursements was provided to Papua New Guinea (PNG), Australia's main aid recipient, 12 per cent to other South Pacific island countries, 38 per cent to countries in Asia, notably the ASEAN countries, and the remainder to a number of countries in other regions, including Sub-Saharan Africa. Bilateral ODA remains in principle tied to procurement in Australia except for budget support to Papua New Guinea.

In line with Papua New Guinea's goal of fiscal self-reliance, both the Australian and PNG governments have agreed in a Treaty on Development Co-operation signed in May 1989 that Australian aid to that country be progressively reduced in real terms. It has also been agreed that there will be a shift from general budget support towards defined programme activities. Against this background it was decided to extend budget support at a level of A$275 million per annum until FY 1992/93 which would drop to A$260 million in FY 1993/1994. Project aid is planned to increase at the same time from A$15 million in FY 1988/89 to A$35 million in 1993/94. As regards Sub-Saharan Africa, a three-year A$100 million package of assistance was decided in 1988, focusing on food security and comprising food aid, training, staffing assistance, non-food commodity assistance and assistance through NGOs.

The reorganisation and the reinforcement of the Australian aid administration along the lines recommended in the Jackson Report was virtually completed in 1988. Major changes include the transformation of the former Bilateral Division into the Country Programmes Division, a substantial upgrading of the Policy Division, including the establishment of an Appraisals, Evaluation and Sectoral Studies Branch, and the grouping of commercial, community-based and international programmes in a separate division. The most dramatic change was in the Country Programmes Division, which is responsible for all aid forms programmed for a particular country or region. The restructuring of the division allows AIDAB (the Australian International Development Assistance Bureau) to introduce country programming as the central concept in the formulation of policy and management for the bulk of the aid programme. Another important aspect of the reorganisation is the increased autonomy given to AIDAB, both for aid policy formulation and the control of its own resources.

Austria

Austrian ODA, which had dropped to a low of 0.17 per cent of GNP in 1987, recovered sharply in 1988. ODA net disbursements increased by 44 per cent in real terms to the equivalent of $302 million or to 0.24 per cent of GNP, reflecting higher multilateral contributions (which were exceptionally low in 1987), while bilateral ODA remained unchanged in real terms. Within bilateral ODA, there was a significant fall in the net volume of concessional export credits from a share of 36 per cent to 18 per cent of total ODA in 1988, while development loans and bilateral grants expanded strongly. This sharp reduction of concessional export credits has substantially improved development profiles of Austrian aid. In the past the predominance of concessional export credits had led to relatively hard financial terms, a low level of bilateral untied ODA, a small share of bilateral aid allocated to the least developed and other low-income countries, and a low concentration on priority sectors, such as agriculture and rural development.

The Austrian authorities maintain their intention to reach the DAC average ODA/GNP ratio in the relatively near future, while further improving the quality of their aid programme. Following an extensive parliamentary debate on the Austrian aid programme in October 1988, Parliament instructed the Federal Ministries of Foreign Affairs and Finances to prepare a plan aiming at reaching the DAC average by 1993. Achievement of this objective will depend on the extent to which budgetary allocations for aid — which are currently constrained by the need to reduce public expenditure — can be significantly increased.

It is the intention of the Austrian authorities to base the envisaged expansion of the bilateral programme to an increasing extent on cofinancing arrangements with the World Bank (which benefit mainly Sub-Saharan African countries) and on a limited number of developing countries in Northern Africa, Asia and Latin America, where aid is to be provided in the framework of comprehensive country programming and in sectors where Austria possesses a particular know-how. Early in 1989, a new cofinancing agreement was concluded with the World Bank in the context of the Special Programme of Action (SPA) covering a total Austrian contribution of Sch 1 billion (about $80 million). In order to make the management of the programme more effective, a reorganisation of the aid administration in the Ministry of Foreign Affairs is being undertaken. This includes the establishment of country and regional desks, a strengthening of the functional capacity of the administration, and the setting up of a division responsible for aid planning and programming.

Belgium

Belgian aid, which had increased in 1987, met with a sharp setback in 1988 as disbursements declined by 15.4 per cent in real terms to the equivalent of $597 million. As a share of GNP, ODA decreased from 0.48 per cent in 1987 to 0.40 per cent in 1988, the lowest recorded ratio to date. A sharp fall in contributions to multilateral institutions, reflecting mainly the timing of contributions to IDA (there were none in 1988), accounted for the major part of the decrease in ODA. The level of Belgian aid, however, is expected to recover and to progress significantly, starting in 1990, since the Belgian government has decided to raise aid to 0.7 per cent of GNP by 1993. Some 40 per cent of bilateral aid is untied.

In April 1989, the Minister for Development Co-operation made public a series of recommendations aiming at stimulating a wide-ranging debate on Belgian aid policy. They include entrusting the preparation and implementation of aid activities to recipient countries; the strengthening of local representation; a reduction in the number of main recipient countries (while continuing to concentrate aid on low-income countries, particularly in Sub-Saharan Africa); a better adaptation of technical co-operation to the requirements of recipient countries; the possibility of reimbursing debts owed to Belgium in local currency to be used for financing development activities, particularly in social sectors; improved collaboration with non-governmental organisations; and a reorganisation of the General Administration for Development Co-operation (AGCD). In July 1989, Belgium agreed to forgive Zaire's total outstanding liabilities to the Belgian public sector.

Canada

In 1988 Canadian ODA expanded by 11 per cent in real terms to reach the equivalent of US$2 342 million. In relation to GNP it increased from 0.47 per cent in 1987 to 0.49 per cent in 1988. In April 1989, however, the Government cut its aid programme as part of a general policy of budget restraint and temporarily suspended the ODA volume targets which it had accepted in 1986 (0.50 per cent of GNP until FY 1990/91 and 0.60 per cent in FY 1995/96). Accordingly, Canadian aid appropriations will drop to 0.43 per cent of GNP in the current fiscal year (running from April 1989 to March 1990) but growth will resume in subsequent years. The Canadian Government has retained the principle of formula funding which pegs the aid budget to a percentage of GNP. Aid appropriations will rise by 0.02 per cent of GNP in FY 1990/91 and then by 0.005 per cent for the next three years to reach a figure between 0.46 per cent and 0.47 per cent of GNP in FY 1993/94.

In March 1988 the Canadian Parliament approved an important aid strategy report entitled "Sharing our Future" in which comprehensive policy guidelines were formulated for future Canadian aid. Among the many new initiatives contained in the report are a considerable easing of procurement restrictions (45 per cent of bilateral ODA commitments were untied in 1988), a substantial decentralisation of both CIDA personnel and authority to the field and a planned significant expansion of activities related to human resource development. Poverty alleviation, concentrating aid on poor countries, specific sectors and poor population groups, is given the highest priority in the new aid strategy. While the cuts in the aid programme decided in April 1989 will have a certain impact in operational terms on practically all of CIDA's programmes, the main aspects and basic orientation of the new aid strategy will be maintained. This means that Canada will continue to focus on poverty alleviation, on emphasizing human resource development and women in development, and on finding new ways to assist in promoting environmentally sound development. CIDA's decentralisation will also go ahead as planned to ensure improved programme delivery.

Since April 1986 all new bilateral development assistance has been extended in grant form. Bilateral aid is highly concentrated on very poor developing countries: least developed and other low-income countries account in most years for about 75 per cent of allocable bilateral ODA disbursements. There has been a notable shift of aid in favour of Sub-Saharan Africa, which in 1987 became the largest recipient area of Canadian aid. Canada has adapted its aid programme to the needs of highly indebted low-income countries and quick-disbursing aid forms were expanded in support of recipients' structural adjustment efforts in co-operation with the IMF and the World Bank. The share of Canadian aid channelled through multilateral institutions was 33 per cent in 1987/88. Canada has one of the most extensive systems of collaboration with the private sector including NGOs.

Denmark

In 1988 ODA net disbursements from Denmark remained virtually stable in real terms, amounting to $922 million. At 0.89 per cent the Danish ODA/GNP ratio exceeded again the 0.7 per cent target by a considerable margin. Further vigorous growth is to be expected given the Danish Parliament's decision in 1985 to increase aid appropriations by annual increments of 0.03 per cent of GNP until a 1 per cent of GNP aid appropriation target is achieved in 1992.

Danish development assistance policy remains governed by a set of both quantitative and qualitative principles. These include a strong poverty orientation in Danish assistance. Other important objectives are the integration in the development process of environmental considerations, of women's role in the development process and of respect for human rights. One of the quantitative objectives is that total ODA should be approximately equally divided between bilateral and multilateral aid. Quick-disbursing aid in the form of commodity assistance is provided in support of structural adjustment efforts in co-operation with the IMF and the World Bank. The share of bilateral ODA allocated to Sub-Saharan African countries is approximately 60 per cent.

A major review of Danish development assistance and of Danish aid administration was initiated in 1987 and led to a draft Plan of Action for Danish development assistance for the coming five-year period. This draft was elaborated by DANIDA, the Danish International Development Agency in the Ministry of Foreign Affairs. It was submitted to Parliament in the summer of 1988 and thoroughly debated in the public at large and subsequently by Parliament. A number of proposals, contained in the Plan, were approved by Parliament in November 1988 and implemented as of January 1989. They comprise the decision to abandon loans and thus to provide future aid entirely in grant form. It was also decided to move to a further decentralisation of both DANIDA personnel and authority to the field, to concentrate aid on a smaller number of recipients (20-25) over a five-year period, and to introduce comprehensive country programming for all aid recipients based on specific country analyses, and aid sector strategies for each of them. The continued strong Danish support for multilateral aid was also confirmed. While Denmark maintains its policy of requiring that about one-half of Danish bilateral aid be procured in Denmark, it has introduced a more flexible procurement policy as well as a new country programme system so as to avoid any negative effects of this policy.

European Economic Community

Aid from the European Economic Community (EEC), which had decreased in 1987, recovered very strongly in 1988. ODA disbursements rose by 45.6 per cent in ECUs (which corresponds to an increase in real terms of about 42 per cent) to a high of $2 909 million in 1988. Virtually all of the Community's ODA is in grant form. Approximately half of EEC aid is extended to 66 African, Caribbean and Pacific (ACP) States within the framework of the Lomé Convention. Since the majority of the ACP States (which are also recipients of Community food aid) are located in Sub-Saharan Africa this region receives a substantial part of EEC ODA; the Community is one of the major sources of aid to African countries south of the Sahara. The remainder of EEC aid is spread over a large number of other developing countries. Aid to Mediterranean and Central American developing countries is extended as part of multi-year agreements. ODA to the ACP States is free for procurement in the twelve member countries of the Community and in the ACP States; that to other countries is tied to procurement in EEC countries or in the recipient country. The EEC devoted a substantial share of its aid to agriculture and rural development in support to structural adjustment efforts, for which policy was defined in May 1988 by a Resolution of the Council of Ministers. Food aid accounts for a significant if fluctuating share in ODA. Fluctuations have also been a feature of disbursements under the Stabex and Sysmin schemes which respectively aim at stabilizing export earnings from agricultural products and at maintaining or restoring the viability of the mining capacity of recipient countries.

Negotiations for the renewal of the current Convention (Lomé III, covering the period 1986-90) between the Community and the ACP States are continuing. The new Convention is likely to emphasize demographic issues, environmental considerations and a strengthening of support for structural adjustment efforts.

Finland

Following the decision taken by the Finnish Government in 1980 to achieve 0.7 per cent of GNP in terms of ODA appropriations by the end of the decade, the growth of Finnish ODA has been one of the most rapid and sustained among DAC countries. In 1988 ODA net disbursements increased by 26 per cent in real terms to $608 million and the ODA/GNP ratio rose from 0.49 per cent in 1987 to 0.59 per cent in 1988. Budgetary aid appropriations for 1989 have been fixed at a level to reach 0.7 per cent of GNP in 1989. However, as it seems that the growth of GNP in current prices in 1989 may be faster than originally estimated, the ODA/GNP target may only be reached in 1990 in terms of appropriations. Since aid disbursements are normally relatively close to appropriations, it can be expected that the 0.7 per cent ODA disbursement target will be attained in the same year or at latest in 1991. This would make Finland the fifth DAC Member whose ODA disbursements reach the target of 0.7 per cent of GNP. There are no firm plans for expanding ODA beyond 0.7 per cent of GNP.

The Finnish aid programme remains characterised by a relatively high multilateral share, high concessionality and a large concentration of bilateral assistance on very poor recipients with a notable emphasis on countries in Sub-Saharan Africa. The bilateral programme retains a relatively narrow sectoral and sub-sectoral concentration, but in order to raise the share of socially-oriented activities some modifications have been decided in the sectoral distribution: one-third of bilateral assistance is to be channelled to agriculture and forestry, one-third to infrastructure and industrial development, and one-third to social development, including education and health.   Within the total sectoral distribution, assistance to forestry and forest industries is being given a specially high priority in view of Finland's growing concern for environmental protection.   Finland is prepared to act as a lead agency in the forestry sector in some recipient countries and has already accepted this role in Nepal.   Finland has continued and expanded its support for structural adjustment efforts, particularly in Sub-Saharan African countries.   High priority has been accorded to the strengthening of the Finnish aid programme at the operational level and there have been extensive improvements of the aid management system, although the country programming unit at FINNIDA may need some further strengthening.

A significant part of bilateral assistance is tied to procurement in Finland.   It is Finnish policy to concentrate ODA on sectors where Finland is internationally competitive.   A high procurement ratio of bilateral aid is seen as a means to contribute, among other things, to sustained public support for a rapidly growing aid programme.   In 1987 a new system of associated financing became operational, whereby the terms of export credits are softened through interest subsidies financed via the aid budget.   It is expected that these subsidies will increase gradually to about 4-5 per cent of Finnish ODA.

At the end of 1988, the Parliamentary Advisory Committee for Economic Relations between Finland and Developing Countries was renewed for a three-year term.   Its mandate covers broad policy issues related to world economic issues, development and trade and reflects the Government's growing support for a more comprehensive approach to development.   At the same time an independent group of experts was nominated by the Ministry of Foreign Affairs to prepare recommendations on Finnish development assistance during the 1990s.

France

Aid from France continued to expand in real terms in 1988 but at a somewhat slower pace than in 1987.   Total ODA (i.e., including flows to Overseas Departments and Territories — DOM/TOM) rose by 1.4 per cent in real terms to the equivalent of $6 865 million.   Aid to independent countries (i.e., excluding flows to the DOM/TOM) increased by 2.6 per cent as both bilateral aid and contributions to multilateral organisations expanded, the growth of the former being slightly more rapid.   As a share of GNP, French aid to independent countries stood at 0.50 per cent, a slight decline compared with 1987.   Aid disbursements are expected to continue to progress in the coming years since France is committed to raising ODA to independent countries to 0.7 per cent of GNP as soon as possible.   Contributions to multilateral institutions, which have increased substantially during the decade thanks largely to increased contributions to IDA and the regional development banks, are expected to continue to expand.   Higher priority is likely to be given to United Nations institutions, where France's participation has so far been more modest.

France's bilateral aid continues to be focused on African countries south of the Sahara, for which France is the largest source of bilateral aid. France is also a significant partner of the countries of the Maghreb. Technical co-operation, of which France is the largest contributor among DAC countries, accounts for a substantial but decreasing part of bilateral aid.

France supports current international efforts to assist African countries implementing structural adjustment efforts and stresses the importance of taking long-term development factors, including social aspects, into account in implementing these programmes.

The financial terms of French aid are above the concessionality threshold of the DAC Terms Recommendation but France is not in compliance with the Recommendation's sub-target for the least developed countries. Financial terms will soften, however, since structural adjustment loans to low-income countries in France's traditional area of concentration have been extended on IDA terms since the beginning of 1988. The terms of Treasury loans to countries outside this zone have also softened considerably. These loans, which until 1987 were associated with private funds in the framework of mixed credits, can now be extended directly on concessional terms (direct grant aid can also be supplied by the Treasury). About half of bilateral aid is untied.

In May 1989 France announced that it would cancel unconditionally all the outstanding ODA debt, amounting to 16 billion francs ($2.7 billion at 1988 exchange rates) owed to it by 35 poorer Sub-Saharan African countries.

Germany

In 1988, German ODA net disbursements increased by 3.8 per cent in real terms to $4 731 million reflecting a 15.5 per cent increase in multilateral contributions. The increase in multilateral ODA was largely due to higher contributions to the World Bank group and the EEC. In relation to GNP, total ODA remained stable at 0.39 per cent. The increase in German net ODA disbursements reported for 1988 follows a period of several years of decline. Future ODA volume prospects are difficult to predict. While there might be a further small increase in real terms in 1989, current financing prospects going beyond 1989 point to approximate stability in real terms in the volume of German aid. Larger budgetary resources than are currently envisaged would be required to ensure a significant real growth in German aid during the next few years and an increase in the ODA/GNP ratio.

Germany has a significant aid presence in all areas of the developing world. In 1987-88 aid to Sub-Saharan Africa accounted for about 27 per cent of allocable bilateral ODA, aid to South and South-East Asia for 41 per cent and Latin America for 12 per cent, with major aid involvements also in North Africa, the Middle East and European developing countries. The proportion of German aid provided to low-income countries (53 per cent in 1987-88) corresponds roughly to the DAC average. The share of German aid channelled through multilateral institutions is of the order of 30-33 per cent, including contributions to the EEC, and about 20 per cent if these are excluded. About half of bilateral aid is untied.

There is a growing emphasis on measures to protect the environment (with increasing engagement in the forestry sector) and on anti-poverty actions, including some interesting innovative approaches to channel aid for self-help measures through non-governmental institutions in developing countries. A relatively large share of bilateral aid supports basic infrastructure projects in energy, communication and transportation. The volume of technical assistance is comparatively large, but includes a significant proportion of cultural assistance and imputed students' costs. Commodity assistance and local-cost financing tended to increase during the recent past. Disbursements of commodity aid under IMF/World Bank led structural adjustment programmes are still small, but they are expected to increase during the next few years.

The average grant element of German aid meets the DAC terms objectives but remains below the DAC average. Steps have been taken recently, however, to improve financial terms together with debt relief actions. Very substantial resources are mobilised by German NGOs (0.06 per cent of GNP compared with a DAC average of 0.03 per cent).

Among new initiatives taken in the recent past are the decision to grant further debt relief to a selected group of low-income countries and an improvement in the financial terms of loans to all low-income countries. From 1989 onwards recipients other than least developed countries can be given grants for self-help-oriented measures to fight poverty and for projects in the field of social infrastructure and environmental protection. Together more than one-third of the recipients of German development assistance will see the terms of their financial assistance improved. Other new initiatives are a reorganisation of the Ministry of Economic Co-operation and of the implementing institution for technical co-operation (GTZ), aiming at strengthening their capacity for a more strategically oriented country focus approach. Germany has traditionaly concentrated overseas aid representation in its embassies, with a view to integrate all relevant aspects under the responsibility of the ambassador. While it has been possible to increase the number of field staff during the reporting period, the number of aid representatives in the field seems still to be relatively small compared to the size and complexity of the German activities.

Ireland

Ireland's aid increased by 5.1 per cent in real terms to the equivalent of $57 million in 1988 and, expressed as a share of GNP, rose from 0.19 per cent to 0.20 per cent. A rise in contributions to IDA (due to timing factors) and to the EEC compensated for a steep fall in bilateral aid and in voluntary contributions to multilateral organisations. The outlook for aid volume over the next few years remains highly uncertain since the Government is determined to reduce the budget deficit.

Multilateral contributions excluding those to the EEC accounted for close to a quarter of total ODA in 1987/88; if contributions to the EEC are included the share of multilateral in total aid rises to slightly over one half. Bilateral aid, which is extended on an all-grant basis, consists mainly of technical co-operation in agriculture, rural development and education, and is highly concentrated on four Sub-Saharan African countries, three of which are among the least-developed. About half of bilateral aid is untied.

Italy

Italy's aid, which had decreased in 1987, recovered in 1988. Net ODA disbursements increased by 16.1 per cent in real terms to reach the equivalent of $3 183 million; expressed as a share of GNP, they rose from 0.35 per cent in 1987 to 0.39 per cent in 1988. A rise of 22.4 per cent in bilateral aid, reflecting increased grant and loan disbursements, accounted for the totality of the growth in ODA. The financial terms of Italy's ODA remain concessional and meet the general provisions of the DAC Terms Recommendation (to which Italy has not subscribed, however). Net lending represented 33 per cent of bilateral ODA in 1987-88. The bulk of bilateral aid is tied to procurement in Italy. Sub-Saharan African countries continue to receive the major part of bilateral ODA and Italy is a significant contributor of concessional flows to these countries and participates actively in international efforts to assist their structural adjustment programmes. Contributions to multilateral organisations remained stable in real terms. Other multilateral contributions, however, in particular those to regional development banks and funds, rose markedly. Contributions to multilateral organisations represented 17 per cent of total ODA in 1987-88; if account is taken of contributions to the EEC this share rises to 27 per cent. ODA can be expected to continue to expand in 1989, since the Italian authorities have indicated that their objective is to achieve an ODA/GNP ratio of 0.40 per cent.

Japan

In 1988 Japanese net ODA disbursements increased by 9.8 per cent in real terms to the equivalent of $9 134 million. This corresponds to 0.32 per cent of GNP, slightly up from the 1987 ratio of 0.31 per cent. Growth was more balanced than in 1987, when the rise in ODA mainly reflected a very strong expansion of bilateral lending. In 1988 bilateral aid expanded by 10.3 per cent in real terms as grants rose by 21.7 per cent, including a marked increase in technical assistance, while net bilateral loans increased by 2.4 per cent. Contributions to multilateral organisations and programmes increased by 8.4 per cent. 1988 was the first year of the 1988-92 period during which Japan intends to raise the share of Japan's ODA in total DAC ODA to a level commensurate with the share of Japan in DAC GNP and to disburse more than $50 billion (its 4th medium-term target). Aid disbursements are expected to continue to increase given the determination of the Japanese authorities to reach their aid volume targets.

Multilateral contributions accounted for 30 per cent of total ODA in 1987-88. Although interest rates on ODA loans have tended to decline, and those for loans to the least developed countries have been lowered to 1 per cent, Japan did not comply with the DAC Recommendation on the Financial Terms of Assistance. About two-thirds of ODA loans commitments are untied for world-wide procurement and the remainder is untied for procurement in developing countries. About 40 per cent of grants are untied. Further steps were taken in the direction of untying in 1988 when Japan decided gradually to untie the engineering services components of ODA loans and to allow foreign consultants to participate in Japanese grant-financed development surveys. Restrictions on local-cost financing were eased in 1988. The share of low-income countries in Japan's ODA is above the DAC average. The major part of bilateral aid is extended to Asian developing countries. Japan is expected to be the principal participant in the Multilateral Aid Initiative in favour of the Philippines. A substantial amount of aid is also directed to Sub-Saharan Africa, much of it as part of Japan's contribution to international action in support of structural adjustment efforts. In June 1989 Japan announced the launching in FY 1990 of a three-year $600 million untied grant programme in favour mainly of low-income Sub-Saharan African countries to succeed an earlier $500 million effort. In 1989 the Japan International Development Organisation (JAIDO) was established, with public and private funds, to help promote direct private investment in developing countries. Measures taken to strengthen aid co-ordination and management include the setting up in 1988 of a cabinet-level Council for Economic Co-operation, consisting of 14 ministers, a strengthening of staff both in Japan and in overseas representations, and the creation in 1989 of the Japan International Co-operation System with a view to improving the procurement and maintenance of equipment financed with JICA grants and others. A revised recycling plan amounting to $65 billion, to supersede the current $30 billion one, was announced at the 1989 Western Economic Summit meeting. It will make use of public and private funds to contribute to a further easing of the socio-economic difficulties of the developing countries, including $10 billion earmarked for the countries to which the "Strengthened Debt Strategy" applies. Japan also announced at the 1989 Western Economic Summit Meeting that it would expand and strengthen its bilateral and multilateral aid for environmental preservation over the next three years with an approximate target of Y 300 billion (about $2.25 billion).

Netherlands

In 1988, net ODA disbursements, which have on average represented close to 1 per cent of GNP for the past ten years, increased by 2.3 per cent in real terms to $2 231 million. The ODA/GNP ratio remained stable at 0.98 per cent, exceeding the 0.7 per cent of GNP target, as it has done every year since 1976. ODA is expected to remain in the vicinity of 1 per cent of GNP; the long-term policy is to devote 1.5 per cent of net national income to development co-operation. Contributions to multilateral institutions, excluding those to the EEC, represent about one quarter of total aid (if contributions to the EEC are included this ratio rises to slightly over 30 per cent). The financial terms of aid are highly concessional. About 40 per cent of total ODA is untied. Some 40 per cent of bilateral aid is extended to ten low-income "programme countries"; substantial amounts of ODA, mainly in the form of sector assistance, are given to other developing countries. The shares of the least developed and other low-income countries in GNP and in ODA are well above the DAC average. High priority is given to aid to agriculture and rural development. The Netherlands participates in international actions in favour of low-income debt-distressed countries by means of flexibly administered policy-related assistance, mainly in the framework of co-financing with multilateral institutions.

A report on Development Co-operation Policy in the 1990s will be submitted to Parliament in 1989. It focuses on the quality and management of the aid programme and contains recommendations aimed at better adapting the Netherlands aid to future requirements.

New Zealand

In 1988 New Zealand ODA remained virtually stable in real terms to reach $105 million. As a result of GNP decline the ODA/GNP ratio increased slightly from 0.26 per cent in 1987 to 0.27 per cent. In 1986 the New Zealand Government had adopted a target for ODA appropriations of 0.51 per cent of GNP to be reached in FY 1990/91. Given the present policy of general budget restraint, it is not likely that the target will be reached by the date foreseen. Aid appropriations account for about 0.6 per cent of the total central budget, a percentage well below that for most other DAC countries.

All New Zealand aid is extended in grant form. Multilateral contributions accounted for about 17 per cent of total ODA in 1987/88, significantly below the DAC average of 24.7 per cent (excluding contributions to the EEC). The bilateral programme shows a relatively narrow geographic concentration. Close to 90 per cent of allocable bilateral ODA is disbursed to the South Pacific Island countries, where lack of natural resources, small size, isolation, and an insufficient number of trained people pose serious development problems. Most of the remaining aid is provided to the ASEAN region, with small amounts allocated to Sub-Saharan African countries. The strategy for New Zealand's bilateral assistance programme to Africa was recently revised. To make New Zealand's contributions to African development more effective, they will be targetted to specific sectors in which New Zealand has a comparative advantage, such as dairying, forestry, energy and water resource management. About half of bilateral aid is untied.

The New Zealand aid administration in the Ministry of Foreign Affairs was completely restructured in 1988. The most signficant features of this reorganisation are the application of increased resources to systematic country programming, a more comprehensive planning of sector priorities, and an upgrading of the economic analytical strength of the staff at the level of project identification, appraisal and evaluation. This will enable the aid administration to develop country strategies based on improved economic and social impact analysis.

Norway

After a slight decline in 1987, ODA net disbursements increased by 3.7 per cent to reach $985 million in 1988. The ODA/GNP ratio rose from 1.09 per cent in 1987 to 1.10 per cent in the following year and remained the highest among DAC Member countries. Aid appropriations amounted in 1988 to $951 million, corresponding to 2.3 per cent of the central government budget and to 1.11 per cent of GNP. In the Long-Term Programme covering the years 1990-93 it is the Government's stated policy that the appropriations will be maintained at the present level measured as a share of GNP.

42 per cent of bilateral ODA was extended to least developed countries in 1988; Sub-Saharan Africa accounted for 55 per cent. Norway supports structural adjustment programmes implemented by the World Bank and IMF in its main partner countries while endeavouring, at the same time, to mitigate harmful social effects of such action. Multilateral contributions, whether measured as a share of total ODA or of GNP, are

168

substantial by DAC standards and in 1988 they equalled 42 per cent of total ODA (total DAC 31 per cent) and 0.47 per cent of GNP (total DAC 0.11 per cent). Norwegian ODA is almost entirely extended in grant form. About 60 per cent of bilateral aid is untied.

The Government has remained committed to a strengthening of international co-operation in environment, activities in this area being identified as a vital element in Norwegian development co-operation. Renewed emphasis has also been placed on initiatives aimed at promoting women in development, particularly in the agricultural sector.

Through a restructuring of Norway's aid administration, which became effective in March 1989, NORAD was re-established as an autonomous executing agency, placed administratively under the Ministry of Development Co-operation; furthermore, NORAD was reorganised along geographical instead of functional/sectoral lines to allow a strengthening of its programme management capacity and country-specific expertise.

Sweden

Sweden was the first DAC Member country to reach the international 0.7 per cent target (in 1975) and has since then attained this target for 14 consecutive years. In recent years the ODA volume has grown roughly at the same pace as GNP, fluctuations in individual years being due mainly to the timing of contributions to certain multilateral agencies. In 1988, ODA net disbursements remained virtually unchanged in real terms from the previous year to reach $1 529 million. The ODA/GNP ratio declined marginally from 0.88 per cent to 0.87 per cent but remained one of the highest among DAC Member countries. ODA is likely to stay at a high level given the Government's declared intention to maintain appropriations at a ratio of 1 per cent of GNP.

The share of multilateral contributions accounted in 1988 for 31 per cent of total ODA (thus coinciding with the total DAC average). The Swedish ODA programme remains characterised by the provision of aid funds almost exclusively in grant form. In Sweden's geographical distribution policy, emphasis has so far been placed on poorer developing countries and in 1988, 46 per cent of bilateral ODA was channelled to least developed countries. Sub-Saharan Africa accounted for 57 per cent of Swedish bilateral ODA in the same year. Two-thirds of bilateral aid is untied.

One of the five principal objectives established for Swedish development co-operation refers to environmental protection and states that ODA should contribute to the sustainable use of natural resources. In line with this objective, SIDA, the main executing agency for bilateral ODA, has recently adopted a plan of action for activities related to environmental issues. Emphasis is also placed on a fuller integration of women in development concerns into ODA projects and programmes. In FY 1988/89 a new type of assistance for special projects in debt-distressed countries was introduced, comprising bilateral aid in the form of balance-of-payments support extended in joint action with other donors as well as contributions through multilateral institutions such as the World Bank and IMF. Humanitarian assistance aimed at promoting democracy and human rights, particularly in southern Africa and Latin America, has become an important element in the bilateral aid programme over the last few years.

A review of organisation and working methods within the bilateral programme was initiated in April 1989 with a view to strengthening the structure for implementation of the growing volume of development aid channelled to recipients outside the group of 17 so-called programme countries, including an increasing number of recipients in the middle-income category.

Switzerland

Switzerland's aid continued to rise in 1988. ODA increased by 7.5 per cent in real terms to the equivalent of $617 million in 1988 as both bilateral aid and contributions to multilateral organisations expanded; the ODA/GNP ratio increased from 0.31 per cent to 0.32 per cent. Aid is expected to continue to expand and according to the Confederation's financial plan it should reach the DAC average ODA/GNP ratio early in the 1990s.

Multilateral contributions accounted for 28 per cent of ODA in 1987/88. More than half of bilateral aid, which is on an all-grant basis, is extended to African countries south of the Sahara and the shares of the least developed and other low-income countries in Swiss aid are above the DAC average. Marked emphasis is given to aid to agriculture. The share of programme assistance is expanding steadily. About 60 per cent of bilateral ODA is untied.

United Kingdom

The aid volume of the United Kingdom has declined in real terms over the past several years and its ODA/GNP ratio is now below the DAC average. In 1988, however, United Kingdom net disbursements of ODA increased sharply, rising by 22 per cent in real terms to $2 645 million, with increases in both bilateral and multilateral ODA. This reflects a 13 per cent increase in aid appropriations for FY 1988/89 over the previous fiscal year, as well as higher disbursements to some major recipients, including India, which drew most of their FY 1987/88 allocations in the first quarter of 1988, and to higher contributions to the World Bank Group and the EEC. As a share of GNP, ODA rose from 0.28 per cent in 1987 to 0.32 per cent in 1988, the highest ODA/GNP ratio since 1985. Future aid figures announced in the statement on public expenditure of November 1988 indicate an increase in aid expenditure averaging 5.4 per cent per annum during the fiscal year period 1988/89-1991/92. This should allow some increase in the real value of British aid but would not be sufficient to increase the ODA/GNP ratio.

The programme remains characterised by high concessionality, a large concentration on very poor developing countries and a strong emphasis on environmentally sound development. The share of United Kingdom aid channelled through multilateral institutions is relatively large: 46 per cent, including contributions to the EEC, in 1987-88, and 27 per cent if these are excluded. The United Kingdom's aid administration is notable for a strong economic analytical capacity in the areas of country and sector programming and project appraisal.

The United Kingdom has made considerable efforts to adapt its aid programme to the needs of highly indebted low-income countries. There has been a considerable expansion of quickly disbursable programme assistance and technical co-operation in support of recipients' structural adjustment efforts in co-operation with the IMF and the World Bank. The share of bilateral aid disbursed to Sub-Saharan African countries was of the order of 40 per cent in 1987-88 and registered a sharp increase over the past few years.

The bulk of British bilateral aid remains tied to procurement in Britain and the United Kingdom continues to have one of the highest tying ratios of bilateral aid among DAC Members. In spite of a recent more extensive use of the Aid and Trade Provision (ATP), the volume of associated financing is not planned to grow as a proportion of the British aid programme.

United States

In 1988 the United States, whose aid had fallen in 1987, recorded an increase in net ODA disbursements of 9.6 per cent in real terms to $10 141 million. As a result of buoyant GNP growth, however, the ODA/GNP ratio rose only to 0.21 per cent. The increase in aid, which substantially exceeded the average rate of growth in recent years, was due — as in the case of other DAC countries — to a number of special factors including, mainly, the timing of contributions to multilateral organisations. These increased by two-thirds largely because of the payment during the calendar year of two instalments on the contribution to IDA. Contributions to regional development banks and funds also increased. Bilateral aid, on the other hand, decreased by 6.6 per cent in real terms in spite of a marked rise in technical assistance disbursements. The level of appropriations for aid in recent years suggests that ODA disbursements may remain roughly stable in current prices in the near future. Longer-term volume prospects are uncertain given the need to reduce the federal budget deficit.

The financial terms of ODA are above the concessionality threshold of the DAC Recommendation on the Financial Terms of Assistance but the United States is not in compliance with the Recommendation because ODA commitments are too low. ODA extended as part of the programmes of AID (Economic Support Fund and Development Assistance) has since October 1988 consisted exclusively of grants; ODA loans are now limited to the PL 480 food aid programme. The United States is one of the DAC Member countries whose multilateral contributions have fluctuated most sharply as a result of the timing of legislation (in recent years the share of these contributions in total ODA has ranged from 13 to 33 per cent). The Economic Support Fund with appropriations of roughly $3.3 billion in FY 1989 remains the largest component of bilateral ODA but its share in bilateral aid has tended to decrease in recent years. Extended mainly to countries of special political and security interest to the United States it has tended to be concentrated on the Middle East but also serves as a source of quick-disbursing programme aid to countries undertaking structural adjustment reforms. AID's Development Assistance programme, which is designed primarily to support economic growth and its equitable distribution and places strong emphasis on environmental considerations, is extended mainly to low-income countries in the form of technical

171

assistance and project aid.   The Development Fund for Africa was established in FY 1988 to provide policy-related assistance in a flexible manner to countries of that region (which also receive ESF financing and PL 480 food aid).   Food aid loans and grants are extended primarily to low-income countries.   The share of the least developed and other low-income countries in United States ODA and GNP are below the DAC average.   About one-third of bilateral ODA is not tied to procurement in the United States.   Beginning in FY 1990, ODA debt relief is to be extended to low-income African coutries on a case-by-case basis.

The United States development assistance policies and programmes have recently been extensively reviewed by the Administration, by the Congress and by private bodies. New legislation to replace the Foreign Assistance Act of 1961, which with amendments has been the legislative base for much of the United States aid programme, is being enacted.

II

AID FROM NON-DAC SOURCES

1. OVERVIEW

The OECD tries to maintain a full picture of international aid flows including assistance from non-DAC resources.   Aid from these sources, mainly CMEA and Arab countries but also some non-DAC OECD countries and other developing countries, now stands at about $8 billion.   As can be seen from Table 1 in the Statistical Annex (Basic Aid Data) the proportion of "world ODA" coming from non-DAC sources has fluctuated considerably, primarily because of the rise and subsequent decline of Arab aid, and is now back at some 15 per cent.   The Soviet Union and Saudi Arabia are the largest single non-DAC sources of aid; the two together accounted for over 80 per cent of all non-DAC aid in 1987 and 1988.   In relation to GNP, Saudi Arabia remains the leading donor.   No comparable figures are available for the USSR.

Arab aid, which was a major additional aid source for the decade after the oil price rises, has been declining since 1981, except in 1986 and thus has had a depressing effect on total world ODA availability in recent years.   In interpreting these trends, however, it is important to keep in mind the quite exceptional circumstances during the surplus years.   The remainder of this chapter provides more detailed information on aid from the various non-DAC donor groups.

2. NON-DAC OECD COUNTRIES

A number of OECD countries, although not members of the DAC, have aid programmes or at least contribute to multilateral development assistance institutions.

Iceland's development assistance declined in 1988 to $1.4 million, equivalent to 0.02 per cent of GNP.   The decline is due to lower multilateral contributions.   Bilateral assistance is mainly extended to Cape Verde.   Special amounts were also set aside for Ethiopia and Central America in 1988.

ODA from *Luxembourg* has more than doubled in absolute figures over the past four years.   It increased from $7 million in 1984 to $18 million in 1988.   It went up

173

from 0.22 to 0.29 per cent of GNP over the same period. Most of this aid continues to be channelled through multilateral organisations, particularly the programmes of the EEC. IDA also received fairly substantial contributions from Luxembourg in 1987 and 1988, while contributions to United Nations agencies remained low. In spite of the fact that multilateral contributions doubled from $5.5 million in 1984 to $11 million in 1988, their share in total ODA fell from around three-quarters on average until 1986 to 60 per cent in 1988. This can be explained by the fact that in December 1985 the Government introduced legal and administrative arrangements enabling it to establish a development co-operation programme which is constantly increasing. Bilateral aid thus rose from less than $2 million in 1984 to over $7 million in 1988. The bulk of this aid is administered by a Development Co-operation Fund set up within the Ministry of Foreign Affairs at the end of 1985. The fund runs the Ministry's bilateral projects, cofinances projects submitted by Luxembourg NGOs, and contributes to the financing of experts and, to some extent, trainees. The fund is financed by annual budgetary appropriations and occasionally from budget surpluses. Finance for operations by the Development Co-operation Fund is generally in the form of grants. Other ministries are also involved in the development co-operation effort of Luxembourg, particularly the Ministries of Treasury, Finance and Education. In 1988, the main recipients of bilateral aid from Luxembourg were, in order of importance, Senegal, Tanzania, Cape Verde, Burundi, India and Burkina Faso. Most projects concerned health, social and agricultural aid, technical assistance, vocational training and feasibility studies.

Spain's gross ODA disbursements rose from $172 million in 1987 to $240 million in 1988, and from 0.06 to 0.07 per cent of GNP. The increase resulted from larger

Table 3-5. AID FROM NON-DAC DONORS

	1980	1985	1986	1987	1988
$ billion (current prices)					
Non-DAC OECD countries[a]	0.17	0.23	0.27	0.23	0.38
CMEA countries[b]	2.83	3.62	4.64	5.01	4.69
Arab countries[c]	9.54	3.61	4.50	3.29	2.34
Other LDC donors[d]	0.71	0.44	0.65	0.49	0.41
Total	13.25	7.90	10.06	9.02	7.82
Share of aid in GNP (per cent)					
Non-DAC OECD countries	0.06	0.10	0.09	0.06	(0.08)
Arab countries	3.26	1.33	1.83	1.25	0.86
Share in World ODA (per cent)					
Non-DAC OECD countries	0.4	0.6	0.6	0.5	0.7
CMEA countries..................	7.0	9.7	9.9	9.9	8.4
Arab countries	23.5	9.7	9.6	6.5	4.2
Other LDC donors...............	1.8	1.2	1.4	1.0	0.7
Total	32.7	21.2	21.5	17.9	14.0

a) Greece, Iceland, Luxembourg, Portugal and Spain.
b) Bulgaria, CSSR, GDR, Hungary, Poland, Romania and USSR.
c) Algeria, Iraq, Kuwait, Libya, Qatar, Saudi Arabia and UAE.
d) China, India, Israel, Korea, Nigeria, Venezuela and Yugoslavia.

multilateral contributions, which were primarily due to a doubling of the EEC aid budgets, and larger gross disbursements of concessional export credits. *Net* disbursements will have been lower but data on repayments of concessional export credits are not available. Bilateral grants declined, mainly as a result of delays in the aid programme for Equatorial Guinea. Main recipients of Spanish aid in 1988 were, in order of magnitude, Ecuador, China, Nicaragua, Bolivia and Venezuela. In 1988, the Spanish Government established an Agency for International Co-operation for the implementation of its development co-operation projects and programmes. The agency operates under the authority of the Foreign Ministry. Spain also signed a protocol with the Inter-American Development Bank for the creation of a $500 million fund at the Bank. It will provide $150 million additionally to subsidise the interest rate of the loans to be extended from the fund, and about $25 million in grants for the provision of technical assistance related to projects financed by the fund.

3. CMEA COUNTRIES

The volume of CMEA aid in 1988 is estimated to have declined to $4.7 billion. The USSR continued to provide 90 per cent of total estimated net ODA disbursements, i.e. $4.2 billion. The Eastern European countries, mainly the German Democratic Republic (GDR), Czechoslovakia and Bulgaria, extended about $0.5 billion in net aid to the developing countries. Hungary also provided some development assistance. Aid figures stated by the USSR and several East European countries in various UN fora are much higher. These data include forms of economic co-operation which fall outside the DAC definition of ODA. They comprise, moreover, types of contribution which are difficult to quantify. The USSR, however, is considering a redefinition of its aid concept together with a review of its statistical reporting practices.

Growing budget deficits, combined with internal priorities such as the reorganisation of the economy and in the case of the USSR the reconstruction of Armenia, will limit the resources available for aid. Multi-year commitments, however, towards some of the major recipients of CMEA aid (i.e., Cuba, Mongolia and Viet Nam), should mitigate the decline.

1988 witnessed further progress in the USSR's new approach to international economic and political relations, and increasing attention is being paid to regional co-operation and organisations. In order to integrate its economy more closely into international economic relations and to enhance the efficiency of its aid programme, the USSR showed growing interest in and support for multilateral organisations and aid co-ordination. In May 1989 it participated for the first time in a joint World Bank-UNDP chaired meeting of aid donors to Guinea Bissau, a relatively small recipient of Soviet aid. On this occasion, the USSR stated its intention to attend all future meetings concerned with developing countries for which it is an aid donor, including UNDP Round Tables and, if possible, World Bank consultative group meetings. The USSR also indicated willingness to participate in local aid co-ordination and might envisage cofinancing arrangements with both the World Bank and bilateral donors. The USSR contributed for the first time in 1988 to the United Nations Population Fund, but total contributions to the UN organisations remained, nevertheless, very small ($7 million).

Table 3-6. CMEA COUNTRIES' ESTIMATED NET DISBURSEMENTS
TO DEVELOPING COUNTRIES AND MULTILATERAL AGENCIES

$ million

	1980	1985	1986	1987	1988
USSR	2 313	3 064	4 118	4 485	4 210
Eastern Europe	514	554	521	521	480
Total..............................	2 827	3 618	4 639	5 006	4 690
of which: Bilateral	2 813	3 605	4 625	4 988	4 666
Multilateral	14	13	14	18	24

In 1989, the USSR attended, as an observer, the annual meeting of the Asian Development Bank for the third consecutive time and is seeking to become a member of this institution.   It has also applied for membership in the Pacific Economic Co-operation Council.   Bulgaria and Czechoslovakia are envisaging membership in the IMF and the World Bank, institutions of which Hungary, Poland and Romania are already members.

To compensate for a stagnating and possibly declining aid volume, emphasis continued to be laid on more efficiency both in the Soviet aid administration and in the recipient countries.   Better quality of aid and higher returns for the Soviet economy are other priorities.   The aid administration was reorganised at the beginning of 1988 and lies now with the Ministry of Foreign Economic Relations.

Following the restructuring of the economy, Soviet enterprises are expected to be self-financing and profitable and to implement projects directly in countries receiving Soviet assistance.   In countries that continue to have a centrally planned economy, such as Cuba, this may create problems, because they will have to adapt their system and deal directly with the newly independent Soviet factories and agencies.   Furthermore, since a number of Soviet firms may retain part of the hard currency earned from business relations with foreign customers, they are likely to prefer producing for Western markets rather than for the aid administration, which will only pay in roubles.

New forms of economic co-operation other than concessional aid have been worked out and are increasingly put into operation.   They consist mainly of joint ventures, the financing of projects the output of which is entirely destined for the developed CMEA countries' markets, the provision of labour for the development of remote areas in the USSR, etc.   A large number of students and trainees who have studied in Czechoslovakia and the GDR are working for about two years after termination of their training in their host countries, thus reimbursing the scholarships.

Although most repayments on CMEA countries' loans are made in local goods, debt reschedulings have been increasing.   Mr. Gorbatchev announced in December 1988 the USSR's intention to grant a debt moratorium of up to 100 years on debt owed by the least developed countries and in some cases to write it off altogether. Reportedly Angola, Ethiopia, Mozambique and Yemen AR will have their debt written off, as well as 18 other countries, which have not been named. Zambia benefitted from a debt moratorium, although it is not a least developed country. Other countries which were granted debt relief in 1988 were Afghanistan ($134 million) and Peru ($905 million, including military aid). Among the East European countries, Bulgaria rescheduled the debt owed by Tanzania and Poland rescheduled the debt service owed by Morocco in 1987 and 1988.

Despite dissatisfaction over the economic performance of the main recipients, CMEA aid in 1988 remained concentrated on Cuba, Mongolia and Viet Nam. More-over, Mongolia and Viet Nam have again been running large deficits in their trade with the USSR and a few Eastern European countries, which are automatically converted to long-term low-interest credits which can be rolled over and are eventually written off altogether. By contrast, Cuba has recorded a surplus for a number of years. The other communist developing countries (Afghanistan, Kampuchea, Korea Dem. and Laos) also continued to receive large amounts of CMEA assistance. Given the dete-riorating economic situation of these countries, this trend is likely to continue in the near future. Economic aid to Afghanistan will remain high, in particular since the USSR has pledged Rb 400 million in humanitarian assistance to be channelled through the UN System. Nicaragua might see its aid receipts stagnate or even decline in the near future, although the USSR promised to continue to provide 60 per cent of the country's needs of oil and oil products in 1989. In 1988, the USSR extended a $17 million long-term loan for the development of the fishing industry and a $4 million food aid grant.

Among the other developing countries India remained by far the largest recipient of Soviet aid. In 1988 it obtained for the fourth consecutive year a large new frame credit ($5.2 billion) at relatively soft terms (53 per cent grant element). The credit, the largest ever extended to India by the USSR, is to be used for the construction of two nuclear power stations and a thermal power station. Various joint projects are currently under negotiation with China, including the construction of a railway line and the modernisation of a Soviet-built iron and steel works. The USSR reportedly offered a $125 million loan for this purpose. The USSR also resumed its aid activities in Egypt, which was offered up to Rb 1.5 billion. Out of this amount, over $200 million were earmarked for the expansion of the iron and steel works at Helwan and $140 million for a power plant. A large loan ($1 billion, probably at non-concessional terms) was extended to Brazil for the construction of a railway line and an irrigation project. In 1989 the Soviet Union reportedly offered Iran up to $1.9 billion in credits to finance joint industrial projects.

Assistance to Sub-Saharan Africa remained small. In 1988 the USSR granted $30 million worth of food aid to Ethiopia, extended a $17 million grant to Guinea and provided two loans to Mali totalling $19 million. Mozambique was promised a $12 million grant for consumer goods and a $28 million loan for the purchase of petroleum products. In May 1989 the USSR signed an agreement with Canada for joint studies of Africa's aid and development needs and for the holding of a conference of Soviet, Canadian and African experts in Moscow in 1990.

Main recipients of known East European new loan commitments were Burkina

Faso, which received $17 million from Czechoslovakia, and Tanzania, which was granted a $10 million loan from Bulgaria. Kampuchea and Laos received commodity grants from Czechoslovakia and the GDR. The latter also extended aid to Nicaragua and Afghanistan. Hungary extended a food aid grant to Ethiopia.

4. ARAB COUNTRIES

Arab aid in 1988 amounted to $2.3 billion, equivalent to 0.86 per cent of GNP, which is the lowest level so far recorded. In the pre-oil boom years 1970 to 1972, Arab aid exceeded 2 per cent of GNP. For the Gulf Arab countries the corresponding ratios were 1.7 per cent and about 5 per cent. The further decline of Arab aid resulted primarily from the cessation of large amounts of general support assistance to Jordan and Syria. At the Arab Summit Meeting in Baghdad in 1978, Arab donors had pledged an annual amount of $3.5 billion for Jordan, Syria and the Palestinians for a ten-year period. The number of contributing countries declined over the years, but Saudi Arabia, which had committed $1 billion annually, paid its share in full and Kuwait which had committed $550 million, honoured most of its commitment. New commitments in 1988 were relatively small and in no way compensated for the cessation of the large sums pledged in Baghdad. Repayments on loans also rose somewhat in 1988, which further reduced net disbursements. The cessation of the Gulf War and the increase in the price of oil, however, should permit a rise of Arab aid in 1989 and beyond.

Table 3-7.   ODA NET DISBURSEMENTS BY ARAB DONORS

$ million

	1980	1985	1986	1987	1988
Saudi Arabia	5 682	2 629	3 517	2 888	2 098
Kuwait	1 140	771	715	316	108
UAE	1 118	122[a]	91[a]	19[a]	4[a]
Other Arab donors[b]	734	118	201	105	147

a) Incomplete data.
b) Algeria, Libya and Qatar; excluding Iraq for which net disbursements in recent years were negative.

The cessation of "Baghdad" aid is likely to have major repercussions for the geographic and sectoral distribution of Arab aid since it was largely responsible for the high share of aid extended to Arab countries, the concentration of aid on a limited number of recipients, and the dominant position of non-project assistance in total bilateral ODA. In 1988, however, Jordan was still by far the largest recipient of known Arab net disbursements. Sudan ranked second. Other relatively important recipients were Algeria, Morocco, Senegal and the Palestinians. Following the cessation of the Gulf

War and the major reconstruction effort undertaken in Iraq, this country is likely to become the largest recipient in 1989.

Total *Saudi Arabian* net disbursements, as communicated to the OECD by the Saudi Arabian Finance Ministry, declined to $2.1 billion. Saudi multilateral aid rose from $224 million in 1987 to $280 million in 1988. The latter consisted mainly of note deposits for IDA, which amounted to $193 million (encashment by IDA amounted to $99 million). Other multilateral institutions which received over $10 million included IFAD, the African Development Fund and the WFP. Part of the bilateral assistance was provided or administered by the *Saudi Fund for Development*. Net disbursements by the Fund fell from $103 million in 1987 to $28 million in 1988. In addition, the Fund administered $15 million on behalf of the Government. Commitments by the Fund continued to fall, to $64 million, the lowest annual level since the Fund was established, but the grant element of commitments softened significantly to 54 per cent. All new commitments were made in favour of African countries, except one, and concerned primarily agricultural development and structural adjustment.

Kuwait reported a further decline of its aid to $108 million, and in relation to GNP to 0.4 per cent, the lowest aid volume since aid statistics were collected. Bilateral aid shrank to $61 million, multilateral contributions to $47 million ($74 million on a note encashment basis). The largest multilateral contributions were made in favour of IFAD, IDA and UNWRA. The main recipients of bilateral assistance were, in order of magnitude, Yemen, Indonesia, Yemen PDR and Sri Lanka. The decline of Kuwaiti aid is primarily attributable to grants by the Ministry of Finance, which became very small. Another important factor in the continuing decline is the *Kuwait Fund*. In 1988, for the first time, repayments exceeded disbursements. Commitments, on the other hand, remained unchanged at $295 million in 1988. The latter were extended to 17 countries and three multilateral organisations. The grant element of commitments was 50 per cent, marginally softer than in 1987. The General Board for the Gulf and Southern Arabia, the aid agency of the Foreign Ministry, maintained its aid at close to $40 million and became the main source of bilateral aid from Kuwait.

Table 3-8. ODA NET DISBURSEMENTS BY NATIONAL ARAB AID AGENCIES INCLUDING LOANS AND GRANTS ADMINISTERED ON BEHALF OF THE GOVERNMENT

	1980	1985	1986	1987	1988
$ million					
Abu Dhabi Fund	135.5	29.2	50.2	4.4	− 6.3
Kuwait Fund	357.0	311.3	321.6	99.2	− 0.3
of which: Bilateral	279.4	228.2	239.4	88.1	− 6.9
Saudi Fund	491.3	97.7	190.0	142.2	42.8
Total	938.8	438.2	543.8	245.8	36.2
As % of GNP					
Abu Dhabi Fund	0.49	0.11	0.23	0.02	− 0.03
Kuwait Fund	1.10	1.28	1.31	0.39	—
Saudi Fund	0.42	0.11	0.25	0.19	0.06

Figures for total aid from the *UAE/Abu Dhabi* in 1988 are not available. Known net disbursements were close to zero in 1987 and 1988. Project assistance, which is carried out by the *Abu Dhabi Fund*, was negative in 1988, while contributions to multilateral organisations totalled $10 million. The reasons for the Fund's negative net disbursements are on the one hand resource constraints and on the other hand a shift in recent years towards domestic activities. Out of five new loan commitments in 1988, four concerned projects in Abu Dhabi.

No official information is available for bilateral disbursements by the *other Arab donors*, but it is estimated that Libyan bilateral aid more than doubled in 1988 to exceed $110 million. Libya thus is the only Arab donor to have increased its aid in 1988. Multilateral payments by Algeria, Iraq, Libya and Qatar totaled $35 million.

Table 3-9. MAIN RECIPIENTS OF KNOWN NET DISBURSEMENTS
OF BILATERAL AND MULTILATERAL ARAB AID

					$ million
	1980	1985	1986	1987	1988
Syria	1 609	567	643	574	(9)
Jordan	1 147	451	434	390	292
Sudan	183	215	208	228	127
Morocco	647	412	69	67	46
Yemen AR	351	147	95	147	19

Table 3-10. NET DISBURSEMENTS BY MULTILATERAL ARAB/OPEC FUNDS AND BANKS

					$ million
	1980	1985	1986	1987	1988
ODA					
AFESD	72.8	40.7	72.5	77.2	83.7
BADEA[a]	35.9	4.3	21.0	− 1.3	− 14.6
Isl. Dev. Bank	23.7	37.1	33.4	29.6	27.7
OPEC Fund	143.2	45.4	16.7	− 32.7	− 36.4
Total	275.6	127.5	143.6	72.8	60.3
OOF					
AFESD	9.9	69.4	47.6	28.5	− 4.2
BADEA	11.9	17.1	17.0	8.9	8.1
Isl. Dev. Bank	89.9	204.2	− 207.2	− 127.2	− 84.9
OPEC Fund	16.2	− 4.8	5.1	− 11.1	− 3.3
Total	127.9	285.9	− 137.5	− 100.9	− 84.3
AMF	23.9	18.8	7.3	− 102.4	227.9

a) Including repayments on SAAFA loans.

180

Among the four *Arab/OPEC multilateral development finance agencies* only the Arab Fund for Economic and Social Development (AFESD) remained a relatively significant source of aid. Total and ODA net disbursements by the Arab Bank for Economic Development in Africa (BADEA) were negative. Resource flows from the other two institutions, the Islamic Development Bank and the OPEC Fund, continued to be negative, although ODA net disbursements by the Islamic Develoment Bank were still positive. On the other hand, commitments at ODA terms by the four institutions almost doubled in 1988 to $580 million, and the grant element of these commitments softened marginally to 46 per cent. The increase was primarily due to AFESD.

5. OTHER DONORS

Available data on co-operation between developing countries are insufficient to draw a comprehensive picture of its scope and the financial efforts involved. There is, evidence, however, that a growing number of developing countries extend assistance in one form or another.

Argentina decided in 1988 to step up economic co-operation with Sub-Saharan Africa. To this effect it is currently setting up a special co-operation agency and has launched a technical co-operation campaign with the help of the UNDP special TCDC unit. Argentina signed various technical assistance agreements with Angola, Côte d'Ivoire and Ghana and offered scholarships and training courses for students from Sub-Saharan Africa, mainly in the field of agriculture and health services. Furthermore, it extended a $2 million loan to Angola and a credit line to Senegal for the purchase of goods and services.

Given its own financial constraints development assistance extended by *Brazil* in 1988 was rather limited. Bilateral assistance consisted mainly of technical co-operation, which received new impetus in 1988 through the setting up of a specialised agency, the Brazilian Co-operation Agency (ABC). The agency has its own budget and employs a staff of 35. Activities mainly consist in helping the developing countries to restructure their administrations, the transfer of technologies and know-how adapted to the recipient countries' needs and the training of students and qualified personnel. Emphasis is laid on Sub-Saharan Africa, in particular the lusophone countries. Equipment is provided on a grant basis, but these grants are limited. Multilateral contributions in 1988 were very small.

China became the second largest "southern" donor in 1988, following the further decline of Kuwaiti aid, which traditionally occupied this position. Bilateral net disbursements remained at about $160 million while contributions to multilateral organisations declined from $50 million in 1987 to $25 million in 1988. In 1989 aid disbursements are expected to remain at their present level, although bilateral commitments fell from $280 million in 1987 to $125 million in 1988. The largest commitments in 1988 were extended to Yemen ($40 million), Guinea and Mozambique ($13 million each). China also extended aid to new recipients as it continued to expand its aid activities, in particular in Latin America, the Caribbean and the Pacific Islands. The most recent recipients include Bolivia, Granada, Belize, Cook Islands, Solomon Islands and Uruguay. In all, 88 countries received aid in 1988. As to sectors, China has no particular preferences and provides its assistance in many fields, including the construction of sports stadiums (there are three new commitments in 1988 for this purpose), since the Chinese authorities believe that sport is part of the development process. Other commitments in 1988 concern cost overruns for projects in Guinea and Niger and rehabilitation of projects in Tanzania. Rehabilitation and maintenance of earlier projects, in particular in Sub-Saharan Africa, are getting increased attention. Contrary to past practice, China now assumes responsibility for completed projects by providing the senior management or by turning them into joint ventures. Many projects which had been unprofitable now produce sizeable profits after their management has been entrusted to Chinese personnel. China also stepped up the training of local managerial and technical personnel, and the delivery of spare parts. Assisting developing countries in managing completed projects will become an important feature of Chinese foreign aid. This decision is in line with the intention of the Chinese authorities to diversify the forms of their aid and to render their assistance more versatile.

By the end of 1988, China was involved in 1 540 aid projects of which 1 233 were completed, involving 470 000 Chinese personnel. Eighty-five per cent of total commitments was disbursed. In 1988, 5 500 Chinese experts worked in developing countries, not including medical and educational personnel. Medical teams were dispatched to 42 countries involving 1 300 medical personnel.

Aid loans are in principle still interest-free, but a few countries were charged 3 to 5 per cent interest. Loan agreements stipulate that recipients should use the loan within five years. After that period the recipients enjoy another five years before repayments are due over a ten-year period. Repayments are either in local goods or in convertible currency, but very few countries repay in convertible currency. Goods delivered by the recipient in repayment of aid loans are valued according to the world market price at the moment of repayment. Only a few loans are repaid in time since China is always willing to extend the repayment period. Since 1983, China has provided convertible currency for the local-cost component of projects, since the previous practice of providing goods for local-cost financing proved inefficient and resulted in delays in project implementation.

India's net aid disbursements in 1988 are estimated to have declined to $126 million from $150 million in 1987. This fall resulted from lower multilateral contributions, while bilateral aid, according to preliminary data, increased to $108 million. As in previous years, the latter was mainly extended to Bhutan and Nepal, which together accounted for nearly three-quarters of total bilateral net aid in 1988. Sri Lanka received a grant of close to $20 million for reconstruction and rehabilitation. Other recipients in 1988 were Botswana, Mozambique and Tanzania. Viet Nam obtained a loan in January 1989, and benefitted from a rescheduling of repayments on earlier credits. Multilateral contributions in 1988 amounted to $18 million, less than half their previous year's level.

Korea, which established an Economic Development Co-operation Fund for the provision of aid in June 1987, signed its first loan agreement in May 1989. The loan, which was extended to Nigeria, amounted to $12 million and carried a grant element of 33 per cent.   The fact that it took two years to sign the first loan agreement is primarily due to constraints Korea faces in project evaluation, since the number of requests for aid received by Korea is relatively large.   As to technical assistance and other bilateral grants for which information is incomplete, they are estimated to have amounted to less than $10 million in 1988.   Multilateral contributions, which had reached $35 million in 1987 fell to $13 million, of which more than half was extended to the World Bank group.

Taiwan established in 1989 an Overseas Economic Co-operation Fund with an authorised capital of NT$30 billion (US$1.1 billion), of which NT$5.05 billion (US$184 million) was paid in by June 1989.   The purpose of the Fund is i) to assist the economic development of friendly developing countries; ii) to promote trade with these countries; and iii) to encourage Taiwanese enterprises to make investments in these countries and to provide technical assistance.   The Fund has already received requests for aid from several countries.   An amount of $3.6 million has been allocated by the Fund for technical assistance activities in fiscal year 1989/90.   Apart from the Fund, Taiwan has an International Technical Co-operation Programme financed by the Ministry of Foreign Affairs.   The budget of this programme amounted to NT$750 million (US$26 million) in 1988.   More than half of this amount was spent on 32 agricultural aid missions comprising 292 experts in 24 countries.   Under its International Technical Co-operation Programme Taiwan also conducts various technical training courses in Taiwan to advance the agricultural skills of developing-country personnel.   Eighty-eight persons received training in Taiwan in 1988.   Taiwan extended a $10 million loan to Paraguay for a fertilizer processing plant and the construction of the Ministry of Education.

Venezuela's net aid more than doubled in 1988 to $50 million, and increased in relation to GNP to 0.08 per cent.   Over 80 per cent of total net aid was extended to multilateral organisations, in particular to IFAD, which accounted for two-thirds of Venezuela's multilateral aid.   Bilateral aid, which was mainly extended to Costa Rica, Honduras and El Salvador, declined to an estimated $7 million.

III

MULTILATERAL AID: A TREND CONTINUES

1. DONORS' ATTITUDES AND CONTRIBUTIONS

Donors' basic attitudes to the role of multilateral agencies, in the context of evolving priorities for the 1990s, are set out in Chapter XII of Part 2 (Section 7). There is general agreement that a strong multilateral system is essential to the working of the whole international development co-operation system, even more so in the light of the new perceptions that have become dominant in the past few years.

This chapter reviews the present trends in terms of funding by donors and disbursements by individual agencies. It then briefly sketches some new features in the climate for replenishing the concessional resources of the main multilateral development banks and characterises the various policy review processes that have recently been initiated within these institutions.

The trend of recent years has been one of increasing consolidation of multilateral aid at about one-quarter of total aid from DAC Members. The figures for DAC funding of multilateral agencies constitute the hard evidence by which donors' attitudes can be judged.

Contributions to multilateral agencies by individual donors, as recorded in the DAC statistics, fluctuate sharply from year to year. This is largely an accident of their respective budgetary processes. Annual fluctuations in the total are largely a reflection of fluctuations in the figures for a few major donors. To some extent, these fluctuations cancel each other out in the aggregate figures. The fluctuations in any case follow a two-year cycle in most instances, so that two-year averages provide a reasonable indication of the trend. (See Chapter I of Part 3, especially Section 2 and Table 3-2, for details of the most recent annual figures.)

Total DAC contributions to multilateral agencies (excluding contributions to the programmes of the EEC, which are a special case) are shown in Table 3-11. After a brief dip in the period 1985-87, multilateral contributions seem to have steadied again at the level of about 25 per cent of total DAC ODA, which became fixed as the normal level in the early 1980s after the very rapid rise of the late 1970s.

In the course of the brief dip and subsequent recovery in total DAC multilateral contributions, there has been a significant shift in the relative weight of individual DAC Members. As noted in the 1988 Report, the most striking feature of the changing

185

Table 3-11. TOTAL ODA CONTRIBUTIONS TO MULTILATERAL DEVELOPMENT AGENCIES
AND FUNDS[a] FROM DAC MEMBER COUNTRIES 1979-88

	1979-80 average	1984	1985	1986	1987	1988	1987-88 average
Total							
$ million	6 436	7 569	6 095	8 762	9 691	12 349	11 020
Percentage of total DAC ODA..............	25.7	26.3	20.7	23.9	23.3	25.7	24.6

a) Excluding EEC.

pattern has been the emergence of Japan as a dominant contributor alongside the United States. These two countries now account for nearly a half of total DAC multilateral contributions. Other important features of the pattern are the continued maintenance of a strong commitment to multilateral agencies on the part of the Nordic countries, and the addition of other major donors as significant sources of support. Table 3-12 suggests that the shifts may not have been as sharp as they seemed, though broadly the new pattern is sustained, notably the continuing growth in the significance of Japan as a source of support for multilateral agencies.

The trend in recent years has been marked, also, by a propensity on the part of donors to give greater weight to their assessments of the relative efficiency and effectiveness of individual agencies, on top of their preference for particular sectors or particular regions. A firm and objective way of comparing the performance of individual agencies is still lacking, so the judgments made by donors remain somewhat impressionistic. Still, it is noteworthy that discussion of the role of individual agencies has moved quite sharply in the DAC to the relevant operational contexts, where a realistic assessment of each agency's capacity is usually implicit. The role of the principal agencies concerned is almost automatically on the agenda of any discussion of sectoral approaches or of issues such as aid co-ordination, which was far from being the case five years or so ago. The role of multilateral agencies as a whole, however, is discussed less frequently. It was a major topic of discussion in the DAC in 1987, when some general conclusions were reached which still stand (see 1987 Report, Chapter IX).

Within the UN system for technical co-operation, the principal test of donors' attitudes that has figured in this report in recent years has been the proportion of funds allocated to the UNDP compared with the proportion allocated to individual agencies in a variety of extra-budgetary forms. In recent years, the central position of the UNDP has been strengthened, after a long period of erosion. The scattering of funds in extra-budgetary contributions, however, continues to be a problem, and reflects a degree of inconsistency with the view of multilateral aid which donors themselves profess. The positions of individual donors are reflected in Table 3-13. In terms of total DAC funding of UN technical co-operation, the relative importance of extra-budgetary contributions channelled directly through the agencies has increased during the 1980s, from the equivalent of 34 per cent of contributions to the UNDP to 43 per cent. Within this total, there are several clearly defined groups. Among major contributors to the

Table 3-12. DAC MEMBERS' ODA CONTRIBUTIONS TO MULTILATERAL DEVELOPMENT AGENCIES AND FUNDS AS PERCENTAGE[a] OF TOTAL ODA, GNP AND OF TOTAL DAC MULTILATERAL ODA, 1980-88

	As % of ODA			As % of GNP			As % of total DAC multilateral ODA, excluding EEC		
	1980-81 average	1985-86 average	1987-88 average	1980-81 average	1985-86 average	1987-88 average	1980-81 average	1985-86 average	1987-88 average
Australia	21.4	30.2	33.0	0.10	0.14	0.14	2.1	3.1	2.6
Austria	21.6	29.2	36.5	0.06	0.08	0.08	0.6	0.9	0.8
Belgium	14.1 (29.5)	19.8 (35.7)	16.0 (33.8)	0.08 (0.16)	0.10 (0.18)	0.07 (0.15)	1.2	1.3	0.9
Canada	38.0	38.3	32.9	0.16	0.19	0.16	6.4	8.6	6.3
Denmark	39.1 (47.0)	41.3 (47.9)	40.9 (47.4)	0.29 (0.35)	0.35 (0.41)	0.36 (0.42)	2.6	3.1	3.3
Finland	41.4	39.8	38.3	0.10	0.17	0.21	0.8	1.4	1.8
France	7.0 (16.0)	10.8 (18.4)	10.7 (18.4)	0.05 (0.11)	0.08 (0.14)	0.08 (0.13)	4.4	6.6	6.5
Germany	18.9 (32.3)	18.8 (31.8)	17.6 (31.3)	0.08 (0.15)	0.08 (0.14)	0.07 (0.12)	9.5	8.6	7.3
Ireland	23.4 (65.3)	26.8 (58.3)	22.8 (54.3)	0.04 (0.11)	0.07 (0.15)	0.04 (0.11)	0.1	0.2	0.1
Italy	51.7 (81.0)	23.7 (35.2)	16.3 (26.1)	0.08 (0.13)	0.08 (0.12)	0.06 (0.10)	5.2	5.6	4.3
Japan	34.5	32.1	29.9	0.10	0.09	0.09	16.8	20.4	22.3
Netherlands	16.9 (24.5)	24.3 (32.5)	23.3 (31.3)	0.17 (0.25)	0.23 (0.31)	0.23 (0.31)	4.0	4.7	4.6
New Zealand	26.4	19.9	16.9	0.08	0.06	0.05	0.3	0.2	0.1
Norway	42.4	41.2	41.4	0.36	0.45	0.46	3.0	3.8	3.5
Sweden	30.0	29.7	32.9	0.24	0.25	0.29	4.2	3.8	4.3
Switzerland	30.6	23.9	28.4	0.07	0.07	0.09	1.1	1.2	1.5
United Kingdom	19.5 (34.4)	23.4 (42.7)	27.2 (46.0)	0.08 (0.13)	0.08 (0.14)	0.08 (0.14)	5.9	5.1	5.6
United States	32.8	16.8	27.8	0.08	0.04	0.06	31.7	21.4	24.1
Total DAC	25.3 (31.3)	22.5 (27.2)	24.6 (29.5)	0.09 (0.11)	0.08 (0.10)	0.09 (0.10)	100.0	100.0	100.0

a) Excluding EEC. Figures including EEC contributions are in brackets.

187

Table 3-13. DAC MEMBERS' SHARES OF TOTAL DAC FUNDING OF THE UNDP
AND OF DAC EXTRA-BUDGETARY FINANCING OF THE SPECIALISED AGENCIES, 1981-88

	1981-82			1987-88		
	UNDP	Specialised agencies	Ratio: specialised agencies/UNDP	UNDP	Specialised agencies	Ratio: specialised agencies/UNDP
	%			%		
Australia................	2.1	1.6	0.3	1.4	0.7	0.2
Austria	1.0	0.8	0.3	1.0	0.6	0.2
Belgium	2.3	7.3	1.1	1.9	4.4	1.0
Canada................	6.4	1.5	0.1	6.5	1.6	0.1
Denmark	7.0	9.5	0.5	8.5	7.8	0.4
Finland................	1.3	1.9	0.5	3.5	3.1	0.4
France.................	4.0	1.4	0.1	5.0	2.7	0.2
Germany...............	7.6	7.7	0.3	8.6	6.7	0.3
Ireland	0.2	0.4	0.8	0.1	0.1	0.2
Italy...................	3.3	9.3	1.0	6.5	18.1	1.2
Japan	7.9	4.7	0.2	8.7	7.8	0.4
Netherlands	10.2	17.1	0.6	9.2	13.3	0.6
New Zealand	0.2	—	—	0.2	0.1	0.1
Norway................	8.4	7.5	0.3	8.3	8.5	0.4
Sweden	9.4	18.5	0.7	9.3	10.6	0.5
Switzerland	2.7	3.8	0.5	3.9	4.6	0.5
United Kingdom	5.4	1.5	0.1	4.6	3.9	0.4
United States	20.6	5.3	0.1	12.7	5.6	0.2
Total	100.0	100.0	0.34	100.0	100.0	0.43

UNDP, the United States, Canada, the United Kingdom and France stand out as donors whose extra-budgetary funding at the beginning of the decade was the equivalent of only one-tenth of their contributions to the UNDP, though all but Canada have lately increased this ratio.   These four donors, therefore, have been in practice the main supporters of the UNDP's central funding role, at least in the limited sense implied by the test used here.   The major sources of extra-budgetary funding tend also to be strong supporters of UN programmes as a whole, including the UNDP, e.g., Denmark, the Netherlands, Norway and Sweden.   In most cases, however, with Denmark now as the main exception, their support for extra-budgetary funding, expressed as a share of the DAC total, is even stronger than their support for the UNDP.   In the case of Belgium and Italy, the preference for extra-budgetary funding is even more marked.   Among these donors, only Sweden convincingly reduced its relative support for extra-budgetary funding during the 1980s, with a sharp fall in the ratio of extra-budgetary funding to contributions to the UNDP.

The question of central funding for UN technical co-operation has recently been a preoccupation of the UN Director-General for Development and International Economic Co-operation.   It was one of the issues identified by the General Assembly at the end of 1987 in a blanket resolution calling for a thoroughgoing review of the UN operational system. The view that seems to be emerging is that the whole question of funding needs to be reconsidered in the light of changing demands on the UN system.

2. TRENDS IN DISBURSEMENTS

In recent years, the trend in net disbursements by multilateral agencies has been characterised by three main elements: a lack of growth in the total flow at current prices and exchange rates, and therefore a decline in real terms; steady growth in concessional flows, and therefore a shift from non-concessional to concessional flows within the total; and a geographical shift to Africa, including rapid growth in resource flows from the African Development Bank. In sectoral terms, multilateral programmes have consistently come closer than bilateral programmes to reflecting the priorities that bilateral donors, among others, profess. There was a very early shift, for instance, to greater concentration on agriculture, and more recently policy-related financing has been of growing significance.

These trends can be seen reflected in the changing composition of the flow of resources through multilateral agencies, both in their receipts and in their commitments and disbursements. The figures are shown in detail in Tables 24-27 in the Statistical Annex. The composition of multilateral disbursements by individual agencies (Table 26 of the Statistical Annex) is translated into constant prices and exchange rates and into percentages, for 1981-82 and 1987-88, in Table 3-14. Several striking facts emerge. First, the previously recorded decline in the relative significance of non-concessional flows through multilateral agencies is almost entirely attributable to a decline in net lending by the IBRD. Second, concessional flows have stagnated in real terms, with a shift in their composition from UN technical co-operation and relief programmes to the financial institutions. Among financial institutions, the African and Asian Development Banks are of growing importance, the combined increase in their concessional disbursements being greater than the increase in disbursements from the far larger IDA. Among the UN agencies, there is as yet no clear trend.

The trend within the UN operational system has been less clear. As already noted, the impact of donors' preferences on the volume of extra-budgetary financing has varied from one donor to another. The composition of resource flows through the UN system is shown in Table 3-15. The recently improved resource position of the UNDP is beginning to show up in disbursements, but the trend is not yet solidly established, and the UNDP still has a long way to go before one will be able to say that it has recovered the central funding role which is the cornerstone of the UN operational system as at present designed, and which it had in the 1970s.

3. CURRENT REPLENISHMENTS OF THE DEVELOPMENT BANKS

In recent years, the World Bank and the three main regional development banks have accounted for about 60 per cent of DAC Members' total contributions to multilateral agencies (excluding the EEC), or 15 per cent of their total ODA (see Statistical Annex,

189

Table 3-14. THE COMPOSITION OF NET DISBURSEMENTS OF CONCESSIONAL
AND NON-CONCESSIONAL FLOWS FROM THE MAIN MULTILATERAL AGENCIES,
1981-82 AND 1987-88

	1981-82		1987-88	
	Annual amount $ million at 1987 prices and exchange rates	Percentages	Annual amount $ million at 1987 prices and exchange rates	Percentages
	Concessional flows (excluding EEC and OPEC)			
Major financial institutions				
IDA.............................	2 978	37.1	3 430	42.4
IBRD	102	1.3	x	—
IDB.............................	558	7.0	123	1.5
African Development Fund	147	1.8	351	4.3
Asian Development Fund	224	2.8	578	7.1
IFAD	124	1.5	231	2.9
Sub-total......................	4 133	51.5	4 712	58.2
United Nations				
WFP	790	9.8	770	9.5
UNDP..........................	1 044	13.0	820	10.1
UNHCR	558	7.0	386	4.8
UNRWA	282	3.5	202	2.5
UNICEF........................	290	3.6	369	4.6
UNTA[b].........................	282	3.5	282	3.5
UNFPA	168	2.1	114	1.4
Other UN.......................	477	6.0	437	5.4
Sub-total......................	3 891	48.5	3 377	41.8
Total concessional[a]..................	8 024	100.0	8 090	100.0
	Non-concessional flows (excluding EEC and OPEC)			
IBRD	5 660	70.8	3 792	59.6
IFC	554	7.0	270	4.2
IDB.............................	1 026	12.8	974	15.3
African Development Bank	129	1.6	500	7.9
Asian Development Bank	600	7.5	406	6.4
Others..........................	20	0.3	418	6.6
Total non-concessional	7 989	100.0	6 359	100.0

a) Excluding IMF Trust Fund, which was a significant element in total concessional multilateral flows in 1981.
b) Technical assistance financed from the regular budget of the UN, as voted by the General Assembly.

Table 3-15. COMPOSITION OF GRANT EXPENDITURES ON OPERATIONAL
ACTIVITIES FOR DEVELOPMENT OF THE UNITED NATIONS SYSTEM, 1980-81 TO 1988

	In percentages			
	1980-81	1986	1987	1988
Financed from regular budgets of agencies	6.1	10.3	11.8	8.8
Financed by UNDP	34.2	27.4	25.6	26.7
Financed from funds administered by UNDP	2.5	3.8	3.6	3.1
Financed by UNFPA	6.8	4.1	3.9	4.2
Financed by UNICEF	11.2	13.1	13.5	13.0
Financed by specialised agencies and other organisations from extra-budgetary resources	12.4	15.3	15.1	15.8
Financed by WFP	26.4	26.0	26.5	28.5
Total	100.0	100.0	100.0	100.0
Annual amounts, $ million.......................	2046.6	2488.5	2709.9	3083.8
UNDP as a percentage of UN technical co-operation[a]	54.8	51.2	48.5	50.8

a) Excluding UNICEF and WFP.
Source: United Nations.

Table 58).   Replenishments are effected, usually every three years, through the negotiation of scales of contributions, which then constitute a contractual obligation.   Understandably, the periodic replenishment of the funds of these institutions and discussions
concerning the level and orientation of their operations have given rise to complicated
international negotiations, which were particularly troublesome in the climate of the
early 1980s.   In the second half of the 1980s, however, the dynamics of the process
began to change.   This was reflected in the negotiation of IDA-8, which came into
effect relatively smoothly under adverse circumstances.

In the coming year (1990), funding exercises will have been completed for all the
main multilateral sources of concessional finance — the International Development
Association (IDA — the soft-loan arm of the World Bank), the regional development
banks, and the European Development Fund.   This collinearity has sharpened donors'
awareness of the place of the funding process in the general pattern of international
development co-operation.   The next replenishment of IDA is scheduled to be in place
by the end of June 1990, and the usual series of meetings of donors' representatives to
consider the replenishment is well under way.   The replenishments of the concessional
resources of the regional development banks should all come into effect six months
later, at the end of the year.

The early discussions on IDA-9 were focused on IDA's role and operational programme, in the light of current policy priorities (such as allocations and eligibility criteria,
and support for adjustment, poverty alleviation, and the environment).   Some illustra-
tive figures were tabled and discussed.   In principle, a specific funding level should
emerge as a conclusion from agreement on the outline of an operational programme.
In practice, it has in the past proved difficult to make this connection.   Funding levels

have been determined by a range of factors, in which the breakdown of burden-sharing has been a source of increasing contention in the 1980s. And the task has been, as in the replenishments of other financial institutions, to find a figure which is attainable within the political and budgetary constraints of the time. The process has been made even more complex by technical ambiguities in the meaning of whatever figures are proposed, when translated into the realities of commitment authority and disbursement capability (see the 1983 Report, Chapter VII, for a technical discussion).

In the run-up to IDA-9, formal meetings on IDA funding have been supplemented by a round of bilateral explorations with individual contributors. By the middle of 1989 a consensus was evolving around the goal of maintaining IDA-9 in real terms at the level of IDA-8. The key question was whether the US could agree to lift its contribution in nominal terms in line with this objective. In principle, it was expected that negotiations would be completed at a final meeting scheduled to take place in Kyoto in November.

The first of the current replenishments to be completed ended with a lower figure than was hoped. The third replenishment of the International Fund for Agricultural Development (IFAD) was provisionally concluded at a level of $522 million, against a target of $750 million and a hope that the figure would be at least $600 million. The shortfall was due essentially to the problems facing the "Category II" oil-producing countries; in particular, the two largest OPEC donors cut their contributions, while some of the poorer OPEC donors maintained their previous levels. In contrast, OECD countries agreed to a new formula for matching the convertible-currency contributions of "Category III" developing countries at a ratio of three to one. This led to contributions amounting to $52 million in convertible currencies from developing countries. Furthermore, the shortfall was partially offset by a shortening of the period covered, from three to two-and-a-half years, so in terms of annual lending capacity the effects of the shortfall have been mitigated.

4. RECENT POLICY REVIEWS

Over the past year, there have been major policy reviews in most of the leading multilateral agencies. In the case of the regional development banks, these have taken the form of reports presented by specially convened groups of prominent personalities. Elsewhere, the reviews have been more internal and managerial, and are best seen as part of the continuing process of reflection, reorganisation and reorientation which has been a marked feature of the workings of multilateral agencies since 1986 or thereabouts.

In general, the reviews of the regional development banks have adopted an incrementalist tone. While they certainly do not represent any agreed institutional view, and are in no way binding either on the managements or the members of the regional banks, they should be seen as a reflection of a wider consultative process that is slowly gathering momentum. There is widespread recognition of the operational implications of new or changing priorities, in relation to perceived issues such as policy-related lending, the environment, the role of women in development, and the promotion of the private sector. At the same time, within some characteristic differences of institutional style and of regional contexts, there is an established view that the financial institutions should build on their existing strengths. The main debate on structural adjustment, policy reform and aid co-ordination is now well advanced, though important questions remain concerning the conclusions in terms of the operational roles of individual institutions. The next task is to define the operational roles of individual agencies within that framework, taking account of their particular qualities.

As regards the World Bank, there is some discussion over the extent to which the Bank's emphasis on structural adjustment has led it into "quick-disbursing" operations, but this has led on to a reconsideration of the long-term development processes that the Bank exists to support, rather than back into the narrow traditional concept of project lending. The emphasis on specific policy priorities, such as poverty alleviation, support for adjustment programmes, the environmental aspects of development, and the scope for development of the private sector, has become very strong.

From the donors' point of view, the evolving role of multilateral agencies, and particularly of the development banks, raises a still unresolved issue concerning the need for complementarity between the World Bank and the regional banks. This has equally been a preoccupation of the regional banks themselves. They have always had a dilemma. On the one hand, with their specifically regional identities, they cannot be expected simply to follow the World Bank's lead. On the other, as each of them moves away from traditional project lending to a more strategic approach at the sectoral or country level, harmonization is clearly required.

In the case of the Inter-American Development Bank (IDB), a panel under the chairmanship of Mr. John R. Petty, former chairman of the Marine Midland Bank, declared roundly that the institution had "lost its spark". It called on the Bank to "change its limited perspective, change the quality of its presence, and change its posture from reactive to active". Thus, in the report's view, the Bank could recover "the character of an architect shaping the region's development" and its "mission of fostering growth through modernization". The report called basically for renewal through reforms in internal structure, organisation and procedures. At the same time, the report reflected some significant shifts in thinking about the Bank's role and operational methods, including a recommendation that the Bank should move into policy-related lending. Operationally, the panel's report reached back into the thinking that had underlain the Bank's origins, modified in the light of current problems and opportunities, notably in the light of new perceptions of the scope for more active support of the private sector. At the Bank's annual meeting in March 1989, the same mood was in evidence. The main outcome of the meeting was a resolution of the long-lasting dispute over the proposed increase in the Bank's capital stock, by an amount equivalent to $26.5 billion for the four-year period 1990-93, which was made possible by agreement on new guidelines on lending policy and other issues, including, crucially, guidelines on policy-related lending and on the handling of contentious proposals.

For the Asian Development Bank (AsDB), the report of a panel under the chairmanship of Dr. Saburo Ohita of Japan was even more overtly incrementalist in tone. The panel recognised the crucial importance of the policy environment and the need for the Bank to maintain and expand the policy dialogue with its borrowers. But it advocated caution in any further move towards policy-related programme lending, with no increase above the current ceiling of 15 per cent of total commitments. It proposed more attention to environmental issues, to new initiatives in support for the private sector, and to the need for greater sensitivity towards the economics of poverty alleviation; and in these respects it was firmly in line with current thinking. (It should be noted that the AsDB, like most multilateral agencies, makes a point of including in discussion of the private sector the role of the informal sector, particularly in the amelioration of urban poverty, and the role of non-governmental organisations.) All in all, perhaps the most important change suggested by the panel was implicit rather than explicit — a change in the institutional style of the Bank, away from being basically an efficient executor of investment projects, towards a broader perception of underlying development problems and issues. The panel's report explicitly calls for a reorganisation of the Bank's structure in this direction, with a strengthening of staff capabilities in policy analysis, social infrastructure, poverty alleviation, environmental protection, and the operations of the private sector.

The trend within the African Development Bank (AfDB) is more difficult to pin down. In recent funding, the AfDB has been strongly supported by donors, as an expression of their more general concern with Africa's special problems. But the extent to which bilateral donors and international agencies are now themselves concentrating their efforts on Africa creates a situation in which the particular role of the AfDB may be difficult to define. Although it is widely recognised that there has been in recent years a significant rapprochement between donors and recipients in Africa concerning the essentials of development strategy, there are still traces of the former view of Africa as a region where deficiencies in domestic policy-making left donors little choice but to act as best they could on their own initiative. To the extent that this has now changed, it must be partly attributed to the massive effort that the World Bank has put into the negotiation of structural adjustment programmes with individual countries. In that historical context, there is an unanswered question concerning the role of the AfDB as a regional institution.

It is a question that has received a bold response from a panel established under the chairmanship of Mr. Mamoun Beheiry, who was the Bank's first president. The panel's review goes somewhat further in breaking new ground than the reviews of the IDB and the AsDB, as was perhaps inevitable under the pressure of an extraordinarily rapid increase in lending, which doubled between 1985 and 1987 from about $1 billion to more than $2 billion a year. The review confronts the special problems of Africa in their historical context. It proposes a concentrated effort to strengthen the Banks's existing capacities in resource mobilisation, project preparation and implementation, country programming, and the development of new initiatives in areas of current concern. On this basis, within quite a short period, from 1992 onwards, the review sees the AfDB moving progressively into a central position as an organism for analysis and advice across the whole range of economic and social policy in Africa. In this context, it is worth recording that the AfDB has already moved quite sharply in the direction of policy-related lending, and sectoral and structural adjustment lending now accounts for 26 per cent of total commitments. The role of the AfDB in policy-related lending remains a matter of considerable debate.

In the UNDP, the evolving strategy was reflected in the Administrator's report to the meeting of the Governing Council in June 1989. In his view of the UNDP, in which he is broadly supported by the donors, its role lies mainly in support for developing countries' efforts to enhance their capacities in the management of the development process. It is a view that finds its most concrete expression in the UNDP's Management Development Programme, but it imbues the whole range of the UNDP's operations. More widely still, its realisation will in time require an improvement in the analytical and managerial capacity of the specialised agencies at the country level, both in the field and at headquarters, as a resource on which the UNDP can draw in its central funding and co-ordinating role. This wider context is implicitly recognised in the UNDP's guidelines for the Management Development Programme, where a connection is made with the UNDP's evolving role in aid co-ordination. At the meeting of the UNDP's Governing Council, the increasing need for capacity-building and the concomitant need to strengthen the capacity of UN agencies at the country level, within the field network of the UNDP, were among the main themes advanced by the Director-General for Development and International Economic Co-operation. More specifically, the elements of the Management Development Programme, in the present thinking of the UNDP, will be focused on the following areas: organisation of the public sector; policy-making capacity; organisation of the civil service; monitoring and evaluation; resource management; and training and research.

To develop the UNDP along these lines will not be an easy task. Past attempts to develop a sharper operational role for the UNDP on its own account have given rise to controversy over possible conflicts of interest between the UNDP in its operational role and the UNDP in its central funding role vis-à-vis other UN agencies. The old attitudes of the agencies to the UNDP persist. It has for some years seemed clear that the solution to this puzzle, if there is one, has to be found at the country level, in further development of the role of the resident co-ordinator. Also, a concerted effort to strengthen the management capacity of the recipient countries should in principle have the effect of giving greater reality to the principle that the recipient should take the lead in aid co-ordination, accompanied by a sharp increase, which has already begun, in government execution of UNDP-funded projects. In countries with relatively weak administrations, already overburdened with extra administrative tasks thrust upon them by donors, this is a line to be pursued with some caution. Still, in the long run, as the experience of several Asian countries has already shown, the development of effective machinery of government in developing countries is the best way to bring order to the aid process and is in any case fundamental for development progress. Help and encouragement to that end is therefore central; and the UNDP's "mission", as noted above, is focused precisely here. To the extent that it succeeds, the old problem of inter-agency competition should also diminish.

STATISTICAL ANNEX

TABLE OF CONTENTS

Part I : **BASIC AID DATA**

1. Long-term Trends in Aid from all Sources 204
2. ODA Performance of DAC Countries in 1988 and recent years 206
3. Other Burden Sharing Indicators 207
4. Financial Terms of ODA Commitments 208
5. Tying Status of ODA and ODA Used for Associated Financing by Individual DAC Members, 1987 209
6. Multilateral Assistance and Geographical Distribution 210
7. Concessional and Non-Concessional Disbursements of the Main Multilateral Organisations, 1986-87 211
8. Geographical Distribution of ODA by Individual DAC Donors and Multilateral Agencies .. 212
9. Major Aid Uses by Individual DAC Donors and Multilateral Organisations 213
10. Relative Importance and Composition of Technical Co-operation 214
11. Non-ODA Economic/Financial Relations with Developing Countries 215
12. Economic Indicators for DAC Member Countries 216
13. Total Net Resource Flows to Developing Countries by Types of Flow 217
14. Net Resource Flows to Developing Countries by Region 218
15. Aggregate Net Financial Transfer by Region (Current $ billion) 219
16. Aggregate Net Financial Transfer by Region ($ billion at 1987 prices and exchange rates) .. 219
17. Debt Service Ratios by Region 220
18. Aid Reliance Ratios and per Capita Income of Developing Countries 221
19. Aid by Non-DAC Donors in 1988 222

Part II : **REFERENCE STATISTICS**

Section A

BASIC RESOURCE FLOW DATA

20. The Total Net Flow of Financial Resources from DAC Countries to Developing Countries and Multilateral Agencies, 1970, 1975, 1980, 1986 to 1988 224
21. The Total Net Flow of Resources from DAC Countries to Developing Countries and Multilateral Agencies, 1977-79 average, 1980, 1984 to 1988 225
22. The Net Flow of Private Capital from DAC Countries to Developing Countries and Multilateral Agencies, 1977-79 average, 1980, 1984 to 1988 226
23. Net Official Development Assistance from DAC Countries to Developing Countries and Multilateral Agencies, 1977-79 average, 1980, 1984 to 1988 227

199

Section B
MULTILATERAL AID

24. ODA from DAC Countries to Multilateral Agencies, 1988 228
25. Capital Subscriptions to Multilateral Agencies, on a Deposit and an Encashment Basis, 1980, 1985-88 229
26. Net Disbursements of Concessional and Non-Concessional Flows by Multilateral Agencies, 1970-71, 1975-76, 1980, 1982 to 1988 230
27. Commitments of Concessional and Non-Concessional Flows by Multilateral Agencies, 1970, 1975, 1980, 1984 to 1988 231

Section C
PURPOSE AND TYING STATUS OF ODA

28. Aid by Major Purposes (Commitments), 1988 232
29. Tying Status of ODA by Individual DAC Members, $ million, 1988 234

Section D
TECHNICAL CO-OPERATION

30. Technical Co-operation Expenditure, 1970, 1980, 1984 to 1988 235
31. Students and Trainees, 1970, 1980, 1983 to 1987 236
32. Experts and Volunteers, 1970, 1980, 1983 to 1987 237

Section E
GEOGRAPHICAL DISTRIBUTION

33. Total Net ODA from DAC Countries, Multilateral Organisations and Arab Countries to Developing Countries and Territories, 1985 to 1988 238
34. Total Net Receipts of ODA from Major Sources by Region and Selected Developing Countries . 240
35. Net Disbursements of ODA to Sub-Saharan Africa by Donor, 1978, 1984-88 242
36. ODA Commitments to Sub-Saharan Africa by Donor, 1984-88 243
37. Net Disbursements of ODA from all Sources, by income group, to Countries in Sub-Saharan Africa, 1978, 1984-88 244
38. Commitments of ODA from all Sources to Countries in Sub-Saharan Africa, 1978, 1984-87 . 245
39. Aid from DAC Countries to Least Developed Countries, 1981-82, 1987-88 246
40. Major Recipients of Individual DAC Members' Aid : annual averages, 1970-71, 1980-81, 1987-88 247

Section F
ARAB AND CMEA AID

41. Concessional Assistance by Arab Countries, 1970, 1975, 1980, 1983 to 1988 ($ million) 257
42. Concessional Assistance by Arab Countries, 1970, 1975, 1980, 1983 to 1988 (% of GNP) ... 257
43. Concessional Assistance by Arab Countries in 1987 258
44. Concessional Assistance by Arab Countries in 1988 258
45. Concessional Assistance by Arab Countries to Multilateral Organisations in 1987 259
46. Concessional Assistance by Arab Countries to Multilateral Organisations in 1988 259
47. Geographic Distribution of Bilateral Concessional Assistance from Arab Countries to Developing Countries and Territories, 1985-88 260
48. Estimated USSR Disbursements, 1970, 1975, 1980, 1983 to 1988 262
49. Estimated East European Disbursements, 1970, 1975, 1980, 1983 to 1988 263

Section G
REFERENCE TABLES

Detailed DAC Data

50. Comparison of Flows by Type in 1987 264
51. Comparison of Flows by Type in 1988 266
    The Flow of Financial Resources to Developing Countries and Multilateral Agencies,
    by Type of Flow, from Individual DAC Countries
52. Australia, Austria, Belgium 268
53. Canada, Denmark, Finland 270
54. France, Germany, Ireland 272
55. Italy, Japan, Netherlands 274
56. New Zealand, Norway, Sweden 276
57. Switzerland, United Kingdom, United States 278
58. Total DAC Countries 280
59. EEC 281
60. GNP Deflators for DAC Countries, 1971 to 1988 283
61. Gross National Product and Population of DAC Member Countries, 1981-82 average, 1986
    to 1988 284

Indicators of Developing Countries

62. The Level of GNP and Population of Developing Countries and Territories in 1987
    and Annual Average Growth of Real GNP per capita 1977-87 285

The data in this report were submitted up to 10th October 1989. At this date, some Member's submissions were incomplete. Where possible, the Secretariat has incorporated earlier provisional estimates supplied in May or June 1989, indicated by ( ); in some instances, absence of reporting is indicated by . .

In compiling tables of the resources channelled to individual recipient countries, allowance was made for missing data by assuming that the 1987 distribution for the donors concerned was applicable to the actual or estimated 1988 outflow.

SIGNS USED

( )	Secretariat estimate in whole or in part
– or 0.00	Nil or negligible
. .	Not available
. . .	Not available separately but included in total
x	Less than half the smallest unit shown
n.a.	Not applicable
.	Incomplete
p	Provisional

Slight discrepancies in totals are due to rounding.

More detailed information on the source and destination of aid and resource flows including firm data received after this annex was prepared, is contained in the statistical report on the *Geographical Distribution of the Flow of Resources to Developing Countries 1985-1988*, to be published shortly.

Part I

BASIC AID DATA

Basic Aid Data

Table 1. LONG-TERM TRENDS IN AID FROM ALL SOURCES

	Volume of ODA (net) ($ million at 1987 prices and exch. rates)				Share of world ODA				ODA as per cent of GNP			
	1970-71	75-76	80-81	87-88	1970-71	75-76	80-81	87-88	1970-71	75-76	80-81	87-88
United States	8 006	7 997	8 480	9 376	25.8	18.1	16.3	18.3	0.31	0.26	0.27	0.20
EEC members combined[a]	10 749	12 508	16 574	19 617	34.7	28.3	31.9	38.2	0.42	0.45	0.39	0.49
EEC members excl. DOM-TOM	9 384	11 343	14 453	17 592	30.3	25.7	27.8	34.2	0.38	0.40	0.34	0.44
of which: France (incl. DOM-TOM)	3 779	4 101	5 257	6 572	12.2	9.3	10.1	12.8	0.66	0.62	0.52	0.73
France (excl. DOM-TOM)	2 414	2 936	3 136	4 547	7.8	6.7	6.0	8.9	0.46	0.38	0.31	0.51
Germany	2 620	3 345	4 598	4 473	8.5	7.6	8.8	8.7	0.33	0.38	0.45	0.39
Italy	658	524	1 036	2 827	2.1	1.2	2.0	5.5	0.17	0.12	0.16	0.37
Netherlands	863	1 300	2 005	2 118	2.8	2.9	3.9	4.1	0.60	0.79	0.80	0.98
United Kingdom	2 076	2 156	2 305	2 077	6.7	4.9	4.4	4.0	0.42	0.39	0.39	0.30
Denmark	278	418	619	864	0.9	0.9	1.2	1.7	0.40	0.57	0.59	0.88
Belgium	475	644	714	634	1.5	1.5	1.4	1.2	0.48	0.55	0.38	0.44
Ireland	–	20	40	52	–	x	x	0.1	–	0.14	0.15	0.20
Japan	2 677	3 062	5 463	7 700	8.6	6.9	10.5	15.0	0.23	0.22	0.30	0.31
Canada	936	1 425	1 407	1 986	3.0	3.2	2.7	3.9	0.41	0.50	0.50	0.48
Sweden	436	1 041	1 105	1 381	1.4	2.4	2.1	2.7	0.41	0.82	0.60	0.88
Norway	146	376	567	906	0.5	0.9	1.1	1.8	0.33	0.68	0.76	1.10
Australia	638	685	675	764	2.1	1.6	1.3	1.5	0.59	0.53	0.46	0.41
Switzerland	187	280	380	568	0.6	0.6	0.7	1.1	0.13	0.19	0.22	0.32
Finland	44	104	176	489	0.1	0.2	0.3	1.0	0.09	0.17	0.22	0.55
Austria	56	151	300	246	0.2	0.3	0.6	0.5	0.07	0.17	0.24	0.21
New Zealand	54	130	93	87	0.2	0.3	0.2	0.2	0.23	0.47	0.26	0.27
Total DAC	23 929	27 758	35 220	43 120	77.2	62.9	67.7	84.1	0.34	0.35	0.34	0.35
Spain	(17)	(78)	269	198	(0.1)	(0.2)	0.5	0.4	(0.01)	0.04	0.11	0.07
Greece	–	–	3	30	–	–	x	0.1	–	–	–	0.06
Portugal	(250)	–	7	(54)	(0.8)	–	x	(0.1)	1.05	–	0.03	(0.14)
Luxembourg	(7)	8	7	16	x	x	x	x	(0.17)	0.12	0.12	0.27
Iceland	–	–	3	2	–	–	x	x	(–)	(0.03)	0.06	0.03
Total non-DAC OECD	(274)	(86)	289	300	(0.9)	(0.2)	0.5	(0.6)	(0.16)	(0.03)	0.08	(0.07)
Arab donors												
Saudi Arabia	685	5 660	7 534	2 423	2.2	12.8	14.5	4.7	5.25	6.66	4.05	3.27
Kuwait	451	1 669	1 550	209	1.5	3.8	3.0	0.4	4.57	5.81	3.58	0.83
UAE	99	2 017	1 290	12	0.3	4.6	2.5	x	3.98	9.58	3.34	0.05
Other	231	1 338	1 580	95	0.7	3.0	3.0	0.2	0.53	1.42	1.02	0.07
Total Arab donors	1 466	10 684	11 954	2 739	4.7	24.2	23.0	(5.3)	2.13	4.68	2.83	1.05

CMEA countries												
USSR	(2 858)	2 476	3 101	4 208	(9.2)	5.6	5.9	8.2	0.15	0.16	0.25	..
GDR	(156)	135	245	184	(0.5)	0.3	0.5	0.4	0.13	0.10	0.20	..
Eastern Europe, other ...	(649)	394	454	300	(2.1)	0.9	0.9	0.6	0.15	0.09	0.12	..
Total CMEA	(3 663)	3 005	3 800	4 692	(11.8)	6.8	7.3	9.1	0.15	0.14	0.20	..
LDC donors												
China	..	699	324	192	..	1.6	0.6	0.4	..	0.11	0.09	0.07
India	..	136	226	134	..	0.3	0.4	0.3	..	0.08	0.11	0.06
Venezuela	-	144	153	35	-	0.3	0.3	0.1	-	0.23	0.19	0.07
Iran	11	1 438	-144	-5	x	3.3	-0.3	-x	0.03	1.20	-0.11	-0.01
Other	..	(176)	214	90	..	(0.4)	(0.4)	0.2	..	..	..	..
Total non-Arab LDC Donors	(1 654)	(2 593)	773	446	(5.3)	(5.9)	(1.5)	(0.9)	..	..	..	..
TOTAL WORLD	(30 986)	44 126	52 036	51 297	100.0	100.0	100.0	100.0	..	..	..	..

a) Excluding Greece, Luxembourg, Portugal and Spain.

Basic Aid Data

Table 2.   ODA PERFORMANCE OF DAC COUNTRIES IN 1988 AND RECENT YEARS

Net disbursements

Countries	$ million			Per cent of GNP						Per cent change 1988/87			Annual average % change in volume[b] 1982/83 1987/88
	1988 actual[a]	1987 actual[a]	1988 at 1987 prices & exchange rates	1975/79 average	1980/84 average	1987/88 average	1986	1987	1988	In national currency	In $	In volume terms[b]	
	(1)	(2)	(3)	(4)	(5)	(6)	(7)	(8)	(9)	(10)	(11)	(12)	(13)
Australia	1 101	627	901	0.51	0.48	0.41	0.47	0.34	0.47	56.8	75.5	43.6	−1.5
Austria	302	201	290	0.22	0.29	0.21	0.21	0.17	0.24	45.5	50.3	44.4	−5.1
Belgium	597	687	581	0.54	0.56	0.44	0.48	0.48	0.40	−14.5	−13.1	−15.4	−3.7
Canada	2 342	1 885	2 087	0.50	0.45	0.48	0.48	0.47	0.49	15.3	24.2	10.7	6.9
Denmark	922	859	868	0.72	0.76	0.88	0.89	0.88	0.89	5.6	7.3	1.0	5.8
Finland	608	433	544	0.18	0.29	0.55	0.45	0.49	0.59	33.6	40.4	25.7	16.4
France incl. DOM-TOM	6 865	6 525	6 618	0.59	0.72	0.73	0.70	0.74	0.72	4.3	5.2	1.4	2.3
France excl. DOM-TOM	4 777	4 489	4 605	0.32	0.47	0.51	0.48	0.51	0.50	5.5	6.4	2.6	3.5
Germany	4 731	4 391	4 556	0.39	0.46	0.39	0.43	0.39	0.39	5.4	7.8	3.8	−1.7
Ireland	57	51	54	0.15	0.20	0.20	0.28	0.19	0.20	7.6	10.3	5.3	−1.6
Italy	3 183	2 615	3 038	0.11	0.20	0.37	0.40	0.35	0.39	22.2	21.7	16.1	16.1
Japan	9 134	7 342	8 058	0.23	0.31	0.31	0.29	0.31	0.32	10.2	24.4	9.8	5.4
Netherlands	2 231	2 094	2 142	0.83	1.01	0.98	1.01	0.98	0.98	4.0	6.5	2.3	2.1
New Zealand	105	87	88	0.39	0.28	0.27	0.30	0.26	0.27	9.5	21.3	1.5	−0.2
Norway	985	890	922	0.83	0.97	1.10	1.17	1.09	1.10	7.0	10.6	3.6	4.9
Sweden	1 529	1 375	1 386	0.86	0.85	0.88	0.85	0.88	0.87	7.5	11.2	0.8	1.4
Switzerland	617	547	588	0.20	0.27	0.32	0.30	0.31	0.32	10.7	12.9	7.5	4.7
United Kingdom	2 645	1 871	2 283	0.45	0.37	0.30	0.31	0.28	0.32	30.0	41.3	22.0	−1.3
United States	10 141	8 945	9 808	0.24	0.24	0.20	0.23	0.20	0.21	13.4	13.4	9.6	−0.1
Total DAC	48 094	41 426	44 813	0.34	0.36	0.35	0.35	0.34	0.36	13.5	16.1	8.2	2.3
Memo :													
Unweighted average	–	–	–	0.44	0.49	0.50	0.51	0.49	0.51	–	–	–	–

a) At current prices and dollar exchange rates.
b) At 1987 exchange rates and prices.

206

Basic Aid Data

Table 3.   OTHER BURDEN SHARING INDICATORS

1987-88 average

Net disbursements

Countries	Share in total DAC		Grant equivalent of total ODA as % of GNP	Aid appropriations as % of central government budget	Multilateral ODA[a] as % of GNP	*Of which :* to IDA, IFAD and UNDP as % of GNP	Aid to LICs[b]	Aid to LLDCs[c]	Private grants
	ODA	GNP					As % of GNP		
Australia	1.9	1.7	0.41	1.31	0.14	0.05	0.20	0.08	0.02
Austria	0.6	0.9	(0.18)	(0.30)	0.08		(0.08)	(0.03)	(0.02)
Belgium	1.4	1.2	0.44	(1.99)	0.07 (0.15)	0.04	0.29	0.12	0.01
Canada	4.7	3.4	0.50	2.07	0.16	0.06	0.29	0.14	(0.05)
Denmark	2.0	0.8	0.91	2.87	0.36 (0.42)	0.14	0.61	0.34	(0.02)
Finland	1.2	0.7	0.54	2.06	0.21	0.07	0.37	0.20	0.03
France	15.0	7.2	0.66	(3.16)	0.08 (0.13)	0.05	0.30	0.14	(0.01)
Germany	10.2	9.1	0.39	2.54	0.07 (0.12)	0.05	0.23	0.11	(0.05)
Ireland	0.1	0.2	0.20	0.40	0.04 (0.11)	0.01	0.06	0.03	0.09
Italy	6.5	6.2	0.34	(1.07)	0.06 (0.10)	0.02	0.26	0.16	x
Japan	18.4	20.6	0.28	1.23	0.09	0.05	0.22	0.07	x
Netherlands	4.8	1.7	0.98	(2.38)	0.23 (0.31)	0.13	0.67	0.31	0.08
New Zealand	0.2	0.3	0.27	0.61	0.05	0.02	0.07	0.04	0.02
Norway	2.1	0.7	1.10	2.31	0.46	0.18	0.74	0.40	0.07
Sweden	3.2	1.3	0.88	2.90	0.29	0.15	0.54	0.30	(0.07)
Switzerland	1.3	1.4	0.31	3.30	0.09	0.03	0.20	0.10	0.05
United Kingdom	5.0	5.9	0.32	1.11	0.08 (0.14)	0.04	0.20	0.10	0.03
United States	21.3	36.7	0.21	0.77	0.06	0.03	0.10	0.04	0.04
Total DAC	100.0	100.0	(0.34)	(1.37)	0.09 (0.10)		0.20	0.09	(0.03)

a) In brackets, including EEC. Capital subscriptions are on a deposit basis.
b) Low-income countries (LICs) are those with per capita income in 1987 of $700 or below. Includes imputed multilateral ODA. Capital subscriptions to multilateral agencies are on a deposit basis.
c) Least developed countries (LLDCs) are the 42 countries in the current United Nations list including Burma and Mozambique. Includes imputed multilateral ODA. Capital subscriptions to multilateral agencies are on a deposit basis.

Basic Aid Data

Table 4. FINANCIAL TERMS OF ODA COMMITMENTS[a]
1987-88 average

Percentages

Countries	Grant element of total ODA Norm : 86% [b]		Grant share of		Grant element of ODA to LLDC's Norm : 90% [c]	Grant element of bilateral ODA to LLDCs	ODA loans with grant element under 50% as percentage of bilateral ODA
	1981-82	1987-88	Bilateral ODA	Total ODA			
			1987-88				
Australia	100.0	100.0	100.0	100.0	100.0	100.0	–
Austria	57.2	(76.2)[e]	(52.8)[e]	(64.6)[e]	100.0	100.0	..
Belgium	98.1	(94.0)[e]	84.4	90.6	99.8	99.8	–
Canada	98.0	99.6	96.1	97.4	100.0	100.0	0.2
Denmark	95.6	99.5	96.7	98.1	100.0	100.0	–
Finland	95.8	97.7	85.7	91.9	98.5	98.0	1.6
France	89.8	(89.3)[e]	(75.3)[e]	(78.2)[e]	79.4	73.5	..
Germany	87.3	86.1	58.2	69.0	97.9	97.1	21.2
Ireland	–	100.0	100.0	100.0	100.0	100.0	–
Italy[d]	90.8	92.0	68.7	76.9	96.2	95.8	–
Japan	75.0	(75.4)[e]	(29.8)[e]	(46.6)[e]	84.1	79.0	..
Netherlands	94.6	94.1	81.3	86.4	99.3	99.1	6.8
New Zealand	99.8	100.0	100.0	100.0	100.0	100.0	–
Norway	99.4	99.6	98.9	99.4	99.6	99.1	..
Sweden	99.8	100.0	100.0	100.0	100.0	100.0	..
Switzerland	96.8	99.9	99.3	99.5	100.0	100.0	–
United Kingdom	97.7	99.0	96.5	97.8	100.0	100.0	2.1
United States	93.9	96.9	88.5	91.2	98.1	96.8	1.1
Total DAC	90.2	(90.4)	(71.1)	(78.4)	94.9	93.0	..

a) *Excluding* debt reorganisation.
b) Countries whose ODA as a percentage of GNP is significantly below the DAC average are not considered as having met the terms target. This provision disqualifies Austria, Ireland, New Zealand and the United States in 1987 and 1988.
c) Including imputed multilateral grant element. Alternative norm : the grant element to each LLDC should on average be at least 86 per cent over a period of three years. In 1988, all countries with the exception of France and Japan met this provision, with respect to the period 1986-88.
d) Italy has not subscribed to the DAC Terms Recommendation, and the figures shown are for information only.
e) 1987 data.

Basic Aid Data

Table 5. TYING STATUS OF ODA AND ODA USE FOR ASSOCIATED FINANCING BY INDIVIDUAL DAC MEMBERS, 1987

Commitments (excluding administrative costs)

Percentage of total ODA of each donor

Countries	Bilateral ODA								Multilateral			Proportion of ODA used for associated financing
			Of which:			Of which:		Of which:	Excluding EEC			
	Untied*[a]	"Cash"*[b]	Untied* technical co-op.	Untied import financing	Partially untied*[c]	Technical co-op.*	Tied[d]	Technical co-op.	Untied	Tied	EEC	
	(1)	(2)	(3)	(4)	(5)	(6)	(7)	(8)	(9)	(10)	(11)	(12)
Australia	32.4	27.5	0.7	3.0	–	–	34.7	20.7	23.5	9.3	–	1.3
Austria	1.8	0.2	0.2	0.9	–	–	72.6	27.1	23.9	1.7	–	–
Belgium	25.0	3.3	3.4	41.1	–	–	32.6	19.1	25.6	–	16.8	0.2
Canada	27.6	–	8.8	..	3.9	–	29.5	0.7	33.4	5.6	–	0.5
Denmark	32.6	0.4	2.2	29.9	–	–	21.6	–	37.4	2.1	6.3	–
Finland	9.9	3.7	–	6.2	–	–	49.1	14.2	34.3	6.7	–	–
France	42.2	20.1	8.8	11.0	3.5	3.5	33.6	23.0	13.4	–	7.3	3.9
Germany	42.2	3.8	18.7	17.1	–	–	33.0	13.5	15.2	–	9.6	–
Ireland	21.5	12.8	–	..	–	–	25.7	24.4	44.7	3.1	5.0	–
Italy	9.5	7.0	1.2	1.2	–	–	61.8	13.7	18.7	0.6	9.3	7.5
Japan	46.9	17.5	–	31.5	16.6	–	11.3	–	25.2	–	–	0.1
Netherlands	30.5	10.8	12.1	6.5	33.7	11.3	6.4	–	21.8	7.3	0.3	4.1
New Zealand	34.5	14.4	2.3	17.9	–	–	32.6	14.1	31.3	1.6	–	–
Norway	29.8	(1.7)	–	..	1.4	–	21.1	..	44.6	3.1	–	0.5
Sweden	41.6	2.6	–	..	–	–	22.3	13.9	33.8	2.3	–	2.9
Switzerland	46.5	37.1	7.6	1.8	–	–	34.3	17.8	17.6	1.6	–	4.8
United Kingdom	13.1	6.3	0.1	..	0.1	–	42.3	23.7	24.9	0.8	18.7	2.1
United States	26.3	26.3	–	–	36.6	14.4	16.3	13.5	19.1	1.7	..	–
Total DAC	33.4	14.6	4.7	..	13.0	3.9	26.7	13.6	21.4	1.4	4.2	1.8

a) Fully and freely available for essentially world-wide procurement.
b) Amounts not directly financing imports: budget and balance-of-payments support, local cost financing and debt relief.
c) Contributions available for procurement from donor and substantially all developing countries.
d) Mainly aid tied to procurement in the donor country, but also includes amounts available for procurement in several countries, but not widely enough to qualify as "partially untied".
* Compliance with revised reporting instructions remains to be verified.

209

Basic Aid Data

Table 6.   MULTILATERAL ASSISTANCE AND GEOGRAPHICAL DISTRIBUTION
1987-88 average

Net disbursements as per cent of total ODA

Countries	ODA to multilateral organisations[a]		ODA to LICs[b]	ODA to LLDCs[c]		ODA to LMICs[d]	ODA to UMICs[e]
				1981-82	1987-88		
Australia	33.0		48.4	19.1	20.3	30.8	8.9
Austria	36.5		(45.1)	12.4	(16.6)	(6.0)	(40.5)
Belgium	16.0	(33.8)	67.5	27.6	26.6	8.3	5.6
Canada	32.9		60.1	28.3	28.1	7.4	5.3
Denmark	40.9	(47.4)	69.3	39.9	38.8	5.1	2.4
Finland	38.3		68.2	34.0	37.4	6.5	3.3
France	10.7	(18.4)	40.4	17.9	19.4	8.5	35.1
Germany	17.6	(31.3)	39.4	28.2	27.8	13.3	14.7
Ireland	22.8	(54.3)	57.9	15.8	35.9	5.3	4.3
Italy	16.3	(26.1)	69.3	36.2	43.6	9.4	6.0
Japan	29.9		69.0	23.7	21.3	9.0	6.8
Netherlands	23.3	(31.3)	68.5	29.8	31.6	6.9	9.1
New Zealand	16.9		25.9	14.2	16.2	18.8	9.8
Norway	41.4		66.5	39.5	36.1	5.5	2.6
Sweden	32.9		61.2	35.9	34.0	6.2	3.4
Switzerland	28.4		62.7	34.5	32.1	6.9	5.0
United Kingdom	27.2	(46.0)	65.8	30.6	32.6	5.3	5.8
United States	27.8		48.8	17.9	18.1	11.1	16.7
Total DAC	24.6	(29.5)	57.7	24.2	25.3	9.6	13.6

a) Figures in brackets : contributions including EEC.
b) Low-income countries comprise least developed countries and all other countries with per capita income in 1987 of $700 or below including imputed multilateral.
c) Least developed countries are the 42 countries in the current United Nations list including Burma and Mozambique. Including imputed multilateral.
d) Lower middle-income countries (LMICs) comprise recipients with a per capita income in 1987 exceeding $700 up to $1 300. Including imputed multilateral.
e) Upper middle-income countries (UMICs) comprise all recipients with a per capita income in 1987 exceeding $1 300. Including imputed multilateral.
Note : Total ODA includes geographically unallocated amounts. Therefore the percentages by income group do not add up to 100 per cent.

Table 7.   CONCESSIONAL AND NON-CONCESSIONAL DISBURSEMENTS, OF THE MAIN MULTILATERAL ORGANISATIONS, 1986-87

	Net flows	Gross flows		% of total
	$ million	$ million	% of concessional or non concessional	
		Concessional		
Major financial institutions				
IDA	3 428	3 577	42.6	15.8
IDB	202	406	4.8	1.8
African Development Fund	323	327	3.9	1.4
Asian Development Fund	478	500	6.0	2.2
IFAD	326	354	4.2	1.6
Other[a]	36	37	0.4	0.2
Sub-total	4 793	5 201	62.0	23.0
United Nations				
UNDP	778	778	9.3	3.4
WFP	684	684	8.2	3.0
UNHCR	392	392	4.7	1.7
UNRWA	197	197	2.4	0.9
UNICEF	345	345	4.1	1.5
UNTA[b]	284	284	3.4	1.3
UNFPA	104	104	1.2	0.5
Other UN	403	403	4.8	1.8
Sub-total	3 187	3 187	38.0	14.1
Total concessional	7 980	8 388	100.0	37.1
		Non-concessional		
IBRD	4 906	10 394	73.1	46.0
IFC	182	624	4.4	2.8
IDB	1 076	1 659	11.7	7.3
African Development Bank	349	460	3.2	2.0
Asian Development Bank	309	652	4.6	2.9
Others[c]	360	432	3.0	1.9
Total non-concessional	7 182	14 221	100.0	62.9
OVERALL TOTAL	15 162	22 609	–	100.0

a) Council of Europe, Caribbean Development Bank, IBRD.
b) Technical assistance financed from the regular budget of the United Nations.
c) Council of Europe, Caribbean Development Bank.

Basic Aid Data

Table 8. GEOGRAPHICAL DISTRIBUTION OF ODA BY INDIVIDUAL DAC DONORS AND MULTILATERAL AGENCIES[a]

Percentage of gross disbursements

Countries	Sub-Saharan Africa			South Asia			Other Asia and Oceania			Middle East and North Africa[b]			Latin America and Caribbean		
	75/76	80/81	87/88	75/76	80/81	87/88	75/76	80/81	87/88	75/76	80/81	87/88	75/76	80/81	87/88
DAC COUNTRIES, BILATERAL															
United States	7.3	15.8	13.9	27.6	12.8	11.6	18.1	9.2	8.1	32.4	50.1	43.4	14.6	12.2	22.9
Japan	5.4	10.0	12.2	32.5	25.8	22.3	49.9	49.1	50.0	7.4	8.3	8.5	4.8	6.9	6.9
France	46.8	48.0	52.4	4.2	2.8	4.5	11.1	12.9	15.6	14.5	12.5	11.1	23.4	23.8	16.4
Germany	20.8	29.4	28.3	27.1	20.6	15.8	9.2	9.4	11.2	30.3	28.8	30.4	12.6	11.8	14.4
Nordic countries, total	46.6	52.6	63.8	26.3	24.9	17.6	18.1	13.9	8.0	5.3	4.8	4.4	3.7	3.8	6.1
of which: Denmark	52.7	51.6	63.6	17.9	31.1	19.1	16.4	8.9	6.8	9.4	6.2	7.4	3.3	2.2	3.2
Finland	75.5	60.6	64.7	2.7	7.5	13.6	9.8	21.0	6.8	2.2	6.7	7.5	9.8	4.2	7.4
Norway	52.6	54.1	66.6	24.5	30.0	21.1	14.5	6.1	4.3	5.1	6.7	0.7	3.3	3.1	7.3
Sweden	40.8	51.5	61.8	31.1	22.2	15.7	20.4	18.4	11.9	4.3	3.2	3.8	3.4	4.7	6.9
Italy	24.1	55.7	65.5	18.1	1.7	5.0	6.8	6.6	6.6	45.2	27.9	12.4	5.8	8.2	10.4
Netherlands	19.5	31.2	39.0	24.0	24.8	20.4	15.6	10.6	16.9	4.3	5.4	5.5	36.6	27.9	18.2
United Kingdom	28.3	37.0	49.1	41.0	40.0	27.6	11.6	8.5	10.2	6.4	8.3	6.2	12.6	6.2	6.9
Canada	35.5	38.6	38.3	41.8	34.8	24.9	6.5	5.8	12.9	6.8	8.0	7.3	9.4	12.8	16.6
Australia	1.9	5.7	7.0	9.9	10.8	4.9	87.8	81.4	86.8	0.3	2.0	1.1	0.1	0.1	0.2
New Zealand	2.2	2.5	1.2	12.3	2.1	1.3	83.8	94.2	96.9	0.1	0.1	–	1.6	1.1	0.6
Other DAC, total	55.9	45.8	58.7	15.3	8.8	8.7	9.7	15.7	9.4	12.1	23.4	12.7	7.0	6.3	10.6
of which: Austria	20.0	7.8	17.0	31.8	5.1	1.3	10.8	29.5	4.7	20.8	53.9	72.9	16.5	3.7	4.2
Belgium	66.6	66.0	75.3	5.8	5.0	2.4	8.9	11.9	10.0	12.5	12.2	5.3	6.2	4.9	7.1
Ireland	79.0	96.2	94.7	12.4	1.0	3.0	–	0.6	1.2	2.9	0.4	0.4	5.7	1.8	0.8
Switzerland	22.4	39.9	48.4	48.6	26.7	18.6	12.8	6.5	10.7	8.4	12.0	5.5	7.8	14.9	16.8
Total DAC	23.3	29.7	32.6	23.5	17.5	14.2	20.2	17.7	21.2	18.9	22.0	17.9	14.1	13.1	14.1
MULTILATERAL INSTITUTIONS															
EEC	58.4	60.1	52.8	20.3	16.9	11.5	1.9	4.9	10.9	14.1	11.8	13.2	5.4	6.3	11.6
IFIs[c]	14.8	21.5	38.0	43.3	44.3	39.2	10.3	11.0	12.5	6.5	4.7	1.5	25.1	18.5	8.9
UN agencies[d]	30.6	32.5	40.9	23.3	18.2	21.5	12.4	19.3	16.0	19.0	18.7	9.1	14.7	11.3	12.5
NON-DAC FLOWS															
Arab countries, bilateral	8.6	11.3	23.4	12.9	7.0	4.1	1.5	1.2	3.9	74.2	78.7	68.4	2.8	1.8	0.2
Arab countries multilateral	42.1	47.5	46.0	–	10.4	12.7	–	2.7	1.5	57.9	33.2	38.9	–	6.2	0.7
CMEA countries	2.9	4.3	4.4	7.5	14.1	10.7	44.4	47.3	60.6	18.7	10.9	5.7	26.5	23.4	18.6
China	n.a.	56.4	63.9	n.a.	18.1	20.3	n.a.	–	2.1	n.a.	22.9	9.0	n.a.	2.6	4.7
OVERALL TOTAL	19.5	25.1	30.7	21.2	18.4	16.6	16.9	16.7	23.3	29.7	28.1	16.1	12.7	11.7	13.3

a) Excluding unspecified.
b) For the purpose of this analysis, includes small amounts to Southern Europe.
c) International financial institutions. Includes IDA, regional banks' soft windows and IFAD.
d) Includes UNDP, UNICEF, UNWRA, WFP, UNHCR and UNFPA.
Note: Percentages in lines add up to 100 per cent for regional distribution in each two-year period for each individual country/institution.

Basic Aid Data

Table 9. MAJOR AID USES BY INDIVIDUAL DAC DONORS AND MULTILATERAL ORGANISATIONS[a]

Percentage of total commitments

	Social and administrative infrastructure		Economic infrastructure		Agriculture		Industry and other production		Food aid		Programme assistance		*Memo:* Share of ODA through NGO's[b]
	75-76	86-87	75-76	86-87	75-76	86-87	75-76	86-87	75-76	86-87	75-76	86-87	86-87
Australia	17.5	28.6	7.1	5.5	4.3	9.9	1.9	1.7	9.2	6.7	60.0	47.6[c]	0.6
Austria	7.4	33.8	31.7	49.4	3.3	4.0	56.0	2.6	–	1.6	1.6	8.5	0.5
Belgium	4.9	44.1	31.8	12.9	2.7	14.9	32.4	5.8	2.9	2.0	25.3	20.3	6.5
Canada[d]	16.5	9.0	20.0	22.7	8.4	27.2	9.1	6.1	20.6	12.9	25.4	22.1	8.9
Denmark	14.0	21.2	7.5	28.1	11.4	11.8	17.0	11.2	3.4	0.6	46.7	27.0	0.8
Finland[d]	10.9	31.9	9.0	14.7	3.6	27.0	11.0	8.8	7.3	–	58.2	17.6	2.5
France	53.7	41.6	17.4	17.7	7.0	9.7	10.9	6.1	1.1	0.8	9.9	24.1	0.3
Germany	23.4	32.8	19.2	22.3	7.5	10.5	16.2	7.7	3.1	3.1	30.6	23.6	6.9
Ireland	–	40.3	–	0.8	–	17.1	–	3.0	–	–	–	38.8	5.6
Italy	14.0	20.6	14.8	23.6	2.9	17.1	15.5	8.7	–	5.8	52.8	24.2	2.6
Japan	3.3	15.4	37.7	43.9	6.0	10.0	20.6	7.6	0.5	1.3	31.9	21.8	1.6
Netherlands	34.6	23.7	13.7	14.8	20.9	22.9	9.5	3.8	1.6	2.0	19.7	32.8	6.5
New Zealand	14.5	36.0	35.3	8.3	23.7	12.3	4.5	1.2	5.5	0.6	16.5	41.6[c]	0.7
Norway	22.9	34.4	24.4	21.1	25.9	12.2	15.1	13.5	–	1.9	11.7	16.9	6.3
Sweden	22.2	15.9	2.6	15.5	9.0	7.5	14.5	9.6	8.4	0.5	43.3	51.0	4.5
Switzerland	12.3	16.5	21.4	12.3	17.9	21.5	13.6	5.4	10.6	5.8	24.2	38.5	13.5
United Kingdom	4.7	22.5	28.2	18.9	4.3	8.8	28.8	14.4	–	1.2	34.0	34.2	0.5
United States	8.1	20.2	2.6	4.1	8.1	10.0	4.5	0.5	29.5	14.0	47.2	51.2[c]	11.9
Total DAC	19.9	24.7	14.4	20.0	8.2	12.1	11.5	5.8	12.7	5.4	33.3	32.0[c]	5.4
World Bank	..	16.9	..	31.9	..	21.9	..	18.7	..	–	..	10.6	–
IDA	..	21.3	..	20.8	..	27.2	..	8.2	..	–	..	22.5	–
EEC	..	12.3	..	15.5	..	30.6	..	9.6	..	11.5	..	20.5	–
UN agencies[d]	..	26.8	..	15.2	..	9.6	..	5.0	..	20.7	..	22.7	–
Other agencies	..	14.9	..	36.8	..	31.4	..	13.8	..	–	..	3.1	–
Total multilateral	..	17.6	..	28.5	..	24.1	..	14.2	..	3.1	..	12.5[e]	–
OVERALL TOTAL	..	21.3	..	24.1	..	17.9	..	9.8	..	4.3	..	22.6	–

a) Multilateral commitments are for official development finance i.e., including non-concessional loans except IDA whose commitments are at concessional terms.
b) On a disbursements basis.
c) Aid to concentrated country programmes in 1987 as a share of total bilateral commitments was 36.6 per cent for Australia, 30.6 per cent for New Zealand, an estimated 19.9 per cent for the United States and 8.7 per cent for total DAC. Total programme assistance of DAC countries combined in 1986-87 amounted to $10.8 billion.
d) 1986 data.
e) Sectoral programme assistance has been allocated by sector.

Basic Aid Data

Table 10.   RELATIVE IMPORTANCE AND COMPOSITION OF TECHNICAL CO-OPERATION[a]

1986-87 average

Percentage of total bilateral disbursements

Countries	Total[a]	Students		Trainees	Experts & volunteers	Research	Other
		Total	Memo : Imputed costs 1987				
Australia	(34.0)	(15.0)	10.3	2.17	10.0	3.9	3.0
Austria	30.5	19.8	19.3	(0.9)	(7.5)	(0.3)	(2.0)
Belgium	39.1	4.4*	5.6	2.6	16.8	0.7	14.6
Canada[b]	(21.5)	(2.3)	..	(1.3)	(8.2)	(6.4)	(3.3)
Denmark	(17.8)	(2.9)	..	(3.7)	(6.6)	(0.0)	(4.6)
Finland	19.4	1.2	..	1.2	2.4	1.5	13.1
France[c,e]	44.5	(2.2)[e]	..	(2.1)[e]	(21.4)[e]	(0.0)[e]	(1.1)[e]
Germany	34.5	4.2	6.0	3.0	15.9	2.5	8.9
Ireland[b]	(50.2)	(3.4)	..	(3.0)	(21.3)	(2.7)	(19.8)
Italy	20.6	3.0	..	1.6	6.4	3.0	6.6
Japan	15.0	1.5	..	3.3	7.6	0.2	2.4
Netherlands	35.7	1.0	..	0.4	6.3	1.4	26.6
New Zealand	(15.1)	(3.8)	(11.8)[d]	(3.8)	(6.0)	(0.0)	(1.5)
Norway	13.6	(0.9)	..	(0.4)	4.4	1.8	6.1
Sweden	13.5	(0.1)	..	(0.0)	4.9	2.7	5.8
Switzerland	..	..	..	..	..	..	..
United Kingdom	41.1	7.8	..	1.9	11.4	3.2	16.8
United States[b]	(18.5)	(0.8)	..	(0.8)	(12.8)	(3.7)	(0.4)
Total DAC	(21.5)	(2.3)	..	(1.6)	(10.9)	(2.1)	(4.6)

a) Excluding equipment.
b) 1986 only.
c) 1987 only.
d) Not included in total.
e) Partial figures.

214

Basic Aid Data

Table 11. NON-ODA ECONOMIC/FINANCIAL RELATIONS WITH DEVELOPING COUNTRIES

1986-87 average

Per cent of reporting country's GNP

Countries	Total net flows	Total non-ODA flows	Of which: Export credits	Bank lending	Non-bank portfolio	Direct investment	OOF excl. export credits	Private voluntary agencies	Non-ODA debt claims[a] on LDCs	Non-oil imports from LDCs	Imports of manufactures	Exports to LDCs
Australia	0.62	0.22	0.04	–	0.18	0.29	0.01	0.02	0.52	2.43	1.95	4.17
Austria	0.14	-0.05	-0.09	–		0.01	–	0.02	1.58	2.03	1.19	2.80
Belgium	-0.43	-0.92	-0.30	-0.47	0.19	0.18	0.15	0.02	1.90	4.52	1.47	6.79
Canada	0.52	-0.05	-0.02	-0.07	0.03	x	x	0.04	1.03	1.93	1.48	1.87
Denmark	0.75	-0.17	-0.09	–	–	0.09	-0.01	0.02	1.00	2.24	1.36	2.71
Finland	0.65	0.17	0.09	–	–	0.04	x	0.04	0.22	1.64	0.88	2.15
France	1.11	0.39	x	0.12	0.11	0.08	0.17	0.01	3.63	2.03	1.12	3.55
Germany	0.83	0.42	0.05	0.10	0.09	0.05	0.11	0.06	1.77	2.88	1.78	3.97
Ireland	0.47	0.23	0.13	–	–	–	–	0.10	..	3.19	1.94	4.73
Italy	0.34	-0.03	-0.19	–	x	0.05	0.12	x	1.46	1.90	0.93	3.21
Japan	1.01	0.71	-0.01	0.35	0.09	0.24	0.01	x	0.85	1.62	0.66	3.63
Netherlands	1.57	0.58	-0.16	0.07	0.44	0.12	x	0.08	2.10	4.25	1.99	4.93
New Zealand	0.39	0.12	x	–	–	0.09	–	0.02	0.01	2.18	1.48	5.73
Norway	1.10	-0.03	-0.10	–	–	0.01	0.02	0.08	1.19	2.45	1.63	2.57
Sweden	1.15	0.28	0.17	–	–	0.08	x	0.03	1.62	2.18	1.45	3.39
Switzerland	-0.02	-0.32	-0.37	0.16	0.91	0.10	x	0.05	1.86	2.11	1.19	5.15
United Kingdom	0.72	0.43	0.08	0.08	–	0.31	0.03	0.03	2.56	2.78	1.83	3.84
United States	0.36	-0.15	-0.06	-0.03	-0.10	0.13	0.03	0.04	1.03	2.58	2.05	1.76
Total DAC	0.64	0.29	-0.04	0.05	0.01	0.14	0.04	0.03	1.39	2.35	1.53	2.91
Memo: EEC Members	..	..	..	..	..	..	..	..	..	2.75	1.36	4.41

a) Credits outstanding.

Basic Aid Data

Table 12. ECONOMIC INDICATORS FOR DAC MEMBER COUNTRIES

Countries	GNP per capita 1988 $	GNP[a] annual average growth rate 1985-88	Inflation annual average rate 1985-88	Unemployment rate in 1988	1987 Budget Surplus (+) or deficit (−) as % of GNP	Current external balance % of GNP 1988	Total government outlays as % of GDP 1987
	(1)	(2)	(3)	(4)	(5)	(6)	(7)
Australia	14 200	3.9	7.9	7.2	−0.6	−4.4	38.3
Austria	16 600	2.4	2.1	3.5	−4.1	−0.4	52.5
Belgium	15 200	2.3	2.2	10.2	−7.2	2.0	52.3
Canada	18 200	4.1	4.1	7.7	−4.6	−1.9	45.6
Denmark	20 100	1.6	4.2	8.6	2.0	−1.7	58.3
Finland	20 700	3.6	4.5	4.5	−0.9	−2.9	42.0
France	17 000	2.4	3.6	10.1	−2.0	−0.4	51.8
Germany	19 700	2.3	0.8	6.2	−1.8	4.0	46.8
Ireland	8 000	0.9	3.6	16.7	−9.9	2.3	(54.7)
Italy	14 300	3.0	6.2	11.8	−10.5	−0.5	50.7
Japan	23 300	4.4	0.7	2.5	−0.6	2.8	33.2
Netherlands	15 400	2.2	0.6	9.5	−6.1	2.3	60.1
New Zealand	11 600	0.8	12.6	6.0	..	−1.8	..
Norway	21 000	3.9	7.1	3.2	4.6	−4.0	51.6
Sweden	20 800	1.9	5.4	1.6	4.1	−1.4	59.9
Switzerland	28 600	3.1	1.8	0.7	..	3.5	30.1
United Kingdom	14 300	3.7	4.7	8.3	−1.5	−3.2	(45.9)
United States	19 700	3.4	3.3	5.4	−2.3	−2.8	36.7
Total DAC	18 900	3.4	2.8	6.3	−2.2	−0.4	41.1

a) At constant prices.
Source: OECD Economic Outlook, June 1989 and country submissions.

216

Basic Aid Data

Table 13. TOTAL NET RESOURCE FLOWS[a] TO DEVELOPING COUNTRIES[b] BY TYPE OF FLOW

	1980	1981	1982	1983	1984	1985	1986	1987	1988	1980	1985	1988
	Current $ billion									Per cent of total		
I. OFFICIAL DEVELOPMENT FINANCE (ODF)	45.6	45.6	44.3	42.4	47.7	49.0	56.1	61.7	65.7	35.5	58.5	64.7
1. Official development assistance (ODA)	37.8	36.9	34.0	33.9	35.0	37.4	44.3	48.4	51.3	29.5	44.6	50.5
of which: Bilateral disbursements	30.0	29.0	26.4	26.3	27.2	28.9	34.8	38.3	40.0	23.4	34.5	39.4
Multilateral disbursements	7.8	7.9	7.6	7.6	7.8	8.5	9.5	10.1	11.3	6.1	10.1	11.1
2. Other ODF	7.8	8.7	10.3	8.5	12.7	11.6	11.8	13.3	14.4	6.1	13.8	14.2
of which: Bilateral disbursements	3.0	3.0	3.7	1.3	4.5	3.7	4.0	6.6	8.0	2.3	4.4	7.9
Multilateral disbursements	4.8	5.7	6.6	7.2	8.2	7.9	7.8	6.7	6.4	3.7	9.4	6.3
II. TOTAL EXPORT CREDITS	16.5	17.6	13.7	4.6	6.2	4.0	-0.6	-0.7	3.0	12.9	4.8	2.9
1. DAC countries	15.4	16.2	12.7	3.9	5.2	3.4	-0.8	-1.0	2.6	12.0	4.1	2.6
of which: Medium and long-term	13.6	13.3	9.7	7.4	4.9	0.2	-3.8	-5.1	-1.0			
Short-term	1.8	2.9	3.0	-3.5	0.3	3.2	3.0	4.1	3.6			
2. Other countries	1.1	1.4	1.0	0.7	1.0	0.6	0.2	0.3	0.4	0.9	0.7	0.4
III. PRIVATE FLOWS	66.2	74.5	58.3	48.1	31.7	30.8	28.2	35.6	32.9	51.6	36.8	32.4
1. Direct investment (OECD)	11.2	17.2	12.8	9.3	11.3	6.6	11.3	20.2	19.0	8.7	7.9	18.7
of which: Offshore centres	3.0	4.1	4.1	3.7	3.8	3.7	6.8	12.0	··			
2. International bank lending	49.0	52.0	37.6	34.7	16.4	13.6	5.0	5.6	4.7	38.2	16.2	4.6
of which: Short-term	26.0	22.0	15.0	-25.0	-6.0	12.0	-4.0	5.0	··			
3. Total bond lending	1.6	1.5	5.0	1.2	0.3	4.8	3.3	1.0	1.6	1.2	5.7	1.6
4. Other private	2.0	1.8	0.6	0.6	1.1	2.9	5.3	5.5	4.0	1.6	3.5	3.9
5. Grants by non-governmental organisations	2.4	2.0	2.3	2.3	2.6	2.9	3.3	3.3	3.6	1.9	3.5	3.5
TOTAL NET RESOURCE FLOWS (I + II + III)	128.3	137.7	116.3	95.1	85.6	83.8	83.7	96.6	101.6	100.0	100.0	100.0
Related data :												
Use of IMF credit, net	2.6	6.1	6.3	12.5	5.4	0.8	-1.4	-4.7	-4.3			
Interest and dividends paid by LDCs, gross	63.6	86.4	94.0	80.6	86.8	88.7	76.2	74.7	86.0			
	At 1987 prices and exchange rates											
Total net resource flows	169.4	188.9	163.5	134.1	123.4	119.4	96.3	96.6	94.8			
Total official development finance	60.2	62.6	62.3	59.8	68.8	69.8	64.5	62.0	61.3			
Total ODA receipts from all sources	49.9	50.6	47.8	47.8	50.4	53.3	51.0	48.4	47.9			
Private flows	87.4	102.2	82.0	67.8	45.7	43.9	32.4	35.6	30.7			
Total DAC ODA (bilateral and multilateral)	36.0	35.1	39.1	38.9	41.4	41.9	42.2	41.5	44.8			

a) Flows from all sources, i.e. including DAC, CMEA, Arab and other LDC donors.
b) Excluding Taiwan.

Table 14.   NET RESOURCE FLOWS TO DEVELOPING COUNTRIES BY REGION
At constant 1987 prices and exchange rates

$ billion

		1980	1983	1984	1985	1986	1987	1988ᴾ
Sub-Saharan Africa	ODA	12	13	14	16	15	15	16
	Total	21	18	18	21	22	22	24
of which : LICs	ODA	9	10	10	12	12	11	12
	Total	14	16	11	12	16	14	16
North Africa and Middle East	ODA	11	9	10	11	8	7	7
	Total	19	16	15	16	14	9	10
Asian LICs	ODA	12	12	13	13	14	13	13
	Total	19	20	26	31	24	27	28
Other Asia	ODA	2	2	2	2	2	2	2
	Total	13	22	11	8	3	1	2
Western Hemisphere	ODA	5	6	7	8	7	7	7
	Total	76	39	43	31	21	22	21
Otherᵃ and unallocated	ODA	8	5	5	4	5	4	1
	Total	21	18	11	12	12	16	11
Total developing countries	ODA	50	48	50	53	51	48	48
	Total	169	134	123	119	96	97	96
Total LICs	ODA	27	28	30	33	31	31	33
	Total	43	48	50	57	53	52	50
of which : LLDCs	ODA	11	13	13	14	14	13	13
	Total	15	16	14	16	15	15	15
Total LMICs	ODA	7	7	7	7	7	7	7
	Total	19	18	16	14	12	12	13
Total UMICs	ODA	11	10	10	11	10	9	9
	Total	100	65	53	44	25	26	30

a) Includes Europe and Oceania.
Note : Includes Secretariat estimates to allocate large amounts of reported "unallocated" of DAC ODA and direct investment.

Table 15.   AGGREGATE NET FINANCIAL TRANSFERS BY REGION[a]

Current $ billion

	Average 1980-82	1983	1984	1985	1986	1987	1988[p]
Sub-Saharan Africa	11	8	7	10	15	17	19
North Africa and Middle Ea.: . . .	−6	−4	−5	−2	0	−2	−4
Asian LICS	8	5	9	12	11	16	17
Other Asia	3	6	−4	−6	−7	−10	−10
Western Hemisphere	25	−5	−7	−18	−14	−6	−9
Other[b]	5	4	−2	−1	2	7	4
Total LDCs[c]	46	15	−1	−5	8	23	17
For reference : Least developed countries	10	10	9	10	11	13	14

Table 16.   AGGREGATE NET FINANCIAL TRANSFERS BY REGION[a]
At 1987 prices and exchange rates

$ billion

	Average 1980-82	1983	1984	1985	1986	1987	1988[p]
Sub-Saharan Africa	15	11	11	14	17	17	17
North Africa and Middle East . . .	−9	−5	−7	−3	0	−2	−4
Asian LICS	11	7	13	17	13	16	16
Other Asia	4	8	−6	−8	−8	−10	−9
Western Hemisphere	35	−6	−10	−25	−16	−6	−9
Other[b]	7	5	−3	−1	3	7	4
Total LDCs[c]	63	20	−2	−7	9	23	15
For reference : Least developed countries	13	14	13	14	13	13	13

a) Net Financial Transfers are defined as total Net Resource Flows *minus* investment income payments (interest and dividends) by developing countries. Total net flows include official and private grants (including technical co-operation), direct investment and total long- and short-term loans *minus* loan repayments. For further explanation on Net Financial Transfers, see Financing and External Debt of Developing Countries, 1988 Survey (Chapter VI), OECD, Paris, 1989.
b) European LDCs, Oceania.
c) Excluding Taiwan.

Basic Aid Data

Table 17.   DEBT SERVICE RATIOS[a] BY REGION

	1982	1983	1984	1985	1986	1987
SUB-SAHARAN AFRICA	23	25	25	27	28	21
of which : LLDCs	20	22	23	21	26	17
Nigeria	20	22	24	31	23	18
Other countries	26	27	27	33	31	24
LATIN AMERICA AND CARIBBEAN ..	46	37	34	38	40	35
of which : Argentina	56	35	38	50	63	54
Brazil	79	61	39	43	48	39
Jamaica	33	28	31	36	55	44
Mexico	52	42	46	53	55	60
Peru	47	35	37	42	37	21
ASIA	16	18	17	25	24	25
of which : China	18	10	5	8	10	11
India	11	13	15	28	31	37
Indonesia	17	18	20	30	33	36
Korea	21	22	23	32	27	34
Malaysia	1	11	12	33	21	20
Philippines	38	38	27	33	32	31
Thailand	22	26	28	31	30	23
NORTH AFRICA AND MIDDLE-EAST .	11	15	15	13	14	13
of which : Algeria	33	42	36	37	62	...
Egypt	34	34	33	32	34	26
Morocco	41	40	29	36	40	33
Tunisia	19	24	24	28	30	26
OVERALL TOTAL	22	23	22	25	25	24
of which : Major debtor countries[b]	45	38	35	39	40	34
LLCDs	16	18	20	21	26	19

a)   Long and short term interest plus amortization payments (including to IMF) as per cent of exports of goods and services (including private transfers).
b)   Argentina, Bolivia, Brazil, Chile, Colombia, Côte d'Ivoire, Ecuador, Mexico, Morocco, Nigeria, Peru, Philippines, Uruguay, Venezuela, Yugoslavia.

Table 18.   AID RELIANCE RATIOS AND PER CAPITA INCOME

Countries shown in descending order of ODA/GNP ratio

Regions and recipients	ODA[a] as % of GNP 1987-88	Per capita income 1987 $	Regions and recipients	ODA[a] as % of GNP 1987-88	Per capita income 1987 $
SUB-SAHARAN AFRICA	7.5	350	ASIA	1.2	430
LICs	8.6	280	LICs	1.4	310
of which : Somalia LD ...	32.0	290	of which : Nepal LD	13.6	160
Mozambique** ..	31.1	150	Bangladesh LD ..	9.9	160
Zambia	22.8	240	Sri Lanka	8.5	400
Sahel Group LD .	20.1	270	Indochina**	7.9	230
Lesotho LD	18.2	360	Burma LD	4.7	220
Tanzania LD ...	16.2	220	Pakistan	3.4	350
Ethiopia** LD ..	16.1	120	Afghanistan** LD	3.2	280
Madagascar	14.7	200	Philippines	2.5	590
Rwanda LD ...	12.3	310	Indonesia	2.1	450
Sudan LD	12.2	330	India	0.9	300
Zaire	11.6	160	China	0.6	300
Kenya	9.4	340	LMICs	1.4	870
Ghana	8.0	390	of which : Mongolia**	25.8	780
Uganda LD	7.7	260	Thailand	1.2	840
Liberia	6.9	440	UMICs	0.1	3 480
Zimbabwe	5.2	580	of which : Malaysia	0.9	1 780
Nigeria	0.2	370			
LMICs	2.5	980	OCEANIA	19.8	1 230
of which : Congo	6.8	870	LMICs	19.3	750
Côte d'Ivoire ...	3.8	750	of which : Papua New Guinea	13.6	730
Cameroon	2.2	960	UMICs	17.6	3 310
Angola**	1.5	1 130	of which : New Caledonia .	32.1	5 470
UMICs	9.8	2 860			
of which : Reunion	19.1	5 580	NORTH AFRICA AND MIDDLE-EAST	1.0	2 500
LATIN AMERICA	0.7	1 830	LICs	4.7	660
LICs	8.6	490	of which : Yemen Dem.*/** LD	15.1	420
of which : Bolivia	8.9	610	Yemen* LD ...	6.4	580
Haiti LD	8.2	360	Egypt	4.9	710
LMICs	2.7	1 030	Morocco	3.1	620
of which : El Salvador	10.0	850	LMICs	3.4	1 210
Nicaragua**	8.6	850	of which : Tunisia	3.4	1 210
Honduras	7.9	780	UMICs	0.6	3 760
Jamaica	7.7	960	of which : Jordan*	11.1	1 160
Cuba**	3.5	1 170	Israel	4.0	6 810
Guatemala	3.4	810	Syria*	2.3	1 820
Dominican Republic	2.9	730	Algeria*	0.3	2 760
Ecuador	1.7	1 040			
Colombia	0.2	1 220			
UMICs	0.4	2 100			
of which : Costa Rica	5.1	1 590			
Suriname	2.1	2 360			
Peru	0.8	1 430			
Argentina	0.2	2 370			
Brazil	0.1	2 230			
Mexico	0.1	1 820			

a)   Net ODA from all sources : DAC Members, Arab and CMEA donors and multilateral organisations. Data on CMEA aid and GNP of several recipients are based on Secretariat estimates.

Note :   LICs :   Least developed countries and all other countries with per capita income in 1987 of less than $700.
　　　　LMICs :   Countries with per capita income between $700 and $1 300 in 1987.
　　　　UMICs :   Countries with per capita income exceeding $1 300 in 1987.

LD   Least developed country.
*   Receives more than 10 per cent of ODA from Arab sources.
**   Receives more than 10 per cent of ODA from CMEA sources.

Table 19.   AID BY NON-DAC DONORS IN 1988

	ODA $ million	Of which: Multilateral ODA $ million (a)	Of which: Multilateral ODA $ million (b)	Bilateral ODA $ million	ODA/GNP %	GNP per capita $
OECD countries	380	43	115	222	0.08	7 430
Spain	240	36	64	140	0.07	8 700
Portugal	(83)	2	12	(69)	(0.20)	3 950
Greece	(38)	1	33	(4)	(0.07)	5 300
Luxembourg	18	4	6	8	0.29	17 000
Iceland	1	x	–	1	0.02	22 800
CMEA countries	4 692	24	–	4 668	..	..
USSR	4 212	7	–	4 205	..	..
GDR	180	2	–	178	..	..
Other Eastern Europe	300	15	–	285	..	..
Arab donors	2 357	341	27	1 989	0.86	4 810
Saudi Arabia	2 098	266	14	1 818	2.70	5 535
Kuwait	108	42	5	61	0.41	13 265
Libya	129	14	4	111	0.51	5 910
Algeria	10	4	1	5	0.02	2 670
UAE[c]	4	8	2	−6	0.02	15 470
Qatar	8	7	1	–	0.16	15 150
Other LDC donors	418	115	3	300	..	..
China	185	25	–	160	..	..
India	126	18	–	108	..	..
Venezuela	49	41	1	7	0.08	3 150
Korea (Rep.)	20	13	–	(7)	0.01	3 720
Israel	18	1	–	17	..	..
Nigeria	14	11	2	1	0.05	285
Yugoslavia	6	6	–	..	..	..
OVERALL TOTAL	7 847	523	145	7 179	..	..
Memo:						
DAC	48 007	11 467	2 565	33 110	0.36	18 910

a)   Contributions to UN programmes, the World Bank Group and regional development banks.
b)   Contributions to multilateral Arab/OPEC agencies and the EEC.
c)   Incomplete data.

Part II

REFERENCE STATISTICS

*Section A : **Basic Resource Flows***

Table 20.   THE TOTAL NET FLOW OF FINANCIAL RESOURCES FROM DAC COUNTRIES
TO DEVELOPING COUNTRIES AND MULTILATERAL AGENCIES
1970, 1975, 1980, 1986 to 1988

Net disbursements at current prices and exchange rates

	$ million						Percent of total					
	1970	1975	1980	1986	1987	1988	1970	1975	1980	1986	1987	1988
I. Official Development Assistance	6 949	13 854	27 297	36 663	41 426	48 094	44	31	36	53	63	
1. Bilateral grants and grant-like flows	3 321	6 269	14 135	21 063	23 246	26 035	21	14	19	31	35	
of which : Technical co-operation	1 525	2 922	5 472	7 486	(8 964)	(10 222)	10	7	7	11	14	
2. Bilateral loans at concessional terms	2 351	3 539	3 985	5 151	6 623	7 145	15	8	5	7	10	
3. Contributions to multilateral institutions	1 277	4 046	9 177	10 449	11 556	14 914	8	9	12	15	18	
of which : UN	371	1 199	2 187	2 693	2 998	3 457	2	3	3	4	5	
EEC	158	675	1 580	1 686	1 866	2 565	1	2	2	2	3	
IDA	582	1 318	3 105	3 555	4 204	5 290	4	3	4	5	6	
Regional development banks	101	418	1 717	1 675	1 747	2 264	1	1	2	2	3	
II. Other Official Flows	1 122	3 912	5 270	2 113	2 015		7	9	7	3	3	
1. Bilateral	845	3 833	5 376	2 260	2 158		5	9	7	3	3	
2. Multilateral	276	79	–106	–147	–143		2	x	x	–x	–x	
III. Private Flows	7 018	25 706	40 403	26 734	18 777		44	57	54	39	29	
1. Direct investment	3 690	10 344	10 127	10 968	20 895		23	23	13	16	32	
2. Bilateral portfolio	697	9 291	17 317	13 399	–2 395		4	21	23	19	–4	
3. Multilateral portfolio	474	2 553	1 469	4 040	2 667		3	5	2	6	4	
4. Export credits	2 157	3 518	11 490	–1 673	–2 390		14	8	15	–2	–4	
IV. Grants by Private Voluntary Agencies	860	1 346	2 386	3 334	3 525		5	3	3	5	5	
Total net flows	15 948	44 817	75 356	68 844	65 743		100	100	100	100	100	100
Total net flows in 1987 prices & exchange rates[a]	50 045	93 818	99 493	79 195	65 743							

a) Deflated by total GNP deflator (total flows used as weights).

Table 21.   THE TOTAL NET FLOW OF RESOURCES FROM DAC COUNTRIES TO DEVELOPING COUNTRIES AND MULTILATERAL AGENCIES

1977-79 average, 1980, 1984-88

Net disbursements

$ million and per cent of GNP

Countries	1977-79 average $ million	1977-79 average As % of GNP	1980 $ million	1980 As % of GNP	1984 $ million	1984 As % of GNP	1985 $ million	1985 As % of GNP	1986 $ million	1986 As % of GNP	1987 $ million	1987 As % of GNP	1988 $ million	1988 As % of GNP
Australia	729	0.50	883	0.64	1 514	0.88	1 234	0.80	1 052	0.65	920	0.49		
Austria	411	0.23	251	0.33	56	0.09	161	0.24	134	0.14	248	0.21		
Belgium	2 133	0.54	2 896	2.42	3 518	4.53	1 313	1.63	-808	-0.70	-309	-0.22		
Canada	2 403	0.50	3 225	1.30	2 811	0.87	1 688	0.51	1 557	0.44	2 482	0.62		
Denmark	641	0.67	799	1.24	625	1.19	447	0.82	473	0.60	852	0.87		
Finland	128	0.18	201	0.40	284	0.57	278	0.52	434	0.63	580	0.66	755	0.74
France	7 302	0.59	11 631	1.76	8 897	1.82	8 874	1.74	9 176	1.27	8 671	0.99	11 811	0.98
Germany	6 992	0.39	10 633	1.30	6 507	1.05	5 750	0.92	7 889	0.88	8 843	0.79	261	0.92
Ireland	21	0.17	30	0.16	59	0.37	99	0.61	114	0.52	77	0.29		
Italy	3 100	0.11	4 010	0.88	2 308	0.56	2 195	0.52	2 566	0.43	2 019	0.27	5 075	0.62
Japan	7 947	0.24	6 815	0.66	11 746	0.93	11 619	0.87	14 578	0.74	20 349	0.85	21 424	0.75
Netherlands	2 263	0.85	2 366	1.40	2 048	1.66	2 629	2.11	2 815	1.63	3 217	1.50	2 675	1.18
New Zealand	82	0.35	107	0.48	81	0.37	88	0.41	109	0.43	122	0.36		
Norway	644	0.90	866	1.55	601	1.14	594	1.05	735	1.07	912	1.12	906	1.03
Sweden	1 376	0.91	1 868	1.52	1 262	1.37	1 410	1.45	1 706	1.33	1 756	1.13		
Switzerland	4 220	0.20	2 705	2.56	3 369	3.51	2 504	2.58	1 386	0.98	-1 618	-0.91	1 981	0.51
United Kingdom	9 882	0.48	12 219	2.29	4 831	1.13	2 463	0.54	6 697	1.21	3 430	0.50	2 952	0.36
United States	13 804	0.23	13 852	0.52	28 585	0.78	1 816	0.05	18 231	0.43	13 193	0.29	17 505	0.36
Total DAC	66 078	1.15	75 356	1.03	79 102	0.99	45 163	0.53	68 844	0.66	65 743	0.55		

Section A : **Basic Resource Flows**

Table 22.   THE NET FLOW OF PRIVATE CAPITAL[a] FROM DAC COUNTRIES TO DEVELOPING COUNTRIES
1977-79 average, 1980, 1984-88

Net disbursements

$ million and per cent of GNP

Countries	1977-79 average		1980		1984		1985		1986		1987		1988	
	$ million	As % of GNP	$ million	As % of GNP	$ million	As % of GNP	$ million	As % of GNP	$ million	As % of GNP	$ million	As % of GNP	$ million	As % of GNP
Australia	128	0.12	163	0.12	561	0.33	413	0.27	226	0.14	311	0.17		
Austria	284	0.49	88	0.12	−131	−0.20	−112	−0.17	−148	−0.16	−61	−0.05		
Belgium	1 550	1.62	2 071	1.74	2 840	3.66	759	0.94	−1 415	−1.23	−1 358	−0.95		
Canada	882	0.43	1 386	0.56	802	0.25	21	0.01	−114	−0.03	185	0.05		
Denmark	149	0.27	178	0.28	−42	−0.08	−82	−0.15	−103	−0.13	47	0.05		
Finland	60	0.17	69	0.14	−7	−0.02	19	0.04	83	0.12	125	0.14	112	0.11
France	4 188	0.87	6 742	1.02	3 828	0.78	3 671	0.72	3 031	0.42	−65	−0.01	−783	−0.08
Germany	4 076	0.64	6 016	0.74	2 348	0.38	1 466	0.23	2 378	0.26	2 357	0.21	5 091	0.42
Ireland	−	−	−	−	3	0.02	37	0.23	32	0.14	−	−	−	−
Italy	2 507	0.94	2 823	0.62	538	0.13	321	0.08	−620	−0.10	−1 913	−0.25	1 400	0.17
Japan	4 492	0.51	1 958	0.19	6 644	0.53	8 022	0.60	9 586	0.49	14 723	0.62	12 822	0.45
Netherlands	1 050	0.77	627	0.37	674	0.54	1 380	1.11	929	0.54	947	0.44	260	0.11
New Zealand	9	0.05	26	0.12	19	0.09	24	0.11	26	0.10	26	0.08		
Norway	253	0.64	321	0.58	−11	−0.02	−45	−0.08	−128	−0.19	−40	−0.05	−123	−0.14
Sweden	473	0.51	846	0.69	278	0.30	283	0.29	145	0.11	273	0.17	686	0.39
Switzerland	3 991	4.78	2 377	2.25	3 038	3.16	2 153	2.21	905	0.64	−2 249	−1.26	1 283	0.67
United Kingdom	8 033	2.42	10 410	1.95	2 794	0.65	378	0.08	4 447	0.80	1 074	0.16	−255	−0.03
United States	8 818	0.40	4 301	0.16	17 387	0.47	−9 278	−0.23	7 473	0.02	4 395	0.10	3 203	0.07
Total DAC	40 945	0.72	40 403	0.55	41 564	0.52	9 431	0.11	26 734	0.26	18 777	0.16		

a) Excluding grants by voluntary agencies.

Section A : Basic Resource Flows

Table 23.   NET OFFICIAL DEVELOPMENT ASSISTANCE FROM DAC COUNTRIES TO DEVELOPING COUNTRIES AND MULTILATERAL AGENCIES

1977-79 average, 1980, 1984-88

Net disbursements

$ million and per cent of GNP

Countries	1977-79 average [a]		1980		1984		1985		1986		1987		1988	
	$ million	As % of GNP	$ million	As % of GNP	$ million	As % of GNP	$ million	As % of GNP	$ million	As % of GNP	$ million	As % of GNP	$ million	As % of GNP
Australia	539	0.50	667	0.48	777	0.45	749	0.48	752	0.47	627	0.34	1 101	0.47
Austria	131	0.23	178	0.23	181	0.28	248	0.38	198	0.21	201	0.17	302	0.24
Belgium	517	0.54	595	0.50	446	0.58	440	0.55	547	0.48	687	0.48	597	0.40
Canada	1 036	0.50	1 075	0.43	1 625	0.50	1 631	0.49	1 695	0.48	1 885	0.47	2 342	0.49
Denmark	369	0.67	481	0.74	449	0.85	440	0.80	695	0.89	859	0.88	922	0.89
Finland	65	0.18	110	0.22	178	0.35	211	0.40	313	0.45	433	0.49	608	0.59
France	2 807	0.59	4 162	0.63	3 788	0.77	3 995	0.78	5 105	0.70	6 525	0.74	6 865	0.72
Germany	2 486	0.39	3 567	0.44	2 782	0.45	2 942	0.47	3 832	0.43	4 391	0.39	4 731	0.39
Ireland	21	0.17	30	0.16	35	0.22	39	0.24	62	0.28	51	0.19	57	0.20
Italy	282	0.11	683	0.15	1 133	0.28	1 098	0.26	2 404	0.40	2 615	0.35	3 183	0.39
Japan	2 108	0.24	3 353	0.32	4 319	0.34	3 797	0.29	5 634	0.29	7 342	0.31	9 134	0.32
Netherlands	1 151	0.85	1 630	0.97	1 268	1.02	1 136	0.91	1 740	1.01	2 094	0.98	2 231	0.98
New Zealand	58	0.35	72	0.33	55	0.25	54	0.25	75	0.30	87	0.26	105	0.27
Norway	360	0.90	486	0.87	540	1.03	574	1.01	798	1.17	890	1.09	985	1.10
Sweden	850	0.91	962	0.78	741	0.80	840	0.86	1 090	0.85	1 375	0.88	1 529	0.87
Switzerland	168	0.20	253	0.24	285	0.30	302	0.31	422	0.30	547	0.31	617	0.32
United Kingdom	1 579	0.48	1 854	0.35	1 429	0.33	1 530	0.33	1 737	0.31	1 871	0.28	2 645	0.32
United States	5 010	0.23	7 138	0.27	8 711	0.24	9 403	0.24	9 564	0.23	8 945	0.20	10 141	0.21
Total DAC	19 536	0.34	27 297	0.37	28 742	0.36	29 429	0.35	36 663	0.35	41 426	0.34	48 094	0.36

a) Excluding administrative costs, except for the United States.

Section B: **Multilateral Aid**

Table 24. ODA FROM DAC COUNTRIES TO MULTILATERAL AGENCIES, 1988

Net disbursements   *$ million*

Countries	World Bank Group			IDB			Asian Development Bank			African Development Fund[b]	EEC		UN agencies			Other	Total
	IBRD[a]	IDA	Total	Ordinary capital	Special Fund	Total	Ordinary capital	Special Fund	Total		Total	of which: EDF	Total	UNDP	WFP		
Australia	7	175	182	–	–	–	–	161	161	–	–	–	108	12	55	28	479
Austria	(17)	(73)	(90)	–	–	–	–	–	–	–	–	–	(21)	(9)	(4)	(28)	(139)
Belgium	3	–	3	–	–	–	1	9	10	–	130	69	26	16	2	5	174
Canada	19	189	208	–	–	–	1	85	86	106	–	–	315	60	181	48	763
Denmark	17	60	77	–	–	–	x	10	10	27	61	29	188	77	30	81	444
Finland	5	37	42	–	–	–	1	8	9	14	–	–	126	33	27	37	228
France	38	262	300	–	–	–	4	103	107	86	605	298	113	43	4	53	1 264
Germany	18	506	524	1	–	1	–	35	35	–	752	329	231	78	22	16	1 559
Ireland	9	5	14	–	–	–	–	–	–	–	18	7	3	x	–	–	35
Italy	42	–	42	–	–	–	10	98	108	3	329	134	203	59	23	90	775
Japan	223	1 340	1 563	27	–	27	520	–	520	156	–	–	378	84	58	68	(2 712)
Netherlands	24	208	232	1	1	2	2	–	2	19	182	86	229	81	47	13	679
New Zealand	–	3	3	–	–	–	1	–	1	–	–	–	5	2	x	3	12
Norway	7	79	86	1	5	6	–	8	8	36	–	–	220	78	25	57	413
Sweden	4	131	135	–	–	–	–	15	15	44	–	–	281	95	58	–	475
Switzerland	–	–	–	–	–	–	1	23	24	34	–	–	95	44	13	19	172
United Kingdom	128	311	439	(–1)	(–)	(–1)	1	49	50	1	488	212	192	44	9	46	1 215
United States	159	1 910	2 069	–	–	–	15	180	195	189	–	–	726	110	185	197	3 376
Total DAC	720	5 289	6 009	29	6	35	557	784	1 341	715	2 565	1 164	3 460	925	743	789	14 914

a) Including IFC and MIGA.
b) Including contributions to the African Development Bank.

Table 25. CAPITAL SUBSCRIPTIONS TO MULTILATERAL AGENCIES[a]
ON A DEPOSIT AND AN ENCASHMENT BASIS

Net disbursements   *$ million*

Countries	Deposit basis					Encashment basis				
	1980	1985	1986	1987	1988	1980	1985	1986	1987	1988
Australia	113	135	133	19	349	34	82	51	66	77
Austria	5	62	35	21	(118)	16	1	..	..	..
Belgium	11	70	90	100	13	38	..	..	..	..
Canada	240	399	394	352	400	91	251	204	336	349
Denmark	62	51	77	99	115	20	..	..	79	..
Finland	29	36	56	66	84	13	..	..	..	..
France	239	337	442	650	494	..	..	..	..	..
Germany	595	420	518	547	561	276	386	483	555	474
Ireland	–	2	13	1	14	–	–	5	7	..
Italy	393	28	536	294	186	290	85	170	262	334
Japan	1 089	957	1 413	1 816	2 294	295	..	..	..	..
Netherlands	104	149	233	297	268	67	99	256	282	183
New Zealand	6	4	8	13	4	5	3	..	..	..
Norway	62	71	95	98	152	..	..	..	..	..
Sweden	25	84	102	206	193	65	..	..	..	..
Switzerland	26	32	36	54	62	26	4	5	..	..
United Kingdom	116	248	262	320	489	202	218	282	312	448
United States	1 844	252	1 132	1 220	2 467	796	1 302	1 481	1 212	1 314
Total DAC	4 959	3 337	5 575	6 173	(8 263)	..	..	..	..	..

a) World Bank, IDA, IDB, African Development Bank, Asian Development Bank and Caribbean Development Bank.

Section B : **Multilateral Aid**

Table 26. NET DISBURSEMENTS OF CONCESSIONAL AND NON-CONCESSIONAL FLOWS BY MULTILATERAL AGENCIES
1970-71, 1975-76, 1980, 1982 to 1988

Net disbursements — $ million

	1970-71	1975-76	1980	1982	1983	1984	1985	1986	1987	1988
CONCESSIONAL FLOWS										
Major Financial Institutions										
IDA	225	1 198	1 543	2 363	2 336	2 492	2 599	3 327	3 530	3 567
IBRD	–	8	107	58	47	41	34	4	x	–
IDB	219	299	326	366	365	438	351	283	121	134
African Dev. Fund	–	7	96	122	158	111	210	272	374	351
Asian Dev. Fund	3	72	149	177	223	304	393	416	540	660
IFAD	–	–	54	104	144	170	270	286	366	102
Sub-total	447	1 584	2 274	3 190	3 272	3 556	3 857	4 588	4 931	4 814
United Nations										
WFP	125	350	539	595	630	679	779	649	720	878
UNDP	219	378	660	714	617	596	635	769	786	914
UNHCR	8	81	465	366	356	397	418	387	398	(400)
UNWRA	45	99	157	235	211	191	187	187	207	(210)
UNICEF	47	114	247	204	246	244	279	326	365	400
UNTA	49	73	35	196	253	217	295	254	314	268
UNFPA	–	–	150	113	122	119	127	101	107	129
Other UN	36	259	235	332	304	319	327	380	426	479
Sub-total	529	1 355	2 487	2 755	2 739	2 763	3 047	3 052	3 322	(3 678)
Other institutions	x	14	1 682	39	35	17	29	29	38	(40)
Total above	976	2 953	6 443	5 984	6 046	6 336	6 933	7 669	8 291	(8 532)
EEC	208	611	1 061	1 143	1 215	1 287	1 407	1 659	1 747	2 723
Arab Funds	–	288	286	398	314	147	133	144	73	60
Total concessional	1 184	3 852	7 790	7 525	7 575	7 770	8 472	9 472	10 111	(11 315)
NON-CONCESSIONAL FLOWS										
Major Financial Institutions										
IBRD	585	1 768	3 166	4 534	5 117	5 628	5 041	5 418	4 395	3 417
IFC	62	180	295	291	166	127	94	156	208	356
IDB	104	247	567	832	957	1 550	1 398	1 224	928	1 093
African Dev. Bank	4	44	97	115	145	110	235	282	416	625
Asian Dev. Bank	29	245	328	473	550	513	400	364	253	598
Others	–	8	10	13	9	14	306	290	431	(433)
Sub-total	785	2 492	4 463	6 258	6 944	7 942	7 474	7 734	6 631	(6 522)
EEC	34	42	257	320	202	84	152	190	140	–3
Arab Funds	–	96	128	48	80	187	286	–137	–101	–84
Total non-concessional	819	2 630	4 848	6 626	7 226	8 213	7 912	7 787	6 670	(6 435)

230

Section B : Multilateral Aid

Table 27. COMMITMENTS OF CONCESSIONAL AND NON-CONCESSIONAL FLOWS FROM MULTILATERAL AGENCIES
1970, 1975, 1980, 1984 to 1988

$ million

Commitments	Concessional								Non-concessional							
	1970	1975	1980	1984	1985	1986	1987	1988	1970	1975	1980	1984	1985	1986	1987	1988
IBRD	–	–	–	–	–	–	–	–	1 508	3 938	8 282	9 273	12 844	13 469	14 148	14 471
IDA	594	1 651	3 784	3 222	3 541	3 373	4 246	4 352	–	–	–	–	–	–	–	–
IFC	–	–	–	–	–	–	–	–	113	158	745	337	550	641	1 016	1 220
IDB	440	580	824	307	251	296	346	120	192	635	1 424	3 195	2 735	2 676	1 929	1 433
African Dev. Bank	–	–	–	–	–	–	–	–	11	105	297	494	709	1 034	1 343	1 405
African Dev. Fund	–	101	273	369	439	586	769	763	–	–	–	–	–	–	–	–
Asian Dev. Bank & Fund	40	166	477	684	765	633	1 452	1 094	212	494	958	1 551	1 271	1 368	1 481	2 062
Caribbean Dev. Bank	–	22	27	48	27	37	26	..	–	14	14	14	23	18	10	..
Council of Europe	–	–	–	9	9	6	4	13	–	–	–	–	328	330	500	571
EEC/EIB	93	486	1 570	1 535	1 249	1 878	3 846	4 785	(2)	58	517	380	247	376	218	615
of which: Grants	92	433	1 117	1 342	1 193	1 787	3 611	4 572	–	–	–	–	–	–	–	–
UN (all grants)	499	1 457	2 487	2 763	3 048	3 051	3 322	(3 678)	–	–	–	–	–	–	–	–
IFAD	–	–	396	203	149	156	233	250	–	–	–	–	–	–	–	–
Arab Funds	–	259	421	424	288	427	295	579	–	84	531	924	755	861	897	666
of which: Grants	–	7	28	44	38	28	22	44	–	–	–	–	–	–	–	–
Total	1 666	4 722	10 259	9 555	9 766	10 443	14 539	15 664	2 038	5 486	12 768	16 168	19 462	20 773	21 542	(22 453)
of which: Grants	591	1 897	3 632	4 149	4 279	4 866	7 155	..	–	–	–	–	–	–	–	–

Section C: Purpose and Tying Status of ODA

Table 28. AID BY MAJOR PURPOSES (COMMITMENTS), 1988

Per cent of total

	Australia	Austria[a]	Belgium[a]	Canada	Denmark	Finland	France[a]	Germany[a]	Ireland	Italy	Japan[a]
Social and administrative infrastructure	23.6	33.9	42.6	15.6	7.4	17.2	45.1	32.1	39.7	11.9	14.0
Education[b]	15.8	28.8	23.7	6.7	3.4	3.8	24.3	19.0	18.7	–	6.2
Health & population	1.6	3.5	9.8	1.9	0.5	5.2	9.6	2.4	9.1	3.2	2.3
Planification and public administ.	4.8	0.4	4.3	0.5	0.1	1.5	5.3	3.1	5.9	–	0.6
Other (including water supply)	1.4	1.2	4.8	6.5	3.4	6.7	5.9	7.6	6.0	8.7	4.9
Economic infrastructure	8.0	49.1	11.7	17.0	22.5	23.2	13.7	26.2	2.3	32.1	49.2
Transport and communication	7.9	1.7	8.9	9.1	12.4	11.6	9.6	15.5	2.3	12.4	28.2
Energy	0.1	1.2	2.2	4.8	10.1	11.6	3.9	10.6	–	16.3	18.1
Other	–	46.2	0.6	3.1	–	–	0.2	0.1	–	3.4	2.9
Production	8.1	6.7	29.5	16.7	36.3	18.8	14.6	22.7	28.8	32.5	15.1
Agriculture	6.1	3.5	17.3	12.6	26.2	14.1	9.7	10.8	22.4	9.8	9.0
Industry, mining and construction	1.3	3.1	6.0	3.7	10.0	3.4	4.5	9.1	1.8	22.7	5.4
Trade, banking, tourism	0.7	–	6.2	0.4	0.1	1.3	0.4	2.8	3.7	–	0.6
Other	–	–	–	–	–	–	–	–	0.9	–	0.1
Multisector	1.2	–	2.2	5.2	7.4	1.7	7.5	4.7	2.3	–	1.4
Programme assistance	50.2	–	–	8.7	–	15.7	3.6	4.7	–	6.2	14.3
Debt relief	–	0.1	3.6	2.9	1.3	10.7	2.7	0.8	–	17.3	1.6
Food aid	3.3	1.2	3.3	12.1	–	0.4	0.7	2.9	5.5	–	1.3
Emergency aid (other than food aid)	0.8	4.0	0.5	3.2	0.4	3.2	–	0.7	13.7	–	–
Administrative expenses	2.6	3.7	5.7	7.5	4.7	4.3	3.3	1.5	7.7	–	2.9
Unspecified	2.2	1.3	0.8	11.1	19.9	4.8	8.7	3.6	–	–	0.2
TOTAL	100.0	100.0	100.0	100.0	100.0	100.0	100.0	100.0	100.0	100.0	100.0
Of which[a]: Technical assistance[c]	34.2	45.3	53.6	13.8	(20.0)	24.4	(46.5)	35.7	(48.4)	15.7	11.4
Students and trainees	16.0	30.5	10.2	2.3	..	1.8	(6.4)	8.0	..	2.6	3.4
Experts and volunteers	9.5	12.2	13.6	5.3	..	2.0	(39.2)	11.1	..	3.4	5.2
Research	3.7	0.7	1.1	4.1	..	0.3	–	1.9	..	1.7	0.1
Other	5.0	1.8	28.7	2.1	..	20.2	(0.9)	14.7	..	7.9	2.7
Memo item:											
Contributions to NGOs (included in above)	1.1	1.7	10.8	9.4	3.9	3.9	0.3	7.4	3.7	2.8	1.5

a) Year 1987.
b) Including students and trainees.
c) Excluding equipment. Calculated from disbursements data.

Table 28 (Cont'd).   AID BY MAJOR PURPOSES (COMMITMENTS), 1988

Per cent of total[a]

	Nether-lands[a]	New Zealand	Norway[a]	Sweden	Switzer-land	United Kingdom[a]	United States[a]	Total DAC	Multilateral finance (ODF)[a]			
									Total	EEC	World Bank	UN agencies
Social and administrative infrastructure	18.9	60.6	36.7	23.7	23.0	18.1	23.4	24.9	19.9	11.3	20.8	27.9
Education[b]	5.0	52.6	10.1	6.6	7.5	10.3	4.9	11.0	4.3	3.8	4.9	2.6
Health & population	3.3	1.7	10.5	5.4	4.5	2.5	9.1	5.3	7.8	2.6	6.1	19.1
Planning and public administ.	1.2	3.2	–	7.2	–	1.9	3.7	2.6	0.5	–	–	4.4
Other (including water supply).	9.4	3.1	16.1	4.5	11.0	3.4	5.7	6.0	7.3	4.9	9.8	1.8
Economic infrastructure	17.0	2.9	16.7	7.7	6.4	17.0	4.8	21.7	30.4	16.8	35.0	5.9
Transport and communication.	14.1	2.2	1.5	4.0	6.0	11.6	1.8	12.6	11.3	9.9	12.8	3.8
Energy	0.7	0.6	14.3	3.4	0.4	5.3	3.0	7.9	18.8	5.8	22.2	–
Other	2.2	0.1	0.9	0.3	–	0.1	–	1.2	0.3	1.1	–	2.1
Production	30.1	14.1	25.0	12.1	27.2	25.8	13.0	17.9	36.6	40.2	36.3	16.6
Agriculture	23.3	6.8	13.0	6.8	21.4	9.1	8.9	10.8	23.2	24.3	23.3	9.6
Industry, mining and construction	4.8	1.0	11.9	4.1	2.0	15.8	0.6	5.4	9.3	10.3	8.0	3.8
Trade, banking, tourism	2.0	6.3	–	1.1	3.8	0.9	3.5	1.7	3.8	5.6	5.0	1.2
Other	–	–	0.1	0.1	–	–	–	–	0.2	–	–	2.0
Multisector	2.1	0.2	6.0	1.9	2.8	–	0.1	2.8	–	–	–	–
Programme assistance	12.4	13.3	9.0	16.2	11.6	14.4	32.5	15.1	5.4	11.7	7.5	–
Debt relief	1.8	–	–	–	–	3.0	0.6	2.0	–	–	–	–
Food aid	1.7	0.2	1.3	3.0	4.5	1.3	16.4	5.3	3.3	13.0	–	20.7
Emergency aid (other than food aid)	1.6	0.6	4.8	11.2	7.3	1.5	1.5	1.3	2.4	1.4	–	19.6
Administrative expenses	4.1	5.4	–	5.6	–	4.5	6.6	3.9	0.2	3.2	–	–
Unspecified	10.3	2.6	0.5	18.6	16.1	14.3	1.1	5.1	1.8	2.4	0.4	9.3
TOTAL	100.0	100.0	100.0	100.0	100.0	100.0	100.0	100.0	100.0	100.0	100.0	100.0
Of which[a] :												
Technical assistance[c]	31.8	24.4	(21.0)	20.5	(16.2)	32.2	16.6	24.6				
Students and trainees	1.3	(17.5)	.	0.1	.	7.5	1.4	3.8				
Experts and volunteers	5.4	6.9	.	4.9	.	8.7	10.7	11.8				
Research	1.2	–	.	4.1	.	2.6	3.0	1.8				
Other	23.9	–	.	11.5	.	13.4	1.5	7.2				
Memo item:												
Contributions to NGOs (included in above)	(8.0)	(1.3)	(14.2)	8.4	17.0	0.4	9.0	.				

a) Year 1987.
b) Including students and trainees.
c) Excluding equipment. Calculated from disbursements data.

Section C: Purpose and Tying Status of ODA

Table 29. TYING STATUS OF ODA BY INDIVIDUAL DAC MEMBERS, 1988

Commitments (excluding administrative costs) — $ million

Countries	Bilateral ODA — Untied[a]	Bilateral ODA — Of which: "Cash"[b]	Bilateral ODA — Of which: Untied technical co-op.	Bilateral ODA — Untied import financing	Bilateral ODA — Partially untied[c]	Bilateral ODA — Of which: Technical co-op.	Bilateral ODA — Tied[d]	Bilateral ODA — Of which: Technical co-op.	Multilateral ODA — Excluding EEC: Untied	Multilateral ODA — Excluding EEC: Tied	Multilateral ODA — EEC	Total ODA	Associated financing[e]
	(1)	(2)	(3)	(4)	(5)	(6)	(7)	(8)	(9)	(10)	(11)	(12)	(13)
Australia	508	461	x	16	-	-	395	235	269	36	-	1 208	35
Austria	..	..	..	..	..	..	..	..	..	..	..	..	..
Belgium	..	..	..	..	..	..	..	..	..	..	..	..	..
Canada	..	..	..	..	..	..	..	..	..	..	..	..	..
Denmark	441	8	113	324	9	9	162	..	304	35	74	1 025	..
Finland	106	58	..	48	-	-	293	-	194	32	-	625[f]	17
France	2 615	245	1 197	1 051	-	-	2 160	732	876	25	975	6 651	-
Germany	..	..	..	..	..	..	..	..	..	..	..	..	..
Ireland	..	..	..	..	..	..	..	..	..	..	..	..	..
Italy	..	..	..	..	..	..	..	..	..	..	..	..	..
Japan	..	..	..	..	..	..	..	..	..	..	..	..	..
Netherlands	739	145	327	221	814	306	255	..	467	48	208	2 532[f]	19
New Zealand	37	16	3	19	9	9	32	-	10	-	-	88[f]	-
Norway	..	..	..	..	..	..	..	..	..	..	..	..	..
Sweden	665	5	-	66	42	42	320	185	489	-	-	1 516	47
Switzerland	..	..	..	..	..	..	..	..	..	..	..	..	..
United Kingdom	281	104	7	74	-	-	1 329	636	662	14	580	2 866	331
United States	..	..	..	..	..	..	..	..	..	..	..	..	..
Total DAC	..	..	..	..	..	..	..	..	..	..	..	..	..

a) Fully and freely available for essentially world-wide procurement.
b) Amounts not directly financing imports: budget and balance-of-payments support, local cost financing and debt relief.
c) Contributions available for procurement from donor and substantially all developing countries.
d) Mainly aid tied to procurement in the donor country, but also includes amounts available for procurement in several countries, but not widely enough to qualify as "partially untied".
e) On a disbursement basis.
f) Including administrative costs.

Table 30.   TECHNICAL CO-OPERATION EXPENDITURE[a]
1970, 1980, 1984 to 1988

Net Disbursements — *$ million*

Countries	1970	1980	1984	1985	1986	1987	1988
Australia	13	54	164	189	176	180	203
Austria	3	31	26	27	39	52	68
Belgium	51	226	99	105	137	162	176
Canada	41	99	102	251	234	(309)	(403)
Denmark	12	105	51	48	70	65	94
Finland	1	33	41	54	70	21	25
France	438	1 825	1 511	1 521	1 975	2 369	2 422
Germany	190	991	877	876	1 230	1 535	1 594
Ireland	..	5	6	7	13	13	13
Italy	15	55	210	267	412	404	286
Japan	22	278	438	422	599	740	1 093
Netherlands	38	328	268	266	386	543	631
New Zealand	3	27	10	10	14	15	49
Norway	4	42	41	43	57	84	86
Sweden	21	109	108	121	103	185	207
Switzerland	2	34	36	31	60	75	102
United Kingdom	109	507	311	333	405	462	643
United States	562	724	1 608	1 458	1 506	1 749	2 127
Total DAC	1 525	5 472	5 908	6 029	7 486	(8 963)	(10 222)

a) Including technical co-operation loans.

Table 31. STUDENTS AND TRAINEES
1970, 1980, 1983 to 1987

Number of persons

Countries	1970	1980	1983	1984	1985	1986	1987
Australia	2 769	3 393	4 382	21 195[a]	20 969	21 396	19 794
Austria	367	5 351	6 496	6 457	5 748	5 840	..
Belgium	3 258	3 258	2 630	(2 082)	2 457	..	2 672
Canada	2 757	1 723	1 705	3 570	6 291	7 941	
Denmark	383	556	481	527	536	592	444
Finland	66	394	429	577	535	702	420
France	14 191	..	..	12 955	14 220	8 573	16 000
Germany	19 646	38 414	15 431	12 101	12 846	15 321	15 179
Ireland	..	..	..	..	..	194	..
Italy	1 512	2 077	5 525	7 461	6 977	8 423	6 390
Japan	3 675	9 342	12 394	15 460	15 114	17 823	19 165
Netherlands	1 209	1 256	1 396	1 400	1 324	1 455	1 457
New Zealand	992	1 058	1 116	1 209	1 340	893	893
Norway	276	1 260	1 761	1 662	1 298	1 060	966
Sweden	1 315	..	..	..	119	152	167
Switzerland	743	832	1 123	..	..	..	..
United Kingdom	12 056	15 507	12 195	13 515	12 144	12 160	6 808
United States	18 272	6 854	9 294	10 846	13 790	12 617	20 225
Total DAC	82 495	(105 800)	(89 700)	(112 400)	(117 000)	(119 500)	(126 000)

a) From 1984, including students partly financed by Australia.

Section D : Technical Co-operation

Table 32.   EXPERTS AND VOLUNTEERS
Publicly financed technical co-operation personnel by individual donors

Number of persons

Countries	1970	1980	1983	1984	1985	1986	1987
Australia	1 024	1 356	1 755	1 965	1 860	1 392	251[a]
Austria	288	555	458	449	471	434	..
Belgium	3 199	3 022	3 051	2 944	3 512	..	3 220
Canada	3 080	2 057	3 454	698	4 309	4 647	..
Denmark	774	1 045	1 159	1 281	1 129	627	1 118
Finland	98	117	176	147	133	108	114
France	38 122	..	..	17 291	15 877	14 200	14 035
Germany	6 344	5 850	5 629	5 827	5 414	6 365	7 117
Ireland	..	..	..	..	..	709	..
Italy	1 507	1 597	2 445	2 736	2 907	3 064	3 374
Japan	2 629	8 215	11 094	11 094	12 721	15 491	15 370
Netherlands	1 177	2 963	2 942	3 254	2 912	2 865	2 976
New Zealand	..	608	439	460	519	303	286
Norway	505	433	459	549	564	524	550
Sweden	658	510	(560)	581	553	645	726
Switzerland	729	1 060	1 028	..	..	..	..
United Kingdom	17 354	7 614	5 765	5 364	5 544	5 318	3 162
United States	22 417	11 447	17 186	19 771	19 887	21 093	..
Total DAC	99 905	(68 700)	(75 000)	(75 000)	(80 000)	(82 300)	(79 000)

a)   Volunteers only.

Table 33. TOTAL ODA NET FROM DAC COUNTRIES, MULTILATERAL ORGANISATIONS

Net Disbursements

	1985	1986	1987	1988
EUROPE				
Cyprus	37	35	41	36
Gibraltar	29	21	15	16
Greece	13	21	34	34
Malta	18	7	-1	-3
Portugal	102	139	64	106
Turkey	181	340	379	286
Yugoslavia	11	19	35	41
Europe Unallocated	22	16	4	3
TOTAL	*414*	*597*	*570*	*519*
NORTH OF SAHARA				
Algeria	173	165	214	137
Egypt	1791	1717	1774	1537
Libya	5	11	7	5
Morocco	785	403	447	481
Tunisia	163	223	279	326
North of Sahara Unall.	13	0	21	16
TOTAL	*2931*	*2518*	*2743*	*2504*
SOUTH OF SAHARA				
Angola	92	131	135	157
Benin	96	138	138	161
Botswana	96	102	156	150
Burkina Faso	197	284	281	297
Burundi	143	188	202	183
Cameroon	159	225	213	286
Cape Verde	70	109	88	85
Central African Rep.	104	139	176	197
Chad	182	165	198	264
Comoros	48	46	54	51
Congo	71	110	152	88
Côte d'Ivoire	125	187	254	439
Djibouti	81	115	105	94
Equatorial Guinea	17	22	43	43
Ethiopia	715	636	635	912
Gabon	61	79	83	106
Gambia	50	101	100	82
Ghana	203	372	373	474
Guinea	119	175	213	262
Guinea-Bissau	58	71	106	98
Kenya	438	455	572	808
Lesotho	94	88	108	108
Liberia	91	97	78	64
Madagascar	188	316	321	304
Malawi	113	198	280	335
Mali	380	372	366	427
Mauritania	209	225	170	184
Mauritius	29	56	65	59
Mayotte	21	28	39	43
Mozambique	300	421	651	882
Namibia	6	16	17	21
Niger	304	307	353	371
Nigeria	32	59	69	119
Reunion	383	506	574	608
Rwanda	181	211	245	247
St. Helena	12	14	20	27
Sao Tome & Principe	13	12	17	24
Senegal	294	567	641	566
Seychelles	22	29	24	21
Sierra Leone	66	87	68	102
Somalia	353	511	580	447
Sudan	1129	945	898	923
Swaziland	25	35	45	37
Tanzania	487	681	882	975
Togo	114	174	125	199
Uganda	182	197	279	353
Zaire	325	448	627	580
Zambia	329	465	430	477
Zimbabwe	237	225	294	270
East African Community	11	2	1	1
DOM/TOM Unallocated	–	–	–	–
EAMA Unallocated	–	–	–	–
South of Sahara Unall.	471	392	513	645

TOTAL . . . .
Africa Unspecified . . . .
AFRICA TOTAL . . . .

N.& C. AMERICA
Aruba . . . .
Bahamas . . . .
Barbados . . . .
Belize . . . .
Bermuda . . . .
Costa Rica . . . .
Cuba . . . .
Dominican Republic . . . .
El Salvador . . . .
Guadeloupe . . . .
Guatemala . . . .
Haiti . . . .
Honduras . . . .
Jamaica . . . .
Martinique . . . .
Mexico . . . .
Netherlands Antilles . . . .
Nicaragua . . . .
Panama . . . .
St. Pierre & Miquelon . . . . . .
Trinidad & Tobago . . . .
Anguilla . . . .
Antigua and Barbuda . . . . . .
Cayman Islands . . . .
Dominica . . . .
Grenada . . . .
Montserrat . . . .
St. Kitts-Nevis . . . .
St. Lucia . . . .
St. Vincent and Gr. . . . .
Turks & Caicos Islands . . . . .
Virgin Islands . . . .
West Indies Unall. . . . .
DOM/TOM Unallocated . . . .
N.& C. America Unall. . . . . . .
TOTAL

SOUTH AMERICA
Argentina . . . .
Bolivia . . . .
Brazil . . . .
Chile . . . .
Colombia . . . .
Ecuador . . . .
Falkland Islands . . . .
Guiana . . . .
Guyana . . . .
Paraguay . . . .
Peru . . . .
Suriname . . . .
Uruguay . . . .
Venezuela . . . .
South America Unall. . . . .
TOTAL
America Unspecified . . . .
AMERICA TOTAL

MIDDLE EAST
Bahrain . . . .
Iran . . . .
Iraq . . . .
Israel . . . .
Jordan . . . .
Kuwait . . . .
Lebanon . . . .
Oman . . . .
Qatar . . . .
Saudi Arabia . . . .
Syria . . . .

AND ARAB COUNTRIES TO DEVELOPING COUNTRIES AND TERRITORIES

$ Million

1985	1986	1987	1988		1985	1986	1987	1988
9526	*11533*	*13058*	*14659*	United Arab Emirates	4	34	115	-12
389	383	454	375	Yemen	283	257	348	226
12846	*14434*	*16255*	*17537*	Yemen, Dem.	114	72	84	76
				Middle East Unall.	67	36	48	44
				TOTAL	*3904*	*3972*	*3418*	*2452*
12	40	21	19					
1	6	1	4	**SOUTH ASIA**				
7	4	6	3	Afghanistan	17	2	45	72
22	24	24	23	Bangladesh	1152	1456	1636	1590
1	0	0	0	Bhutan	24	40	42	41
280	196	228	188	Burma	356	416	368	451
18	18	30	20	India	1592	2124	1843	2099
207	93	130	118	Maldives	9	16	19	27
345	341	426	419	Nepal	236	301	347	399
165	206	181	266	Pakistan	802	970	879	1439
83	135	241	232	Sri Lanka	485	570	502	592
153	175	218	147	South Asia Unall.	104	129	15	32
273	283	258	323	*TOTAL*	*4776*	*6024*	*5695*	*6743*
169	178	168	193					
293	380	399	461	**FAR EAST ASIA**				
145	252	156	173	Brunei	1	3	3	5
65	58	64	53	China	940	1134	1462	1973
102	150	141	209	Hong Kong	20	18	19	18
69	52	41	22	Indonesia	603	711	1246	1626
17	21	28	36	Kampuchea	13	13	14	18
7	19	34	8	Korea	-9	-17	11	7
3	3	4	4	Korea, Dem.	6	6	17	10
3	5	6	8	Laos	37	48	58	77
0	2	2	13	Macao	0	0	0	0
17	11	14	19	Malaysia	229	192	363	103
35	24	20	23	Mongolia	3	5	3	3
2	4	3	6	Philippines	486	956	770	854
4	6	7	14	Singapore	24	29	23	22
7	12	11	14	Taiwan	-10	-10	-9	-9
6	12	13	15	Thailand	481	496	504	557
6	9	10	8	Viet Nam	114	146	111	150
2	1	2	2	Far East Asia Unall.	22	38	39	76
9	32	105	78	*TOTAL*	*2962*	*3768*	*4636*	*5491*
–			–	Asia Unspecified	142	1701	1357	267
121	83	45	86	*ASIA TOTAL*	*11784*	*15466*	*15106*	*14953*
2649	*2834*	*3037*	*3206*					
				OCEANIA				
				Cook Islands	10	26	11	12
39	88	99	152	Fiji	32	42	36	54
202	321	319	392	Kiribati	12	13	18	16
123	178	289	210	Nauru	0	0	0	0
40	-5	21	44	New Caledonia	145	207	283	261
62	63	78	61	Niue	4	4	7	5
136	146	204	136	Pacif. Isl.(trust Tr.)	159	232	186	149
14	15	13	8	Papua New Guinea	259	263	323	377
90	137	147	145	Polynesia, French	172	248	294	331
27	31	29	27	Solomon Islands	21	30	57	58
50	66	81	75	Tokelau	2	2	2	4
316	272	292	272	Tonga	14	15	21	19
11	14	22	21	Tuvalu	3	4	26	14
5	27	18	41	Vanuatu	22	24	51	39
11	16	19	18	Wallis & Futuna	0	0	1	1
29	23	23	35	Western Samoa	19	23	35	31
1155	*1392*	*1653*	*1637*	TOM Oceania Unall.	–	–	–	–
181	168	278	272	Oceania Unallocated	26	23	61	61
3986	*4395*	*4968*	*5116*	*TOTAL*	*900*	*1159*	*1412*	*1434*
72	100	0	-3	LDCS Unspecified	3432	3495	4602	6649
16	27	71	67					
26	33	91	9	**TOTAL,ALL LDCS**	**33361**	**39546**	**42913**	**46207**
1978	1937	1251	1241					
538	564	579	431					
4	5	3	6					
83	62	101	141					
78	84	16	1					
2	2	3	2					
29	31	22	19					
610	728	684	205					

Section E: Geographical Distribution

Table 34. TOTAL NET RECEIPTS OF ODA FROM MAJOR SOURCES BY REGION AND SELECTED DEVELOPING COUNTRIES

Regions and recipients	Percentage of total ODA			Percentage of DAC bilateral ODA 1988 %	Share in total population 1987 %	ODA receipts		ODA as percentage of LDCs GNP		Per capita income 1987 $	GNP annual average growth per capita %
	1975-76 %	1980-81 %	1987-88 %			1988 $ billion	Annual real % change 1980-88	1980-81 %	1987-88 %		
SUB-SAHARAN AFRICA	19.7	25.8	34.5	34.9	11.7	14.0	7.3	4.1	7.5	350	-1.5
of which: Sahel[a]	4.0	4.5	6.0	5.5	1.0	2.4	7.7	14.5	20.1	270	-0.2
Sudan	1.4	2.0	2.4	1.8	0.6	0.9	5.1	8.7	12.2	330	-4.2
Tanzania	1.6	2.2	2.4	2.9	0.6	1.0	4.6	12.5	16.2	220	-1.2
Ethiopia	0.8	1.0	2.1	2.0	1.2	0.9	16.8	7.2	16.1	120	-1.0
Mozambique	0.3	0.5	2.1	2.6	0.4	0.9	22.5	7.2	31.1	150	-6.1
Kenya	0.8	1.4	1.8	2.2	0.6	0.8	9.3	6.3	9.4	340	0.1
Zaire	1.1	1.3	1.6	1.5	0.9	0.6	3.9	4.3	11.6	160	-2.8
Reunion	1.6	1.8	1.5	2.1	0.0	0.6	2.6	29.5	19.1	5 580	1.7
Somalia	0.8	1.3	1.3	1.1	0.1	0.4	0.4	44.0	32.0	290	0.8
Zambia	0.4	0.9	1.2	1.5	0.2	0.5	5.2	7.5	22.8	240	-4.4
Ghana	0.5	0.5	1.1	0.9	0.4	0.5	12.0	3.9	8.0	390	-1.7
Côte d'Ivoire	0.6	0.5	0.9	0.8	0.3	0.4	9.6	2.0	3.8	750	-0.2
Madagascar	0.4	0.8	0.8	0.8	0.3	0.3	2.3	8.4	14.7	200	-3.5
Uganda	0.2	0.4	0.8	0.6	0.4	0.4	15.3	4.3	7.7	260	-3.1
Zimbabwe	0.0	0.6	0.7	0.9	0.2	0.3	6.4	3.3	5.2	580	0.4
Cameroon	0.7	0.7	0.6	0.9	0.3	0.3	1.0	3.3	2.2	960	5.9
Rwanda	0.5	0.5	0.6	0.5	0.2	0.2	6.0	12.4	12.3	310	1.3
Congo	0.4	0.3	0.3	0.3	0.1	0.1	-0.5	4.9	6.8	870	3.8
Nigeria	0.4	0.1	0.2	0.4	2.8	0.1	16.5	0.0	0.2	370	-2.6
ASIA	34.2	31.8	33.4	30.1	68.7	12.1	2.5	1.2	1.2	430	4.8
of which: India	8.6	6.7	5.4	3.5	20.8	2.1	-0.5	1.3	0.9	300	2.6
China	.	0.9	4.4	4.3	27.9	2.0	52.9	0.1	0.6	300	8.0
Bangladesh	4.5	3.8	4.2	3.4	2.8	1.6	2.6	8.8	9.9	160	1.4
Indonesia	3.8	3.0	3.6	5.5	4.4	1.6	7.5	1.1	2.1	450	2.7
Indochina[b]	5.5	4.6	3.5	0.5	2.0	0.2	-19.2	11.5	7.9	230	1.3
Pakistan	4.9	3.3	3.0	3.7	2.7	1.4	2.0	3.7	3.4	350	2.9
Philippines	1.0	1.1	2.1	2.9	1.5	0.9	13.9	0.9	2.5	590	-0.9
Sri Lanka	0.9	1.2	1.4	1.6	0.4	0.6	5.4	9.2	8.5	400	2.7
Thailand	0.7	1.3	1.4	1.9	1.4	0.6	3.7	1.2	1.2	840	3.2
OCEANIA	3.3	3.2	3.5	4.5	0.1	1.4	3.9	15.3	19.8	1 230	0.0

NORTH AFRICA AND MIDDLE EAST	29.2	24.6	14.3	14.7	5.8	4.9	-5.8	1.5	1.0	2 500	-2.1
of which: Egypt	12.2	4.1	4.2	5.2	1.3	1.5	1.8	5.7	4.9	710	3.4
Israel	3.1	2.7	3.2	4.5	0.1	1.2	4.2	4.4	4.0	6 810	2.5
Jordan	2.5	3.8	1.3	0.5	0.1	0.4	-12.7	34.3	11.1	1 160	2.1
Morocco	1.3	3.1	1.2	1.5	0.6	0.5	-7.5	6.2	3.1	620	0.3
Syria	3.7	5.2	1.2	0.6	0.3	0.2	-23.3	11.8	2.3	1 820	1.3
Tunisia	1.2	0.8	0.8	0.9	0.2	0.3	3.2	3.0	3.4	1 210	2.0
Yemen	1.2	1.4	0.7	0.6	0.2	0.2	-8.9	13.9	6.4	580	4.9
LATIN AMERICA	12.2	11.3	13.0	14.1	10.9	4.6	3.6	0.5	0.7	1 830	0.3
of which: El Salvador	0.2	0.4	1.1	1.4	0.1	0.4	20.2	3.8	10.0	850	-2.8
Martinique	1.0	1.6	1.1	1.6	0.0	0.5	-2.6	36.4	26.5	5 020	1.7
Bolivia	0.4	0.6	0.9	0.8	0.2	0.4	10.3	6.1	8.9	610	-3.9
Peru	0.5	0.8	0.7	0.9	0.5	0.3	1.9	1.1	0.8	1 430	-0.3
Honduras	0.3	0.3	0.7	0.9	0.1	0.3	15.3	4.4	7.9	780	-0.6
Costa Rica	0.2	0.2	0.5	0.6	0.1	0.2	14.2	1.7	5.1	1 590	-0.9
Mexico	0.3	0.3	0.4	0.5	2.1	0.2	15.1	0.0	0.1	1 820	1.1
SOUTH EUROPE	1.5	3.3	1.4	1.6	2.6	0.5	-9.7	0.5	0.3	2 010	1.3
of which: Turkey	0.7	2.7	0.8	1.0	1.4	0.3	-13.9	1.5	0.5	1 200	1.2
Portugal	0.2	0.3	0.2	0.2	0.3	0.1	-1.2	0.4	0.3	2 890	2.1
Cyprus	0.2	0.2	0.1	0.1	0.0	0.0	-6.0	2.3	1.1	5 200	5.4
Gibraltar	0.0	0.0	0.0	0.1	0.0	0.0	4.8	6.8	12.4	4 240	0.3
TOTAL	100.0	100.0	100.0	100.0	100.0	37.6	2.2	1.2	1.4	740	1.6

Note: Net ODA from all sources : DAC Members, Arab and CMEA donors and multilateral organisations. Data on CMEA aid and on GNP for several LDCs are based on Secretariat estimates. Excludes unallocated amounts by region.

a) Burkina Faso, Cape Verde, Chad, Gambia, Mali, Mauritania, Niger and Senegal.
b) Kampuchea, Laos and Viet Nam.

Table 35. NET DISBURSEMENTS OF ODA TO SUB-SAHARAN AFRICA BY DONOR, 1978, 1984-1988

Countries	In $ million at 1987 prices and exchange rates[a]						In percentage of donor's programme					
	1978	1984	1985	1986	1987[p]	1988	1978	1984	1985	1986	1987	1988
DAC BILATERAL												
Australia	16	43	39	29	35	34	3	7	6	5	7	7
Austria	10	23	26	15	29	:	5	10	9	9	19	–
Belgium	282	284	311	307	287	280	70	63	67	70	67	68
Canada	289	378	372	318	365	342	29	34	34	28	29	24
Denmark	131	212	192	251	230	266	40	55	50	56	51	59
Finland	38	101	106	121	139	183	90	59	54	54	54	54
France	1 686	2 336	2 347	2 316	2 420	2 591	47	45	45	47	46	48
Germany	726	953	1 014	948	939	919	31	30	30	29	30	30
Ireland	6	15	17	16	17	14	59	62	64	55	61	69
Italy	27	619	755	1 148	1 148	1 302	61	59	57	64	61	57
Japan	217	406	466	524	593	832	8	10	11	12	11	15
Netherlands	293	468	410	526	510	527	27	33	33	39	37	36
New Zealand	2	0	1	1	0	1	2	0	1	1	1	1
Norway	150	220	239	312	307	293	51	54	55	56	58	55
Sweden	284	353	398	459	380	432	42	43	45	50	42	45
Switzerland	62	155	167	198	147	154	37	41	42	49	38	36
United Kingdom	437	359	436	378	380	516	27	31	35	30	38	42
United States	459	938	1 397	911	783	747	8	13	16	12	11	11
Total DAC	5 114	7 863	8 692	8 780	8 710	(9 460)	25	26	27	29	29	30
MULTILATERAL AGENCIES[b]												
IBRD	44	13	9	1	0	–	36	22	18	28	100	–
IDA	488	1 091	1 226	1 579	1 631	1 321	30	30	33	41	46	40
Af DF	63	152	294	301	369	323	100	95	98	96	99	99
EDF	777	998	1 053	993	816	1 385	61	54	53	52	47	57
IMF Trust Fund	528	–	–	–	–	–	38	–	–	–	–	–
UNDP	199	284	318	294	262	288	30	33	36	34	34	34
UNTA	52	50	70	54	57	41	29	16	17	19	18	17
UNICEF	51	110	144	128	130	129	19	31	36	34	36	35
WFP	196	403	503	258	259	294	30	41	45	35	36	36
UNHCR	52	233	297	208	162	151	26	41	50	47	41	41
Other UN	88	131	142	122	124	121	14	21	22	22	23	21
IFAD	–	62	110	108	130	46	–	25	29	33	35	49
Arab Financed Agencies	173	108	72	100	44	12	11	51	40	60	60	22
TOTAL MULTILATERAL	2 711	3 638	4 236	4 147	3 983	4 112	28	32	35	38	39	39
Arab Countries[b]	816	704	855	511	349	185	8	13	20	12	12	10
CMEA	3	20	22	4	1	–	5	12	13	3	1	–
OVERALL TOTAL[c]	8 644	12 225	13 805	13 442	13 043	13 757	22	26	29	29	30	32

a) Bilateral disbursements deflated by the price index of each individual DAC country.
b) Deflated by the general DAC price index.
c) Differs from the total given in table 37 because the figures in that table were deflated with the general DAC price index.

Section E :   **Geographical Distribution**

Table 36.   ODA COMMITMENTS TO SUB-SAHARAN AFRICA BY DONOR, 1984-88

$ million at 1987 prices and exchange rates

Countries	1984	1985	1986	1987	1988P
Australia	67	41	25	47	38
Austria	16	21	30	18	. .
Belgium	160	123	276	264	270
Canada	856	498	344	488	520
Denmark	159	230	336	266	258
Finland	111	177	188	119	205
France	2 637	2 393	2 390	2 613	. .
Germany	994	1 101	1 014	1 058	. .
Ireland	13	16	16	17	14
Italy	595	800	1 875	1 845	1 460
Japan	414	369	612	680	. .
Netherlands	417	317	542	580	539
New Zealand	0	1	1	1	2
Norway	302	268	374	267	. .
Sweden	391	373	446	14	446
Switzerland	102	200	147	159	213
United Kingdom	361	392	420	503	628
United States	1 898	1 748	1 196	826	832
Total DAC	9 495	9 069	10 232	9 764	(10 300)
Af. D.F.	513	582	656	724	682
EDF	1 223	941	1 009	2 360	2 716
IDA	1 609	1 803	1 881	1 915	2 140
IFAD	111	105	85	123	113
Total UN	1 213	1 473	1 065	993	. .
Arab Agencies	355	149	203	108	149
TOTAL MULTILATERAL	5 024	5 053	4 899	6 223	(6 800)
ARAB COUNTRIES	1 010	838	626	396	196
CMEA	576	482	379	397	. .
OVERALL TOTAL	16 105	15 442	16 136	16 780	(17 700)

Table 37. NET DISBURSEMENTS OF ODA FROM ALL SOURCES, BY INCOME GROUP, TO COUNTRIES IN SUB-SAHARAN AFRICA, 1978, 1984-88

$ million at 1987 prices and exchange rates

Countries	1978	1984	1985	1986	1987	1988ᵖ
LICS South of Sahara						
Of which :						
Sudan	570	908	1 617	1 159	902	923
Tanzania	686	804	695	795	882	975
Mozambique	174	432	524	654	750	882
Ethiopia	238	748	1 197	902	730	912
Senegal	344	530	419	652	641	566
Zaire	505	450	463	515	627	580
Somalia	313	505	502	587	580	447
Kenya	395	593	624	524	572	808
Zambia	296	350	468	534	429	477
Mali	262	484	546	431	371	427
Niger	249	232	434	353	353	371
Ghana	182	306	285	424	370	474
Madagascar	146	233	280	375	334	304
Burkina Faso	254	272	281	327	281	297
Malawi	157	228	161	228	280	335
Uganda	57	235	264	227	279	353
Rwanda	200	237	258	242	245	247
Burundi	119	202	200	213	200	183
Mauritania	380	252	298	258	170	184
Chad	199	166	259	190	198	264
Guinea	104	116	158	177	194	262
Central African Rep.	82	164	148	159	176	197
Botswana	110	148	137	118	156	150
Benin	97	112	137	159	138	161
Togo	163	159	162	201	125	199
Guinea-Bissau	81	88	82	77	108	98
Lesotho	82	146	134	101	108	108
Djibouti	160	147	116	132	105	94
Gambia	57	77	71	116	100	82
Cape Verde	60	92	101	129	88	85
Liberia	77	192	129	112	78	64
Sierra Leone	64	90	94	107	68	102
Comoros	21	59	68	53	54	51
Equatorial Guinea	1	22	25	25	43	43
Mayotte	21	20	30	33	39	43
St. Helena	11	14	17	16	20	27
Sao Tome & Principe	7	17	19	15	18	24
Total	6 923	9 830	11 404	11 322	10 811	11 802
LMICS South of Sahara						
Of which :						
Zimbabwe	15	430	339	259	294	270
Côte d'Ivoire	209	184	178	215	254	439
Cameroon	287	269	226	259	213	286
Angola	100	141	139	166	156	157
Congo	131	136	93	125	150	88
Nigeria	68	48	46	68	69	119
Mauritius	70	51	41	65	65	59
Swaziland	71	43	36	40	45	37
Total	951	1 301	1 097	1 196	1 245	1 455
UMICS South of Sahara						
Of which :						
Reunion	601	499	546	582	574	608
Gabon	70	109	87	91	83	106
Seychelles	26	25	33	37	27	21
Namibia	–	–	9	18	17	21
Total	697	633	675	727	700	756
South of Sahara Unallocated	329	374	687	453	286	646
TOTAL	8 900	12 138	13 863	13 699	13 043	14 659

Table 38. COMMITMENTS OF ODA FROM ALL SOURCES TO COUNTRIES IN SUB-SAHARAN AFRICA, 1978, 1984-87

$ million at 1987 prices and exchange rates

Countries	1978	1984	1985	1986	1987
LICS					
Of which :					
Tanzania	1 230	746	662	1 047	1 169
Mozambique	161	519	584	673	1 033
Sudan	1 261	1 038	1 855	1 499	1 016
Senegal	373	642	446	734	935
Zaire	671	542	551	691	834
Ethiopia	276	1 032	1 245	1 161	820
Ghana	259	414	598	416	727
Somalia	271	601	555	904	697
Kenya	727	958	569	717	661
Zambia	511	495	642	533	480
Madagascar	261	398	390	450	469
Niger	299	499	372	526	441
Uganda	64	445	214	248	436
Guinea	160	510	262	241	376
Mali	294	614	629	416	362
Rwanda	225	232	284	264	352
Burkina Faso	331	355	356	303	331
Chad	247	208	299	293	331
Malawi	425	207	316	305	316
Mauritania	369	276	356	231	260
Benin	211	238	136	146	207
Burundi	135	178	285	183	203
Central African Rep.	99	140	167	200	202
Guinea-Bissau	138	110	89	77	169
Liberia	155	209	123	115	160
Togo	98	181	334	204	158
Botswana	245	159	161	166	133
Sierra Leone	68	122	161	104	130
Lesotho	104	180	131	161	101
Djibouti	145	160	108	176	101
Cape Verde	85	136	88	103	101
Gambia	59	118	47	131	87
Comoros	32	73	37	40	61
Equatorial Guinea	1	39	58	48	59
St. Helena	13	14	17	16	48
Sao Tome & Principe	22	22	20	48	46
Mayotte	23	20	28	24	38
Total	10 050	12 831	13 177	13 593	14 051
LMICS South Sahara					
Of which :					
Cameroon	452	439	238	311	336
Angola	91	224	169	159	294
Zimbabwe	14	460	237	321	252
Côte d'Ivoire	164	244	165	390	247
Congo	78	103	83	198	168
Nigeria	77	80	85	76	86
Mauritius	22	59	43	68	71
Swaziland	131	57	40	62	50
Total	1 030	1 665	1 060	1 586	1 505
UMICS South Sahara					
Of which :					
Reunion	926	762	552	407	593
Gabon	120	133	95	78	104
Seychelles	26	23	40	29	18
Namibia	–	–	19	13	9
Total	1 073	918	707	527	724
South of Sahara Unallocated	371	692	518	445	501
TOTAL	12 522	16 106	15 462	16 150	16 780

Table 39. AID FROM DAC COUNTRIES TO LEAST DEVELOPED COUNTRIES[a]
1981-82, 1987-88

Net disbursements

Countries	1981/82			1987			1988[b]		
	$ million	Per cent of donor's total	Per cent of donor's GNP	$ million	Per cent of donor's total	Per cent of donor's GNP	$ million	Per cent of donor's total	Per cent of donor's GNP
Australia	147	19	0.09	94	15	0.05	257	23	0.11
Austria	28	12	0.04	41	21	0.04	(41)	(21)	(0.04)
Belgium	148	28	0.16	195	28	0.14	146	24	0.10
Canada	338	28	0.12	546	29	0.14	643	27	0.14
Denmark	163	40	0.30	319	37	0.32	373	40	0.36
Finland	47	34	0.10	154	36	0.18	236	39	0.23
France	733	18	0.13	1 260	19	0.14	1 334	19	0.14
Germany	893	28	0.13	1 200	27	0.11	1 339	28	0.11
Ireland	6	16	0.03	18	36	0.07	(18)	(36)	(0.07)
Italy	267	36	0.07	1 188	45	0.16	1 338	42	0.16
Japan	734	24	0.07	1 584	21	0.07	1 951	21	0.07
Netherlands	444	30	0.32	664	32	0.31	704	32	0.31
New Zealand	9	14	0.04	19	21	0.06	12	12	0.03
Norway	203	39	0.37	309	35	0.38	368	37	0.42
Sweden	342	36	0.33	450	33	0.29	541	35	0.31
Switzerland	84	34	0.08	177	32	0.10	196	32	0.10
United Kingdom	610	31	0.12	620	33	0.09	854	32	0.10
United States	1 254	18	0.04	1 484	16	0.03	1 947	19	0.04
Total DAC	6 452	24	0.09	10 322	25	0.09	12 298	26	0.09

a) Including allowance for contributions through multilateral organisations, calculated using the geographical distribution of multilateral disbursements in 1981/82 and 1987 respectively.
b) 1987 coefficients.

Table 40. MAJOR RECIPIENTS OF INDIVIDUAL DAC MEMBERS' AID

Gross disbursements		Australia		Percentage of total ODA	
1970-71		**1980-81**		**1987-88**	
Papua New Guinea	66.9	Papua New Guinea	42.9	Papua New Guinea	26.5
Indonesia	8.2	Indonesia	7.0	Indonesia	6.9
India	2.2	Bangladesh	3.0	Malaysia	4.4
Thailand	2.0	Philippines	1.9	Philippines	2.7
Malaysia	1.6	Pakistan	1.8	Thailand	2.2
Viet Nam	1.5	Fiji	1.7	China	2.0
Pakistan	0.8	Burma	1.6	Fiji	1.8
Laos	0.6	Thailand	1.3	Ethiopia	1.3
Kampuchea	0.6	Egypt	1.3	Bangladesh	1.1
Sri Lanka	0.6	Malaysia	1.2	Vanuatu	1.0
Fiji	0.5	Sri Lanka	1.0	Burma	1.0
Burma	0.4	Tanzania	1.0	Solomon Islands	0.9
Nepal	0.4	Solomon Islands	0.9	Mozambique	0.9
Singapore	0.3	Tonga	0.7	Western Samoa	0.8
Bangladesh	0.3	Kenya	0.6	Tonga	0.7
Nigeria	0.1	Kampuchea	0.6	Hong Kong	0.7
Korea	0.1	Sudan	0.6	Egypt	0.6
Western Samoa	0.1	Vanuatu	0.5	Laos	0.5
Zambia	0.1	Western Samoa	0.5	Tuvalu	0.5
Philippines	0.1	India	0.4	Singapore	0.4
Tonga	0.1	Kiribati	0.4	Nepal	0.4
Ghana	0.1	Ethiopia	0.4	Tanzania	0.3
Mauritius	0.1	Mauritius	0.4	Mauritius	0.3
Malawi	0.1	Uganda	0.4	Kiribati	0.2
Uganda	0.1	Zimbabwe	0.4	Sri Lanka	0.2
Total above	87.8	Total above	72.6	Total above	58.4
Multilateral ODA	10.9	Multilateral ODA	21.3	Multilateral ODA	33.0
Unallocated	0.8	Unallocated	4.1	Unallocated	6.2
Total ODA $ million	214	Total ODA $ million	662	Total ODA $ million	864

		Austria		Percentage of total ODA	
1970-71		**1980-81**		**1987-88**	
Thailand	13.8	Indonesia	17.7		
Pakistan	11.3	Algeria	15.3		
India	11.1	Turkey	10.1		
Algeria	7.3	Lebanon	6.8		
Sudan	5.0	Malaysia	6.8		
Israel	2.4	Jordan	4.7		
Brazil	1.5	India	4.4		
Tunisia	0.8	Cyprus	3.6		
Turkey	0.8	Tunisia	2.9		
Kenya	0.6	Egypt	2.1		
Nigeria	0.6	Iran	2.1		
Bolivia	0.4	Philippines	1.8		
Mexico	0.3	Nigeria	1.7		
Burkina Faso	0.3	Tanzania	1.6		
Guatemala	0.2	Greece	1.4		
Iran	0.2	Yugoslavia	1.0		
Costa Rica	0.2	Zambia	0.8		
Zaire	0.2	Guatemala	0.6		
Ethiopia	0.1	Cuba	0.5		
Afghanistan	0.1	Mozambique	0.5		
Tanzania	0.1	Brazil	0.4		
Peru	0.1	Mexico	0.4		
Congo	0.0	Cape Verde	0.4		
Madagascar	0.0	Viet Nam	0.4		
Colombia	0.0	Taiwan	0.4		
Total above	57.4	Total above	88.4	Total above	
Multilateral ODA	29.0	Multilateral ODA	23.8	Multilateral ODA	
Unallocated	13.4	Unallocated	-18.2	Unallocated	
Total ODA $ million	21	Total ODA $ million	209	Total ODA $ million	

Section E. Geographical Distribution of ODA
Table 40. MAJOR RECIPIENTS OF INDIVIDUAL DAC MEMBERS' AID

Gross disbursements | **Belgium** | *Percentage of total ODA*

1970-71		1980-81		1987-88	
Zaire	39.9	Zaire	25.0	Zaire	20.1
Rwanda	9.0	Rwanda	5.5	Rwanda	4.8
Burundi	7.4	Burundi	4.3	China	3.1
Indonesia	3.5	Indonesia	3.0	Burundi	2.8
India	3.3	Morocco	2.5	Indonesia	1.5
Tunisia	2.5	Tunisia	2.1	Cameroon	1.4
Pakistan	1.6	Niger	1.9	Zambia	0.9
Turkey	1.6	India	1.9	Niger	0.9
Morocco	1.2	Philippines	1.6	Senegal	0.9
Chile	1.0	China	1.6	Morocco	0.9
Peru	0.5	Turkey	1.6	Bangladesh	0.8
Philippines	0.4	Côte d'Ivoire	1.3	Turkey	0.7
Senegal	0.3	Senegal	1.0	Côte d'Ivoire	0.7
Argentina	0.3	Bangladesh	0.9	Ethiopia	0.7
Brazil	0.2	Tanzania	0.8	Tanzania	0.7
Cameroon	0.2	Peru	0.8	Peru	0.6
Côte d'Ivoire	0.2	Algeria	0.8	Ecuador	0.5
Algeria	0.2	Cameroon	0.7	Tunisia	0.5
Colombia	0.2	Sudan	0.5	Cape Verde	0.5
Bolivia	0.1	Pakistan	0.5	Mali	0.5
Iran	0.1	Egypt	0.5	Gabon	0.5
Egypt	0.1	Bolivia	0.4	Thailand	0.4
Niger	0.1	Viet Nam	0.4	Kenya	0.4
Benin	0.1	Malaysia	0.3	Egypt	0.4
Mexico	0.1	Lebanon	0.3	Bolivia	0.4
Total above	74.3	Total above	60.1	Total above	45.6
Multilateral ODA	23.7	Multilateral ODA	29.4	Multilateral ODA	33.2
Unallocated	0.9	Unallocated	4.7	Unallocated	13.7
Total ODA $ million	134	Total ODA $ million	590	Total ODA $ million	654

Canada | *Percentage of total ODA*

1970-71		1980-81		1987-88	
India	29.0	Bangladesh	5.0	Bangladesh	5.0
Pakistan	11.0	India	4.2	Pakistan	2.7
Nigeria	2.7	Pakistan	3.7	India	2.4
Sri Lanka	1.9	Sri Lanka	2.7	Indonesia	2.0
Ghana	1.9	Tanzania	2.0	Tanzania	1.8
Algeria	1.5	Kenya	2.0	Jamaica	1.6
Tunisia	1.5	Egypt	1.8	China	1.6
Niger	1.3	Indonesia	1.6	Kenya	1.4
Turkey	1.2	Cameroon	1.5	Zambia	1.3
Morocco	1.2	Mali	1.1	Mozambique	1.2
Tanzania	1.1	Zambia	1.0	Egypt	1.2
Cameroon	1.0	Ghana	1.0	Sri Lanka	1.2
Senegal	0.9	Zaire	0.9	Ethiopia	1.2
Colombia	0.9	Senegal	0.9	Thailand	1.2
Jamaica	0.9	Jamaica	0.9	Senegal	1.2
Guyana	0.9	Turkey	0.9	Niger	1.0
Malaysia	0.8	Malawi	0.8	Morocco	1.0
Indonesia	0.7	Tunisia	0.7	Burkina Faso	1.0
Kenya	0.6	Burkina Faso	0.7	Philippines	1.0
Viet Nam	0.6	Thailand	0.6	Ghana	0.9
Burma	0.6	Madagascar	0.6	Peru	0.9
Côte d'Ivoire	0.5	Haiti	0.6	Mali	0.8
Chile	0.5	Rwanda	0.5	Zaire	0.7
Trinidad & Tobago	0.5	Nepal	0.5	Costa Rica	0.7
Uganda	0.5	Ethiopia	0.5	Cameroon	0.6
Total above	64.0	Total above	36.6	Total above	35.5
Multilateral ODA	22.6	Multilateral ODA	37.6	Multilateral ODA	31.9
Unallocated	8.4	Unallocated	17.7	Unallocated	21.4
Total ODA $ million	363	Total ODA $ million	1143	Total ODA $ million	2171

Section E.   Geographical Distribution of ODA
Table 40. MAJOR RECIPIENTS OF INDIVIDUAL DAC MEMBERS' AID

Gross disbursements		**Denmark**		*Percentage of total ODA*	
1970-71		**1980-81**		**1987-88**	
Tanzania	5.5	Tanzania	7.1	Tanzania	6.9
India	4.7	Bangladesh	5.5	India	4.3
Egypt	4.2	India	4.7	Kenya	3.5
Kenya	3.5	Kenya	3.8	Bangladesh	3.3
Zaire	3.0	Sudan	3.0	China	2.3
Uganda	2.8	Mozambique	2.3	Egypt	2.3
Zambia	2.4	Burma	1.9	Malawi	2.1
Pakistan	2.0	Egypt	1.8	Mozambique	1.7
Tunisia	2.0	Viet Nam	1.5	Botswana	1.6
Kampuchea	1.9	Philippines	1.4	Yemen, Dem.	1.2
Malaysia	1.8	Sri Lanka	1.0	Nicaragua	1.2
Peru	1.7	Pakistan	0.9	Zimbabwe	1.1
Malawi	1.5	Botswana	0.9	Somalia	1.0
Côte d'Ivoire	1.3	Malawi	0.8	Benin	1.0
Indonesia	1.2	Angola	0.8	Sudan	0.9
Colombia	1.1	Jordan	0.8	Nepal	0.9
Bolivia	1.0	Togo	0.8	Uganda	0.9
Thailand	0.8	Zambia	0.8	Zambia	0.8
Chile	0.7	Indonesia	0.7	Mauritania	0.7
Turkey	0.7	Zimbabwe	0.7	Sri Lanka	0.7
Jordan	0.6	Nepal	0.5	Niger	0.7
Korea	0.6	Burkina Faso	0.4	Ghana	0.6
Morocco	0.6	Bolivia	0.4	Burkina Faso	0.6
Sri Lanka	0.6	Afghanistan	0.3	Thailand	0.6
Ghana	0.5	Gambia	0.3	Swaziland	0.6
Total above	46.4	Total above	43.1	Total above	41.4
Multilateral ODA	44.3	Multilateral ODA	45.7	Multilateral ODA	44.9
Unallocated	7.0	Unallocated	7.2	Unallocated	7.5
Total ODA $ million	67	Total ODA $ million	455	Total ODA $ million	927

		Finland		*Percentage of total ODA*	
1970-71		**1980-81**		**1987-88**	
Tanzania	4.7	Tanzania	13.7	Tanzania	9.7
India	3.6	Viet Nam	8.7	Zambia	4.8
Kenya	1.1	Zambia	6.0	Kenya	4.0
Pakistan	1.0	Mozambique	2.7	Egypt	2.9
Ethiopia	0.9	Kenya	2.7	Somalia	2.9
Tunisia	0.5	Egypt	2.1	Sri Lanka	2.8
Jordan	0.2	Bangladesh	1.8	Mozambique	2.7
Zambia	0.2	Peru	1.1	Sudan	2.6
Nigeria	0.2	Somalia	1.0	Nicaragua	2.4
Uganda	0.2	Sri Lanka	1.0	Viet Nam	2.3
Turkey	0.2	Turkey	0.9	Ethiopia	2.1
Yemen	0.1	Burma	0.7	Bangladesh	2.0
Syria	0.1	Sudan	0.7	Nepal	1.5
Peru	0.1	Uganda	0.6	Zimbabwe	1.0
Lebanon	0.1	Liberia	0.5	Namibia	1.0
Thailand	0.1	Philippines	0.5	Peru	1.0
Chile	0.1	Ethiopia	0.4	Uganda	0.8
Algeria	0.0	Indonesia	0.3	Turkey	0.7
Egypt	0.0	Honduras	0.3	Indonesia	0.5
Ghana	0.0	Kampuchea	0.3	Angola	0.4
		Thailand	0.3	Burma	0.4
		Nicaragua	0.2	China	0.3
		China	0.2	Cape Verde	0.3
		Zimbabwe	0.2	Rwanda	0.2
		Colombia	0.1	India	0.2
Total above	13.7	Total above	47.0	Total above	49.5
Multilateral ODA	78.0	Multilateral ODA	41.2	Multilateral ODA	38.1
Unallocated	8.3	Unallocated	10.1	Unallocated	10.7
Total ODA $ million	10	Total ODA $ million	123	Total ODA $ million	521

Table 40. MAJOR RECIPIENTS OF INDIVIDUAL DAC MEMBERS' AID

France

Gross disbursements 1970-71		1980-81		Percentage of total ODA 1987-88	
Reunion	9.7	Reunion	13.0	Reunion	8.1
Algeria	8.8	Martinique	11.7	Martinique	6.1
Martinique	7.0	New Caledonia	4.2	Polynesia, French	4.7
Guadeloupe	5.7	Polynesia, French	3.6	New Caledonia	4.2
New Caledonia	2.9	Morocco	3.3	Guadeloupe	3.2
Morocco	2.8	Senegal	2.7	Morocco	2.8
Côte d'Ivoire	2.6	Côte d'Ivoire	2.3	Côte d'Ivoire	2.8
Madagascar	2.2	Guiana	2.2	Senegal	2.6
Tunisia	2.2	Cameroon	2.1	Guiana	2.0
Guiana	2.1	Algeria	1.8	Madagascar	1.6
Indonesia	2.1	Tunisia	1.6	Cameroon	1.5
Polynesia, French	1.9	Central African Rep.	1.6	Egypt	1.3
Senegal	1.8	Burkina Faso	1.5	China	1.3
India	1.8	Brazil	1.5	Congo	1.3
Gabon	1.6	Guadeloupe	1.5	Gabon	1.2
Cameroon	1.5	Niger	1.3	Central African Rep.	1.1
Chad	1.5	Mali	1.3	Chad	1.1
Niger	1.4	Madagascar	1.3	Mali	1.0
Burkina Faso	1.0	Egypt	1.2	India	1.0
Djibouti	1.0	Indonesia	1.1	Niger	1.0
Iran	0.9	Congo	1.1	Algeria	1.0
Congo	0.8	Gabon	0.9	Guinea	1.0
Egypt	0.8	Mexico	0.8	Zaire	0.9
Central African Rep.	0.8	Zaire	0.8	Burkina Faso	0.9
Benin	0.7	India	0.7	Tunisia	0.9
Total above	65.5	Total above	64.8	Total above	54.3
Multilateral ODA	10.2	Multilateral ODA	15.2	Multilateral ODA	17.5
Unallocated	16.9	Unallocated	6.8	Unallocated	12.9
Total ODA $ million	1135	Total ODA $ million	4407	Total ODA $ million	6925

Germany

1970-71		1980-81		Percentage of total ODA 1987-88	
India	10.7	Turkey	8.5	Turkey	5.6
Pakistan	7.3	Bangladesh	6.9	India	4.6
Israel	5.1	India	4.1	Egypt	3.7
Indonesia	5.0	Sudan	3.3	Indonesia	3.1
Turkey	4.2	Indonesia	3.2	Israel	2.1
Brazil	3.8	Tanzania	3.1	Brazil	2.1
Morocco	3.1	Egypt	2.2	Pakistan	2.0
Tunisia	1.9	Israel	1.9	China	1.6
Afghanistan	1.8	Brazil	1.8	Tanzania	1.2
Nigeria	1.7	Yemen	1.4	Bangladesh	1.2
Chile	1.6	Peru	1.4	Morocco	1.2
Argentina	1.6	Pakistan	1.4	Peru	1.1
Egypt	1.2	Thailand	1.3	Kenya	1.1
Peru	1.1	Tunisia	1.2	Portugal	1.0
Viet Nam	1.1	Somalia	1.0	Zaire	1.0
Iran	0.9	Kenya	0.9	Tunisia	1.0
Côte d'Ivoire	0.9	Zaire	0.9	Sudan	0.9
Ghana	0.9	Ghana	0.8	United Arab Emirates	0.9
Colombia	0.9	Portugal	0.8	Nepal	0.9
Yemen	0.8	Burkina Faso	0.8	Zambia	0.8
Kenya	0.8	Syria	0.8	Sri Lanka	0.8
Thailand	0.7	Burma	0.8	Zimbabwe	0.8
Burma	0.7	Mali	0.7	Cameroon	0.8
Tanzania	0.7	Niger	0.7	Syria	0.8
Togo	0.7	Colombia	0.7	Somalia	0.8
Total above	59.2	Total above	50.3	Total above	41.5
Multilateral ODA	22.0	Multilateral ODA	25.9	Multilateral ODA	27.3
Unallocated	4.9	Unallocated	5.9	Unallocated	6.9
Total ODA $ million	766	Total ODA $ million	4226	Total ODA $ million	5249

Table 40. MAJOR RECIPIENTS OF INDIVIDUAL DAC MEMBERS' AID

Gross disbursements	**Ireland**	*Percentage of total ODA*
1970-71	1980-81	1987-88

1970-71		1980-81		1987-88	
		Lesotho	11.6	Lesotho	7.3
		Sudan	3.0	Tanzania	6.3
		Tanzania	2.6	Zambia	5.7
		Zambia	2.2	Sudan	4.5
		Swaziland	0.6	Zimbabwe	1.6
		Kenya	0.4	Bangladesh	0.5
		Rwanda	0.4	Rwanda	0.4
		Burundi	0.3	Uganda	0.3
		Bangladesh	0.2	Kenya	0.3
		Nigeria	0.1	Burundi	0.3
		Liberia	0.1	Ethiopia	0.3
		Mauritius	0.1	Swaziland	0.2
		Thailand	0.1	Sierra Leone	0.1
		Gambia	0.1	India	0.1
		India	0.1	Afghanistan	0.1
		Sierra Leone	0.1	Jordan	0.1
		Cameroon	0.1	Gambia	0.1
		Zimbabwe	0.1	Peru	0.1
		Peru	0.1	Liberia	0.1
		Yemen	0.1	Ghana	0.1
		Papua New Guinea	0.0	Indonesia	0.1
		Ecuador	0.0	Mozambique	0.1
		Paraguay	0.0	China	0.1
		Burkina Faso	0.0	Philippines	0.1
		Argentina	0.0	Botswana	0.1
Total above		Total above	22.5	Total above	28.7
Multilateral ODA		Multilateral ODA	65.5	Multilateral ODA	54.4
Unallocated		Unallocated	11.9	Unallocated	16.3
Total ODA $ million		Total ODA $ million	29	Total ODA $ million	54

	Italy	*Percentage of total ODA*
1970-71	1980-81	1987-88

1970-71		1980-81		1987-88	
Indonesia	15.1	Somalia	3.9	Mozambique	7.4
Egypt	9.6	Malta	2.8	Somalia	7.3
Yugoslavia	8.7	Ethiopia	1.7	Ethiopia	6.2
Turkey	7.4	Tanzania	0.9	Tanzania	4.7
Somalia	4.0	Mozambique	0.8	China	3.7
Pakistan	3.7	Indonesia	0.7	Tunisia	2.8
Ethiopia	2.8	Egypt	0.6	Sudan	2.6
Mexico	2.7	Libya	0.5	Egypt	2.6
Tanzania	2.3	Zimbabwe	0.5	India	1.7
Algeria	2.2	Nicaragua	0.4	Senegal	1.6
Guinea	2.0	Zaire	0.4	Zaire	1.6
Tunisia	1.3	Algeria	0.4	Pakistan	1.3
India	1.2	Yugoslavia	0.3	Zambia	1.3
Kenya	1.2	Viet Nam	0.3	Kenya	1.2
Sri Lanka	0.9	Zambia	0.3	Argentina	1.0
Madagascar	0.7	Guinea	0.3	Angola	0.9
Syria	0.6	Morocco	0.2	Mali	0.9
Morocco	0.6	Lebanon	0.2	Peru	0.9
Benin	0.5	Tunisia	0.2	Burkina Faso	0.9
Cameroon	0.4	Thailand	0.2	Niger	0.8
Chile	0.4	Brazil	0.2	Uganda	0.8
Libya	0.3	Sudan	0.2	Zimbabwe	0.7
Kampuchea	0.2	Pakistan	0.2	Brazil	0.7
Yemen	0.2	Peru	0.1	Bolivia	0.6
Sudan	0.1	Mexico	0.1	Ecuador	0.6
Total above	69.0	Total above	16.2	Total above	54.9
Multilateral ODA	28.3	Multilateral ODA	76.7	Multilateral ODA	25.6
Unallocated	1.7	Unallocated	4.7	Unallocated	8.6
Total ODA $ million	230	Total ODA $ million	713	Total ODA $ million	2939

Table 40. MAJOR RECIPIENTS OF INDIVIDUAL DAC MEMBERS' AID

Gross disbursements | **Japan** | *Percentage of total ODA*

1970-71		1980-81		1987-88	
Indonesia	22.9	Indonesia	11.2	Indonesia	11.9
Korea	19.8	Korea	6.9	China	6.6
India	10.2	Thailand	5.9	Philippines	5.7
Pakistan	7.9	Bangladesh	5.0	Thailand	4.3
Philippines	4.4	Philippines	4.7	Bangladesh	3.9
Burma	3.5	Burma	4.1	India	3.6
Thailand	2.9	Pakistan	3.6	Pakistan	2.7
Taiwan	2.5	Egypt	2.7	Malaysia	2.6
Iran	1.4	Malaysia	2.3	Burma	2.5
Sri Lanka	1.3	India	2.2	Korea	2.4
Malaysia	1.3	Sri Lanka	1.4	Sri Lanka	1.8
Singapore	1.1	Zaire	1.3	Turkey	1.8
Nigeria	1.1	Tanzania	1.1	Egypt	1.6
Kampuchea	0.9	Turkey	0.9	Kenya	1.2
Viet Nam	0.9	Nepal	0.8	Brazil	0.9
Laos	0.9	Brazil	0.8	Syria	0.9
Kenya	0.3	Kenya	0.8	Zambia	0.8
Tanzania	0.2	Bolivia	0.7	Tanzania	0.8
Peru	0.1	Paraguay	0.6	Nepal	0.8
Afghanistan	0.1	Peru	0.6	Sudan	0.7
Uganda	0.1	China	0.4	Paraguay	0.6
Brazil	0.1	Zambia	0.4	Bolivia	0.5
Bolivia	0.1	Madagascar	0.4	Malawi	0.5
Nepal	0.1	Tunisia	0.4	Ghana	0.5
Ethiopia	0.1	Iran	0.4	Honduras	0.4
Total above	84.1	Total above	59.7	Total above	60.1
Multilateral ODA	14.9	Multilateral ODA	31.5	Multilateral ODA	26.4
Unallocated	0.3	Unallocated	2.2	Unallocated	3.8
Total ODA $ million	555	Total ODA $ million	3592	Total ODA $ million	9303

	Netherlands			*Percentage of total ODA*	
1970-71		1980-81		1987-88	
Indonesia	22.1	India	9.6	Indonesia	7.7
Suriname	11.9	Suriname	6.6	India	6.2
Netherlands Antilles	11.0	Indonesia	5.1	Tanzania	3.4
India	6.7	Netherlands Antilles	5.0	Bangladesh	3.0
Pakistan	1.5	Tanzania	5.0	Netherlands Antilles	3.0
Nigeria	1.3	Bangladesh	3.4	Sudan	2.8
Kenya	1.3	Kenya	2.6	Kenya	2.7
Chile	0.9	Sudan	2.6	Mozambique	2.6
Tanzania	0.7	Sri Lanka	2.2	Pakistan	1.6
Colombia	0.7	Pakistan	1.7	Yemen	1.4
Tunisia	0.6	Peru	1.6	Sri Lanka	1.3
Cameroon	0.6	Zambia	1.4	Zimbabwe	1.3
Bangladesh	0.6	Jamaica	1.3	Burkina Faso	1.2
Turkey	0.6	Yemen	1.2	Zambia	1.2
Peru	0.6	Burkina Faso	1.2	Peru	1.2
Viet Nam	0.5	Egypt	1.2	Egypt	1.1
Uruguay	0.4	Mozambique	1.1	Philippines	1.1
Thailand	0.4	Nicaragua	0.9	Mali	1.0
Côte d'Ivoire	0.3	Guinea-Bissau	0.8	Nicaragua	1.0
Rwanda	0.3	Uganda	0.8	Aruba	0.9
Uganda	0.3	Colombia	0.7	China	0.9
Brazil	0.3	Viet Nam	0.7	Bolivia	0.8
Philippines	0.3	Mali	0.6	Senegal	0.8
Zambia	0.3	Cape Verde	0.6	Ghana	0.7
Korea	0.3	Zimbabwe	0.5	Ethiopia	0.6
Total above	64.2	Total above	58.5	Total above	49.4
Multilateral ODA	25.3	Multilateral ODA	23.6	Multilateral ODA	29.7
Unallocated	8.3	Unallocated	8.0	Unallocated	9.5
Total ODA $ million	209	Total ODA $ million	1631	Total ODA $ million	2275

Table 40. MAJOR RECIPIENTS OF INDIVIDUAL DAC MEMBERS' AID

Gross disbursements	**New Zealand**		*Percentage of total ODA*
1970-71	1980-81		1987-88
	Cook Islands	12.6	Cook Islands 8.9
	Western Samoa	5.6	Niue 5.8
	Indonesia	5.4	Western Samoa 4.1
	Fiji	5.4	Tuvalu 4.0
	Niue	4.8	Tonga 3.0
	Papua New Guinea	3.8	Fiji 2.9
	Tonga	3.7	Tokelau 2.6
	Thailand	2.5	Papua New Guinea 2.4
	Tokelau	2.3	Indonesia 2.3
	Philippines	1.8	Vanuatu 1.9
	Tanzania	1.3	Kiribati 1.8
	Solomon Islands	0.9	Solomon Islands 1.6
	Malaysia	0.8	Thailand 1.2
	Nepal	0.6	Philippines 1.0
	Peru	0.6	Tanzania 0.3
	Tuvalu	0.5	China 0.2
	Kiribati	0.5	Malaysia 0.2
	Vanuatu	0.5	India 0.1
	India	0.4	Peru 0.1
	Zimbabwe	0.3	Botswana 0.1
	Bangladesh	0.2	Singapore 0.1
	Singapore	0.2	Bangladesh 0.1
	Jamaica	0.1	Nepal 0.1
	Korea	0.1	Kenya 0.1
	Sri Lanka	0.1	Ecuador 0.1
Total above —	Total above	54.7	Total above 45.3
Multilateral ODA 21.4	Multilateral ODA	26.5	Multilateral ODA 16.9
Unallocated 78.6	Unallocated	18.4	Unallocated 37.3
Total ODA $ million 15	Total ODA $ million	70	Total ODA $ million 96

	Norway		*Percentage of total ODA*
1970-71	1980-81		1987-88
India 9.4	Tanzania	8.8	Tanzania 8.2
Kenya 7.0	India	4.4	Mozambique 4.3
Tanzania 5.4	Bangladesh	4.4	Zambia 3.8
Pakistan 4.1	Kenya	4.4	Bangladesh 3.7
Bangladesh 3.3	Pakistan	3.1	Kenya 3.3
Uganda 2.7	Mozambique	2.4	India 3.1
Zambia 2.1	Botswana	2.3	Zimbabwe 2.4
Nigeria 1.1	Sri Lanka	2.0	Botswana 1.9
Madagascar 1.0	Zambia	2.0	Nicaragua 1.8
Turkey 0.7	Portugal	1.7	Sri Lanka 1.7
Tunisia 0.4	Sudan	1.7	Ethiopia 1.5
Ghana 0.4	Zimbabwe	1.2	Pakistan 1.2
Ethiopia 0.4	Turkey	1.1	China 1.0
Zaire 0.3	Viet Nam	1.0	Mali 0.7
Korea 0.3	Madagascar	0.9	Sudan 0.7
Sri Lanka 0.2	Jamaica	0.8	Madagascar 0.6
Egypt 0.2	Papua New Guinea	0.6	Philippines 0.5
Iran 0.2	Burma	0.6	Thailand 0.4
Algeria 0.2	Indonesia	0.5	Nepal 0.4
Sierra Leone 0.1	Philippines	0.4	Uganda 0.3
Thailand 0.1	Ethiopia	0.3	Jamaica 0.3
Burundi 0.1	Benin	0.3	Angola 0.3
Botswana 0.1	Cameroon	0.3	Gambia 0.3
Indonesia 0.1	Thailand	0.2	Ghana 0.3
Philippines 0.1	Rwanda	0.2	Bhutan 0.3
Total above 39.7	Total above	45.7	Total above 42.8
Multilateral ODA 58.5	Multilateral ODA	42.4	Multilateral ODA 41.2
Unallocated 1.5	Unallocated	8.9	Unallocated 12.5
Total ODA $ million 40	Total ODA $ million	477	Total ODA $ million 940

Gross disbursements **Sweden** *Percentage of total ODA*

1970-71		1980-81		1987-88	
Pakistan	6.9	Viet Nam	8.7	Tanzania	6.0
India	6.5	Tanzania	8.2	Mozambique	4.7
Tanzania	6.4	India	6.2	India	3.4
Ethiopia	4.9	Mozambique	3.6	Viet Nam	3.2
Kenya	2.3	Zambia	3.2	Ethiopia	3.0
Tunisia	2.2	Bangladesh	2.8	Nicaragua	2.3
Viet Nam	1.7	Ethiopia	2.7	Zambia	2.1
Turkey	1.2	Sri Lanka	2.4	Bangladesh	2.0
Brazil	0.9	Kenya	2.3	Angola	1.9
Sri Lanka	0.6	Angola	2.0	Zimbabwe	1.9
Zambia	0.5	Botswana	1.5	Kenya	1.9
Afghanistan	0.4	Guinea-Bissau	1.2	Botswana	1.2
Sudan	0.4	Pakistan	1.2	Laos	1.1
Nigeria	0.4	Zimbabwe	1.2	Algeria	1.0
Korea	0.3	Laos	1.2	Guinea-Bissau	0.9
Botswana	0.3	Cape Verde	0.8	Sri Lanka	0.9
Cuba	0.2	Turkey	0.6	China	0.9
Swaziland	0.1	Nicaragua	0.6	Afghanistan	0.7
Lesotho	0.1	Kampuchea	0.6	Cape Verde	0.7
Jordan	0.1	Somalia	0.6	Lesotho	0.5
Sierra Leone	0.1	Tunisia	0.5	Uganda	0.3
Burundi	0.1	Lesotho	0.4	Pakistan	0.3
Malaysia	0.1	Uganda	0.3	Yemen	0.2
Liberia	0.1	Portugal	0.3	Jordan	0.2
Zaire	0.1	Swaziland	0.3	Sudan	0.2
Total above	36.8	Total above	53.4	Total above	41.7
Multilateral ODA	52.6	Multilateral ODA	29.9	Multilateral ODA	33.0
Unallocated	10.4	Unallocated	14.6	Unallocated	23.4
Total ODA $ million	138	Total ODA $ million	941	Total ODA $ million	1462

Switzerland *Percentage of total ODA*

1970-71		1980-81		1987-88	
India	14.6	India	4.5	India	3.9
Bangladesh	5.0	Bangladesh	4.3	Madagascar	3.3
Nigeria	4.4	Tanzania	4.0	Indonesia	3.1
Rwanda	2.7	Nepal	3.6	Bolivia	3.0
Pakistan	2.1	Turkey	2.9	Tanzania	2.7
Cameroon	1.9	Rwanda	2.6	Mozambique	2.5
Peru	1.7	Mali	1.6	Nepal	1.9
Turkey	1.7	Honduras	1.3	Rwanda	1.9
Ecuador	1.6	Indonesia	1.3	Mali	1.6
Brazil	1.5	Senegal	1.1	Pakistan	1.6
Jordan	1.3	Peru	1.1	Senegal	1.5
Paraguay	1.2	Madagascar	1.1	China	1.4
Nepal	1.2	Thailand	1.0	Ethiopia	1.4
Tunisia	1.1	Bolivia	1.0	Ghana	1.2
Tanzania	1.0	Egypt	0.9	Peru	1.2
Madagascar	0.9	Burkina Faso	0.8	Chad	1.1
Benin	0.7	Sudan	0.8	Niger	1.1
Kenya	0.6	Kampuchea	0.8	Cameroon	1.0
Israel	0.6	Kenya	0.8	Honduras	1.0
Indonesia	0.6	Somalia	0.7	Egypt	1.0
Colombia	0.5	Niger	0.7	Uganda	0.9
Burundi	0.5	Mozambique	0.7	Thailand	0.8
Chad	0.5	Pakistan	0.7	Nicaragua	0.8
Bolivia	0.5	Cameroon	0.7	Kenya	0.8
Laos	0.5	Paraguay	0.6	Bangladesh	0.8
Total above	48.8	Total above	39.6	Total above	41.6
Multilateral ODA	34.3	Multilateral ODA	30.4	Multilateral ODA	28.2
Unallocated	9.4	Unallocated	20.6	Unallocated	18.4
Total ODA $ million	30	Total ODA $ million	247	Total ODA $ million	586

Table 40. MAJOR RECIPIENTS OF INDIVIDUAL DAC MEMBERS' AID

Gross disbursements		**United Kingdom**		*Percentage of total ODA*	
1970-71		**1980-81**		**1987-88**	
India	20.5	India	12.1	India	6.0
Kenya	4.0	Bangladesh	5.0	Bangladesh	2.8
Pakistan	3.6	Tanzania	2.9	Kenya	2.7
Nigeria	3.5	Sri Lanka	2.9	Tanzania	2.1
Malawi	3.4	Kenya	2.7	Malawi	2.0
Malta	3.2	Sudan	2.6	Mozambique	1.9
Singapore	3.0	Zimbabwe	2.6	Ghana	1.8
Malaysia	2.4	Pakistan	2.3	Sudan	1.7
Ghana	2.4	Zambia	1.9	Pakistan	1.6
Turkey	2.2	Turkey	1.7	Zambia	1.5
Sri Lanka	2.0	Malawi	1.3	Uganda	1.3
Uganda	1.7	Ghana	1.2	Sri Lanka	1.1
Indonesia	1.6	Egypt	1.0	Ethiopia	1.0
Zambia	1.5	Indonesia	0.9	Zimbabwe	1.0
Botswana	1.4	Solomon Islands	0.9	China	1.0
Solomon Islands	1.2	Uganda	0.8	St. Helena	1.0
Guyana	1.1	Botswana	0.8	Egypt	1.0
Fiji	1.1	Nepal	0.7	Indonesia	0.8
Seychelles	0.9	Malaysia	0.7	Nepal	0.7
Jamaica	0.9	Vanuatu	0.7	Gibraltar	0.7
Tanzania	0.8	Burma	0.6	Malaysia	0.6
Belize	0.8	Jamaica	0.6	Botswana	0.6
Jordan	0.8	Morocco	0.6	Somalia	0.5
Lesotho	0.7	Jordan	0.6	Gambia	0.5
Swaziland	0.7	Swaziland	0.5	Nigeria	0.5
Total above	65.6	Total above	48.5	Total above	36.2
Multilateral ODA	18.0	Multilateral ODA	31.2	Multilateral ODA	42.9
Unallocated	8.4	Unallocated	9.9	Unallocated	11.8
Total ODA $ million	629	Total ODA $ million	2232	Total ODA $ million	2390

		United States		*Percentage of total ODA*	
1970-71		**1980-81**		**1987-88**	
India	13.9	Egypt	12.6	Israel	12.0
Viet Nam	10.5	Israel	11.5	Egypt	9.4
Indonesia	7.8	India	3.3	El Salvador	3.3
Pakistan	5.0	Turkey	2.8	Pakistan	2.7
Korea	4.5	Bangladesh	2.2	Philippines	1.8
Brazil	3.6	Indonesia	2.1	India	1.7
Turkey	3.6	Pacif. Isl.(trust Tr.)	1.7	Pacif. Isl.(trust Tr.)	1.6
Colombia	3.0	Pakistan	1.4	Honduras	1.5
Israel	1.7	El Salvador	1.0	Guatemala	1.4
Laos	1.6	Peru	0.9	Costa Rica	1.3
Pacif. Isl.(trust Tr.)	1.5	Portugal	0.9	Bangladesh	1.3
Morocco	1.4	Sudan	0.9	Sudan	1.0
Nigeria	1.3	Somalia	0.9	Jordan	0.9
Tunisia	1.3	Kenya	0.8	Indonesia	0.9
Thailand	1.1	Philippines	0.8	Morocco	0.9
Philippines	1.0	Liberia	0.7	Jamaica	0.8
Dominican Republic	0.9	Jordan	0.7	Bolivia	0.8
Chile	0.9	Nicaragua	0.7	Peru	0.7
Jordan	0.7	Sri Lanka	0.7	Haiti	0.7
Bolivia	0.7	Korea	0.6	Dominican Republic	0.6
Ghana	0.7	Jamaica	0.6	Mexico	0.6
Peru	0.5	Dominican Republic	0.6	Mozambique	0.6
Panama	0.5	Haiti	0.5	Zaire	0.5
Ethiopia	0.5	Senegal	0.5	Kenya	0.5
Nicaragua	0.5	Morocco	0.5	Tunisia	0.5
Total above	68.6	Total above	50.0	Total above	48.1
Multilateral ODA	11.4	Multilateral ODA	30.4	Multilateral ODA	25.9
Unallocated	11.3	Unallocated	10.5	Unallocated	16.8
Total ODA $ million	3328	Total ODA $ million	6973	Total ODA $ million	10186

Section E. Geographical distribution of ODA

Table 40. MAJOR RECIPIENTS OF DAC MEMBERS' AID

Gross disbursements — **Total DAC** — *Percentage of total ODA*

1970-71		1980-81		1987-88	
India	11.5	Egypt	4.2	Indonesia	3.7
Indonesia	7.2	India	3.9	Egypt	3.4
Viet Nam	4.8	Bangladesh	3.4	India	2.9
Pakistan	4.6	Indonesia	3.4	Israel	2.8
Korea	3.4	Israel	3.1	China	2.2
Turkey	2.5	Turkey	2.5	Bangladesh	2.0
Brazil	2.0	Tanzania	2.0	Pakistan	1.9
Papua New Guinea	1.8	Reunion	2.0	Philippines	1.8
Colombia	1.4	Martinique	1.8	Tanzania	1.6
Algeria	1.4	Pakistan	1.6	Mozambique	1.4
Reunion	1.4	Sudan	1.3	Kenya	1.2
Morocco	1.4	Kenya	1.2	Reunion	1.2
Tunisia	1.3	Thailand	1.1	Thailand	1.2
Nigeria	1.3	Korea	1.1	Turkey	1.1
Israel	1.2	Zaire	1.1	Sudan	1.0
Martinique	1.0	Sri Lanka	1.1	Ethiopia	0.9
Zaire	1.0	Papua New Guinea	1.1	Martinique	0.9
Laos	0.9	Philippines	1.0	Sri Lanka	0.9
Thailand	0.9	Morocco	0.9	Morocco	0.9
Guadeloupe	0.8	Burma	0.8	El Salvador	0.8
Philippines	0.8	Zambia	0.7	Zaire	0.8
Egypt	0.8	Senegal	0.7	Zambia	0.8
Kenya	0.7	Peru	0.7	Senegal	0.8
Ghana	0.7	Tunisia	0.7	Somalia	0.8
Chile	0.7	Brazil	0.6	Polynesia, French	0.7
Total above	55.3	Total above	42.0	Total above	37.5
Multilateral ODA	16.1	Multilateral ODA	28.9	Multilateral ODA	27.5
Unallocated	9.6	Unallocated	7.9	Unallocated	11.4
Total ODA $ million	7884	Total ODA $ million	28720	Total ODA $ million	47656

EEC — *Percentage of total ODA*

1970-71		1980-81		1987-88	
Cameroon	8.8	India	9.4	India	5.9
Zaire	8.2	Sudan	4.0	Ethiopia	5.7
Senegal	8.0	Egypt	3.5	Côte d'Ivoire	5.3
Madagascar	5.9	Bangladesh	3.4	Egypt	3.3
Côte d'Ivoire	4.8	Senegal	3.4	Senegal	3.2
Burkina Faso	4.1	Somalia	3.1	Papua New Guinea	2.6
India	3.6	Ethiopia	2.9	Sudan	2.6
Niger	3.4	Zaire	2.7	Kenya	2.3
Mali	3.3	Mali	2.6	Bangladesh	2.1
Gabon	2.9	Tanzania	2.6	Mozambique	2.1
Chad	2.9	Kenya	2.4	Chad	2.0
Turkey	2.7	Zambia	1.9	Tunisia	1.7
Togo	2.6	Madagascar	1.9	Uganda	1.6
Algeria	2.1	Guinea	1.7	Tanzania	1.6
Benin	2.1	Rwanda	1.6	Reunion	1.5
Mexico	2.0	Morocco	1.6	Portugal	1.5
Pakistan	2.0	Côte d'Ivoire	1.6	Malawi	1.5
Congo	1.9	Turkey	1.5	Zaire	1.4
Egypt	1.8	Burundi	1.5	Rwanda	1.4
Burundi	1.8	Pakistan	1.4	Mali	1.3
Somalia	1.7	Uganda	1.4	Zambia	1.2
Netherlands Antilles	1.7	Malawi	1.4	China	1.2
Rwanda	1.5	Indonesia	1.3	Madagascar	1.2
Bangladesh	1.4	Burkina Faso	1.2	Turkey	1.0
Central African Rep.	1.4	Mauritania	1.1	Cameroon	1.0
Total above	82.6	Total above	61.1	Total above	56.2
Multilateral ODA	0.0	Multilateral ODA	0.0	Multilateral ODA	0.0
Unallocated	3.5	Unallocated	10.4	Unallocated	17.2
Total ODA $ million	208	Total ODA $ million	1265	Total ODA $ million	2205

Table 41. CONCESSIONAL ASSISTANCE BY ARAB COUNTRIES

Net disbursements   *US$ million*

	1970	1975	1980	1983	1984	1985	1986	1987	1988ᵖ
Algeria	1	31	81	37	52	54	114	26	10
Iraq	–	265	864	−9	−23	−32	−21	−35	−19
Kuwait	148	910	1 140	997	1 020	771	715	316	108
Libya	64	275	376	144	25	58	68	76	129
Qatar	–	307	277	20	9	8	19	4	8
Saudi Arabia	172	2 699	5 682	3 259	3 194	2 629	3 517	2 888	2 098
United Arab Emirates	–	929	1 118	351	88	122	91	19	4
Total	385	5 417	9 539	4 797	4 366	3 609	4 503	3 292	2 337
Total 1987 prices and exchange rates	1 425	11 339	12 594	6 763	6 293	5 142	5 180	3 292	2 181

Section F : **Arab and CMEA Aid**

Table 42. CONCESSIONAL ASSISTANCE BY ARAB COUNTRIES

Net disbursements   *As percentage of GNP*

	1970	1975	1980	1983	1984	1985	1986	1987	1988ᵖ
Algeria	0.02	0.22	0.20	0.08	0.10	0.10	0.19	0.04	0.02
Iraq	–	2.01	2.36	−0.02	−0.05	−0.07	(−0.05)	(−0.07)	(−0.04)
Kuwait	6.19	6.91	3.52	3.83	3.85	3.17	2.91	1.23	0.41
Libya	1.89	2.43	1.16	0.51	0.10	0.24	0.34	0.30	0.51
Qatar	–	14.17	4.16	0.40	0.18	0.15	0.49	0.08	0.16
Saudi Arabia	5.57	7.60	4.87	2.69	3.20	2.98	4.67	3.88	2.70
United Arab Emirates	–	10.38	4.06	1.26	0.32	0.45	0.43	0.08	0.02
Total	2.19	5.49	3.26	1.63	1.54	1.33	1.83	1.25	0.86

Table 43.   CONCESSIONAL ASSISTANCE BY ARAB COUNTRIES IN 1987

$ million

Donor country	Commitments			Net disbursements			
	Bilateral	Multi-lateral	Total	Bilateral	Multi-lateral	Total	As % of GNP
Algeria	2.0	0.8	2.8	(12.2)	13.3	(25.5)	(0.04)
Iraq	–	–	–	−35.4	0.1	−35.3	(−0.07)
Kuwait	402.6	38.7	441.3	226.5	89.6	316.1	1.23
Libya	68.0	27.8	95.8	(49.1)	26.7	(75.8)	(0.30)
Qatar	..	–	..	(1.4)	2.1	(3.5)	(0.08)
Saudi Arabia	2 752.0	181.5	2 933.5	2 664.1	223.5	2 887.7	3.88
United Arab Emirates	35.7	0.3	36.1	16.0	2.9	18.9	0.08
Total	3 260.3	249.2	3 509.5	(2 933.8)	358.2	(3 292.0)	(1.25)

Note :   Bilateral data for the UAE are incomplete.

Section F: **Arab and CMEA Aid**

Table 44.   CONCESSIONAL ASSISTANCE BY ARAB COUNTRIES IN 1988

$ million

Donor country	Commitments			Net disbursements			
	Bilateral	Multi-lateral	Total	Bilateral	Multi-lateral	Total	As % of GNP
Algeria	5.0	0.8	5.8	5.0	4.7	9.8	0.02
Iraq	3.0	20.9	23.9	−24.0	5.0	−19.0	−0.04
Kuwait	343.3	32.8	376.3	60.8	46.9	107.7	0.41
Libya	61.3	3.8	65.1	111.3	17.4	128.7	0.51
Qatar	–	7.3	7.3	–	(8.2)	(8.2)	(0.16)
Saudi Arabia	1 900.4	153.8	2 054.2	1 817.8	280.2	2 098.0	2.70
United Arab Emirates	9.8	8.3	18.1	−6.2	10.2	4.0	0.02
Total	2 323.0	227.7	2 550.7	1 964.6	372.6	2 337.2	0.86

Note :   Bilateral data are provisional and for the UAE incomplete.

Table 45. CONCESSIONAL ASSISTANCE BY ARAB COUNTRIES
TO MULTILATERAL ORGANISATIONS IN 1987

$ million

	UN Agencies and Funds			IFAD	IBRD IFC	IDA	AfDB AfDF	OPEC Fund	Arab Aid Agencies	Other	Total
	Total	of which :									
		UNDP	WFP								
COMMITMENTS											
Algeria	0.8	0.5	0.1	–	–	–	–	–	–	–	0.8
Iraq	–	–	–	–	–	–	–	–	–	–	–
Kuwait	3.8	–	0.1	–	11.1	8.3	1.4	–	12.3	1.8	38.7
Libya	0.5	0.5	–	–	21.1	–	6.2	–	–	–	27.8
Qatar	–	–	–	–	–	–	–	–	–	–	–
Saudi Arabia	19.5	3.5	15.0	–	32.5	124.6	0.9	–	–	4.0	181.5
UAE	0.4	0.3	–	–	–	–	–	–	–	–	0.4
Total	25.0	4.8	15.2	–	64.7	132.9	8.5	–	12.3	5.8	249.2
NET DISBURSEMENTS											
Algeria	0.6	0.5	–	–	–	–	10.9	1.8	–	–	13.3
Iraq	0.1	–	–	–	–	–	–	–	–	–	0.1
Kuwait	3.5	–	–	–	11.1	44.0	11.6	6.5	11.1	1.8	89.6
Libya	0.5	0.5	–	5.0	21.1	–	–	–	–	–	26.6
Qatar	–	–	–	–	–	–	–	1.6	0.5	–	2.1
Saudi Arabia	34.0	3.5	28.5	–	32.5	105.0	18.4	18.1	11.5	4.0	223.5
UAE	0.7	–	–	–	–	–	–	1.5	0.7	–	2.9
Total	39.4	4.5	28.5	5.0	64.7	149.0	40.9	29.5	23.8	5.8	358.1

Section F : **Arab and CMEA Aid**

Table 46. CONCESSIONAL ASSISTANCE BY ARAB COUNTRIES
TO MULTILATERAL ORGANISATIONS IN 1988

$ million

	UN Agencies and Funds			IFAD	IBRD IFC MIGA	IDA	AfDB AfDF	OPEC Fund	Arab Aid Agencies	Other	Total
	Total	of which :									
		UNDP	UNRWA								
COMMITMENTS											
Algeria	0.8	0.5	–	–	–	–	–	–	–	–	0.8
Iraq	3.2	–	3.2	2.0	15.7	–	–	–	–	–	20.9
Kuwait	8.3	–	7.6	–	2.0	8.3	11.1	–	1.4	1.6	32.8
Libya	3.8	1.0	2.8	–	–	–	–	–	–	–	3.8
Qatar	2.3	0.2	2.1	5.0	–	–	–	–	–	–	7.3
Saudi Arabia	19.5	3.5	–	–	6.8	124.6	0.9	–	–	2.0	153.8
UAE	3.3	0.3	3.0	5.0	–	–	–	–	–	–	8.3
Total	41.3	5.5	18.7	12.0	24.5	132.9	12.0	–	1.4	3.6	227.7
NET DISBURSEMENTS											
Algeria	0.6	0.5	–	–	–	–	3.2	0.9	–	–	4.7
Iraq	3.3	–	3.2	–	1.7	–	–	–	–	–	5.0
Kuwait	8.3	–	7.6	17.5	2.0	8.3	4.2	3.3	1.7	1.6	46.9
Libya	2.8	–	2.8	11.0	–	–	–	3.6	–	–	17.4
Qatar	2.3	0.2	2.1	5.0	–	–	–	0.4	(0.5)	–	8.2
Saudi Arabia	18.6	3.5	1.2	25.4	6.8	193.4	20.0	9.0	(5.0)	2.0	280.2
UAE	3.0	–	3.0	5.0	–	–	–	1.5	0.7	–	10.2
Total	38.9	4.2	19.9	63.9	10.5	201.7	27.4	18.7	(7.9)	3.6	372.6

Section F : Arab and CMEA Aid

Table 47. GEOGRAPHIC DISTRIBUTION OF BILATERAL CONCESSIONAL ASSISTANCE FROM ARAB COUNTRIES TO DEVELOPING COUNTRIES AND TERRITORIES, 1985-1988

Net disbursements — $ million

	1985	1986	1987	1988		1985	1986	1987	1988
EUROPE					**MIDDLE EAST**				
Cyprus	3.1	0.7	4.3	5.5	Bahrain	71.6	98.2	−0.8	−4.6
Malta	12.5	4.3	−2.4	−3.6	Iran	0.1	−	0.1	−
Turkey	31.8	25.3	−25.9	−2.7	Iraq	−0.3	0.2	10.0	9.1
Yugoslavia	0.0	0.0	−	0.3	Jordan	451.2	433.3	383.3	293.6
Europe Unallocated	−	−	−	0.0	Lebanon	12.2	2.7	18.2	11.2
TOTAL	*47.4*	*30.3*	*−24.1*	*−0.5*	Oman	59.4	52.7	−1.6	−14.8
					Saudi Arabia	−	−	0.0	−
NORTH OF SAHARA					Syria	559.7	631.8	575.2	0.6
Algeria	9.1	27.9	51.6	27.2	United Arab Emirates	1.0	0.0	0.0	−
Egypt	−24.7	54.2	74.5	−16.1	Yemen	138.3	84.0	142.2	14.6
Libya	0.0	−	−	−	Yemen, Dem.	46.3	23.0	19.8	9.2
Morocco	403.9	69.6	61.5	21.4	*TOTAL*	*1 339.6*	*1 326.0*	*1 146.5*	*318.8*
Tunisia	5.2	39.8	31.8	6.6					
TOTAL	*393.5*	*191.5*	*219.4*	*39.2*	**SOUTH ASIA**				
					Afghanistan	−1.5	−3.3	−1.3	−0.6
SOUTH OF SAHARA					Bangladesh	9.6	81.3	26.3	−14.9
Angola	−	0.8	1.5	2.6	Bhutan	2.9	8.3	7.1	3.1
Benin	2.9	2.7	0.7	1.0	Burma	−	−	0.0	−
Botswana	3.2	−1.1	−0.3	0.8	India	28.2	21.3	−18.9	−16.2
Burkina Faso	3.5	10.6	6.6	2.4	Maldives	−1.2	−0.2	−1.9	−0.7
Burundi	6.3	8.4	12.1	2.5	Nepal	−1.5	4.1	3.6	4.3
Cameroon	2.9	3.2	0.1	−3.6	Pakistan	−16.1	−53.3	−29.5	−13.7
Cape Verde	1.8	1.7	1.2	1.2	Sri Lanka	5.5	21.6	2.4	6.4
Central African Rep.	0.4	3.3	8.3	2.3	South Asia Unall.	100.0	126.2	−	−
Chad	−	−	0.0	0.0	*TOTAL*	*125.8*	*206.0*	*−12.2*	*−32.5*
Comoros	4.3	2.4	0.0	0.1					
Congo	−1.1	−0.8	−	−	**FAR EAST ASIA**				
Ivory Coast	0.1	0.0	−	−	China	21.9	22.7	10.8	8.8
Djibouti	12.3	28.9	23.6	3.4	Indonesia	1.2	20.4	11.2	9.1
Equatorial Guinea	0.0	0.1	0.1	−	Korea	−4.5	1.8	5.7	−1.9
Ethiopia	10.0	−1.4	−	−	Malaysia	14.7	8.7	0.1	−5.2
Gabon	−0.2	14.0	4.9	−1.6	Philippines	−0.6	−0.2	−0.4	−0.1
Gambia	0.8	−0.9	0.0	−2.0	Singapore	0.0	0.1	−	−
Ghana	−5.9	3.4	−4.9	13.3	Taiwan	−7.2	−9.1	−9.2	−8.8
Guinea	2.1	4.4	12.0	13.6	Thailand	11.2	8.1	−4.5	−6.8
Guinea-Bissau	3.0	3.6	3.7	5.6	Viet Nam	15.4	4.0	−0.4	−0.7

260

AFRICA

Kenya	21.4	4.7	4.1	3.4
Lesotho	3.1	-0.5	-0.5	-0.7
Liberia	0.1	0.0	–	0.0
Madagascar	-4.8	-1.5	-2.3	-1.5
Malawi	0.0	0.2	0.2	–
Mali	26.8	39.9	7.6	5.4
Mauritania	60.0	62.8	-0.6	-3.6
Mauritius	2.0	1.7	3.5	3.2
Mozambique	6.3	6.8	3.0	3.1
Niger	1.8	5.4	8.6	6.1
Nigeria	0.1	0.1	0.0	0.1
Rwanda	5.2	6.1	5.9	2.8
Senegal	37.8	32.8	30.0	24.2
Seychelles	1.5	1.4	0.7	0.4
Sierra Leone	0.2	5.8	3.7	10.1
Somalia	36.3	-9.3	1.1	4.1
Sudan	214.2	190.6	207.5	103.4
Tanzania	10.0	5.2	–	0.3
Togo	9.1	7.9	2.6	-1.5
Uganda	0.2	3.0	4.1	-0.1
Zimbabwe	-2.6	-2.1	0.5	-3.2
South of Sahara Unall	125.5	–	–	–
TOTAL	*600.3*	*444.3*	*349.3*	*197.7*
Africa Unspecified	–	9.1	20.5	6.4
AFRICA TOTAL	*993.9*	*644.8*	*589.2*	*243.3*

N & C AMERICA

Jamaica	–	0.1	0.6	0.4
TOTAL	*–*	*0.1*	*0.6*	*0.4*

SOUTH AMERICA

Brazil	-1.7	-1.4	-3.4	-0.3
Suriname	5.0	8.0	8.0	–
TOTAL	*3.3*	*6.6*	*4.6*	*-0.3*
AMERICA TOTAL	*3.3*	*6.7*	*5.1*	*0.1*

TOTAL	*52.0*	*56.6*	*13.3*	*-5.5*
Asia unspecified	–	1 524.2	1 162.2	0.3
ASIA TOTAL	*1 517.0*	*3 112.7*	*2 309.8*	*281.1*

OCEANIA

Papua New Guinea	-0.0	-0.2	-0.2	-0.2
Solomon Islands	1.0	2.4	1.2	0.0
Western Samoa	0.0	0.7	2.1	0.5
TOTAL	*1.0*	*2.9*	*3.1*	*0.3*

Arab Countries Unsp.	42.1	44.5	39.3	70.1
LDCs Unspecified	369.3	18.6	11.5	1 370.2
TOTAL, ALL LDCs	*2 975.0*	*3 860.4*	*2 933.8*	*1 964.6*
LLDCs	616.8	584.3	509.1	175.7
OTHER LOW-INCOME	482.2	200.2	139.9	35.2
LOW MIDDLE-INCOME	49.8	76.3	3.3	-3.7
UPPER MIDDLE-INCOME	1 189.3	1 277.0	1 048.1	310.4
UNALLOCATED	636.9	1 722.6	1 233.5	1 447.1

Table 48.   ESTIMATED USSR DISBURSEMENTS

US$ million

	1970	1975	1980	1983	1984	1985	1986	1987	1988P
1. CMEA LDCs									
Cuba	141	535	542	619	708	655	532	656	663
Mongolia	104	150	552	624	568	550	706	804	715
Vietnam	320	500	458	901	914	1 056	1 457	1 811	1 658
Total	565	1 185	1 552	2 144	2 190	2 261	2 695	3 271	3 036
2. Countries having special links									
Afghanistan	28	34	337	373	220	219	283	200	201
Kampuchea	–	–	134	86	87	98	150	161	172
Korea Dem.	145	60	75	26	46	96	123	62	63
Laos	–	–	57	99	77	99	81	110	104
Total	173	94	603	584	430	512	637	533	540
3. Other developing countries	351	389	571	703	651	644	1 101	904	809
4. Scholarships	25	45	130	185	180	190	200	220	220
5. Multilateral contributions	4	5	7	4	4	4	5	7	7
Total, gross	1 118	1 718	2 863	3 620	3 456	3 611	4 638	4 935	4 612
6. Repayments	320	454	550	574	565	547	520	450	400
Of which :									
CMEA LDCs and Korea Dem.	100	110	140	140	140	140	145	150	150
Other LDCs	220	344	410	434	425	407	375	300	250
Total net	798	1 264	2 313	3 046	2 891	3 064	4 118	4 485	4 212

Table 49. ESTIMATED EAST EUROPEAN DISBURSEMENTS

US$ million

	1970	1975	1980	1983	1984	1985	1986	1987	1988ᵖ
1. CMEA LDCs									
Cuba	80	5	150	180	180	180	190	190	190
Mongolia	–	–	10	10	10	10	11	11	11
Vietnam	70	120	150	180	180	180	190	190	190
Total	150	125	310	370	370	370	391	391	391
2. Countries having special links									
Afghanistan	1	1	16	20	15	13	15	23	22
Kampuchea	–	–	22	15	15	15	16	17	16
Laos	–	–	20	20	9	13	20	13	12
Total	1	1	58	55	39	41	51	53	50
3. Other developing countries	125	218	254	130	181	213	129	118	62
4. Scholarships	17	26	70	85	95	100	110	110	110
5. Multilateral contributions	2	5	7	5	22	9	9	11	17
Total, gross	295	375	699	645	707	733	690	683	630
6. Repayments	89	137	185	213	196	179	169	162	150
Of which :									
CMEA LDCs	20	20	33	33	33	33	33	33	33
Other LDCs	69	117	152	180	163	146	136	129	117
Total net	206	238	514	432	511	554	521	521	480

263

	Total DAC Countries	Australia	Austria	Belgium	Canada	Denmark
NET DISBURSEMENTS						
I. Official Development Assistance (ODA), (A + B)	**41426**	**627**	**201**	**687**	**1885**	**859**
ODA as % of GNP	*0.34*	*0.34*	*0.17*	*0.48*	*0.47*	*0.88*
A. Bilateral Official Development Assistance (1 + 2)	29869	535	157	428	1259	459
1. Grants and grant like contributions	23246	535	77	383	1265	391
1.1. Technical assistance	8964	180	52	162	309	65
1.2. Food aid	1479	34	2	8	178	–
1.3. Administrative costs	1444	16	5	23	119	28
1.4. Other grants	11359	305	18	190	660	297
2. Development lending and capital	6623	0	80	45	-5	68
2.1. New development lending	5392	0	80	44	-5	68
2.2. Food aid loans	596	–	–	–	–	–
2.3. Equities and other bilateral assets	634	–	–	1	–	–
B. Contributions to multilateral institutions(1 + 2 + 3)	11557	92	44	259	626	400
1. Grants	5397	74	23	159	274	301
1.1. UN Agencies	2998	58	19	47	233	210
1.2. EEC	1865	–	–	98	–	55
1.3. Other	534	15	4	14	40	37
of which: Food aid grants,total	802	26	–	20	121	32
2. Capital subscription payments and similar to	6173	19	21	100	352	99
2.1. IBRD (incl. IFC)	222	15	-1	5	10	–
2.2. IDA	4204	–	6	72	245	67
2.3. Regional Development Banks	1620	4	12	23	86	2
2.4. Other	127	–	4	–	11	30
3. Concessional lending	-13	–	–	–	–	–
Memo: Subscriptions on an encashment basis	3111	66	–	–	336	79
II. Other Official Flows (OOF), net (A + B)	**2015**	**-58**	**83**	**343**	**219**	**-79**
A. Bilateral Other Official Flows (1 + 2)	2158	-2	83	340	213	-56
1. Official export credits *a*	-4099	-2	83	–	213	-78
2. Equities and other bilateral assets	6257	0	–	340	–	22
B. Multilateral Institutions	-143	-55	–	3	6	-23
of which: IBRD	-95	-55	–	3	-4	-23
Sub-total (I + II): Total Official Flows	*43440*	*570*	*284*	*1030*	*2105*	*780*
III. Grants by Private Voluntary Agencies	**3525**	**40**	**24**	**18**	**193**	**24**
IV. Private Flows at Market Terms (1 to 4)	**18777**	**311**	**-61**	**-1358**	**185**	**47**
1. Direct investment	20895	418	10	238	-82	106
2. Bilateral portfolio investment and other	-2395	-191	–	-1475	169	–
3. Multilateral portfolio investment	2667	–	–	134	-1	–
4. Private export credits	-2389	84	-70	-255	99	-59
IV (5)a. Monetary Sector included in IV *b*	-8645	–	–	-1508	143	–
i) Resident banks *c*: Change in bilateral claims	-8672	–	–	-1508	143	–
ii) Multilateral portfolio investment	27	–	–	–	–	–
V. Total Resource Flows (Balance of Payments Basis) (I to IV)	**65743**	**920**	**247**	**-309**	**2482**	**852**
Total Resource Flows as % of GNP	*0.55*	*0.49*	*0.21*	*-0.22*	*0.62*	*0.87*
IV (5)b. Parent banks and their affiliates *d*	..	..	..	..	..	..
Adjusted Resource Flow, Consolidated Balance Sheet Basis						
(I to IV - IV (5)a. + IV (5)b.)	..	..	..	..	..	..
For reference						
GROSS DISBURSEMENTS						
Total Official	60329	847	334	1077	2554	1131
Official Development Assistance	44441	628	241	694	1916	927
Other Official Flows	15888	220	93	384	638	204
New development lending	8256	–	115	49	25	136
Total debt reorganisation	6664	–	0	282	–	60
ODA grants (debt forgiveness)	191	–	0	–	–	60
ODA lending	511	–	–	–	–	–
OOF lending	5962	–	–	282	–	–
Total food aid	2871	60	2	28	299	32
Official export credits	4305	26	93	–	556	117
Private export credits	17372	452	125	557	143	47
COMMITMENTS						
Official Development Assistance, Total *e*	49118	776	195	661	2296	744
Bilateral	36150	527	147	404	1644	416
of which: Grants	25274	527	78	357	1632	405
Multilateral	12488	249	49	257	652	328
Other Official Flows	22842	229	–	285	822	111
MEMO ITEMS						
1. Total flows to multilateral agencies, net (IB + IIB + IV3)	14080	37	44	396	631	377
2. Official funds in support of private export credits (included in II.A.1. above)	-2114	–	–	–	–	-8
3. Official funds in support of private investment (included in II.A.2. above)	23	0	–	–	–	–
4. Interest received on ODA	2021	–	–	2	0	–
5. Interest received on OOF	1364	34	–	–	–	91

For footnotes see page after table 59

264

Reference Tables

OF FLOWS BY TYPE IN 1987

$ Million

Finland	France	Germany	Ireland	Italy	Japan	Nether-lands	New-Zealand	Norway	Sweden	Switzer-land	United Kingdom	United States	EEC
433	**6525**	**4391**	**51**	**2615**	**7342**	**2094**	**87**	**890**	**1375**	**547**	**1871**	**8945**	**1951**
0.49	*0.74*	*0.39*	*0.19*	*0.35*	*0.31*	*0.98*	*0.26*	*1.09*	*0.88*	*0.31*	*0.28*	*0.20*	–
263	5326	3090	27	1878	5135	1419	66	528	896	389	1008	7007	1747
233	3921	2166	27	1249	2108	1256	66	525	900	363	1093	6688	1696
21	2369	1535	13	404	740	543	15	84	185	75	462	1749	138
2	30	117	–	115	102	34	0	6	3	22	19	808	183
12	182	66	3	62	214	68	2	30	52	12	65	486	73
198	1340	448	11	668	1052	611	48	406	661	254	547	3645	1302
30	1405	924	–	629	3027	162	–	2	-4	26	-85	319	51
28	1244	887	–	468	2855	139	–	2	-3	26	-114	-325	51
–	–	–	–	–	–	–	–	–	–	–	–	596	–
2	161	38	–	161	171	24	–	–	-1	–	29	48	–
170	1199	1300	24	737	2207	676	20	363	479	158	863	1938	204
105	548	762	24	444	391	378	8	264	273	104	544	723	204
98	103	209	7	157	359	211	4	218	231	87	158	590	126
–	420	506	16	240	–	167	–	–	–	–	363	–	–
7	25	47	1	47	31	0	3	46	42	17	22	133	77
22	74	111	7	65	–	49	1	24	31	–	98	121	–
66	650	547	0	294	1816	297	13	98	206	54	320	1220	–
9	7	8	0	5	70	18	1	1	3	–	7	63	–
27	496	389	–	234	1121	207	6	61	157	–	219	895	–
19	148	150	–	55	580	59	5	36	46	50	84	262	–
11	–	–	–	–	45	12	–	–	–	4	10	–	–
–	–	-8	–	–	–	–	–	–	–	–	–	-5	–
–	–	555	7	262	–	282	–	–	–	–	312	1212	–
-18	**2106**	**1451**	–	**1299**	**-1808**	**4**	**1**	**-4**	**2**	**-10**	**264**	**-1780**	**140**
–	2106	1453	–	1290	-1761	4	1	13	–	-10	264	-1780	140
–	–	-102	–	480	-2047	–	1	15	–	–	191	-2852	–
–	2106	1555	–	810	287	4	–	-2	–	-10	73	1072	140
-18	–	-2	–	9	-47	–	–	-17	2	–	–	–	–
–	–	-2	–	4	–	–	–	-17	–	–	–	–	–
415	*8631*	*5841*	*51*	*3915*	*5534*	*2098*	*87*	*886*	*1377*	*537*	*2135*	*7165*	*2091*
41	**106**	**645**	**26**	**18**	**92**	**172**	**8**	**66**	**105**	**94**	**221**	**1633**	–
125	**-65**	**2357**	–	**-1913**	**14723**	**947**	**26**	**-40**	**273**	**-2249**	**1074**	**4395**	–
30	696	661	–	375	7421	259	26	10	92	-332	2952	8016	–
–	-161	978	–	-91	4357	845	–	–	–	5	-2458	-4373	–
–	578	398	–	–	1865	423	–	–	–	-1070	–	340	–
94	-1179	320	–	-2198	1081	-580	–	-49	181	-852	580	412	–
–	-1992	285	–	–	–	162	–	–	–	–	-2362	-3374	–
–	-1996	249	–	–	–	176	–	–	–	–	-2362	-3374	–
–	4	36	–	–	–	-13	–	–	–	–	–	–	–
580	**8671**	**8843**	**77**	**2019**	**20349**	**3217**	**121**	**912**	**1756**	**-1618**	**3430**	**13193**	**2091**
0.66	*0.99*	*0.79*	*0.29*	*0.27*	*0.85*	*1.50*	*0.36*	*1.12*	*1.13*	*-0.91*	*0.50*	*0.29*	–
..	..	879	..	..	..	..	..	..	..	..	424	-5368	–
..	..	9436	..	..	..	..	..	..	..	..	6216	11199	–
415	9449	7924	51	4352	12922	2233	87	944	1382	550	2334	11743	2290
433	6802	5078	51	2654	8262	2197	87	893	1380	550	2014	9635	1986
-18	2647	2847	–	1698	4660	36	1	51	2	–	321	2108	303
28	1500	1543	–	507	3776	241	–	5	–	29	27	276	87
–	2065	1743	–	1159	116	30	–	–	2	–	43	1164	–
–	–	–	–	19	49	17	–	–	2	–	43	–	–
–	181	42	–	161	67	13	–	–	–	–	–	48	–
–	1884	1701	–	979	–	–	–	–	–	–	–	1116	–
24	104	228	7	180	102	83	1	29	34	22	111	1525	183
–	–	727	–	676	1382	–	1	15	–	–	191	522	–
94	–	3117	–	1172	3022	525	–	19	768	579	3402	3351	–
443	6881	5697	51	4368	9739	2383	74	880	1380	572	2613	9365	4176
222	5493	4303	27	3135	7343	1709	51	514	900	462	1441	7412	3846
193	4025	2540	27	1953	2205	1396	51	507	900	455	1375	6646	3611
221	1388	1394	24	1233	2396	674	23	366	–	110	1171	1953	330
6	5403	1688	–	3076	8819	51	1	–	–	–	356	1996	218
152	1777	1697	24	747	4024	1098	20	345	481	-912	863	2278	204
–	–	17	–	-25	-2081	–	–	–	–	–	–	-17	–
–	–	18	–	–	–	–	–	–	–	–	–	5	–
–	–	392	–	27	871	77	–	1	–	3	41	607	27
–	–	173	–	–	–	13	–	7	–	2	59	985	166

		Total DAC Countries	Australia	Austria	Belgium	Canada	Denmark
	NET DISBURSEMENTS						
I.	**Official Development Assistance (ODA), (A + B)**	**48094**	**1101**	**302**	**597**	**2342**	**922**
	ODA as % of GNP	*0.36*	*0.47*	*0.24*	*0.40*	*0.49*	*0.89*
	A. Bilateral Official Development Assistance (1 + 2)	33180	622	163	423	1579	478
	1. Grants and grant like contributions	26035	622	90	371	1651	424
	1.1. Technical assistance	10222	203	68	176	403	95
	1.2. Food aid	1827	33	2	5	231	–
	1.3. Administrative costs	1598	27	–	21	143	21
	1.4. Other grants	12389	360	20	169	874	308
	2. Development lending and capital	7145	–	74	52	-72	54
	2.1. New development lending	6745	–	74	52	-72	54
	2.2. Food aid loans	648	–	–	–	–	–
	2.3. Equities and other bilateral assets	-248	–	–	–	–	–
	B. Contributions to multilateral institutions(1 + 2 + 3)	14914	479	139	174	763	444
	1. Grants	6668	129	21	162	364	329
	1.1. UN Agencies	3457	108	21	26	315	188
	1.2. EEC	2565	–	–	130	–	61
	1.3. Other	646	21	–	6	48	80
	of which: Food aid grants,total	1166	60	–	31	181	32
	2. Capital subscription payments and similar to	8263	349	118	13	400	115
	2.1. IBRD (incl. IFC)	720	7	17	3	19	17
	2.2. IDA	5290	175	73	–	189	60
	2.3. Regional Development Banks	2134	161	26	10	192	0
	2.4. Other	119	7	2	–	–	38
	3. Concessional lending	-16	0	–	–	–	–
	Memo: Subscriptions on an encashment basis	3179	77	–	–	349	–
II.	**Other Official Flows (OOF), net (A + B)**		**49**	**-23**	**..**	**..**	**..**
	A. Bilateral Other Official Flows (1 + 2)		35	–	..	..	..
	1. Official export credits *a*		35	–	–	–	–
	2. Equities and other bilateral assets		0	–	–	–	–
	B. Multilateral Institutions		13	–	–	–	–
	of which: IBRD		13	–	–	–	–
	Sub-total (I + II): Total Official Flows		*1150*	*279*	*..*	*..*	*..*
III.	**Grants by Private Voluntary Agencies**		**45**	**..**	**6**	**..**	**..**
IV.	**Private Flows at Market Terms (1 to 4)**		**2390**	**..**	**..**	**..**	**..**
	1. Direct investment		2152	–	–	–	–
	2. Bilateral portfolio investment and other		193	–	–	–	–
	3. Multilateral portfolio investment		–	–	–	–	–
	4. Private export credits		45	–	–	–	–
	IV (5)a. Monetary Sector included in IV *b*		–	–	–	–	–
	i) Resident banks *c*: Change in bilateral claims		–	–	–	–	–
	ii) Multilateral portfolio investment		–	–	–	–	–
V.	**Total Resource Flows (Balance of Payments Basis) (I to IV)**		**3584**	**..**	**..**	**..**	**..**
	Total Resource Flows as % of GNP		*1.52*	*..*	*..*	*..*	*..*
	IV (5)b. Parent banks and their affiliates *d*	..	..	..	..	..	..
	Adjusted Resource Flow, Consolidated Balance Sheet Basis						
	(I to IV - IV (5)a. + IV (5)b.)	..	..		..	..	..
For reference							
	GROSS DISBURSEMENTS						
	Total Official	67236	1389	–	618	2432	939
	Official Development Assistance	51203	1102	–	618	2432	939
	Other Official Flows	16033	288	–	..	–	–
	New development lending	9213	–	–	71	18	71
	Total debt reorganisation	7360	–	–	–	55	9
	ODA grants (debt forgiveness)	271	–	–	–	55	9
	ODA lending	445	–	–	–	–	–
	OOF lending	6644	–	–	–	–	–
	Total food aid	3567	93	–	37	413	–
	Official export credits	4150	70	–	–	–	–
	Private export credits	16147	482	–	–	–	–
	COMMITMENTS						
	Official Development Assistance, Total *e*		1232	–	719	3033	1054
	Bilateral		927	–	430	1911	642
	of which: Grants		927	–	347	1786	617
	Multilateral		305	–	289	1122	413
	Other Official Flows		277	–	312	–	–
	MEMO ITEMS						
	1. Total flows to multilateral agencies, net (IB + IIB + IV3)	16087	492	139	174	763	444
	2. Official funds in support of private export credits (included in II.A.1. above)	-1510	–	–	–	–	–
	3. Official funds in support of private investment (included in II.A.2. above)	-279	–	–	–	–	–
	4. Interest received on ODA	1637	–	–	4	2	–
	5. Interest received on OOF	1521	30	–	–	–	–

For footnotes see page after table 59

266

Reference Tables
OF FLOWS BY TYPE IN 1988

$ Million

Finland	France	Germany	Ireland	Italy	Japan	Nether-lands	New-Zealand	Norway	Sweden	Switzer-land	United Kingdom	United States	EEC
608	**6865**	**4731**	**57**	**3183**	**9134**	**2231**	**105**	**985**	**1529**	**617**	**2645**	**10141**	**2909**
0.59	*0.72*	*0.39*	*0.20*	*0.39*	*0.32*	*0.98*	*0.27*	*1.10*	*0.87*	*0.32*	*0.32*	*0.21*	–
380	5601	3172	22	2408	6422	1552	93	572	1054	445	1430	6765	2587
334	4175	2305	22	1604	2908	1393	93	570	1058	414	1528	6472	2511
25	2422	1594	13	286	1093	631	49	86	207	103	642	2127	–
1	49	113	–	188	91	40	–	0	29	23	31	990	388
17	189	66	3	82	266	72	5	35	51	13	82	505	104
291	1516	532	6	1049	1458	650	39	449	771	274	773	2850	2020
45	1426	867	–	804	3514	159	–	1	-4	31	-98	293	76
45	1309	806	–	633	3514	145	–	1	-4	31	-128	286	76
–	–	–	–	–	–	–	–	–	–	–	–	648	
–	116	61	–	171	–	14	–	–	–	–	30	-641	–
228	1265	1559	35	775	2712	679	12	413	475	172	1215	3376	322
144	770	1007	21	589	418	411	7	261	285	110	725	913	322
123	113	231	3	203	378	229	5	220	281	95	192	726	214
–	605	752	18	329	–	182	–	–	–	–	488	–	–
21	52	24	–	57	40	1	3	41	4	14	46	187	109
34	–	212	–	110	46	93	–	25	–	15	142	185	–
84	494	561	13	186	2294	268	4	152	194	62	489	2467	–
5	38	19	8	42	224	24	–	7	4	–	128	160	–
37	262	506	5	–	1340	208	3	79	131	–	311	1910	–
23	194	36	–	141	704	26	1	51	59	62	50	397	–
19	–	–	–	3	26	10	–	15	–	–	–	–	–
–	–	-9	–	–	–	–	–	–	–	-3	–	-4	–
–	–	474	–	334	–	183	–	–	–	–	448	1314	–
20	**1028**	**1294**	**182**	**473**	**-639**	**4**	**2**	**-12**	**31**	**-7**	**323**	**1906**	**56**
0	1028	1293	182	472	-428	4	1	1	31	7	323	1906	56
0	571	29	–	185	-1838	–	1	–	31	-7	196	-865	–
–	457	1265	182	287	1410	4	–	1	–	–	127	2771	56
19	–	1	–	1	-211	–	1	-12	–	–	–	–	–
–	–	–	–	–	–	–	–	-12	–	–	–	–	–
627	*7893*	*6025*	*238*	*3656*	*8494*	*2235*	*107*	*973*	*1560*	*610*	*2968*	*12047*	*2965*
15	..	**695**	23	19	107	180	8	56	..	89	239	2255	–
112	**-783**	**5091**	–	**1400**	**12822**	**260**	**30**	**-123**	**686**	**1283**	**-255**	**3203**	–
74	663	1235	–	1053	8190	472	29	28	145	2078	2494	4205	–
–	-481	2858	–	0	2830	573	–	–	–	-77	-1425	-1619	–
–	687	450	–	–	1583	-222	–	–	–	-128	–	-1009	–
39	-1652	548	–	347	219	-563	1	-151	541	-591	-1324	1626	–
–	–	682	–	–	–	-479	–	–	–	-657	–	-5948	–
–	45	848	–	–	-1583	-280	–	–	–	-657	–	-5948	–
–	-45	-165	–	–	1583	-200	–	–	–	–	–	–	–
755	..	**11811**	**261**	**5075**	**21424**	**2675**	**145**	**906**	..	**1981**	**2952**	**17505**	–
0.74	..	*0.98*	*0.92*	*0.62*	*0.75*	*1.18*	*0.38*	*1.03*	..	*0.51*	*0.36*	*0.36*	–
..	..	1884	..	..	..	..	..	..	..	..	..	-8376	–
..	..	13013	..	..	..	..	..	..	..	..	..	15077	–
630	8670	9333	238	3897	15323	2393	107	1025	1568	621	3166	14888	286
610	7081	5434	57	3230	10350	2356	105	988	1537	621	2795	10948	–
20	1590	3898	182	667	4973	37	2	37	31	–	370	3940	286
48	1496	1483	–	680	4731	270	–	5	–	35	21	286	116
43	768	2758	–	497	90	27	–	–	–	–	51	3063	–
43	–	3	–	1	90	27	–	–	–	–	43	–	–
–	145	50	–	171	–	–	–	–	–	–	1	78	–
–	623	2704	–	325	–	–	–	–	–	–	6	2985	–
36	49	325	–	298	137	132	–	0	29	39	172	1823	–
0	967	751	–	311	1339	–	1	–	31	–	196	483	–
78	–	3345	–	1941	2165	514	1	21	997	442	1937	4225	–
625	–	6718	57	4586	13747	2531	88	732	1557	706	2948	11176	4909
399	–	4841	22	3040	12326	1809	78	313	1078	519	1691	7928	4560
345	–	2742	22	2052	3540	1461	78	311	1078	519	1653	6818	4347
226	–	1876	35	1546	1422	723	10	418	479	188	1256	3247	350
0	–	2469	–	2485	9160	26	2	–	31	–	442	3720	615
247	1952	2009	35	776	4083	457	13	401	475	45	1215	2367	322
–	–	-26	–	-19	-1503	–	–	–	–	–	–	37	–
–	–	27	–	–	-310	–	–	1	–	–	–	4	–
–	–	443	–	28	1096	–	–	–	–	–	63	756	–
–	–	274	–	–	–	15	–	5	–	1	75	1120	–

Table 52. THE FLOW OF FINANCIAL RESOURCES TO

Disbursements

	AUSTRALIA				
	1977-1979 average	1985	1986	1987	1988
I. **Official Development Assistance (ODA), (A + B)**	**539**	**749**	**752**	**627**	**1101**
ODA as % of GNP	*0.50*	*0.48*	*0.47*	*0.34*	*0.47*
A. Bilateral Official Development Assistance (1 + 2)	412	535	513	535	622
1. Grants and grant like contributions	413	535	513	535	622
1.1. Technical assistance	43	189	176	180	203
1.2. Food aid	38	23	28	34	33
1.3. Administrative costs	3	14	17	16	27
1.4. Other grants	329	309	291	305	360
2. Development lending and capital	-2	0	0	0	–
2.1. New development lending	-2	0	0	0	–
2.2. Food aid loans	–	–	–	–	–
2.3. Equities and other bilateral assets	–	–	–	–	–
B. Contributions to multilateral institutions(1 + 2 + 3)	127	214	239	92	479
1. Grants	42	79	107	74	129
1.1. UN Agencies	29	64	92	58	108
1.2. EEC	–	–	–	–	–
1.3. Other	13	15	15	15	21
of which: Food aid grants,total	10	28	56	26	60
2. Capital subscription payments and similar to	84	135	133	19	349
2.1. IBRD (incl. IFC)	3	–	9	15	7
2.2. IDA	52	93	85	–	175
2.3. Regional Development Banks	29	41	39	4	161
2.4. Other	–	–	–	–	7
3. Concessional lending	–	–	–	–	0
Memo: Subscriptions on an encashment basis	11	82	51	66	77
II. **Other Official Flows (OOF), net (A + B)**	**21**	**21**	**34**	**-58**	**49**
A. Bilateral Other Official Flows (1 + 2)	22	-7	-52	-2	35
1. Official export credits *a*	22	-7	-52	-2	35
2. Equities and other bilateral assets	0	0	0	0	0
B. Multilateral Institutions	-1	28	86	-55	13
of which: IBRD	-1	32	86	-55	13
Sub-total (I + II): Total Official Flows	*559*	*769*	*786*	*570*	*1150*
III. **Grants by Private Voluntary Agencies**	**41**	**52**	**39**	**40**	**45**
IV. **Private Flows at Market Terms (1 to 4)**	**128**	**413**	**226**	**311**	**2390**
1. Direct investment	88	20	403	418	2152
2. Bilateral portfolio investment and other	4	242	-298	-191	193
3. Multilateral portfolio investment	–	–	–	–	–
4. Private export credits	36	151	122	84	45
IV (5)a. Monetary Sector included in IV b					
i) Resident banks *c*: Change in bilateral claims	–	–	–	–	–
ii) Multilateral portfolio investment	–	–	–	–	–
V. **Total Resource Flows (Balance of Payments Basis) (I to IV)**	**729**	**1234**	**1052**	**920**	**3584**
Total Resource Flows as % of GNP	*0.68*	*0.80*	*0.65*	*0.49*	*1.52*
IV (5)b. Parent banks and their affiliates d					
Adjusted Resource Flow, Consolidated Balance Sheet Basis					
(I to IV - IV (5)a. + IV (5)b.)	..	..	..	..	..
For reference					
GROSS DISBURSEMENTS					
Total Official	567	906	1013	847	1389
Official Development Assistance	542	770	780	628	1102
Other Official Flows	25	136	232	220	288
New development lending	2	–	–	–	–
Total debt reorganisation	0	–	–	–	–
ODA grants (debt forgiveness)	0	–	–	–	–
ODA lending	–	–	–	–	–
OOF lending	–	–	–	–	–
Total food aid	49	51	85	60	93
Official export credits	25	25	40	26	70
Private export credits	137	323	461	452	482
COMMITMENTS					
Official Development Assistance, Total *e*	598	774	689	776	1232
Bilateral	455	532	532	527	927
of which: Grants	455	532	532	527	927
Multilateral	142	243	156	249	305
Other Official Flows	12	157	218	229	277
MEMO ITEMS					
1. Total flows to multilateral agencies, net (IB + IIB + IV3)	126	242	325	37	492
2. Official funds in support of private export credits (included in II.A.1. above)	–	–	–	–	–
3. Official funds in support of private investment (included in II.A.2. above)	–	0	0	0	–
4. Interest received on ODA	1	–	–	–	–
5. Interest received on OOF	5	36	36	34	30

For footnotes see page after table 59

G.
Tables

DEVELOPING COUNTRIES AND MULTILATERAL AGENCIES

$ million

	AUSTRIA					BELGIUM			
1977-1979 average	1985	1986	1987	1988	1977-1979 average	1985	1986	1987	1988
131	**248**	**198**	**201**	**302**	**517**	**440**	**547**	**687**	**597**
0.23	*0.38*	*0.21*	*0.17*	*0.24*	*0.54*	*0.55*	*0.48*	*0.48*	*0.40*
87	174	141	157	163	339	275	359	428	423
34	44	60	77	90	284	240	288	383	371
31	27	39	52	68	185	105	137	162	176
1	4	3	2	2	7	24	1	8	5
2	4	5	5	–	4	15	19	23	21
0	9	14	18	20	87	95	131	190	169
53	130	81	80	74	55	35	71	45	52
52	130	81	80	74	54	33	71	44	52
–	–	–	–	–	–	–	–	–	–
1	–	–	–	–	1	2	0	1	–
44	74	56	44	139	178	165	187	259	174
12	17	21	23	21	103	96	97	159	162
11	17	18	19	21	41	18	9	47	26
–	–	–	–	–	57	72	85	98	130
1	0	3	4	–	5	5	3	14	6
2	4	–	–	–	21	20	19	20	31
32	62	35	21	118	67	70	90	100	13
2	7	-3	-1	17	9	9	11	5	3
20	38	31	6	73	50	45	60	72	–
6	16	8	12	26	9	15	20	23	10
4	–	–	4	2	–	–	–	–	–
–	-5	–	–	–	8	–	–	–	–
–	1	..	–	–	9	..	..	–	–
-18	**6**	**65**	**83**	**-23**	**33**	**91**	**41**	**343**	**..**
-18	6	65	83	–	36	99	55	340	–
-18	6	65	83	–	–	–	–	–	–
–	–	–	–	–	36	99	55	340	–
–	–	–	–	–	-3	-8	-14	3	–
–	–	–	–	–	-4	-3	-14	3	–
113	*254*	*263*	*284*	*279*	*550*	*531*	*587*	*1030*	*..*
14	**18**	**19**	**24**	**..**	**33**	**23**	**20**	**18**	**6**
284	**-112**	**-148**	**-61**	**..**	**1550**	**759**	**-1415**	**-1358**	**..**
17	11	18	10	..	154	116	220	238	..
–	–	–	–	–	786	389	-1293	-1475	–
–	–	–	–	–	-6	205	157	134	–
267	-123	-165	-70	–	617	49	-499	-255	–
–	–	–	–	–	806	377	-1293	-1508	–
–	–	–	–	–	812	377	-1293	-1508	–
–	–	–	–	–	-6	–	–	–	–
411	**161**	**134**	**247**	**..**	**2133**	**1313**	**-808**	**-309**	**..**
0.71	*0.24*	*0.14*	*0.21*	*..*	*2.22*	*1.63*	*-0.70*	*-0.22*	*..*
..	..	..	..	..	..	..	..	..	..
..	..	..	..	..	..	..	..	..	..
140	280	292	334	–	595	596	646	1077	618
133	263	215	241	–	519	447	558	694	618
7	17	78	93	–	75	149	87	384	..
53	140	90	115	–	56	38	80	49	71
1	0	0	0	–	20	57	67	282	–
–	0	0	0	–	–	–	–	–	–
1	–	–	–	–	1	–	–	–	–
–	–	–	–	–	19	57	67	282	–
3	8	3	2	–	28	45	20	28	37
7	17	78	93	–	–	–	–	–	–
332	16	25	125	–	1053	537	221	557	–
141	139	190	195	–	650	262	542	661	719
91	60	126	147	–	421	132	318	404	430
33	39	60	78	–	363	118	248	357	347
50	79	64	49	–	229	130	225	257	289
7	76	6	–	–	58	35	5	285	312
44	74	56	44	139	169	362	330	396	174
–	–	–	–	–	–	–	–	–	–
–	2	–	–	–	4	2	3	2	4
–	–	–	–	–	3	–	–	–	–

Table 53. THE FLOW OF FINANCIAL RESOURCES TO

Disbursements

	1977-1979 average	1985	1986	1987	1988
			CANADA		
NET DISBURSEMENTS					
I. Official Development Assistance (ODA), (A + B)	**1036**	**1631**	**1695**	**1885**	**2342**
ODA as % of GNP	*0.50*	*0.49*	*0.48*	*0.47*	*0.49*
A. Bilateral Official Development Assistance (1 + 2)	572	997	1054	1259	1579
1. Grants and grant like contributions	441	888	958	1265	1651
1.1. Technical assistance	54	251	234	309	403
1.2. Food aid	95	150	152	178	231
1.3. Administrative costs	10	71	83	119	143
1.4. Other grants	283	415	488	660	874
2. Development lending and capital	131	110	97	-5	-72
2.1. New development lending	129	106	97	-5	-72
2.2. Food aid loans	2	–	–	–	–
2.3. Equities and other bilateral assets	0	3	0	–	–
B. Contributions to multilateral institutions(1 + 2 + 3)	463	634	641	626	763
1. Grants	195	235	247	274	364
1.1. UN Agencies	154	203	211	233	315
1.2. EEC	–	–	–	–	–
1.3. Other	40	32	36	40	48
of which: Food aid grants,total	92	113	110	121	181
2. Capital subscription payments and similar to	267	399	394	352	400
2.1. IBRD (incl. IFC)	9	15	13	10	19
2.2. IDA	162	244	192	245	189
2.3. Regional Development Banks	92	141	185	86	192
2.4. Other	3	–	5	11	–
3. Concessional lending	2	0	0	–	–
Memo: Subscriptions on an encashment basis	134	251	204	336	349
II. Other Official Flows (OOF), net (A + B)	**389**	**-134**	**-201**	**219**	..
A. Bilateral Other Official Flows (1 + 2)	401	-145	-198	213	..
1. Official export credits [a]	388	-152	-198	213	–
2. Equities and other bilateral assets	13	7	–	–	–
B. Multilateral Institutions	-11	11	-3	6	–
of which: IBRD	-11	-4	-3	-4	–
Sub-total (I + II): Total Official Flows	*1425*	*1497*	*1495*	*2105*	..
III. Grants by Private Voluntary Agencies	**95**	**171**	**176**	**193**	..
IV. Private Flows at Market Terms (1 to 4)	**882**	**21**	**-114**	**185**	..
1. Direct investment	342	85	104	-82	..
2. Bilateral portfolio investment and other	573	-248	-234	169	–
3. Multilateral portfolio investment	-19	197	-1	-1	–
4. Private export credits	-14	-13	17	99	–
IV (5)a. *Monetary Sector included in IV* [b]	555	43	-246	143	–
i) Resident banks [c]: Change in bilateral claims	559	43	-246	143	–
ii) Multilateral portfolio investment	-4	–	–	–	–
V. Total Resource Flows (Balance of Payments Basis) (I to IV)	**2403**	**1688**	**1557**	**2482**	..
Total Resource Flows as % of GNP	*1.16*	*0.51*	*0.44*	*0.62*	..
IV (5)b. *Parent banks and their affiliates* [d]	..	..	..	..	..
Adjusted Resource Flow, Consolidated Balance Sheet Basis					
(I to IV - IV (5)a. + IV (5)b.)	..	..	..	..	..
For reference					
GROSS DISBURSEMENTS					
Total Official	1935	2247	2227	2554	2432
Official Development Assistance	1109	1662	1727	1916	2432
Other Official Flows	826	584	500	638	–
New development lending	202	137	128	25	18
Total debt reorganisation	81	10	0	–	55
ODA grants (debt forgiveness)	68	–	–	–	55
ODA lending	0	3	0	–	–
OOF lending	13	7	–	–	–
Total food aid	189	263	263	299	413
Official export credits	799	501	423	556	–
Private export credits	55	2	26	143	–
COMMITMENTS					
Official Development Assistance, Total [e]	1302	1770	1770	2296	3033
Bilateral	905	1172	1179	1644	1911
of which: Grants	621	1091	1154	1632	1786
Multilateral	397	598	591	652	1122
Other Official Flows	1219	583	733	822	–
MEMO ITEMS					
1. Total flows to multilateral agencies, net (IB + IIB + IV3)	433	842	637	631	763
2. Official funds in support of private export credits (included in II.A.1. above)	–	–	–	–	–
3. Official funds in support of private investment (included in II.A.2. above)	–	–	–	–	–
4. Interest received on ODA	2	5	5	0	2
5. Interest received on OOF	133	272	239	–	–

For footnotes see page after table 59

270

G.
Tables

DEVELOPING COUNTRIES AND MULTILATERAL AGENCIES

$ million

	DENMARK					FINLAND				
	1977-1979 average	1985	1986	1987	1988	1977-1979 average	1985	1986	1987	1988
	369	**440**	**695**	**859**	**922**	**64**	**211**	**313**	**433**	**608**
	0.67	*0.80*	*0.89*	*0.88*	*0.89*	*0.18*	*0.40*	*0.45*	*0.49*	*0.59*
	208	228	362	459	478	31	128	188	263	380
	151	190	366	391	424	40	115	168	233	334
	63	47	70	65	95	18	54	70	21	25
	6	–	–	–	–	2	2	3	2	1
	4	9	12	28	21	1	6	9	12	17
	78	134	284	297	308	19	54	87	198	291
	57	39	-4	68	54	-9	12	20	30	45
	57	39	-4	68	54	-10	11	19	28	45
	–	–	–	–	–	–	–	–	–	–
	0	–	–	–	–	0	1	1	2	–
	161	211	333	400	444	34	83	125	170	228
	119	160	256	301	329	14	47	69	105	144
	98	101	177	210	188	12	47	69	98	123
	18	33	42	55	61	–	–	–	–	–
	3	26	37	37	80	2	0	–	7	21
	24	25	27	32	32	3	10	18	22	34
	42	51	77	99	115	20	36	56	66	84
	2	13	1	–	17	2	4	8	9	5
	30	16	49	67	60	11	19	24	27	37
	4	7	26	2	0	5	12	17	19	23
	5	14	–	30	38	2	1	8	11	19
	–	–	–	–	–	–	–	–	–	–
	6	..	..	79	–	12	..	..	..	–
	115	**74**	**-131**	**-79**	**..**	**-3**	**35**	**10**	**-18**	**20**
	116	27	-116	-56	–	–	–	–	–	0
	110	21	-119	-78	–	–	–	–	–	0
	5	6	3	22	–	–	–	–	–	–
	-1	48	-16	-23	–	-3	35	10	-18	19
	-1	48	-16	-23	–	–	–	–	–	–
	484	*514*	*564*	*780*	*..*	*61*	*246*	*323*	*415*	*627*
	8	**16**	**12**	**24**	**..**	**7**	**13**	**28**	**41**	**15**
	149	**-82**	**-103**	**47**	**..**	**60**	**19**	**83**	**125**	**112**
	47	42	46	106	–	8	25	39	30	74
	–	–	–	–	–	8	–	–	–	–
	17	–	–	–	–	–	–	–	–	–
	85	-125	-149	-59	–	44	-6	44	94	39
	–	–	–	–	–	8	–	–	–	–
	–	–	–	–	–	8	–	–	–	–
	642	**447**	**473**	**852**	**..**	**128**	**278**	**434**	**580**	**755**
	1.16	*0.82*	*0.60*	*0.87*	*..*	*0.36*	*0.52*	*0.63*	*0.66*	*0.74*
	..	..	..	..	..	..	..	..	..	..
	..	..	..	..	..	..	..	..	..	..
	531	724	961	1131	939	79	247	323	415	630
	404	459	830	927	939	79	211	313	433	610
	127	265	132	204	–	–	35	10	-18	20
	92	58	131	136	71	5	11	19	28	48
	30	14	127	60	9	16	–	–	–	43
	29	14	127	60	9	15	–	–	–	43
	0	–	–	–	–	0	–	–	–	–
	–	–	–	–	–	–	–	–	–	–
	29	25	27	32	–	5	12	21	24	36
	118	177	81	117	–	–	–	–	–	0
	159	166	27	47	–	79	22	44	94	78
	459	572	780	744	1054	90	349	408	443	625
	279	340	480	416	642	48	233	276	222	399
	178	231	300	405	617	42	215	255	193	345
	180	232	301	328	413	42	117	132	221	226
	146	128	99	111	–	–	35	10	6	0
	178	259	317	377	444	30	119	135	152	247
	110	-66	-63	-8	–	–	–	–	–	–
	–	–	–	–	–	–	–	–	–	–
	0	–	–	–	–	0	0	–	–	–
	13	72	54	91	–	–	–	–	–	–

Table 54. THE FLOW OF FINANCIAL RESOURCES TO

Disbursements

		FRANCE			
	1977-1979 average	1985	1986	1987	1988
I. **NET DISBURSEMENTS**					
Official Development Assistance (ODA), (A + B)	**2807**	**3995**	**5105**	**6525**	**6865**
ODA as % of GNP	*0.59*	*0.78*	*0.70*	*0.74*	*0.72*
A. Bilateral Official Development Assistance (1 + 2)	2382	3262	4162	5326	5601
1. Grants and grant like contributions	2105	2536	3177	3921	4175
1.1. Technical assistance	1385	1521	1975	2369	2422
1.2. Food aid	19	41	38	30	49
1.3. Administrative costs	31	93	134	182	189
1.4. Other grants	670	881	1030	1340	1516
2. Development lending and capital	277	726	985	1405	1426
2.1. New development lending	261	572	876	1244	1309
2.2. Food aid loans	–	–	–	–	–
2.3. Equities and other bilateral assets	16	155	109	161	116
B. Contributions to multilateral institutions(1 + 2 + 3)	425	733	943	1199	1265
1. Grants	214	396	501	548	770
1.1. UN Agencies	27	78	109	103	113
1.2. EEC	186	310	385	420	605
1.3. Other	1	9	7	25	52
of which: Food aid grants,total	53	86	84	74	–
2. Capital subscription payments and similar to	204	337	442	650	494
2.1. IBRD (incl. IFC)	18	22	31	7	38
2.2. IDA	129	231	300	496	262
2.3. Regional Development Banks	32	83	108	148	194
2.4. Other	26	0	2	–	–
3. Concessional lending	7	–	–	–	–
Memo: Subscriptions on an encashment basis	..	..	..	..	..
II. **Other Official Flows (OOF), net (A + B)**	**286**	**1143**	**955**	**2106**	**1028**
A. Bilateral Other Official Flows (1 + 2)	286	1143	955	2106	1028
1. Official export credits *a*	–	–	–	–	571
2. Equities and other bilateral assets	286	1143	955	2106	457
B. Multilateral Institutions	–	–	–	–	–
of which: IBRD	–	–	–	–	–
Sub-total (I + II): Total Official Flows	*3093*	*5138*	*6061*	*8631*	*7893*
III. **Grants by Private Voluntary Agencies**	**20**	**65**	**84**	**106**	**..**
IV. **Private Flows at Market Terms (1 to 4)**	**4188**	**3671**	**3031**	**-65**	**-783**
1. Direct investment	453	578	609	696	663
2. Bilateral portfolio investment and other	1782	631	752	-161	-481
3. Multilateral portfolio investment	94	545	867	578	687
4. Private export credits	1860	1918	804	-1179	-1652
IV (5)a. Monetary Sector included in IVᵇ	*1765*	*741*	*–*	*-1992*	*–*
i) Resident banksᶜ: Change in bilateral claims	*1671*	*734*	*-14*	*-1996*	*45*
ii) Multilateral portfolio investment	*94*	*7*	*14*	*4*	*-45*
V. **Total Resource Flows (Balance of Payments Basis) (I to IV)**	**7301**	**8874**	**9176**	**8671**	**..**
Total Resource Flows as % of GNP	*1.52*	*1.74*	*1.27*	*0.99*	*..*
IV (5)b. Parent banks and their affiliatesᵈ	..	..	..	..	
Adjusted Resource Flow, Consolidated Balance Sheet Basis					
(I to IV - IV (5)a. + IV (5)b.)	..	..	..	..	
For reference					
GROSS DISBURSEMENTS					
Total Official	4066	5618	6764	9449	8670
Official Development Assistance	3453	4132	5273	6802	7081
Other Official Flows	612	1486	1492	2647	1590
New development lending	428	685	1026	1500	1496
Total debt reorganisation	58	1111	925	2065	768
ODA grants (debt forgiveness)	–	19	–	–	–
ODA lending	32	175	120	181	145
OOF lending	26	917	805	1884	623
Total food aid	72	128	122	104	49
Official export credits	–	–	–	–	967
Private export credits	4312	6181	804	–	–
COMMITMENTS					
Official Development Assistance, Totalᵉ	3606	4555	5870	6881	–
Bilateral	3058	3756	4822	5493	–
of which: Grants	2615	2559	3146	4025	–
Multilateral	547	799	1048	1388	–
Other Official Flows	631	1504	1882	5403	–
MEMO ITEMS					
1. Total flows to multilateral agencies, net (IB + IIB + IV3)	519	1278	1810	1777	1952
2. Official funds in support of private export credits (included in II.A.1. above)	–	–	–	–	–
3. Official funds in support of private investment (included in II.A.2. above)	–	–	–	–	–
4. Interest received on ODA	57	–	–	–	–
5. Interest received on OOF	55	–	–	–	–

For footnotes see page after table 59

Tables

DEVELOPING COUNTRIES AND MULTILATERAL AGENCIES

$ million

GERMANY					IRELAND				
1977-1979 average	1985	1986	1987	1988	1977-1979 average	1985	1986	1987	1988
2486	**2942**	**3832**	**4391**	**4731**	**21**	**39**	**62**	**51**	**57**
0.39	0.47	0.43	0.39	0.39	0.17	0.24	0.28	0.19	0.20
1598	1980	2642	3090	3172	5	17	25	27	22
909	1427	1799	2166	2305	5	17	25	27	22
680	876	1230	1535	1594	2	7	13	13	13
52	73	104	117	113	–	–	–	–	–
14	37	49	66	66	0	2	3	3	3
163	441	416	448	532	3	8	10	11	6
689	553	844	924	867	–	–	–	–	–
589	498	534	887	806	–	–	–	–	–
–	–	–	–	–	–	–	–	–	–
100	55	310	38	61	–	–	–	–	–
888	962	1189	1300	1559	16	22	37	24	35
421	546	678	762	1007	10	20	24	24	21
126	131	176	209	231	3	5	6	7	3
233	403	471	506	752	7	15	17	16	18
62	12	31	47	24	0	0	0	1	–
104	131	123	111	212	1	8	10	7	–
459	420	518	547	561	5	2	13	0	13
21	–	76	8	19	2	2	0	0	8
329	324	346	389	506	4	0	13	–	5
109	95	97	150	36	–	–	–	–	–
–	–	–	–	–	0	–	–	–	–
8	-4	-6	-8	-9	–	–	–	–	–
82	386	484	555	474	–	..	5	7	–
131	**917**	**1135**	**1451**	**1294**	–	–	–	–	**182**
128	928	1139	1453	1293	–	–	–	–	182
84	248	366	-102	29	–	–	–	–	–
44	680	774	1555	1265	–	–	–	–	182
3	-11	-4	-2	1	–	–	–	–	–
-4	-4	-3	-2	–	–	–	–	–	–
2617	*3860*	*4967*	*5841*	*6025*	*21*	*39*	*62*	*51*	*238*
299	**424**	**545**	**645**	**695**	–	**22**	**20**	**26**	**23**
4076	**1466**	**2378**	**2357**	**5091**	–	**37**	**32**	–	–
896	-143	411	661	1235	–	–	–	–	–
1674	994	970	978	2858	–	–	–	–	–
882	381	471	398	450	–	–	–	–	–
624	235	527	320	548	–	37	32	–	–
1639	641	1037	285	682	–	–	–	–	–
1238	724	957	249	848	–	–	–	–	–
401	-82	80	36	-165	–	–	–	–	–
6992	**5749**	**7889**	**8843**	**11811**	**21**	**99**	**114**	**77**	**261**
1.09	0.92	0.88	0.79	0.98	0.17	0.61	0.52	0.29	0.92
..	-753	-1884	879	1884	..	..	..	..	..
..	4355	4969	9436	13013	..	..	..	..	..
3825	5082	6780	7924	9333	21	39	62	51	238
2937	3411	4587	5078	5434	21	39	62	51	57
888	1671	2193	2847	3898	–	–	–	–	182
1032	954	1268	1543	1483	–	–	–	–	–
384	985	1341	1743	2758	–	–	–	–	–
79	157	36	–	3	–	–	–	–	–
83	36	277	42	50	–	–	–	–	–
222	792	1028	1701	2704	–	–	–	–	–
156	205	227	228	325	1	8	10	7	–
364	660	867	727	751	–	–	–	–	–
2622	1000	1512	3117	3345	–	37	32	–	–
3718	3552	4767	5697	6718	21	39	62	51	57
2726	2427	3337	4303	4841	5	17	25	27	22
1212	1612	2013	2540	2742	5	17	25	27	22
992	1125	1430	1394	1876	16	22	37	24	35
548	834	921	1688	2469	–	–	–	–	–
1773	1332	1656	1697	2009	16	22	37	24	35
-47	-45	-3	17	-26	–	–	–	–	–
–	–	–	18	27	–	–	–	–	–
206	200	435	392	443	–	–	–	–	–
64	55	157	173	274	–	–	–	–	–

Table 55. THE FLOW OF FINANCIAL RESOURCES TO

Disbursements

	1977-1979 average	1985	1986	1987	1988
			ITALY		
NET DISBURSEMENTS					
I. Official Development Assistance (ODA), (A + B)	**283**	**1098**	**2403**	**2615**	**3183**
ODA as % of GNP	*0.11*	*0.26*	*0.40*	*0.35*	*0.39*
A. Bilateral Official Development Assistance (1 + 2)	27	781	1487	1878	2408
1. Grants and grant like contributions	60	621	1211	1249	1604
1.1. Technical assistance	43	267	412	404	286
1.2. Food aid	12	97	189	115	188
1.3. Administrative costs	–	27	57	62	82
1.4. Other grants	5	230	553	668	1049
2. Development lending and capital	-33	160	275	629	804
2.1. New development lending	-42	156	268	468	633
2.2. Food aid loans	–	–	–	–	–
2.3. Equities and other bilateral assets	8	4	7	161	171
B. Contributions to multilateral institutions(1 + 2 + 3)	256	317	917	737	775
1. Grants	134	289	381	444	589
1.1. UN Agencies	18	90	125	157	203
1.2. EEC	106	180	225	240	329
1.3. Other	10	18	31	47	57
of which: Food aid grants,total	35	67	70	65	110
2. Capital subscription payments and similar to	118	28	536	294	186
2.1. IBRD (incl. IFC)	–	–	9	5	42
2.2. IDA	77	–	408	234	–
2.3. Regional Development Banks	42	5	119	55	141
2.4. Other	–	23	–	–	3
3. Concessional lending	3	–	–	–	–
Memo: Subscriptions on an encashment basis	60	85	170	262	334
II. Other Official Flows (OOF), net (A + B)	**309**	**768**	**772**	**1299**	**473**
A. Bilateral Other Official Flows (1 + 2)	297	811	779	1290	472
1. Official export credits[a]	190	74	-29	480	185
2. Equities and other bilateral assets	107	737	808	810	287
B. Multilateral Institutions	12	-43	-7	9	1
of which: IBRD	4	-3	-6	4	–
Sub-total (I + II): Total Official Flows	*592*	*1866*	*3175*	*3915*	*3656*
III. Grants by Private Voluntary Agencies	**1**	**8**	**11**	**18**	**19**
IV. Private Flows at Market Terms (1 to 4)	**2507**	**321**	**-620**	**-1913**	**1400**
1. Direct investment	229	360	302	375	1053
2. Bilateral portfolio investment and other	-5	5	-39	-91	0
3. Multilateral portfolio investment	–	–	–	–	–
4. Private export credits	2283	-44	-883	-2198	347
IV (5)a. *Monetary Sector included in IV[b]*	–	–	–	–	–
i) Resident banks[c]: Change in bilateral claims	–	–	–	–	–
ii) Multilateral portfolio investment	–	–	–	–	–
V. Total Resource Flows (Balance of Payments Basis) (I to IV)	**3099**	**2195**	**2566**	**2019**	**5075**
Total Resource Flows as % of GNP	*1.16*	*0.52*	*0.43*	*0.27*	*0.62*
IV (5)b. *Parent banks and their affiliates[d]*	..	..	..	..	..
Adjusted Resource Flow, Consolidated Balance Sheet Basis (I to IV - IV (5)a. + IV (5)b.)	..	..	..	..	..
For reference					
GROSS DISBURSEMENTS					
Total Official	835	2120	3426	4352	3897
Official Development Assistance	333	1117	2426	2654	3230
Other Official Flows	502	1002	1000	1698	667
New development lending	9	176	291	507	680
Total debt reorganisation	25	490	477	1159	497
ODA grants (debt forgiveness)	–	8	–	19	1
ODA lending	8	4	7	161	171
OOF lending	17	478	470	979	325
Total food aid	48	164	259	180	298
Official export credits	351	233	164	676	311
Private export credits	3197	1446	963	1172	1941
COMMITMENTS					
Official Development Assistance, Total[e]	523	2302	4040	4368	4586
Bilateral	68	1178	2327	3135	3040
of which: Grants	60	867	1926	1953	2052
Multilateral	455	1123	1713	1233	1546
Other Official Flows	2272	2687	2143	3076	2485
MEMO ITEMS					
1. Total flows to multilateral agencies, net (IB + IIB + IV3)	268	273	909	747	776
2. Official funds in support of private export credits (included in II.A.1. above)	89	-42	-41	-25	-19
3. Official funds in support of private investment (included in II.A.2. above)	–	–	–	–	–
4. Interest received on ODA	17	11	16	27	28
5. Interest received on OOF	–	–	–	–	–

For footnotes see page after table 59

DEVELOPING COUNTRIES AND MULTILATERAL AGENCIES

$ million

	JAPAN					NETHERLANDS			
1977-1979 average	1985	1986	1987	1988	1977-1979 average	1985	1986	1987	1988
2108	**3797**	**5634**	**7342**	**9134**	**1151**	**1136**	**1740**	**2094**	**2231**
0.24	0.29	0.29	0.31	0.32	0.85	0.91	1.01	0.98	0.98
1466	2557	3846	5135	6422	821	762	1180	1419	1552
409	1185	1703	2108	2908	698	652	1044	1256	1393
204	422	599	740	1093	241	266	386	543	631
17	53	69	102	91	29	26	30	34	40
16	85	158	214	266	23	40	56	68	72
173	624	878	1052	1458	405	321	571	611	650
1057	1372	2143	3027	3514	124	110	136	162	159
1009	1380	2038	2855	3514	107	106	129	139	145
27	-26	-44	–	–	6	–	–	–	–
21	19	149	171	–	11	4	7	24	14
642	1240	1788	2207	2712	330	374	560	676	679
100	286	377	391	418	232	225	327	378	411
88	266	349	359	378	141	119	182	211	229
–	–	–	–	–	79	101	134	167	182
12	21	29	31	40	12	5	11	0	1
6	–	41	–	46	55	59	79	49	93
548	957	1413	1816	2294	96	149	233	297	268
15	–	7	70	224	7	20	21	18	24
324	562	826	1121	1340	60	106	168	207	208
189	395	574	580	704	13	23	40	59	26
21	–	6	45	26	16	–	4	12	10
-7	-3	-2	–	–	2	–	–	–	–
269	..	..	–	–	13	99	255	282	183
1328	**-302**	**-724**	**-1808**	**-639**	**8**	**15**	**6**	**4**	**4**
1310	-154	-526	-1761	-428	8	15	6	4	4
711	-152	-858	-2047	-1838	–	–	–	–	–
599	-1	332	287	1410	8	15	6	4	4
19	-148	-198	-47	-211	–	–	–	–	–
-9	-130	-164	–	–	–	–	–	–	–
3437	*3495*	*4910*	*5534*	*8494*	*1159*	*1151*	*1746*	*2098*	*2235*
19	**101**	**82**	**92**	**107**	**54**	**98**	**140**	**172**	**180**
4492	**8022**	**9586**	**14723**	**12822**	**1050**	**1380**	**929**	**947**	**260**
911	1046	2761	7421	8190	366	532	224	259	472
2304	5138	5312	4357	2830	543	24	121	845	573
621	2832	1314	1865	1583	-5	757	636	423	-222
656	-994	199	1081	219	146	68	-51	-580	-563
2464	6211	4632	–	–	473	158	-73	162	-479
2008	4627	4061	–	-1583	479	98	-14	176	-280
456	1584	570	–	1583	-5	61	-59	-13	-200
7947	**11619**	**14579**	**20349**	**21424**	**2263**	**2629**	**2815**	**3217**	**2675**
0.90	0.87	0.74	0.85	0.75	1.67	2.11	1.63	1.50	1.18
..	7897	12043	..	..	..	..	..	..	..
..	13305	21990	..	..	..	..	..	..	..
5437	6994	10062	12922	15323	1265	1224	1841	2233	2393
2337	4299	6474	8262	10350	1252	1201	1814	2197	2356
3099	2695	3587	4660	4973	13	24	26	36	37
1231	1834	2783	3776	4731	208	171	203	241	270
10	40	217	116	90	117	19	13	30	27
–	26	39	49	90	110	19	11	17	27
10	13	178	67	–	7	0	2	13	–
–	–	–	–	–	–	–	–	–	–
50	53	110	102	137	90	85	109	83	132
1928	1617	1627	1382	1339	–	–	–	–	–
1675	2442	2513	3022	2165	405	386	620	525	514
3171	5357	6161	9739	13747	1550	1117	1866	2383	2531
2233	4076	4342	7343	12326	1170	731	1299	1709	1809
520	1261	1828	2205	3540	868	630	1180	1396	1461
938	1281	1820	2396	1422	380	386	567	674	723
3138	2886	3166	8819	9160	19	24	22	51	26
1282	3924	2904	4024	4083	324	1130	1195	1098	457
275	-290	-926	-2081	-1503	–	–	–	–	–
602	-46	191	–	-310	–	–	–	–	–
244	447	755	871	1096	32	44	60	77	–
–	–	–	–	–	3	10	12	13	15

Table 56. THE FLOW OF FINANCIAL RESOURCES TO

Disbursements

		NEW ZEALAND			
	1977-1979 average	1985	1986	1987	1988
NET DISBURSEMENTS					
I. **Official Development Assistance (ODA), (A + B)**	**59**	**54**	**75**	**87**	**105**
ODA as % of GNP	0.35	0.25	0.30	0.26	0.27
A. Bilateral Official Development Assistance (1 + 2)	47	43	61	66	93
1. Grants and grant like contributions	48	43	61	66	93
1.1. Technical assistance	16	10	14	15	49
1.2. Food aid	0	0	–	0	–
1.3. Administrative costs	0	2	3	2	5
1.4. Other grants	31	31	44	48	39
2. Development lending and capital	-1	–	–	–	–
2.1. New development lending	-1	–	–	–	–
2.2. Food aid loans	–	–	–	–	–
2.3. Equities and other bilateral assets	–	–	–	–	–
B. Contributions to multilateral institutions(1 + 2 + 3)	12	11	14	20	12
1. Grants	7	7	7	8	7
1.1. UN Agencies	4	5	5	4	5
1.2. EEC	–	–	–	–	–
1.3. Other	3	2	2	3	3
of which: Food aid grants,total	1	1	0	1	–
2. Capital subscription payments and similar to	5	4	8	13	4
2.1. IBRD (incl. IFC)	0	2	2	1	–
2.2. IDA	2	–	3	6	3
2.3. Regional Development Banks	2	2	2	5	1
2.4. Other	0	–	–	–	–
3. Concessional lending	–	–	–	–	–
Memo: Subscriptions on an encashment basis	2	3	..	–	–
II. **Other Official Flows (OOF), net (A + B)**	**7**	**1**	**1**	**1**	**2**
A. Bilateral Other Official Flows (1 + 2)	7	1	1	1	1
1. Official export credits[a]	7	1	–	1	1
2. Equities and other bilateral assets	–	1	2	–	–
B. Multilateral Institutions	–	–	–	–	1
of which: IBRD	–	–	–	–	–
Sub-total (I + II): Total Official Flows	66	55	76	87	107
III. **Grants by Private Voluntary Agencies**	**7**	**8**	**7**	**8**	**8**
IV. **Private Flows at Market Terms (1 to 4)**	**9**	**24**	**26**	**26**	**30**
1. Direct investment	9	24	25	26	29
2. Bilateral portfolio investment and other	–	–	–	–	–
3. Multilateral portfolio investment	–	–	–	–	–
4. Private export credits	0	0	1	–	1
IV (5)a. Monetary Sector included in IV[b]					
i) Resident banks[c]: Change in bilateral claims	–	–	–	–	–
ii) Multilateral portfolio investment	–	–	–	–	–
V. **Total Resource Flows (Balance of Payments Basis) (I to IV)**	**82**	**88**	**109**	**121**	**145**
Total Resource Flows as % of GNP	0.49	0.41	0.43	0.36	0.38
IV (5)b. Parent banks and their affiliates[d]	..	..	..	..	..
Adjusted Resource Flow, Consolidated Balance Sheet Basis (I to IV - IV (5)a. + IV (5)b.)	..	..	..	..	..
For reference					
GROSS DISBURSEMENTS					
Total Official	112	55	76	87	107
Official Development Assistance	60	54	75	87	105
Other Official Flows	52	1	1	1	2
New development lending	0	–	–	–	–
Total debt reorganisation	2	–	–	–	–
ODA grants (debt forgiveness)	2	–	–	–	–
ODA lending	–	–	–	–	–
OOF lending	–	–	–	–	–
Total food aid	1	1	0	1	–
Official export credits	52	–	–	1	1
Private export credits	0	0	1	–	1
COMMITMENTS					
Official Development Assistance, Total[e]	54	63	74	74	88
Bilateral	45	47	34	51	78
of which: Grants	45	47	34	51	78
Multilateral	9	16	40	23	10
Other Official Flows	54	1	1	1	2
MEMO ITEMS					
1. Total flows to multilateral agencies, net (IB + IIB + IV3)	12	11	14	20	13
2. Official funds in support of private export credits (included in II.A.1. above)	7	–	–	–	–
3. Official funds in support of private investment (included in II.A.2. above)	–	–	–	–	–
4. Interest received on ODA	0	–	–	–	–
5. Interest received on OOF	–	–	–	–	–

For footnotes see page after table 59

DEVELOPING COUNTRIES AND MULTILATERAL AGENCIES

$ million

	NORWAY					SWEDEN			
1977-1979 average	1985	1986	1987	1988	1977-1979 average	1985	1986	1987	1988
360	**574**	**798**	**890**	**985**	**850**	**840**	**1090**	**1375**	**1529**
0.90	*1.01*	*1.17*	*1.09*	*1.10*	*0.91*	*0.86*	*0.85*	*0.88*	*0.87*
202	328	479	528	572	537	580	777	896	1054
203	327	474	525	570	607	582	767	900	1058
34	43	57	84	86	83	121	103	185	207
2	8	4	6	0	12	6	6	3	29
–	20	28	30	35	11	36	46	52	51
168	256	384	406	449	501	419	613	661	771
-1	1	5	2	1	-71	-2	10	-4	-4
-1	1	5	2	1	-71	-2	10	-3	-4
–	–	0	–	–	–	–	–	-1	–
158	246	319	363	413	313	260	313	479	475
115	175	224	264	261	198	176	211	273	285
103	138	179	218	220	171	151	181	231	281
–	–	–	–	–	–	–	–	–	–
12	37	45	46	41	27	24	30	42	4
17	19	23	24	25	32	32	29	31	–
43	71	95	98	152	113	84	102	206	194
4	8	10	1	7	4	–	2	3	4
28	43	50	61	79	93	51	62	157	131
10	20	35	36	51	16	33	38	46	59
1	–	–	–	15	0	–	–	–	–
–	–	–	–	–	2	–	–	–	-3
11	..	..	–	–	44	..	..	..	..
5	**13**	**7**	**-4**	**-12**	**8**	**210**	**387**	**2**	**31**
7	13	10	13	1	6	210	385	–	31
3	–	12	15	–	4	210	385	–	31
4	13	-2	-2	1	3	–	–	–	–
-3	–	-3	-17	-12	2	0	2	2	–
-3	–	-3	-17	-12	–	–	–	–	–
364	*588*	*805*	*886*	*973*	*858*	*1050*	*1476*	*1377*	*1560*
26	**52**	**57**	**66**	**56**	**46**	**78**	**85**	**105**	**..**
253	-45	-128	-40	-123	473	283	145	273	686
18	–	4	10	28	123	277	141	92	145
34	–	–	–	–	149	–	–	–	–
–	–	–	–	–	0	–	–	–	–
201	-45	-132	-49	-151	202	6	3	181	541
11	–	–	–	–	135	–	–	–	–
11	–	–	–	–	135	–	–	–	–
644	**594**	**735**	**912**	**906**	**1377**	**1411**	**1706**	**1756**	**..**
1.62	*1.05*	*1.07*	*1.12*	*1.03*	*1.47*	*1.45*	*1.33*	*1.13*	*..*
..	..	..	..	..	..	..	..	..	..
..	..	..	..	..	..	..	..	..	..
378	640	831	944	1025	941	1282	1663	1382	1568
361	576	800	893	988	933	842	1093	1380	1537
17	64	32	51	37	8	440	571	2	31
–	3	7	5	5	12	–	13	–	–
1	–	2	–	–	89	–	48	2	–
1	–	2	–	–	89	–	48	2	–
–	–	0	–	–	–	–	–	–	–
19	27	27	29	0	44	39	35	34	29
3	–	12	15	–	4	440	569	–	31
283	26	3	19	21	345	143	215	768	997
382	622	868	880	732	983	826	1092	1380	1557
210	346	548	514	313	663	566	779	900	1078
210	343	541	507	311	656	566	775	900	1078
172	275	321	366	418	320	260	313	–	479
3	–	–	–	–	8	439	393	–	31
155	246	316	345	401	315	260	315	481	475
3	–	12	–	–	–	–	–	–	–
–	–	–	–	1	3	–	–	–	–
–	1	1	1	–	7	1	1	–	–
–	7	3	7	5	0	–	–	–	–

Disbursements

	SWITZERLAND				
	1977-1979 average	1985	1986	1987	1988
NET DISBURSEMENTS					
I. Official Development Assistance (ODA), (A + B)	**168**	**303**	**422**	**547**	**617**
ODA as % of GNP	*0.20*	*0.31*	*0.30*	*0.31*	*0.32*
A. Bilateral Official Development Assistance (1 + 2)	95	228	323	389	445
1. Grants and grant like contributions	109	217	311	363	414
1.1. Technical assistance	6	31	60	75	103
1.2. Food aid	12	25	24	22	23
1.3. Administrative costs	2	7	10	12	13
1.4. Other grants	89	154	217	254	274
2. Development lending and capital	-14	11	12	26	31
2.1. New development lending	-16	11	12	26	31
2.2. Food aid loans	–	–	–	–	–
2.3. Equities and other bilateral assets	2	–	–	–	–
B. Contributions to multilateral institutions(1 + 2 + 3)	73	75	98	158	172
1. Grants	53	43	62	104	110
1.1. UN Agencies	43	43	61	87	95
1.2. EEC	–	–	–	–	–
1.3. Other	10	1	1	17	14
of which: Food aid grants,total	9	4	6	–	15
2. Capital subscription payments and similar to	18	32	36	54	62
2.1. IBRD (incl. IFC)	–	–	–	–	–
2.2. IDA	–	–	–	–	–
2.3. Regional Development Banks	18	28	36	50	62
2.4. Other	–	4	–	4	–
3. Concessional lending	2	–	–	–	–
Memo: Subscriptions on an encashment basis	..	4	6	–	–
II. Other Official Flows (OOF), net (A + B)	**16**	**-5**	**-7**	**-10**	**-7**
A. Bilateral Other Official Flows (1 + 2)	16	-5	-7	-10	-7
1. Official export credits *a*	–	–	–	–	-7
2. Equities and other bilateral assets	16	-5	-7	-10	–
B. Multilateral Institutions	–	–	–	–	–
of which: IBRD	–	–	–	–	–
Sub-total (I + II): Total Official Flows	*184*	*297*	*415*	*537*	*610*
III. Grants by Private Voluntary Agencies	**45**	**54**	**66**	**94**	**89**
IV. Private Flows at Market Terms (1 to 4)	**3991**	**2153**	**905**	**-2249**	**1283**
1. Direct investment	267	489	475	-332	2078
2. Bilateral portfolio investment and other	2211	424	336	5	-77
3. Multilateral portfolio investment	724	1379	427	-1070	-128
4. Private export credits	788	-139	-332	-852	-591
IV (5)a. Monetary Sector included in IV*b*	1238	123	253	–	-657
i) Resident banks*c*: Change in bilateral claims	1238	123	253	–	-657
ii) Multilateral portfolio investment	–	–	–	–	–
V. Total Resource Flows (Balance of Payments Basis) (I to IV)	**4220**	**2505**	**1386**	**-1618**	**1981**
Total Resource Flows as % of GNP	*5.05*	*2.58*	*0.98*	*-0.91*	*0.51*
*IV (5)b. Parent banks and their affiliates*d	..	..	..	..	..
Adjusted Resource Flow, Consolidated Balance Sheet Basis					
(I to IV - IV (5)a. + IV (5)b.)	..	..	..	..	..
For reference					
GROSS DISBURSEMENTS					
Total Official	211	304	426	550	621
Official Development Assistance	190	304	426	550	621
Other Official Flows	20	0	–	–	–
New development lending	6	13	17	29	35
Total debt reorganisation	45	0	–	–	–
ODA grants (debt forgiveness)	23	–	–	–	–
ODA lending	2	–	–	–	–
OOF lending	20	0	–	–	–
Total food aid	22	29	30	22	39
Official export credits	–	–	–	–	–
Private export credits	1171	580	577	579	442
COMMITMENTS					
Official Development Assistance, Total*e*	239	381	442	572	706
Bilateral	146	307	329	462	519
of which: Grants	130	281	314	455	519
Multilateral	94	74	113	110	188
Other Official Flows	34	–	–	–	–
MEMO ITEMS					
1. Total flows to multilateral agencies, net (IB + IIB + IV3)	798	1454	525	-912	45
2. Official funds in support of private export credits (included in II.A.1. above)	–	–	–	–	–
3. Official funds in support of private investment (included in II.A.2. above)	–	–	–	–	–
4. Interest received on ODA	1	1	1	3	–
5. Interest received on OOF	0	2	2	2	1

For footnotes see page after table 59

DEVELOPING COUNTRIES AND MULTILATERAL AGENCIES

$ million

	UNITED KINGDOM					UNITED STATES			
1977-1979 average	1985	1986	1987	1988	1977-1979 average	1985	1986	1987	1988
1579	1530	1737	1871	2645	5010	9403	9564	8945	10141
0.48	0.33	0.31	0.28	0.32	0.23	0.24	0.23	0.20	0.21
874	860	1011	1008	1430	3482	8182	7602	7007	6765
843	914	1104	1093	1528	2083	7310	7033	6688	6472
303	333	405	462	642	455	1458	1506	1749	2127
19	36	11	19	31	439	781	835	808	990
17	47	53	65	82	..	468	475	486	505
504	499	636	547	773	1189	4603	4217	3645	2850
31	-55	-93	-85	-98	1399	872	569	319	293
31	-56	-97	-114	-128	650	-63	-239	-325	286
–	–	–	–	–	694	898	755	596	648
-1	1	4	29	30	55	37	53	48	-641
705	670	726	863	1215	1528	1221	1962	1938	3376
273	422	465	544	725	467	973	836	723	913
108	101	114	158	192	354	758	631	590	726
144	304	327	363	488	–	–	–	–	–
21	17	24	22	46	113	215	205	133	187
51	101	87	98	142	77	180	136	121	185
432	248	262	320	489	1051	252	1132	1220	2467
9	25	18	7	128	79	30	133	63	160
365	174	196	219	311	704	–	742	895	1910
48	50	33	84	50	268	222	257	262	397
10	–	15	10	–	–	–	–	–	–
0	-1	-1	–	–	10	-4	-5	-5	-4
139	218	282	312	448	763	1302	1481	1212	1314
199	387	322	264	323	1042	178	-559	-1780	1906
199	387	322	264	323	1042	178	-559	-1780	1906
-120	-52	-13	191	196	810	-898	-1787	-2852	-865
318	439	335	73	127	232	1076	1228	1072	2771
–	–	–	–	–	–	–	–	–	–
1777	1917	2059	2135	2968	6052	9581	9005	7165	12047
71	169	191	221	239	933	1513	1753	1633	2255
8033	378	4447	1074	-255	8818	-9278	7473	4395	3203
897	2096	2080	2952	2494	6157	930	3107	8016	4205
6313	-1426	2199	-2458	-1425	2442	-10640	5573	-4373	-1619
–	–	–	–	–	11	314	171	340	-1009
823	-292	168	580	-1324	207	118	-1378	412	1626
6340	-1426	–	-2362	–	2969	-7155	4949	-3374	-5948
6340	-1426	–	-2362	–	2969	-7155	4949	-3374	-5948
–	–	–	–	–	–	–	–	–	–
9881	2463	6697	3430	2952	15804	1816	18231	13193	17505
2.98	0.54	1.21	0.50	0.36	0.73	0.05	0.43	0.29	0.36
..	..	..	424	..	4699	-7916	179	-5368	-8376
..	..	..	6216	..	17533	1055	13461	11199	15077
2035	2117	2244	2334	3166	7912	12718	12628	11743	14888
1694	1645	1870	2014	2795	5647	10115	10460	9635	10948
341	472	374	321	370	2265	2603	2168	2108	3940
145	56	35	27	21	1010	548	466	276	286
38	40	43	43	51	195	1165	1218	1164	3063
35	36	39	43	43	–	–	–	–	–
–	4	4	–	1	55	37	53	48	78
3	–	–	–	6	140	1128	1165	1116	2985
70	137	98	111	172	1294	1859	1726	1525	1823
16	–	–	191	196	1941	1032	405	522	483
3535	2980	3438	3402	1937	1353	3825	2233	3351	4225
1932	1397	1944	2613	2948	6804	10280	10753	9365	11176
1395	731	1081	1441	1691	4744	9157	8746	7412	7928
1238	708	1077	1375	1653	2759	7997	7742	6646	6818
537	666	863	1171	1256	2060	1122	2007	1953	3247
222	469	428	356	442	3806	1879	1961	1996	3720
705	670	726	863	1215	1539	1535	2133	2278	2367
-120	-52	-13	–	–	50	-17	-35	-17	37
–	–	–	–	–	2	-7	-14	5	4
73	31	30	41	63	397	605	657	607	756
10	58	59	59	75	627	1266	1204	985	1120

Table 58. THE FLOW OF FINANCIAL RESSOURCES TO DEVELOPING COUNTRIES

Disbursements AND MULTILATERAL AGENCIES *$ million*

		TOTAL DAC COUNTRIES			
	1977-1979 average	1985	1986	1987	1988
NET DISBURSEMENTS					
I. **Official Development Assistance (ODA), (A + B)**	**19536**	**29429**	**36663**	**41426**	**48094**
ODA as % of GNP	*0.34*	*0.35*	*0.35*	*0.34*	*0.36*
A. Bilateral Official Development Assistance (1 + 2)	13184	21918	26214	29869	33180
1. Grants and grant like contributions	9443	17842	21063	23246	26035
1.1. Technical assistance	3846	6029	7486	8964	10222
1.2. Food aid	762	1351	1498	1479	1827
1.3. Administrative costs	138	981	1215	1444	1598
1.4. Other grants	4696	9482	10865	11359	12389
2. Development lending and capital	3741	4075	5151	6623	7145
2.1. New development lending	2798	2922	3800	5392	6745
2.2. Food aid loans	729	872	711	596	648
2.3. Equities and other bilateral assets	214	281	640	634	-248
B. Contributions to multilateral institutions(1 + 2 + 3)	6352	7512	10448	11557	14914
1. Grants	2710	4192	4888	5397	6668
1.1. UN Agencies	1532	2336	2693	2998	3457
1.2. EEC	831	1417	1686	1865	2565
1.3. Other	347	439	509	534	646
of which: Food aid grants,total	594	890	919	802	1166
2. Capital subscription payments and similar to	3605	3337	5575	6173	8263
2.1. IBRD (incl. IFC)	185	158	346	222	720
2.2. IDA	2440	1948	3555	4204	5290
2.3. Regional Development Banks	891	1189	1634	1620	2134
2.4. Other	90	42	41	127	119
3. Concessional lending	37	-17	-14	-13	-16
Memo: Subscriptions on an encashment basis	1553	2430	2939	3111	3179
II. **Other Official Flows (OOF), net (A + B)**	**3877**	**3419**	**2113**	**2015**	
A. Bilateral Other Official Flows (1 + 2)	3864	3507	2260	2158	
1. Official export credits *a*	2191	-703	-2228	-4099	
2. Equities and other bilateral assets	1672	4210	4490	6257	
B. Multilateral Institutions	13	-88	-147	-143	
of which: IBRD	-29	-64	-122	-95	
Sub-total (I + II): Total Official Flows	*23413*	*32848*	*38776*	*43440*	
III. **Grants by Private Voluntary Agencies**	**1720**	**2884**	**3335**	**3525**	
IV. **Private Flows at Market Terms (1 to 4)**	**40945**	**9431**	**26734**	**18777**	
1. Direct investment	10982	6488	10968	20895	
2. Bilateral portfolio investment and other	18818	-4466	13399	-2395	
3. Multilateral portfolio investment	2319	6609	4040	2667	
4. Private export credits	8825	800	-1673	-2389	
IV (5)a. Monetary Sector included in IV b	18404	-286	9258	-8645	
i) Resident banks c: Change in bilateral claims	17468	-1856	8653	-8672	
ii) Multilateral portfolio investment	936	1570	605	27	
V. **Total Resource Flows (Balance of Payments Basis) (I to IV)**	**66079**	**45163**	**68845**	**65743**	
Total Resource Flows as % of GNP	*1.15*	*0.53*	*0.66*	*0.55*	
IV (5)b. Parent banks and their affiliates d	..	..	..	..	..
Adjusted Resource Flow, Consolidated Balance Sheet Basis					
(I to IV - IV (5)a. + IV (5)b.)	..	..	..	..	..
For reference					
GROSS DISBURSEMENTS					
Total Official	30882	43193	52266	60329	67236
Official Development Assistance	22004	31549	39784	44441	51203
Other Official Flows	8879	11644	12482	15888	16033
New development lending	4490	4824	6558	8256	9213
Total debt reorganisation	1111	3931	4478	6664	7360
ODA grants (debt forgiveness)	451	280	303	191	271
ODA lending	201	273	641	511	445
OOF lending	460	3378	3534	5962	6644
Total food aid	2169	3139	3171	2871	3567
Official export credits	5608	4701	4266	4305	4150
Private export credits	20712	20113	13716	17372	16147
COMMITMENTS					
Official Development Assistance, Total *e*	26222	34357	42320	49118	
Bilateral	18662	25809	30579	36150	
of which: Grants	12011	19115	23150	25274	
Multilateral	7560	8547	11740	12488	
Other Official Flows	12176	11737	11989	22842	
MEMO ITEMS					
1. Total flows to multilateral agencies, net (IB + IIB + IV3)	8685	14033	14341	14080	16087
2. Official funds in support of private export credits (included in II.A.1. above)	367	-512	-1069	-2114	-1510
3. Official funds in support of private investment (included in II.A.2. above)	607	-53	177	23	-279
4. Interest received on ODA	1041	1349	1963	2021	1637
5. Interest received on OOF	915	1778	1765	1364	1521

For footnotes see page after table 59

Table 59. THE FLOW OF FINANCIAL RESSOURCES TO DEVELOPING COUNTRIES AND MULTILATERAL AGENCIES

Disbursements — $ million

	EEC 1977-1979 average	1985	1986	1987	1988
NET DISBURSEMENTS					
I. Official Development Assistance (ODA), (A + B)	**884**	**1510**	**1899**	**1951**	**2909**
ODA as % of GNP	–	–	–	–	–
A. Bilateral Official Development Assistance (1 + 2)	776	1407	1659	1747	2587
1. Grants and grant like contributions	621	1387	1600	1696	2511
1.1. Technical assistance	–	–	–	138	–
1.2. Food aid	167	205	49	183	388
1.3. Administrative costs	13	44	63	73	104
1.4. Other grants	440	1138	1306	1302	2020
2. Development lending and capital	155	20	59	51	76
2.1. New development lending	107	20	59	51	76
2.2. Food aid loans	–	–	–	–	–
2.3. Equities and other bilateral assets	48	–	–	–	–
B. Contributions to multilateral institutions(1 + 2 + 3)	108	103	240	204	322
1. Grants	108	103	240	204	322
1.1. UN Agencies	83	103	149	126	214
1.2. EEC	–	–	–	–	–
1.3. Other	25	–	91	77	109
of which: Food aid grants,total	108	–	–	–	–
2. Capital subscription payments and similar to	–	–	–	–	–
2.1. IBRD (incl. IFC)	–	–	–	–	–
2.2. IDA	–	–	–	–	–
2.3. Regional Development Banks	–	–	–	–	–
2.4. Other	–	–	–	–	–
3. Concessional lending	–	–	–	–	–
Memo: Subscriptions on an encashment basis	–	–	–	–	–
II. Other Official Flows (OOF), net (A + B)	**96**	**152**	**190**	**140**	**56**
A. Bilateral Other Official Flows (1 + 2)	96	152	190	140	56
1. Official export credits [a]	–	–	–	–	–
2. Equities and other bilateral assets	96	–	190	140	56
B. Multilateral Institutions	–	–	–	–	–
of which: IBRD	–	–	–	–	–
Sub-total (I + II): Total Official Flows	*980*	*1661*	*2089*	*2091*	*2965*
III. Grants by Private Voluntary Agencies	–	–	–	–	–
IV. Private Flows at Market Terms (1 to 4)	–	–	–	–	–
1. Direct investment	–	–	–	–	–
2. Bilateral portfolio investment and other	–	–	–	–	–
3. Multilateral portfolio investment	–	–	–	–	–
4. Private export credits	–	–	–	–	–
IV (5)a. Monetary Sector included in IV [b]	–	–	–	–	–
i) Resident banks [c]: Change in bilateral claims	–	–	–	–	–
ii) Multilateral portfolio investment	–	–	–	–	–
V. Total Resource Flows (Balance of Payments Basis) (I to IV)	**980**	**1661**	**2089**	**2091**	–
Total Resource Flows as % of GNP	–	–	–	–	–
IV (5)b. Parent banks and their affiliates [d]	..	..	..	..	
Adjusted Resource Flow, Consolidated Balance Sheet Basis (I to IV - IV (5)a. + IV (5)b.)	..	..	..	..	
For reference					
GROSS DISBURSEMENTS					
Total Official	1017	1730	2218	2290	286
Official Development Assistance	896	1525	1927	1986	–
Other Official Flows	122	205	291	303	286
New development lending	118	35	87	87	116
Total debt reorganisation	–	–	–	–	–
ODA grants (debt forgiveness)	–	–	–	–	–
ODA lending	–	–	–	–	–
OOF lending	–	–	–	–	–
Total food aid	275	205	183	183	–
Official export credits	–	–	–	–	–
Private export credits	–	–	–	–	–
COMMITMENTS					
Official Development Assistance, Total [e]	1334	1334	2284	4176	4909
Bilateral	1230	1249	1878	3846	4560
of which: Grants	936	1193	1787	3611	4347
Multilateral	103	85	407	330	350
Other Official Flows	306	247	376	218	615
MEMO ITEMS					
1. Total flows to multilateral agencies, net (IB + IIB + IV3)	108	103	240	204	322
2. Official funds in support of private export credits (included in II.A.1. above)	–	–	–	–	–
3. Official funds in support of private investment (included in II.A.2. above)	–	–	–	–	–
4. Interest received on ODA	6	–	22	27	–
5. Interest received on OOF	12	55	–	166	–

For footnotes see page after table 59

NOTES TO TABLES 51 TO 60

a) Including funds in support of private export credits.
b) Some portion of the bank lending included in a country's total may be construed as intermediation of resources originating outside the economy of the reporting country. This proportion cannot be satisfactorily ascertained in each case, although it has been suggested that, in global terms, it may be represented by foreign currency lending undertaken by banks (see sub-item IV.5 *(i)*. Care is therefore required when interpreting the relationship of the total shown for a given country, or any sub-total thereof which includes bank sector flows, to the GNP of that country.
c) Includes affiliates in reporting country of banks with headquarters elsewhere.
d) Includes foreign affiliates of parent banks resident in the reporting country.
e) Including debt reorganisation.

Section G : **Reference Tables**

Table 60. GNP DEFLATORS FOR DAC COUNTRIES, 1971-1988[a]

1987 = 100.00

Countries	1971	1972	1973	1974	1975	1976	1977	1978	1979	1980	1981	1982	1983	1984	1985	1986	1988
Australia	34.86	39.71	52.74	62.85	66.28	70.33	69.52	77.30	82.25	93.26	102.36	101.04	97.20	101.35	86.15	88.60	122.19
Austria	21.51	25.04	32.11	36.88	42.21	43.21	49.40	59.20	67.13	72.59	62.17	61.99	61.06	57.43	57.20	80.68	104.14
Belgium	29.15	33.55	40.96	46.22	55.21	56.46	65.25	77.46	86.46	90.40	74.64	65.65	62.17	58.04	59.43	81.99	102.72
Canada	40.02	42.88	46.37	54.79	58.46	65.98	65.53	64.99	69.92	77.62	83.26	89.52	94.54	92.48	90.44	91.48	112.22
Denmark	24.90	28.86	36.76	41.21	49.18	50.94	55.83	66.99	75.59	76.40	66.37	62.73	61.47	57.32	58.87	80.43	106.17
Finland	23.11	25.64	31.45	38.93	45.88	49.35	51.96	54.69	62.17	70.99	68.38	66.78	63.04	62.87	64.94	82.44	111.72
France	27.81	32.14	39.70	40.86	52.06	51.30	54.46	64.90	75.82	85.23	74.17	68.68	64.83	60.55	62.36	84.69	103.73
Germany, Fed. Rep.	26.88	30.82	39.47	43.41	48.78	49.37	55.54	66.62	75.80	79.99	67.14	65.57	64.26	58.79	58.09	81.15	103.83
Ireland	—	—	—	35.03	40.83	40.18	43.92	53.36	64.77	74.62	69.36	70.68	67.23	62.37	65.06	87.90	104.86
Italy	26.04	29.43	32.76	34.82	40.76	37.67	42.39	50.14	59.29	69.28	61.35	60.56	62.20	59.52	59.52	82.35	104.78
Japan	18.81	22.53	26.75	30.19	35.68	38.02	44.45	59.27	58.38	58.16	61.44	55.50	58.60	58.96	59.61	86.01	113.35
Netherlands	25.28	29.84	37.38	42.58	50.27	52.34	59.96	71.49	80.32	85.38	71.92	71.21	67.93	61.99	61.19	83.55	104.14
New Zealand	30.28	35.18	43.27	47.13	46.02	45.35	50.10	59.97	69.91	74.15	76.74	74.22	68.36	64.62	62.74	76.62	119.55
Norway	28.15	31.28	39.01	45.35	52.51	54.16	60.16	65.10	71.60	84.53	83.46	82.30	78.02	74.78	75.00	85.92	106.71
Sweden	32.57	37.34	43.81	44.02	53.84	58.89	63.44	69.27	78.45	88.83	81.58	71.12	63.58	63.59	65.24	84.49	110.33
Switzerland	16.74	19.46	25.93	29.79	36.70	40.63	43.42	60.41	66.37	67.70	61.43	63.39	63.33	58.22	57.05	80.89	104.96
United Kingdom	27.86	31.00	32.53	35.59	43.00	40.02	44.12	53.70	68.36	89.13	86.64	80.52	73.35	67.46	69.08	80.87	115.87
United States	40.27	41.96	43.66	47.47	51.96	54.59	57.81	62.14	67.22	73.33	80.02	84.77	87.99	91.33	94.35	96.81	103.40
DAC Total	29.11	32.50	37.61	41.19	47.77	49.23	53.69	62.75	69.35	75.74	72.88	71.12	70.93	69.38	70.18	86.93	107.14

a) Including the effect of exchange rate changes, i.e. applicable to US dollar figures only.

Table 61. GROSS NATIONAL PRODUCT AND POPULATION OF DAC MEMBER COUNTRIES
Average 1981-82, 1986-88

Countries	Gross National Product ($ billion)				Population (000)			
	1981-82 average	1986	1987	1988	1981-82 average	1986	1987	1988
Australia	157.7	161.5	187.1	235.3	15 053	16 018	16 263	16 538
Austria	66.0	93.6	116.7	125.8	7 568	7 565	7 575	7 595
Belgium	91.8	114.9	143.4	150.3	9 855	9 862	9 868	9 884
Canada	282.7	351.5	402.0	471.5	24 511	25 675	25 652	25 950
Denmark	54.7	78.5	98.1	103.4	5 121	5 121	5 130	5 140
Finland	49.7	69.0	87.7	102.6	4 814	4 918	4 932	4 946
France	560.4	724.2	879.8	949.9	54 331	55 393	55 627	55 869
Germany	670.6	897.7	1 123.4	1 206.5	61 660	61 080	61 094	61 375
Ireland	17.5	22.0	26.5	28.3	3 463	3 541	3 542	3 538
Italy	407.4	600.6	750.9	823.2	56 571	57 221	57 331	57 441
Japan	1 102.9	1 962.7	2 384.4	2 859.7	118 050	121 490	122 091	122 613
Netherlands	139.1	173.0	214.5	226.7	14 280	14 572	14 671	14 765
New Zealand	23.4	25.4	33.1	38.6	3 170	3 279	3 309	3 326
Norway	54.8	68.3	81.3	88.3	4 108	4 169	4 184	4 211
Sweden	104.2	128.7	156.0	175.4	8 325	8 370	8 399	8 438
Switzerland	99.9	141.5	178.6	190.7	6 448	6 573	6 619	6 659
United Kingdom	499.7	555.4	679.4	818.7	56 357	56 763	56 930	57 088
United States	3 039.2	4 219.0	4 502.4	4 864.3	231 329	241 596	243 934	246 329
Total DAC	7 421.7	10 387.7	12 045.4	13 459.2	685 014	703 206	707 151	711 705

Table 62. THE LEVEL OF GNP AND POPULATION IN 1987 AND 1977-87 REAL GROWTH RATE

Countries	1987 GNP/CAP US$	1987 Population Million	1977-87 Real growth rate (%) GNP/CAP	1977-87 Real growth rate (%) GNP	1987 GNP Million US $
LLDCs					
Afghanistan	280	18.9	−1.7	0.7	5 260
Bangladesh	160	105.87	1.4	4.0	17 480
Benin	300	4.32	0.2	3.3	1 650
Bhutan	150	1.35	3.4	5.6	200
Botswana	1 030	1.15	6.5	10.7	1090
Burkina Faso	170	8.33	2.7	5.3	1 930
Burma	220	38.41	2.4	4.4	9 210
Burundi	240	4.98	−0.2	2.3	1 190
Cape Verde	500	0.34	3.8	5.8	170
Central African Rep.	330	2.73	−1.8	0.6	1 060
Chad	150	5.27	−2.5	−0.3	960
Comoros	380	0.42	1.7	5.2	200
Djibouti	1 210	0.37	−1.3	2.1	450
Equatorial Guinea	180	0.39	−1.5	0.4	70
Ethiopia	120	44.79	1.0	3.6	5 020
Gambia	220	0.80	−3.4	−0.1	210
Guinea	320	6.47	−0.1	2.1	2 060
Guinea-Bissau	160	0.92	−0.2	2.6	120
Haiti	360	6.16	−0.3	1.6	2 230
Kiribati	480	0.07	−1.1	0.7	30
Laos	160	3.77	−0.7	1.2	590
Lesotho	360	1.63	−0.3	2.3	640
Malawi	160	7.63	0.6	4.0	1 250
Maldives	300	0.20	3.9	7.0	50
Mali	200	7.77	0.8	3.1	1 930
Mauritania	440	1.86	0.0	2.2	870
Mozambique	150	14.59	−6.1	−3.6	1 240
Nepal	160	17.44	0.6	3.2	2 770
Niger	280	6.80	−1.8	1.2	2 080
Rwanda	310	6.45	1.3	4.6	2 090
Sao Tome & Principe	280	0.11	−2.3	−0.1	20
Sierra Leone	300	3.85	−0.6	1.5	900
Somalia	290	5.71	0.8	3.7	1 660
Sudan	330	23.21	−4.2	−1.5	8 090
Tanzania	220	23.88	−1.2	2.2	5 200
Togo	300	3.25	−1.9	1.1	1 150
Tuvalu	650	0.01	−2.8	−0.3	10
Uganda	260	15.66	−3.1	−0.3	3 760
Vanuatu	1 020	0.14	−1.9	0.6	140
Western Samoa	560	0.17	−1.7	−0.8	90
Yemen	580	8.43	4.9	7.7	4 580
Yemen, Dem.	420	2.28	−3.1	−0.4	940
Total	220	406.87	−0.1	2.5	90 650
Other LICs					
Bolivia	610	6.80	−3.9	−1.2	4 150
China	300	1 068.73	8.0	9.3	291 750
Egypt	710	50.95	3.4	6.2	34 240
Ghana	390	13.60	−1.7	1.3	4 940
Guyana	380	0.81	−5.3	−4.5	250
India	300	797.06	2.6	4.8	247 090
Indonesia	450	169.74	2.7	4.9	65 990
Kampuchea	170	7.64	3.3	4.5	1 280
Kenya	340	22.10	0.1	4.1	7 740
Liberia	440	2.33	−4.3	−1.2	1 060
Madagascar	200	10.89	−3.5	−0.5	1 850
Mayotte	300	0.05	−1.0	1.0	20
Morocco	620	22.97	0.3	2.7	15 640
Nigeria	370	106.70	−2.6	0.4	39 530
Pakistan	350	102.47	2.9	6.1	34 560

Table 62 *(Cont'd).* THE LEVEL OF GNP AND POPULATION IN 1987
AND 1977-87 REAL GROWTH RATE

Countries	1987		1977-87		1987 GNP
	GNP/CAP US$	Population Million	Real growth rate (%) GNP/CAP	GNP	Million US $
Other LICs *(cont'd)*					
Philippines	590	58.28	−0.9	1.8	34 620
Senegal	510	6.97	−0.7	2.2	4 490
Solomon Islands	420	0.29	3.7	7.5	110
Sri Lanka	400	16.36	2.7	4.3	6 530
St. Helena	540	0.01	0.0	0.0	x
Swaziland	700	0.71	1.9	4.1	590
Viet Nam	240	65.00	−1.7	0.8	15 530
Zaire	160	32.66	−2.8	0.3	5 260
Zambia	240	7.20	−4.4	−1.2	1 910
Zimbabwe	580	9.00	0.4	3.8	5 650
Total	330	2 579.31	3.9	5.9	824 790
LMICs					
Albania	790	3.09	1.3	3.3	2 430
Angola	1 130	9.24	0.4	3.3	10 430
Anguilla	850	0.01	−0.3	1.0	10
Belize	1 250	0.17	0.5	3.0	220
Cameroon	960	10.93	5.9	9.3	12 190
Colombia	1 220	29.50	1.9	3.9	33 870
Congo	870	2.02	3.8	7.2	1 890
Cook Islands	1 550	0.02	1.8	2.3	30
Cote d'Ivoire	750	11.07	−0.2	3.9	9 440
Cuba	1 170	10.27	1.4	2.1	12 000
Dominican Republic	730	6.72	−0.8	1.6	4 630
Ecuador	1 040	9.90	−1.1	1.7	9 710
El Salvador	850	4.97	−2.8	−1.3	4 630
Guatemala	810	8.44	−1.9	0.9	6 870
Honduras	780	4.68	−0.6	2.9	3 800
Jamaica	960	2.35	−2.2	−0.6	2 530
Korea, Dem.	970	21.33	−2.0	0.4	20 590
Mongolia	780	2.01	−0.7	2.0	1 580
Namibia	. .	. .	. .	. .	. .
Nicaragua	850	3.50	−5.9	−2.8	2 960
Pacif. Isl. (Trust Tr.)	1 090	0.16	−1.3	1.0	170
Papua New Cuinza	730	3.49	0.2	2.3	2 760
Paraguay	1 000	3.92	1.6	4.9	4 470
St. Vincent and Grenada	1 080	0.11	4.1	5.7	120
Thailand	840	53.54	3.2	5.4	46 840
Tokelau	830	x	0.0	0.0	x
Tonga	730	0.10	2.7	3.7	70
Tunisia	1 210	7.48	2.0	4.4	9 200
Turkey	1 200	52.85	1.3	3.7	65 400
Turks & Caicos Islands	780	0.01	−0.5	1.0	10
Wallis & Futuna	. .	. .	. .	. .	. .
Total	1 010	263.11	1.1	3.5	271 830
UMICs					
Algeria	2 760	23.06	1.5	4.6	65 200
Antigua & Barbuda	2 570	0.08	5.2	6.6	210
Argentina	2 370	31.44	−1.7	−0.2	74 490
Aruba	6 750	0.06	2.9	3.6	400
Bahamas	10 320	0.24	5.2	7.4	2 550
Bahrain	9 740	0.45	−0.7	3.3	4 330
Barbados	5 350	0.25	1.9	2.2	1 350
Bermuda	22 260	0.06	3.0	1.5	1 270
Brazil	2 230	141.24	1.0	3.3	314 640
Brunei	20 760	0.24	−4.4	−0.9	4 980
Cayman Islands	3 480	0.02	−0.7	2.1	70
Chile	1 310	12.54	0.6	2.4	17 110
Costa Rica	1 590	2.71	−0.9	1.7	4 090
Cyprus	5 200	0.68	5.4	6.4	3 740

286

Table 62 *(Cont'd)*. THE LEVEL OF GNP AND POPULATION IN 1987
AND 1977-87 REAL GROWTH RATE

Countries	1987		1977-87		1987 GNP
	GNP/CAP US$	Population Million	Real growth rate (%) GNP/CAP	GNP	Million US $
UMICs *(cont'd)*					
Dominica	1 440	0.08	2.6	3.7	120
Falkland Islands	7 500	x	4.6	4.6	20
Fiji	1 510	0.72	−1.2	0.7	1 120
Gabon	2 760	1.05	−6.7	−3.3	3 060
Gibraltar	4 240	0.03	0.3	0.7	120
Greece	4 350	10.00	1.8	2.5	50 490
Grenada	1 340	0.10	3.9	5.0	130
Guadeloupe	6 390	0.34	2.6	2.9	2 150
Guiana	3 360	0.09	−0.4	3.3	300
Hong Kong	8 260	5.48	6.3	8.4	46 200
Iran	3 530	47.01	−4.0	−1.2	165 930
Iraq	2 340	17.11	−1.7	2.0	40 070
Israel	6 810	4.37	2.5	4.5	33 450
Jordan	1 160	3.75	2.1	5.4	4 670
Korea	2 690	42.03	5.7	7.2	118 000
Kuwait	14 870	1.84	−1.6	3.2	25 760
Lebanon	2 150	2.70	−0.8	−1.0	5 810
Libya	5 500	4.06	−6.8	−3.0	25 500
Macao	3 110	0.41	0.9	4.7	1 280
Malaysia	1 780	16.56	2.7	5.3	29 160
Malta	4 010	0.36	3.5	4.3	1 670
Martinique	5 020	0.33	1.7	1.8	1 650
Mauritius	1 460	1.04	2.6	3.9	1 720
Mexico	1 820	81.95	1.1	3.7	139 230
Montserrat	3 330	0.01	5.2	5.2	40
Nauru	10 230	0.01	−0.3	1.0	80
Netherlands Antilles	6 360	0.19	3.0	3.6	1 210
New Caledonia	5 470	0.15	−2.8	−1.6	840
Niue	1 750	x	4.9	1.9	10
Oman	5 780	1.35	−2.1	2.5	7 160
Panama	2 260	2.27	2.1	4.4	5 130
Peru	1 430	20.73	−0.3	2.7	44 580
Polynesia, French	8 250	0.19	2.8	5.9	1 530
Portugal	2 890	10.21	2.1	2.6	34 870
Qatar	12 360	0.33	−10.5	−5.4	4 210
Reunion	5 580	0.56	1.7	3.1	3 150
Saudi Arabia	5 940	12.46	−6.5	−2.3	69 680
Seychelles	3 180	0.07	1.5	2.1	220
Singapore	7 940	2.61	6.4	7.6	20 550
St. Kitts-Nevis	1 700	0.05	3.3	4.0	80
St. Lucia	1 370	0.14	2.2	4.3	210
St. Pierre & Miquelon	2 310	0.01	0.3	1.8	20
Suriname	2 360	0.41	−3.3	−2.1	1 090
Syria	1 820	11.25	1.3	4.9	21 040
Taiwan	4 480	19.90	6.1	8.0	89 220
Trinidad & Tobago	4 220	1.22	−2.7	−1.2	5 130
United Arab Emirates	15 680	1.46	−3.8	2.5	22 890
Uruguay	2 180	3.01	0.5	1.1	7 220
Venezuela	2 640	18.27	−3.0	−0.1	38 640
Virgin Islands	8 500	0.01	7.4	9.1	120
Yugoslavia	2 480	23.41	1.2	1.9	60 450
Total	2 760	584.75	0.2	2.5	1 631 400
Overall Total	740	3 834.03	1.6	3.7	2 818 660

Note : The figures in the first column, designed to maximise international comparability (Atlas basis) cannot be related to the figures in the last column, which are at current 1987 prices and exchange rates.

Sources : World Bank, supplemented by Secretariat estimates.

WHERE TO OBTAIN OECD PUBLICATIONS
OÙ OBTENIR LES PUBLICATIONS DE L'OCDE

Argentina – Argentine
Carlos Hirsch S.R.L.
Galeria Güemes, Florida 165, 4° Piso
1333 Buenos Aires
Tel. 30.7122, 331.1787 y 331.2391
Telegram: Hirsch-Baires
Telex: 21112 UAPE-AR. Ref. s/2901
Telefax:(541)334-1719
Codigo 93 – Carlos Hirsch SRL

Australia – Australie
D.A. Book (Aust.) Pty. Ltd.
11-13 Station Street (P.O. Box 163)
Mitcham, Vic. 3132   Tel. (03)873.4411
Telex: AA37911 DA BOOK
Telefax: (03)873.5679

Austria – Autriche
OECD Publications and Information Centre
4 Simrockstrasse
5300 Bonn (Germany) Tel. (0228)21.60.45
Telex: 8 86300 Bonn
Telefax: (0228)26.11.04
Gerold & Co.
Graben 31
Wien I   Tel. (1)533.50.14

Belgium – Belgique
Jean De Lannoy
Avenue du Roi 202
B-1060 Bruxelles
Tel. (02)538.51.69/538.08.41
Telex: 63220

Canada
Renouf Publishing Company Ltd.
1294 Algoma Road
Ottawa, Ont. K1B 3W8 Tel. (613)741.4333
Telex: 053-4783 Telefax: (613)741.5439
Stores:
61 Sparks Street
Ottawa, Ont. K1P 5R1   Tel. (613)238.8985
211 Yonge Street
Toronto, Ont. M5B 1M4
Tel. (416)363.3171
Federal Publications
165 University Avenue
Toronto, ON M5H 3B9   Tel. (416)581.1552
Telefax: (416)581.1743
Les Publications Fédérales
1185 rue de l'Université
Montréal, PQ H3B 1R7 Tel.(514)954-1633
Les Éditions La Liberté Inc.
3020 Chemin Sainte-Foy
Sainte-Foy, P.Q. G1X 3V6
Tel. (418)658.3763
Telefax: (418)658.3763

Denmark – Danemark
Munksgaard Export and Subscription Service
35, Norre Sogade, P.O. Box 2148
DK-1016 Kobenhavn K
Tel. (45 33)12.85.70
Telex: 19431 MUNKS DK
Telefax: (45 33)12.93.87

Finland – Finlande
Akateeminen Kirjakauppa
Keskuskatu 1, P.O. Box 128
00100 Helsinki   Tel. (358 0)12141
Telex: 125080 Telefax: (358 0)121.4441

France
OECD/OCDE
Mail Orders/Commandes par correspon-
dance:
2 rue André-Pascal
75775 Paris Cedex 16   Tel. (1)45.24.82.00
Bookshop/Librairie:
33, rue Octave-Feuillet
75016 Paris   Tel. (1)45.24.81.67
(1)45.24.81.81
Telex: 620 160 OCDE
Telefax: (33-1)45.24.85.00
Librairie de l'Université
12a, rue Nazareth
13602 Aix-en-Provence   Tel. 42.26.18.08

Germany – Allemagne
OECD Publications and Information Centre
4 Simrockstrasse
5300 Bonn   Tel. (0228)21.60.45
Telex: 8 86300 Bonn
Telefax: (0228)26.11.04

Greece – Grèce
Librairie Kauffmann
28 rue du Stade
105 64 Athens   Tel. 322.21.60
Telex: 218187 LIKA Gr

Hong Kong
Government Information Services
Publications (Sales) Office
Information Service Department
No. 1 Battery Path
Central   Tel. (5)23.31.91
Telex: 802.61190

Iceland – Islande
Mal Mog Menning
Laugavegi 18, Postholf 392
121 Reykjavik   Tel. 15199/24240

India – Inde
Oxford Book and Stationery Co.
Scindia House
New Delhi 110001   Tel. 331.5896/5308
Telex: 31 61990 AM IN
Telefax: (11)332.5993
17 Park Street
Calcutta 700016   Tel. 240832

Indonesia – Indonésie
Pdii-Lipi
P.O. Box 269/JKSMG/88
Jakarta   12790 Tel. 583467
Telex: 62 875

Ireland – Irlande
TDC Publishers – Library Suppliers
12 North Frederick Street
Dublin 1   Tel. 744835/749677
Telex: 33530 TDCP EI Telefax : 748416

Italy – Italie
Libreria Commissionaria Sansoni
Via Benedetto Fortini, 120/10
Casella Post. 552
50125 Firenze   Tel. (055)645415
Telex: 570466 Telefax: (39.55)641257
Via Bartolini 29
20155 Milano   Tel. 365083
La diffusione delle pubblicazioni OCSE viene
assicurata dalle principali librerie ed anche
da:
Editrice e Libreria Herder
Piazza Montecitorio 120
00186 Roma   Tel. 679.4628
Telex: NATEL I 621427
Libreria Hoepli
Via Hoepli 5
20121 Milano   Tel. 865446
Telex: 31.33.95 Telefax: (39.2)805.2886
Libreria Scientifica
Dott. Lucio de Biasio "Aeiou"
Via Meravigli 16
20123 Milano   Tel. 807679
Telefax: 800175

Japan – Japon
OECD Publications and Information Centre
Landic Akasaka Building
2-3-4 Akasaka, Minato-ku
Tokyo 107   Tel. 586.2016
Telefax: (81.3)584.7929

Korea – Corée
Kyobo Book Centre Co. Ltd.
P.O. Box 1658, Kwang Hwa Moon
Seoul   Tel. (REP)730.78.91
Telefax: 735.0030

**Malaysia/Singapore –
Malaisie/Singapour**
University of Malaya Co-operative Bookshop
Ltd.
P.O. Box 1127, Jalan Pantai Baru 59100
Kuala Lumpur
Malaysia   Tel. 756.5000/756.5425
Telex: 757.3661
Information Publications Pte. Ltd.
Pei-Fu Industrial Building
24 New Industrial Road No. 02-06
Singapore 1953   Tel. 283.1786/283.1798
Telefax: 284.8875

Netherlands – Pays-bas
SDU Uitgeverij
Christoffel Plantijnstraat 2
Postbus 20014
2500 EA's-Gravenhage Tel. (070)78.99.11
Voor bestellingen: Tel. (070)78.98.80
Telex: 32486 stdru Telefax: (070)47.63.51

New Zealand – Nouvelle-Zélande
Government Printing Office
Customer Services
P.O. Box 12-411
Freepost 10-050
Thorndon, Wellington
Tel. 0800 733-406   Telefax: 04 499-1733

Norway – Norvège
Narvesen Info Center – NIC
Bertrand Narvesens vei 2
P.O. Box 6125 Etterstad
0602 Oslo 6
Tel. (02)67.83.10/(02)68.40.20
Telex: 79668 NIC N Telefax: (47 2)68.53.47

Pakistan
Mirza Book Agency
65 Shahrah Quaid-E-Azam
Lahore 3   Tel. 66839
Telex: 44886 UBL PK. Attn: MIRZA BK

Portugal
Livraria Portugal
Rua do Carmo 70-74
1117 Lisboa Codex   Tel. 347.49.82/3/4/5

**Singapore/Malaysia –
Singapour/Malaisie**
See "Malaysia/Singapore"
Voir "Malaisie/Singapour

Spain – Espagne
Mundi-Prensa Libros S.A.
Castello 37, Apartado 1223
Madrid 28001   Tel. 431.33.99
Telex: 49370 MPLI Telefax: 275.39.98
Libreria Bosch
Ronda Universidad 11
Barcelona 7   Tel. 317.53.08/317.53.58

Sweden – Suède
Fritzes Fackboksföretaget
Box 16356, S 103 27 STH
Regeringsgatan 12
DS Stockholm   Tel. (08)23.89.00
Telex: 12387 Telefax: (08)20.50.21
Subscription Agency/Abonnements:
Wennergren-Williams AB
Box 30004
104 25 Stockholm   Tel. (08)54.12.00
Telex: 19937 Telefax: (08)50.82.86

Switzerland – Suisse
OECD Publications and Information Centre
4 Simrockstrasse
5300 Bonn (Germany) Tel. (0228)21.60.45
Telex: 8 86300 Bonn
Telefax: (0228)26.11.04
Librairie Payot
6 rue Grenus
1211 Genève 11   Tel. (022)731.89.50
Telex: 28356
Maditec S.A.
Ch. des Palettes 4
1020 Renens/Lausanne Tel. (021)635.08.65
Telefax: (021)635.07.80
United Nations Bookshop/Librairie des Na-
tions-Unies
Palais des Nations
1211 Genève 10
Tel. (022)734.60.11 (ext. 48.72)
Telex: 289696 (Attn: Sales)
Telefax: (022)733.98.79

Taiwan – Formose
Good Faith Worldwide Int'l. Co. Ltd.
9th Floor, No. 118, Sec. 2
Chung Hsiao E. Road
Taipei   Tel. 391.7396/391.7397
Telefax: 394.9176

Thailand – Thaïlande
Suksit Siam Co. Ltd.
1715 Rama IV Road, Samyan
Bangkok 5   Tel. 251.1630

Turkey – Turquie
Kültur Yayinlari Is-Türk Ltd. Sti.
Atatürk Bulvari No. 191/Kat. 21
Kavaklidere/Ankara   Tel. 25.07.60
Dolmabahce Cad. No. 29
Besiktas/Istanbul   Tel. 160.71.88
Telex: 43482B

United Kingdom – Royaume-Uni
H.M. Stationery Office
Gen. enquiries   Tel. (01) 873 0011
Postal orders only:
P.O. Box 276, London SW8 5DT
Personal Callers HMSO Bookshop
49 High Holborn, London WC1V 6HB
Telex: 297138 Telefax: 873.8463
Branches at: Belfast, Birmingham, Bristol,
Edinburgh, Manchester

United States – États-Unis
OECD Publications and Information Centre
2001 L Street N.W., Suite 700
Washington, D.C. 20036-4095
Tel. (202)785.6323
Telex: 440245 WASHINGTON D.C.
Telefax: (202)785.0350

Venezuela
Libreria del Este
Avda F. Miranda 52, Aptdo. 60337
Edificio Galipan
Caracas 106
Tel. 951.1705/951.2307/951.1297
Telegram: Libreste Caracas

Yugoslavia – Yougoslavie
Jugoslovenska Knjiga
Knez Mihajlova 2, P.O. Box 36
Beograd   Tel. 621.992
Telex: 12466 jk bgd

Orders and inquiries from countries where
Distributors have not yet been appointed
should be sent to: OECD Publications
Service, 2 rue André-Pascal, 75775 Paris
Cedex 16.
Les commandes provenant de pays où
l'OCDE n'a pas encore désigné de dis-
tributeur devraient être adressées à : OCDE,
Service des Publications, 2, rue André-
Pascal, 75775 Paris Cedex 16.

OECD PUBLICATIONS, 2, rue André-Pascal, 75775 PARIS CEDEX 16 - No. 44823 1989
PRINTED IN FRANCE
(43 89 04 1) ISBN 92-64-13300-3